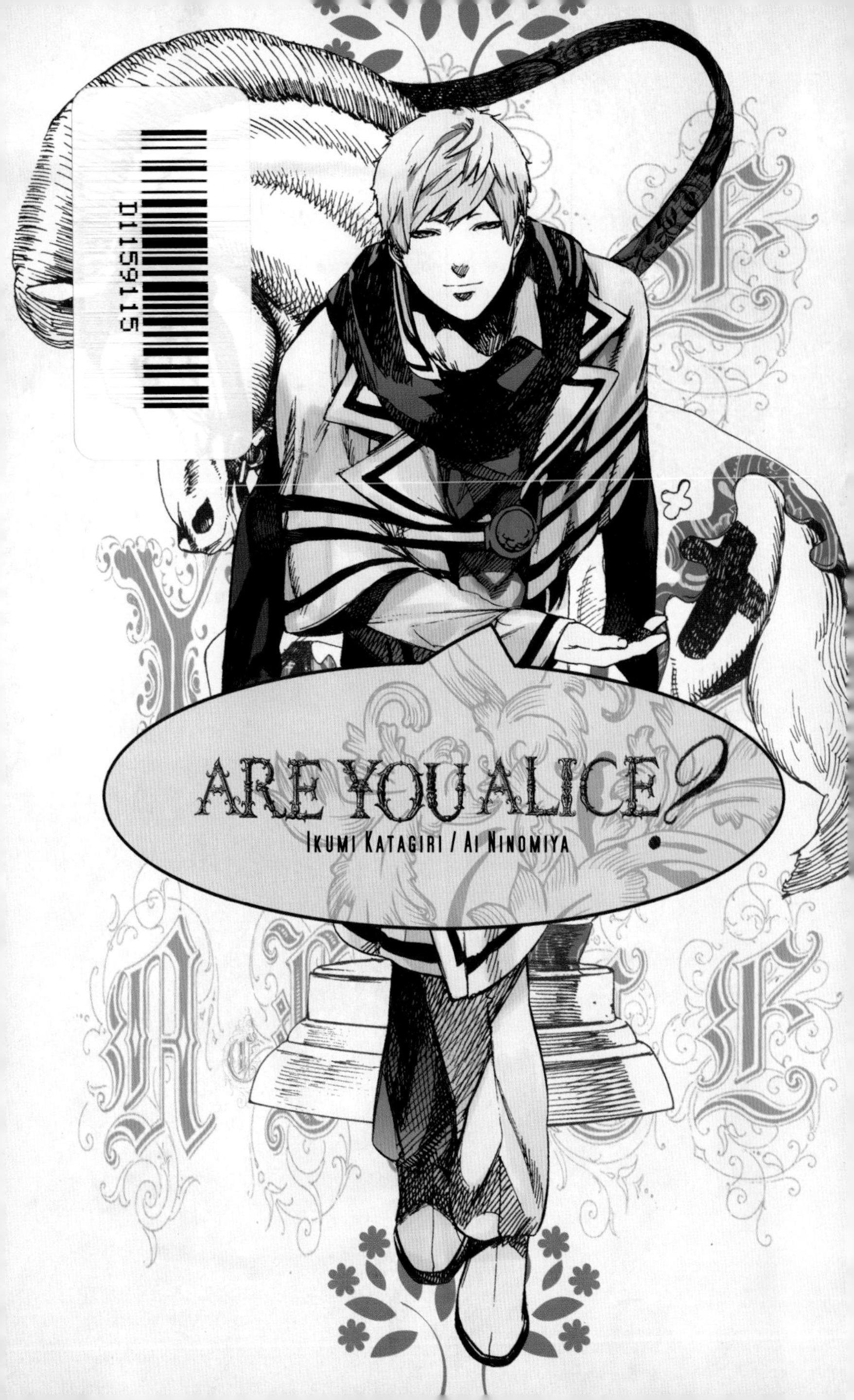
ARE YOU ALICE?
IKUMI KATAGIRI / AI NINOMIYA

Are You Alice?
8
CONTENTS!

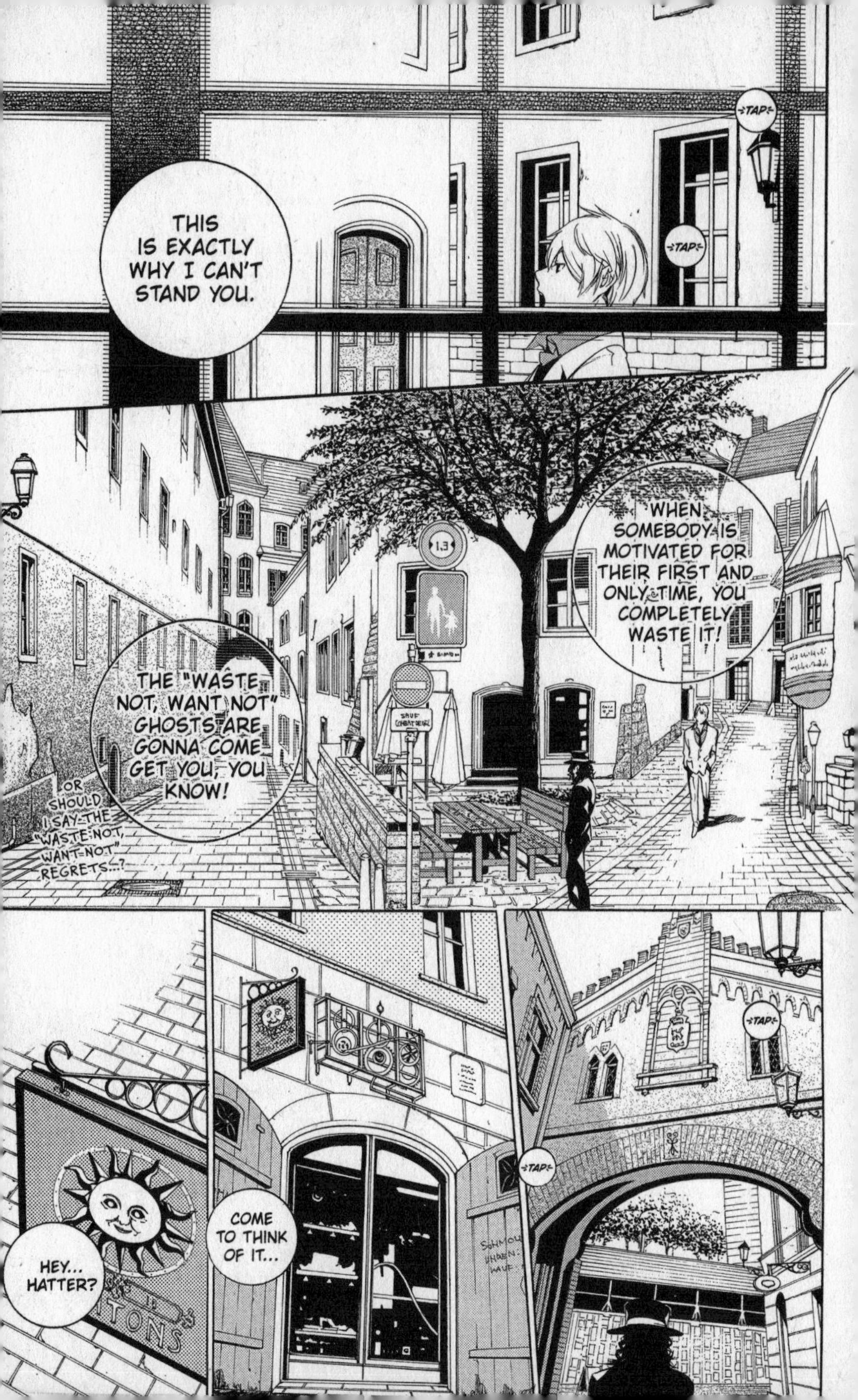

TAP
TAP
THIS IS EXACTLY WHY I CAN'T STAND YOU.
WHEN SOMEBODY IS MOTIVATED FOR THEIR FIRST AND ONLY TIME, YOU COMPLETELY WASTE IT!
THE "WASTE NOT, WANT NOT" GHOSTS ARE GONNA COME GET YOU, YOU KNOW!
OR SHOULD I SAY THE "WASTE NOT, WANT NOT" REGRETS...?
TAP
TAP
COME TO THINK OF IT...
HEY... HATTER?

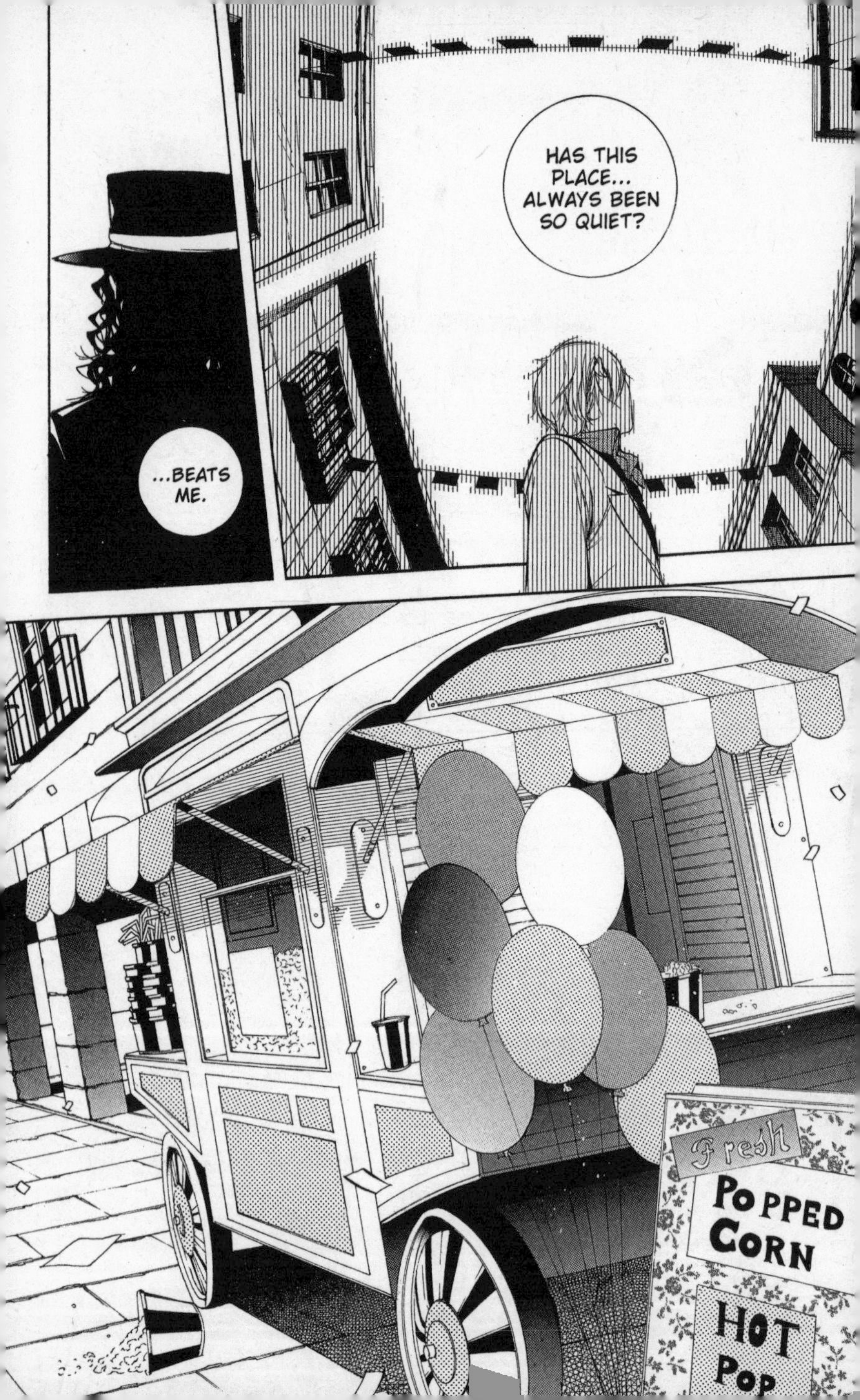
HAS THIS PLACE... ALWAYS BEEN SO QUIET?
...BEATS ME.
Fresh
POPPED CORN
HOT POP

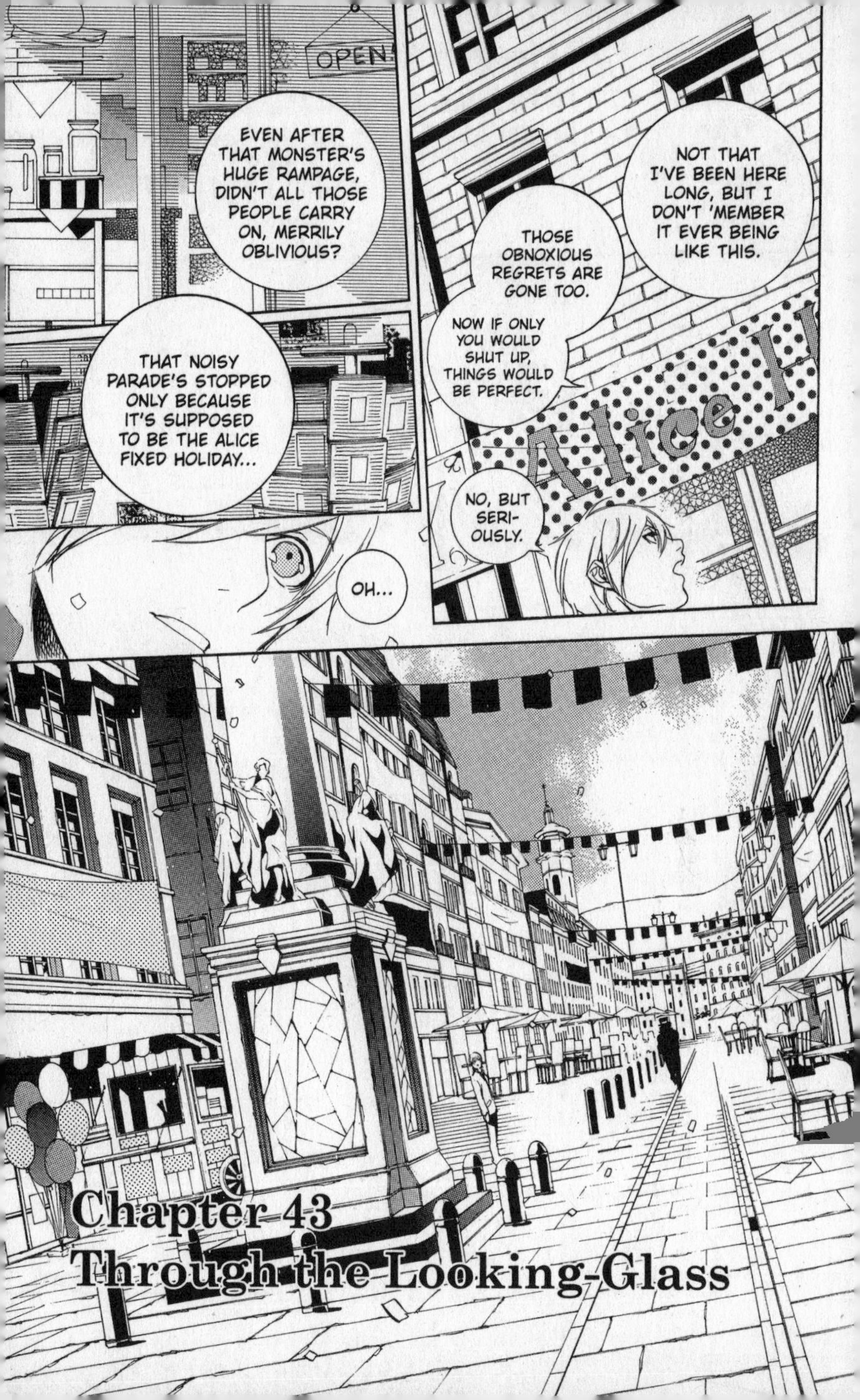
NOT THAT I'VE BEEN HERE LONG, BUT I DON'T 'MEMBER IT EVER BEING LIKE THIS.
THOSE OBNOXIOUS REGRETS ARE GONE TOO.
NOW IF ONLY YOU WOULD SHUT UP, THINGS WOULD BE PERFECT.
Alice
NO, BUT SERIOUSLY.
OPEN
EVEN AFTER THAT MONSTER'S HUGE RAMPAGE, DIDN'T ALL THOSE PEOPLE CARRY ON, MERRILY OBLIVIOUS?
THAT NOISY PARADE'S STOPPED ONLY BECAUSE IT'S SUPPOSED TO BE THE ALICE FIXED HOLIDAY...
OH...
Chapter 43
Through the Looking-Glass

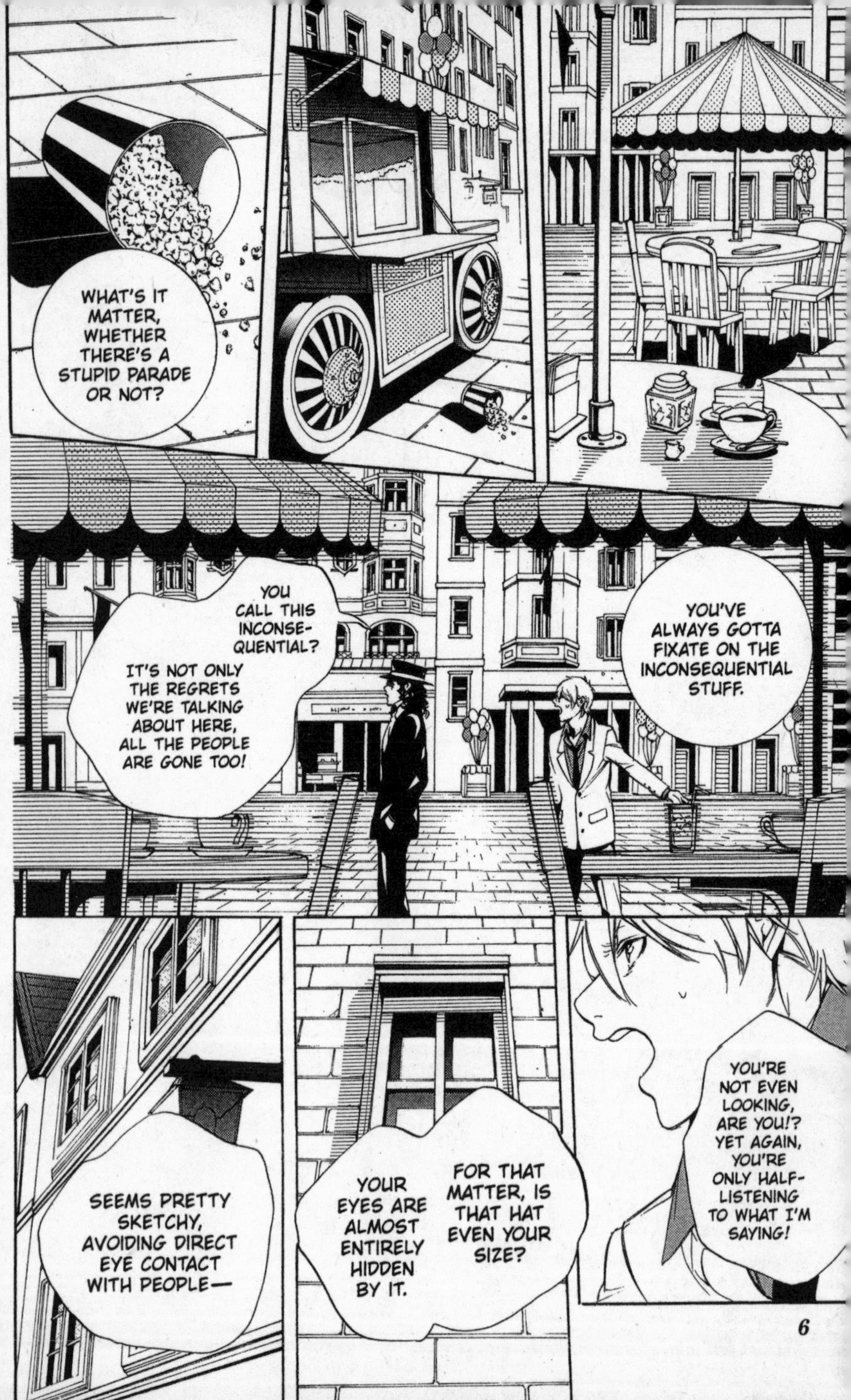
WHAT'S IT MATTER, WHETHER THERE'S A STUPID PARADE OR NOT?
YOU'VE ALWAYS GOTTA FIXATE ON THE INCONSEQUENTIAL STUFF.
YOU CALL THIS INCONSE-QUENTIAL?
IT'S NOT ONLY THE REGRETS WE'RE TALKING ABOUT HERE, ALL THE PEOPLE ARE GONE TOO!
YOU'RE NOT EVEN LOOKING, ARE YOU!? YET AGAIN, YOU'RE ONLY HALF-LISTENING TO WHAT I'M SAYING!
FOR THAT MATTER, IS THAT HAT EVEN YOUR SIZE?
YOUR EYES ARE ALMOST ENTIRELY HIDDEN BY IT.
SEEMS PRETTY SKETCHY, AVOIDING DIRECT EYE CONTACT WITH PEOPLE—

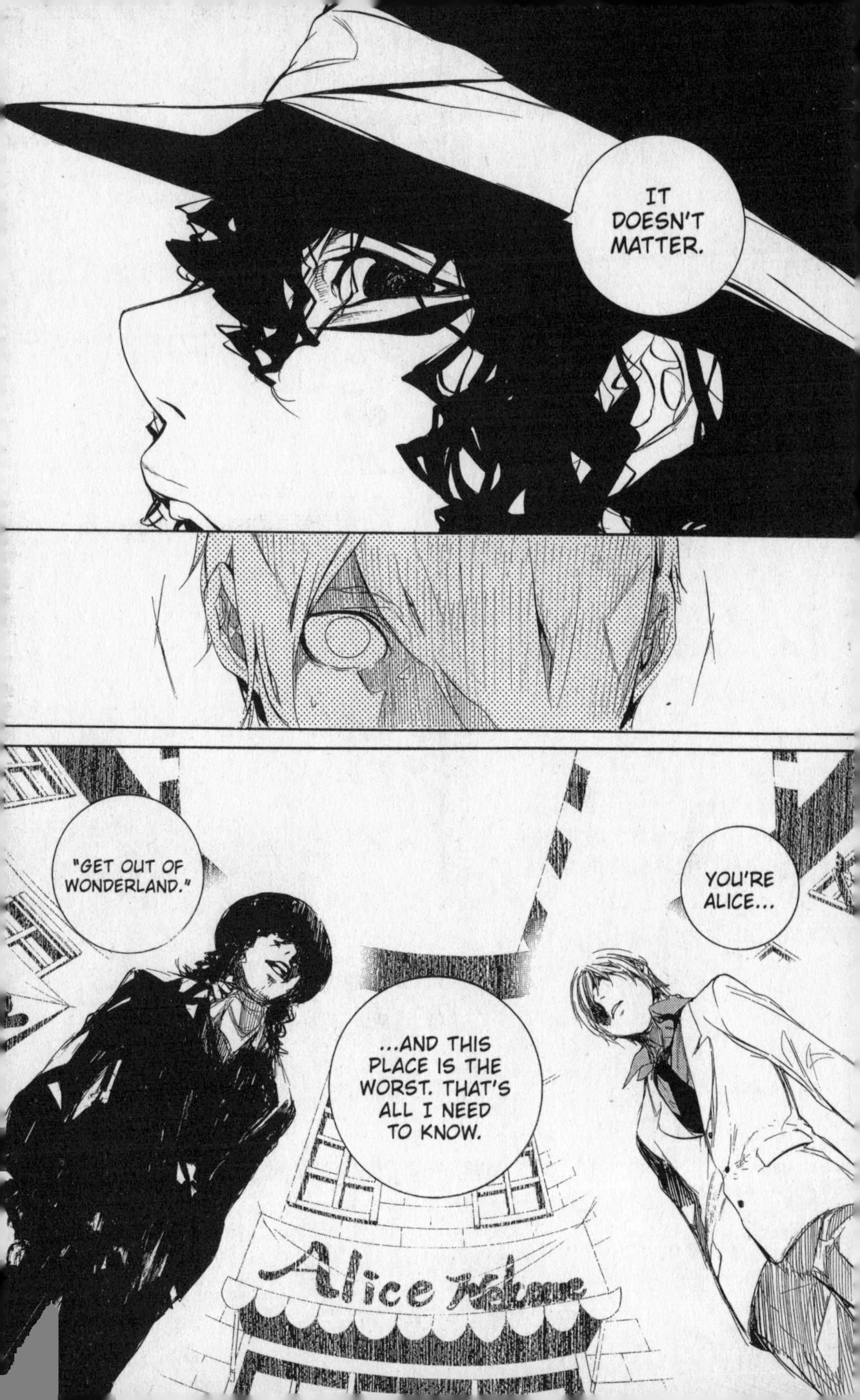
IT DOESN'T MATTER.
YOU'RE ALICE...
"GET OUT OF WONDERLAND."
...AND THIS PLACE IS THE WORST. THAT'S ALL I NEED TO KNOW.
Alice

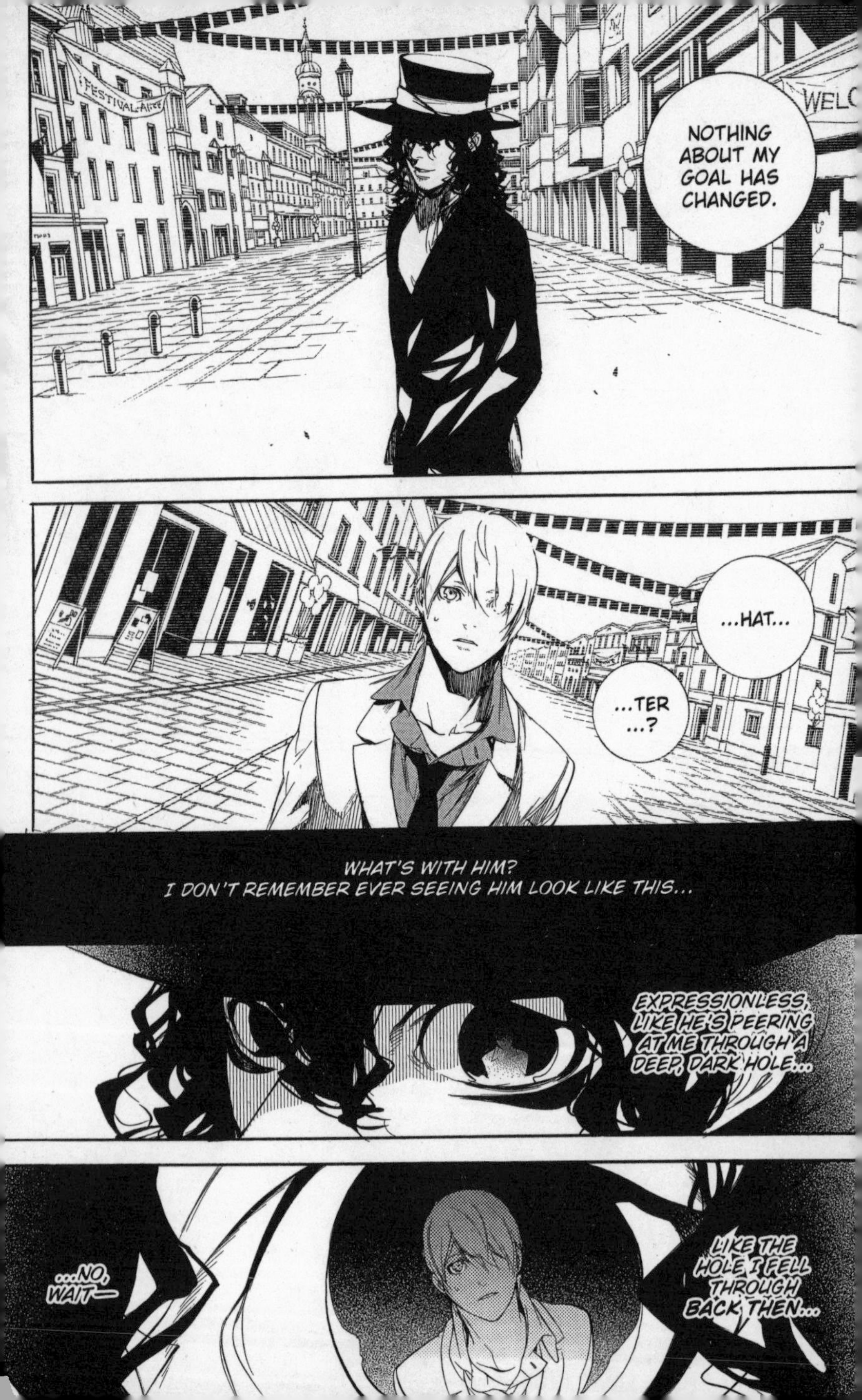
NOTHING ABOUT MY GOAL HAS CHANGED.
...HAT...
...TER ...?
WHAT'S WITH HIM? I DON'T REMEMBER EVER SEEING HIM LOOK LIKE THIS...
EXPRESSIONLESS, LIKE HE'S PEERING AT ME THROUGH A DEEP, DARK HOLE...
LIKE THE HOLE I FELL THROUGH BACK THEN...
...NO, WAIT—

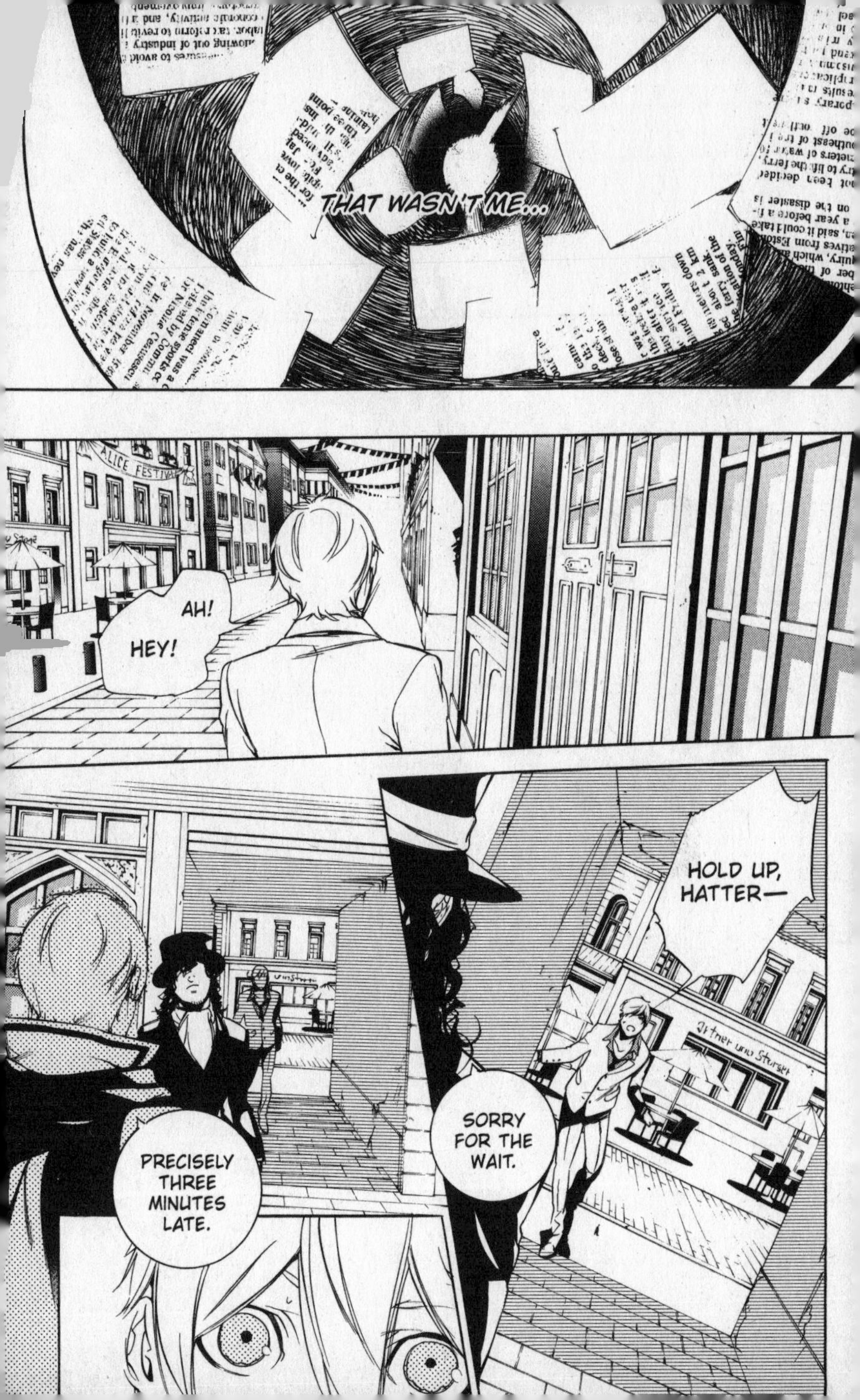
THAT WASN'T ME...
AH!
HEY!
HOLD UP, HATTER—
SORRY FOR THE WAIT.
PRECISELY THREE MINUTES LATE.

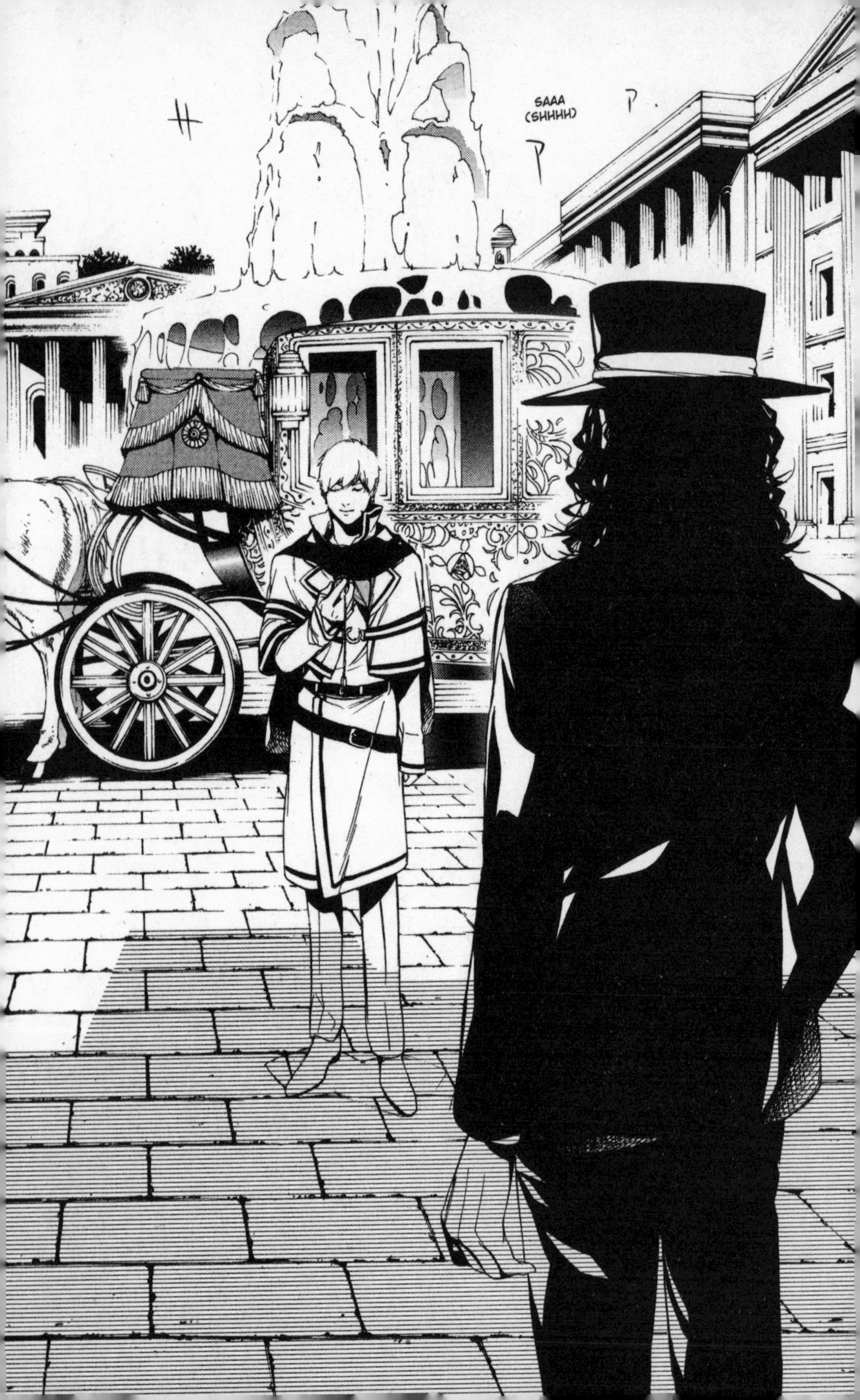
SAAA
(SHHHH)

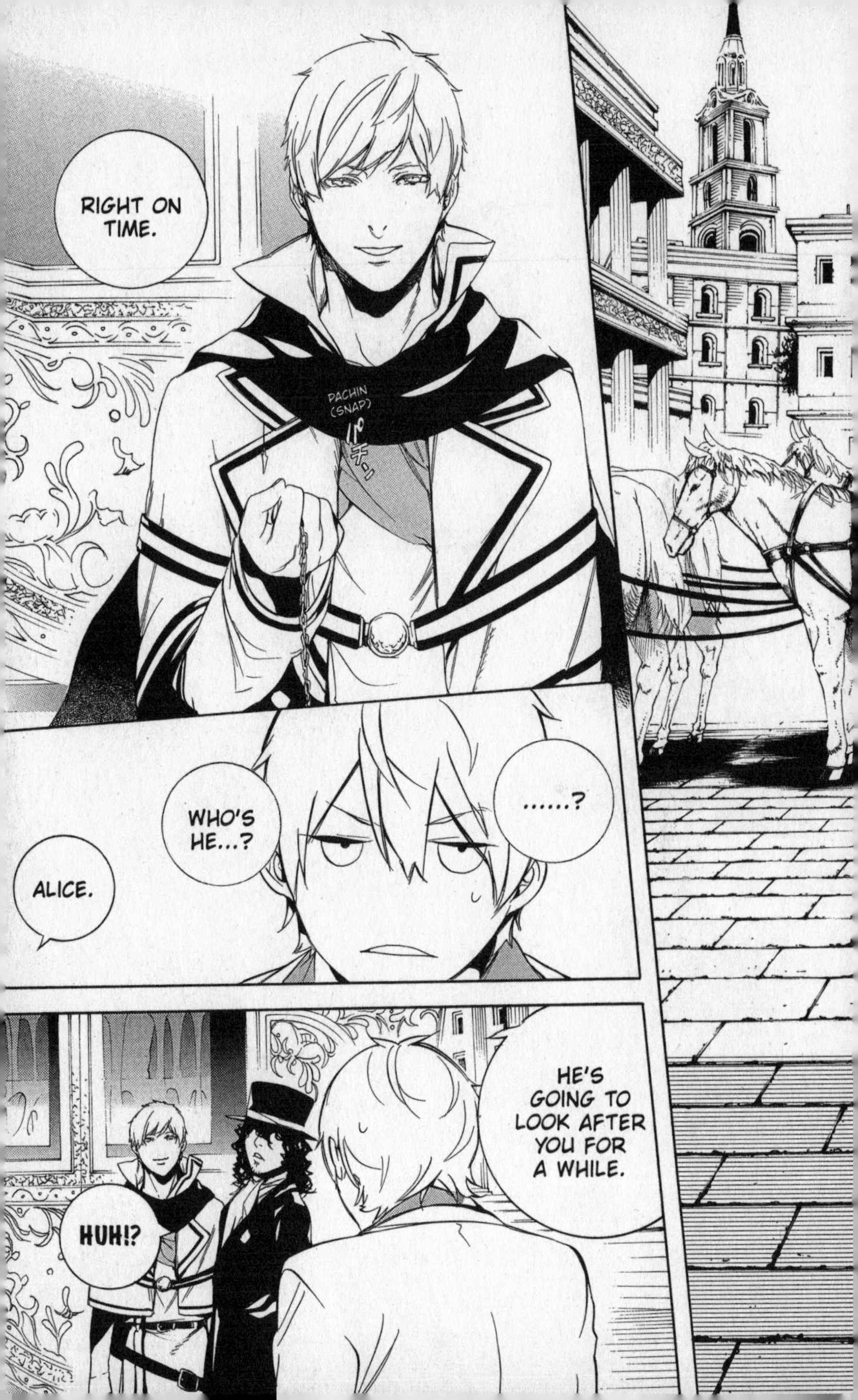
RIGHT ON TIME.
PACHIN (SNAP)
......?
WHO'S HE...?
ALICE.
HE'S GOING TO LOOK AFTER YOU FOR A WHILE.
HUH!?

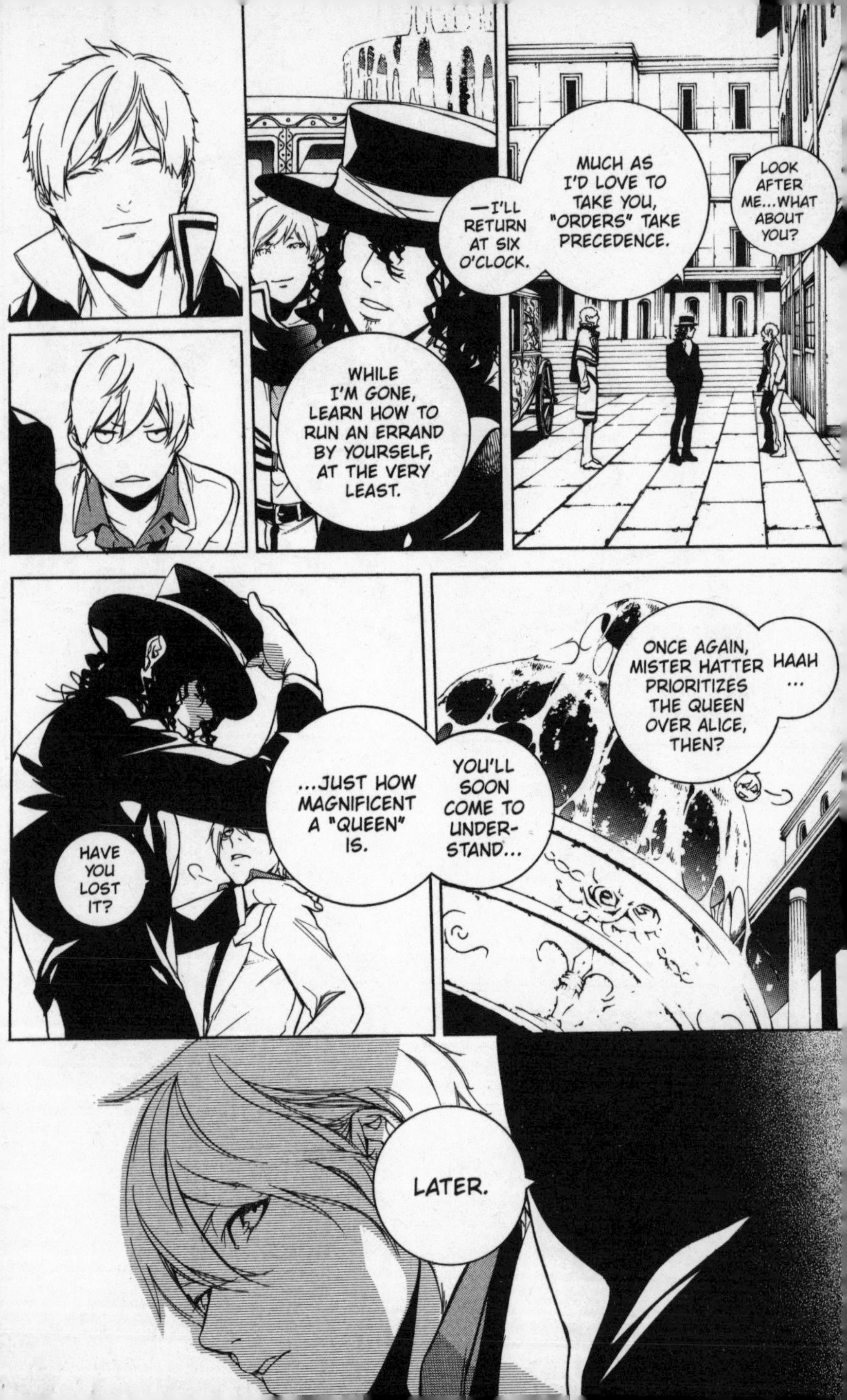
LOOK AFTER ME...WHAT ABOUT YOU?
MUCH AS I'D LOVE TO TAKE YOU, "ORDERS" TAKE PRECEDENCE.
—I'LL RETURN AT SIX O'CLOCK.
WHILE I'M GONE, LEARN HOW TO RUN AN ERRAND BY YOURSELF, AT THE VERY LEAST.
HAAH ...
ONCE AGAIN, MISTER HATTER PRIORITIZES THE QUEEN OVER ALICE, THEN?
YOU'LL SOON COME TO UNDER-STAND...
...JUST HOW MAGNIFICENT A "QUEEN" IS.
HAVE YOU LOST IT?
LATER.

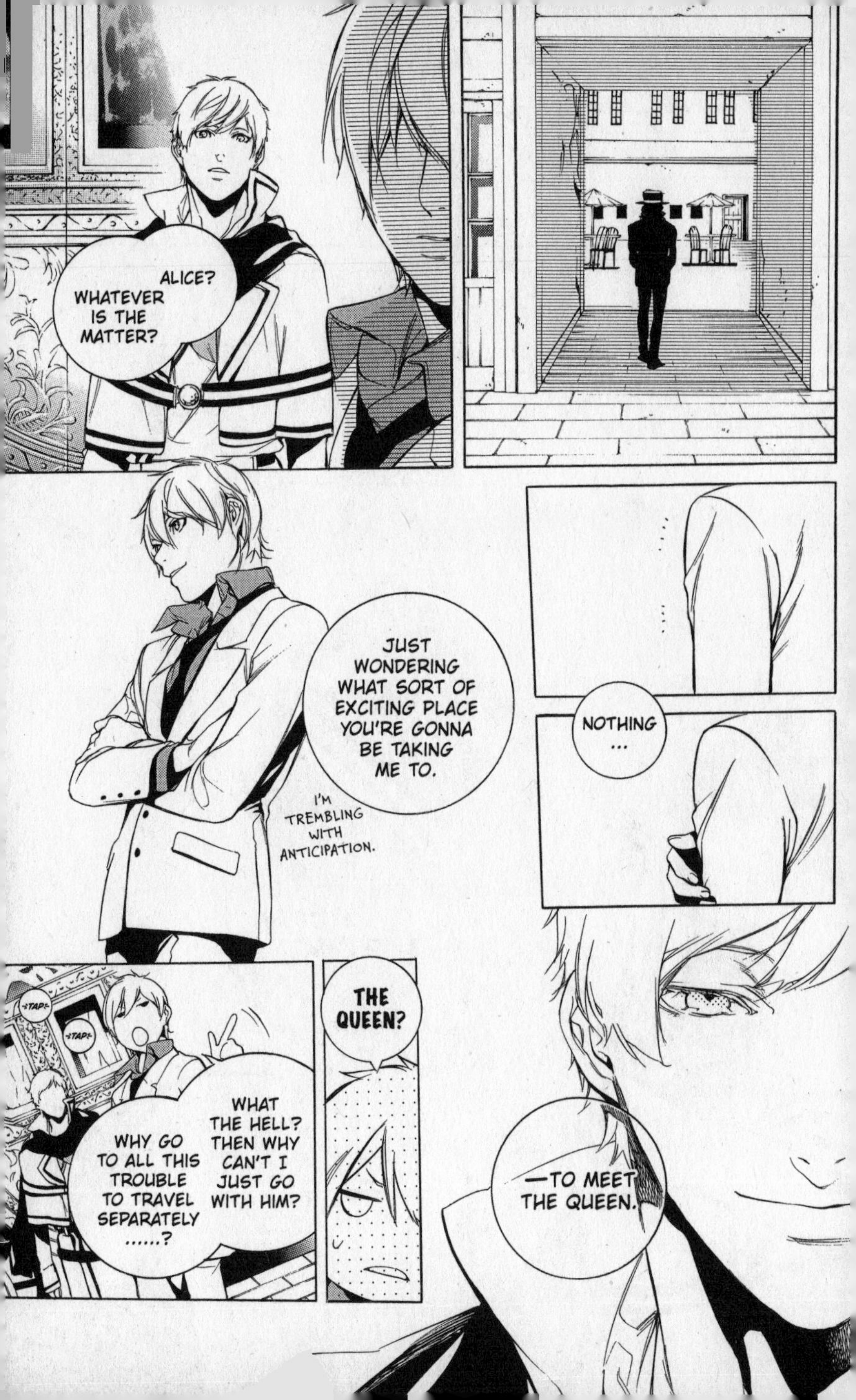
ALICE? WHATEVER IS THE MATTER?
NOTHING ...
JUST WONDERING WHAT SORT OF EXCITING PLACE YOU'RE GONNA BE TAKING ME TO.
I'M TREMBLING WITH ANTICIPATION.
—TO MEET THE QUEEN.
THE QUEEN?
TAP
TAP
WHAT THE HELL? THEN WHY CAN'T I JUST GO WITH HIM?
WHY GO TO ALL THIS TROUBLE TO TRAVEL SEPARATELY ......?

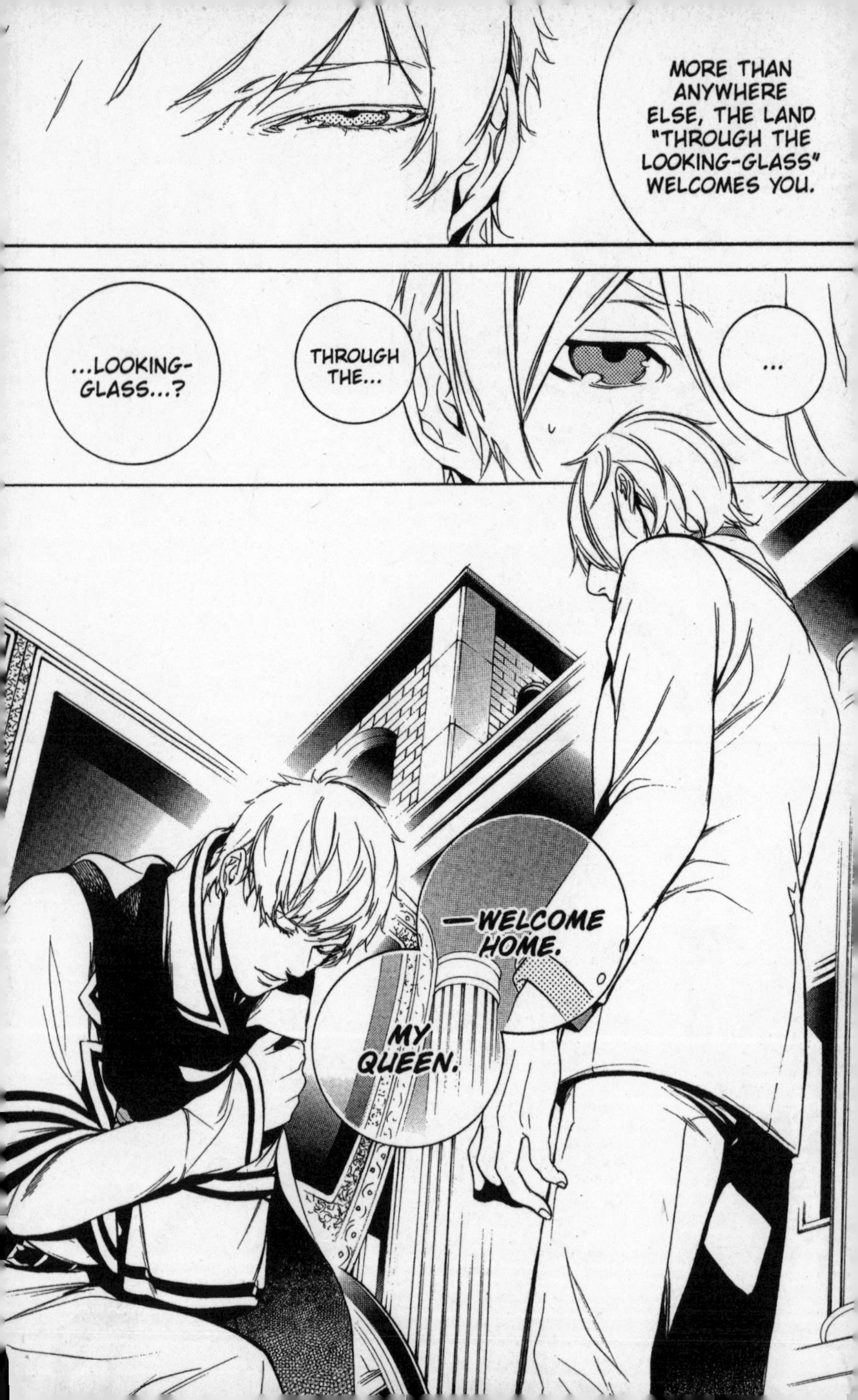
MORE THAN ANYWHERE ELSE, THE LAND "THROUGH THE LOOKING-GLASS" WELCOMES YOU.
...
THROUGH THE...
...LOOKING-GLASS...?
—WELCOME HOME.
MY QUEEN.

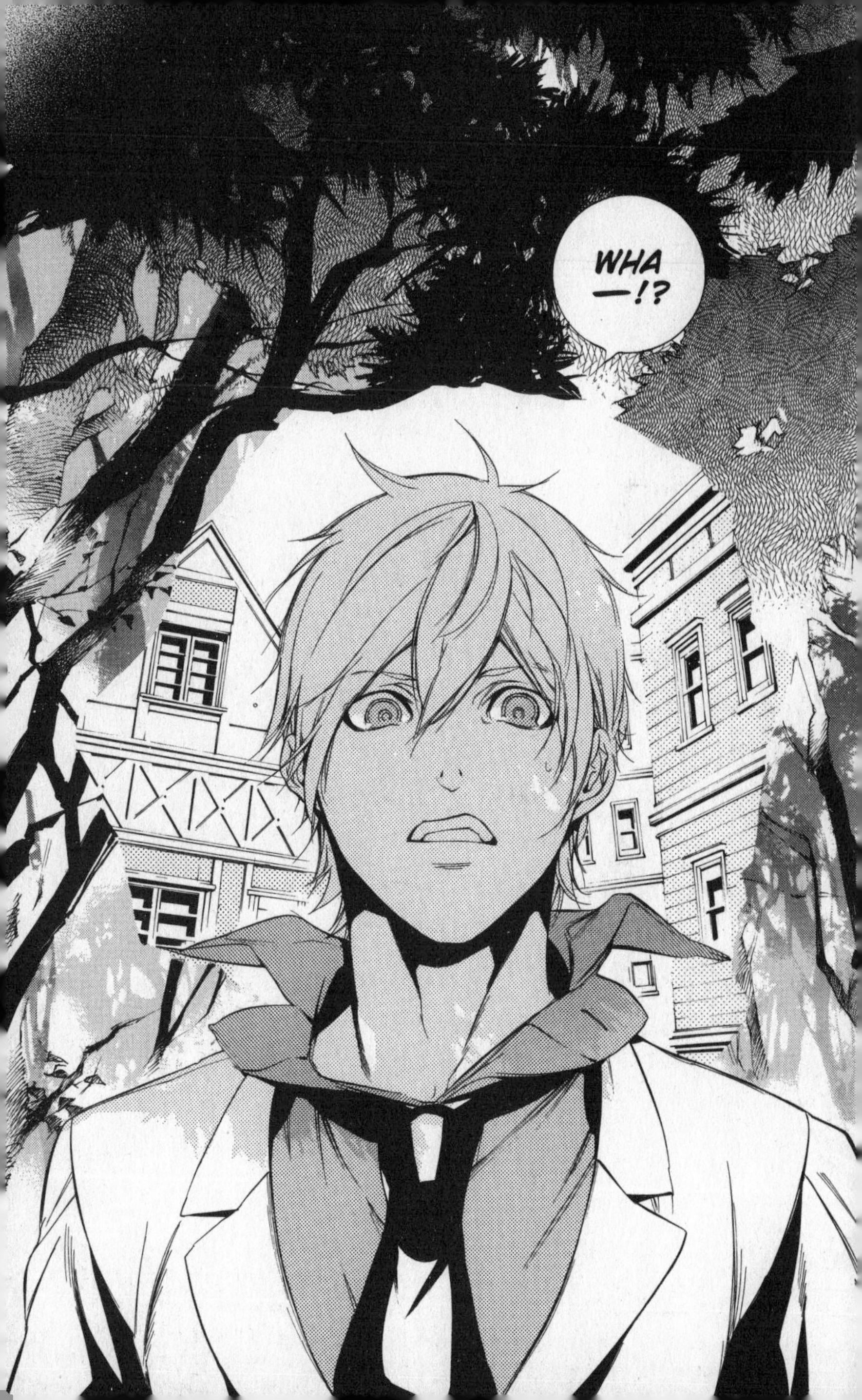
WHA—!?

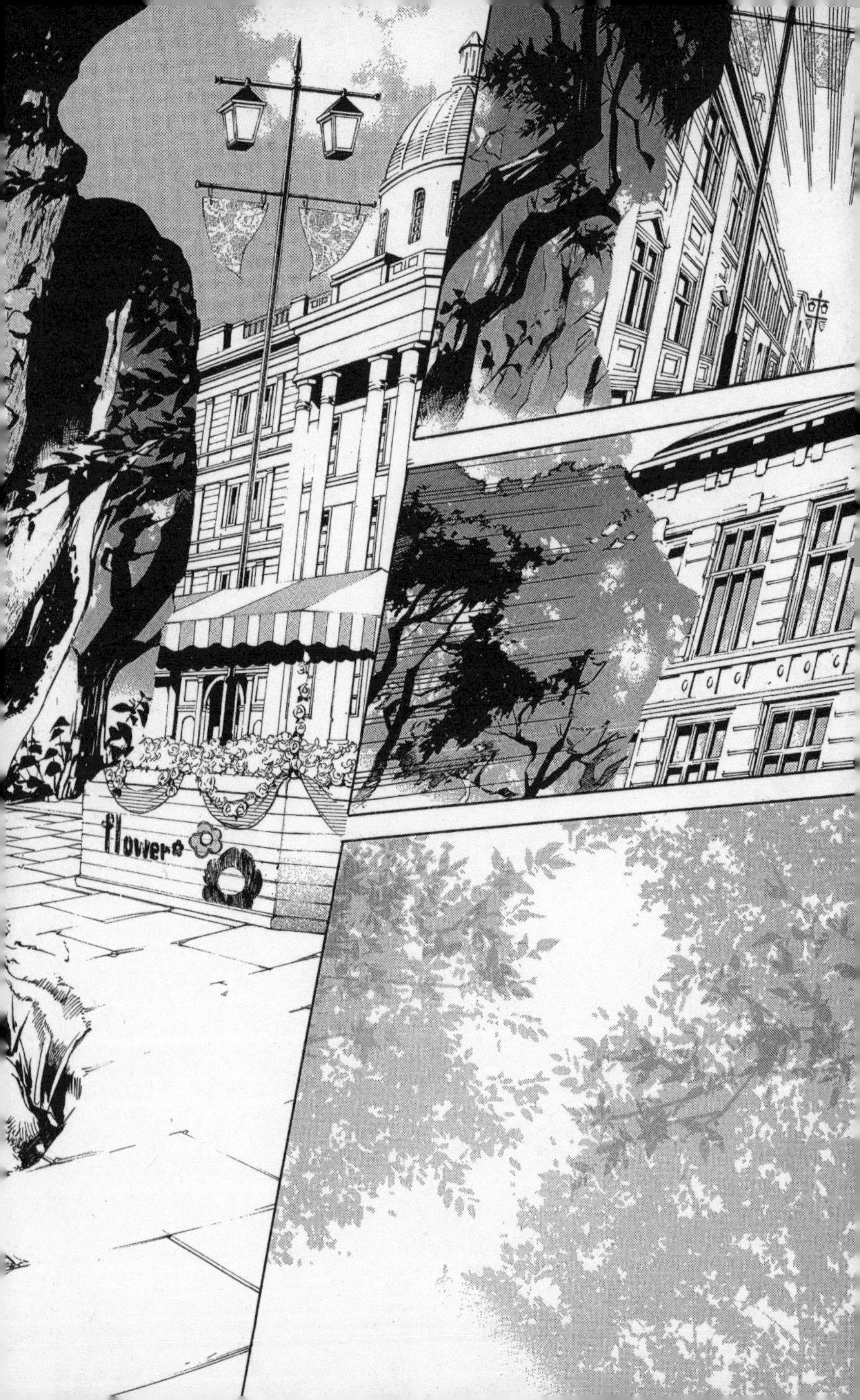
flower

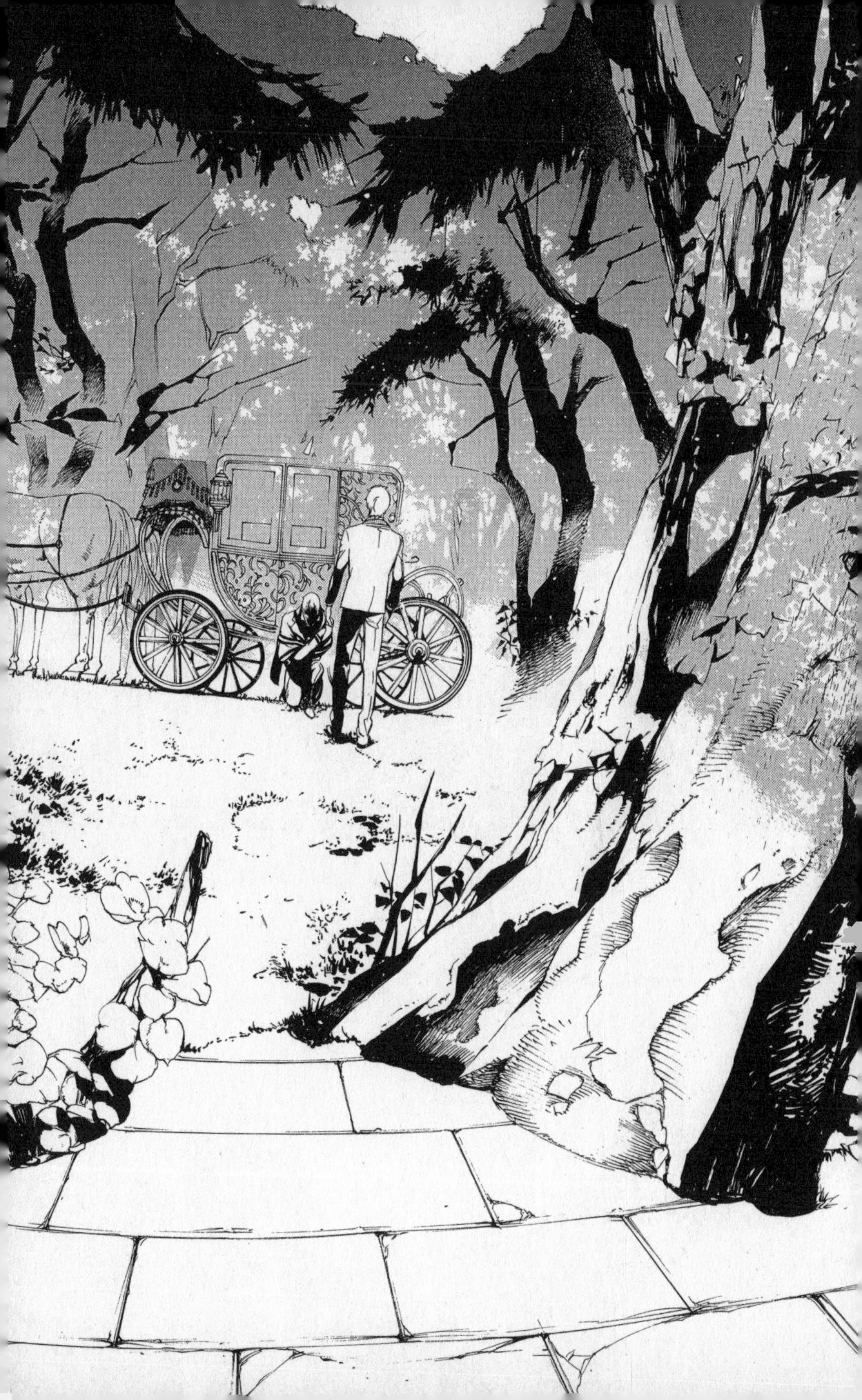

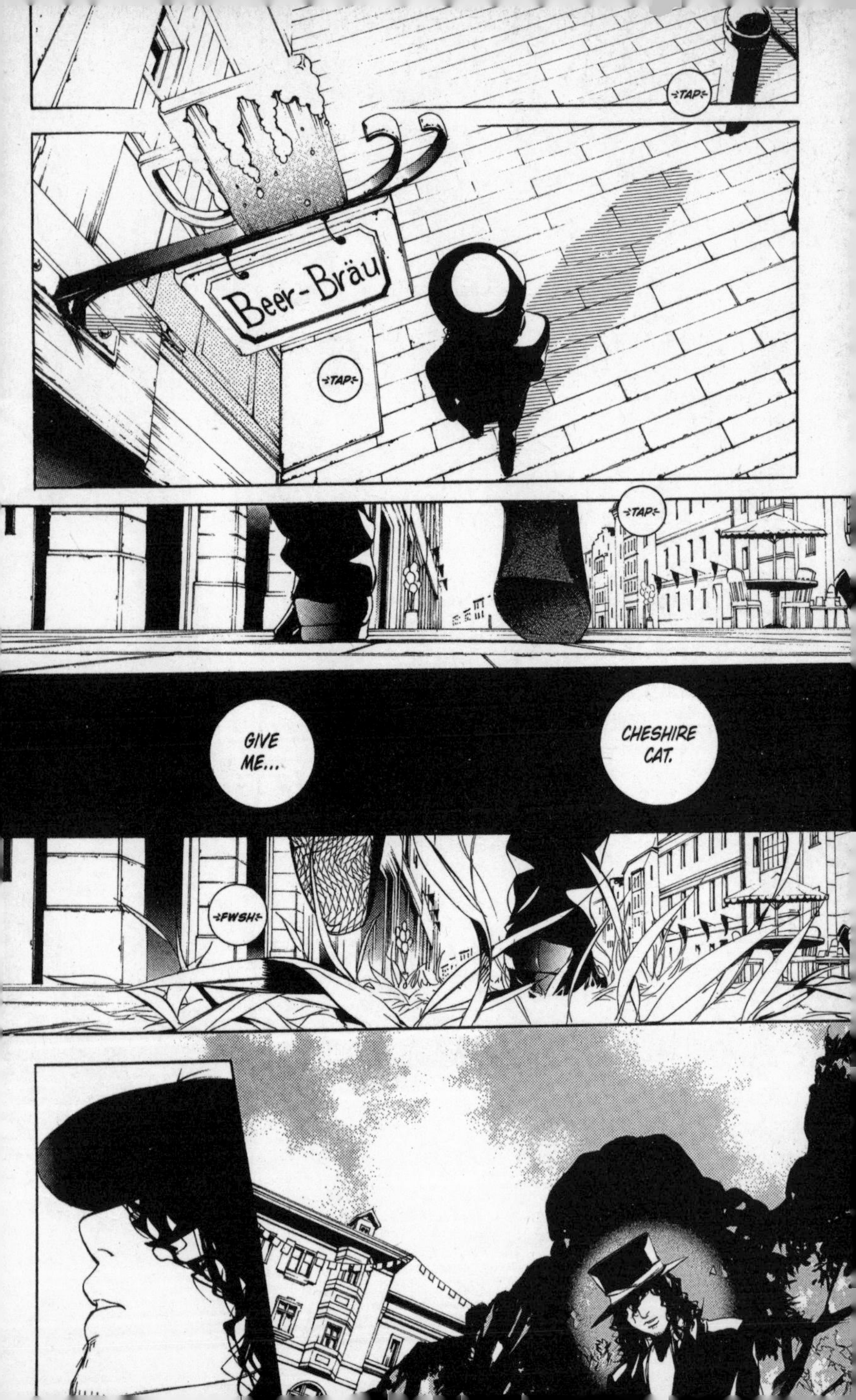
TAP
Beer-Bräu
TAP
TAP
CHESHIRE CAT.
GIVE ME...
FWSH

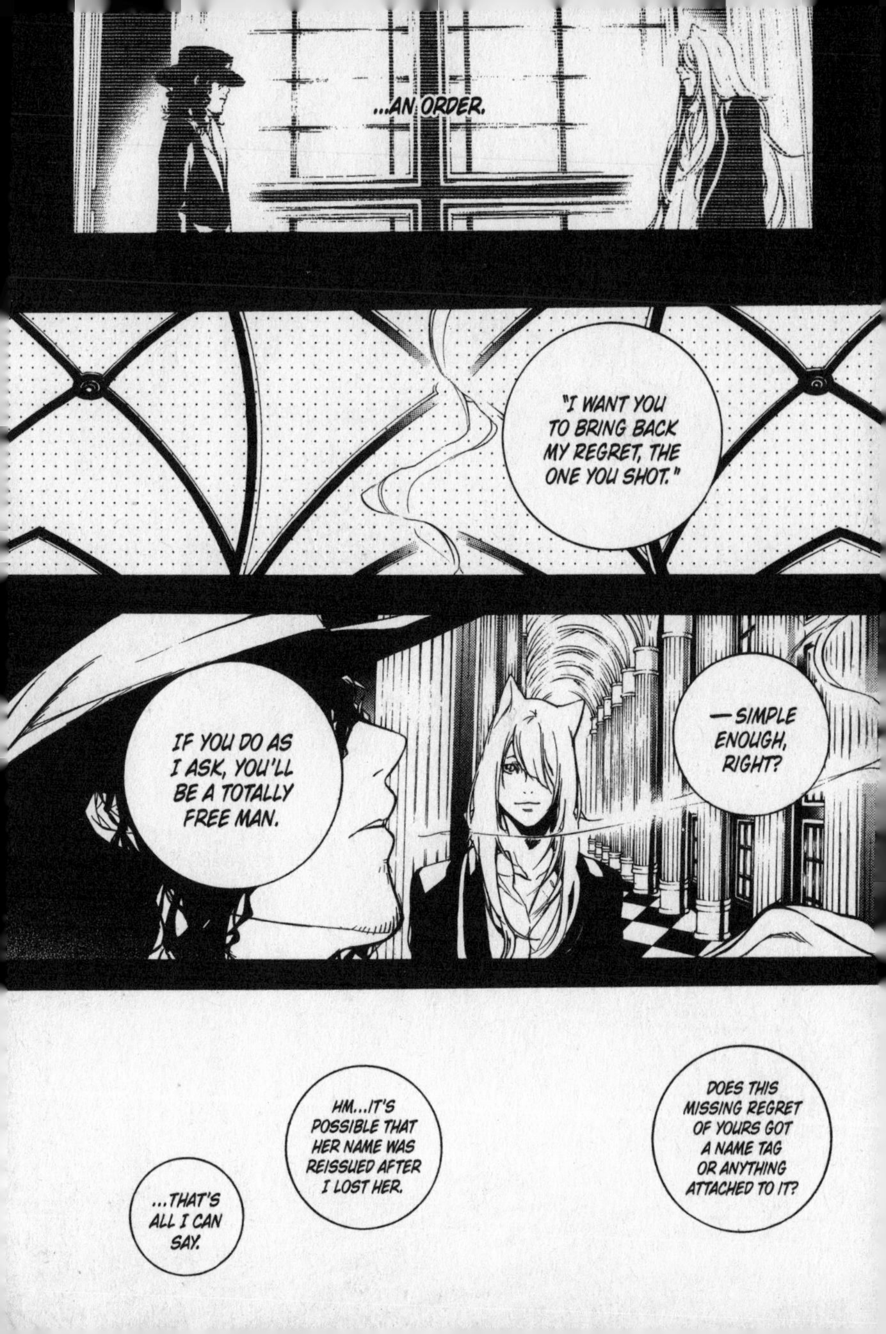
...AN ORDER.
"I WANT YOU TO BRING BACK MY REGRET, THE ONE YOU SHOT."
—SIMPLE ENOUGH, RIGHT?
IF YOU DO AS I ASK, YOU'LL BE A TOTALLY FREE MAN.
DOES THIS MISSING REGRET OF YOURS GOT A NAME TAG OR ANYTHING ATTACHED TO IT?
HM...IT'S POSSIBLE THAT HER NAME WAS REISSUED AFTER I LOST HER.
...THAT'S ALL I CAN SAY.

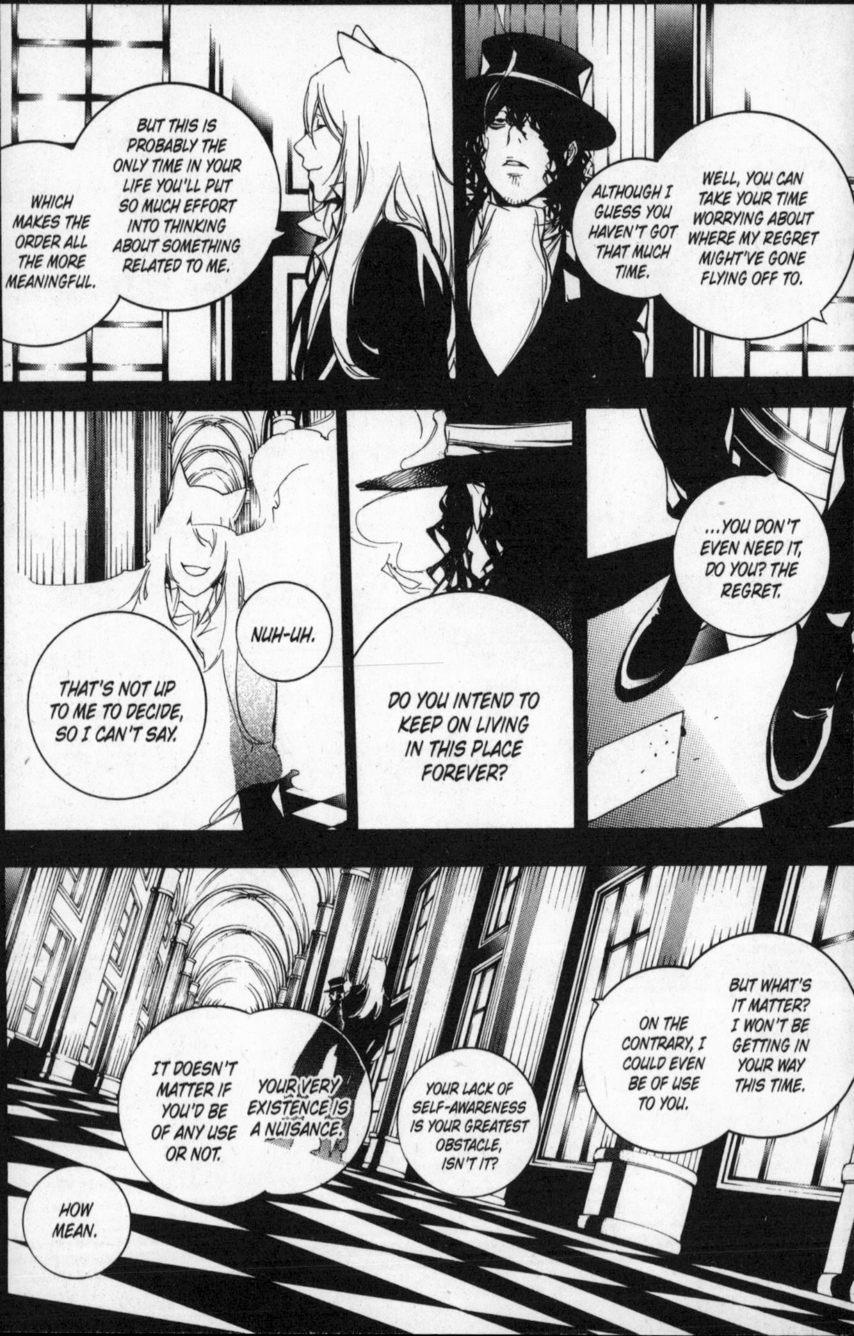
WELL, YOU CAN TAKE YOUR TIME WORRYING ABOUT WHERE MY REGRET MIGHT'VE GONE FLYING OFF TO.
ALTHOUGH I GUESS YOU HAVEN'T GOT THAT MUCH TIME.
BUT THIS IS PROBABLY THE ONLY TIME IN YOUR LIFE YOU'LL PUT SO MUCH EFFORT INTO THINKING ABOUT SOMETHING RELATED TO ME.
WHICH MAKES THE ORDER ALL THE MORE MEANINGFUL.
...YOU DON'T EVEN NEED IT, DO YOU? THE REGRET.
DO YOU INTEND TO KEEP ON LIVING IN THIS PLACE FOREVER?
NUH-UH.
THAT'S NOT UP TO ME TO DECIDE, SO I CAN'T SAY.
BUT WHAT'S IT MATTER? I WON'T BE GETTING IN YOUR WAY THIS TIME.
ON THE CONTRARY, I COULD EVEN BE OF USE TO YOU.
YOUR LACK OF SELF-AWARENESS IS YOUR GREATEST OBSTACLE, ISN'T IT?
YOUR VERY EXISTENCE IS A NUISANCE.
IT DOESN'T MATTER IF YOU'D BE OF ANY USE OR NOT.
HOW MEAN.

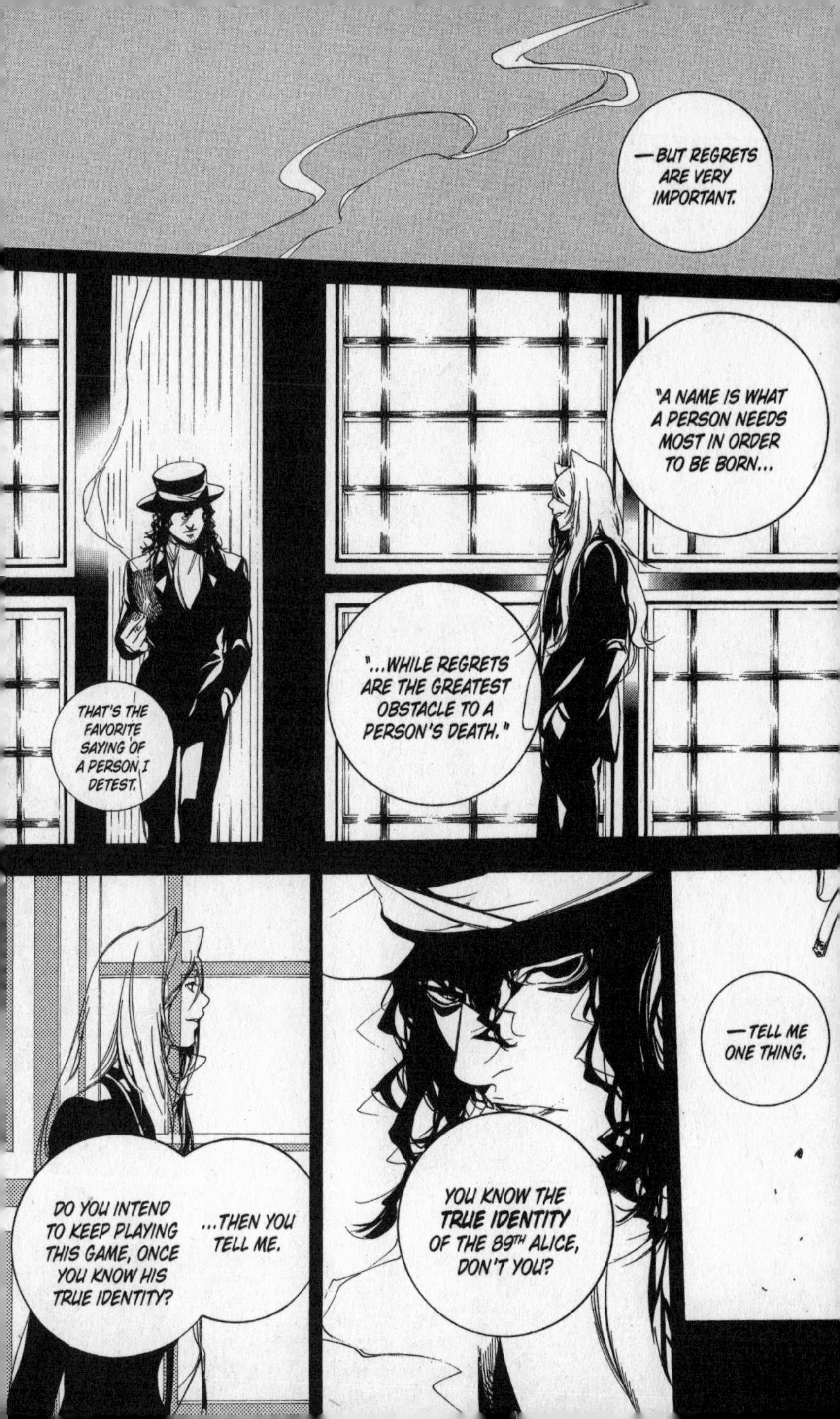
—BUT REGRETS ARE VERY IMPORTANT.
"A NAME IS WHAT A PERSON NEEDS MOST IN ORDER TO BE BORN...
"...WHILE REGRETS ARE THE GREATEST OBSTACLE TO A PERSON'S DEATH."
THAT'S THE FAVORITE SAYING OF A PERSON I DETEST.
—TELL ME ONE THING.
YOU KNOW THE TRUE IDENTITY OF THE 89TH ALICE, DON'T YOU?
...THEN YOU TELL ME.
DO YOU INTEND TO KEEP PLAYING THIS GAME, ONCE YOU KNOW HIS TRUE IDENTITY?

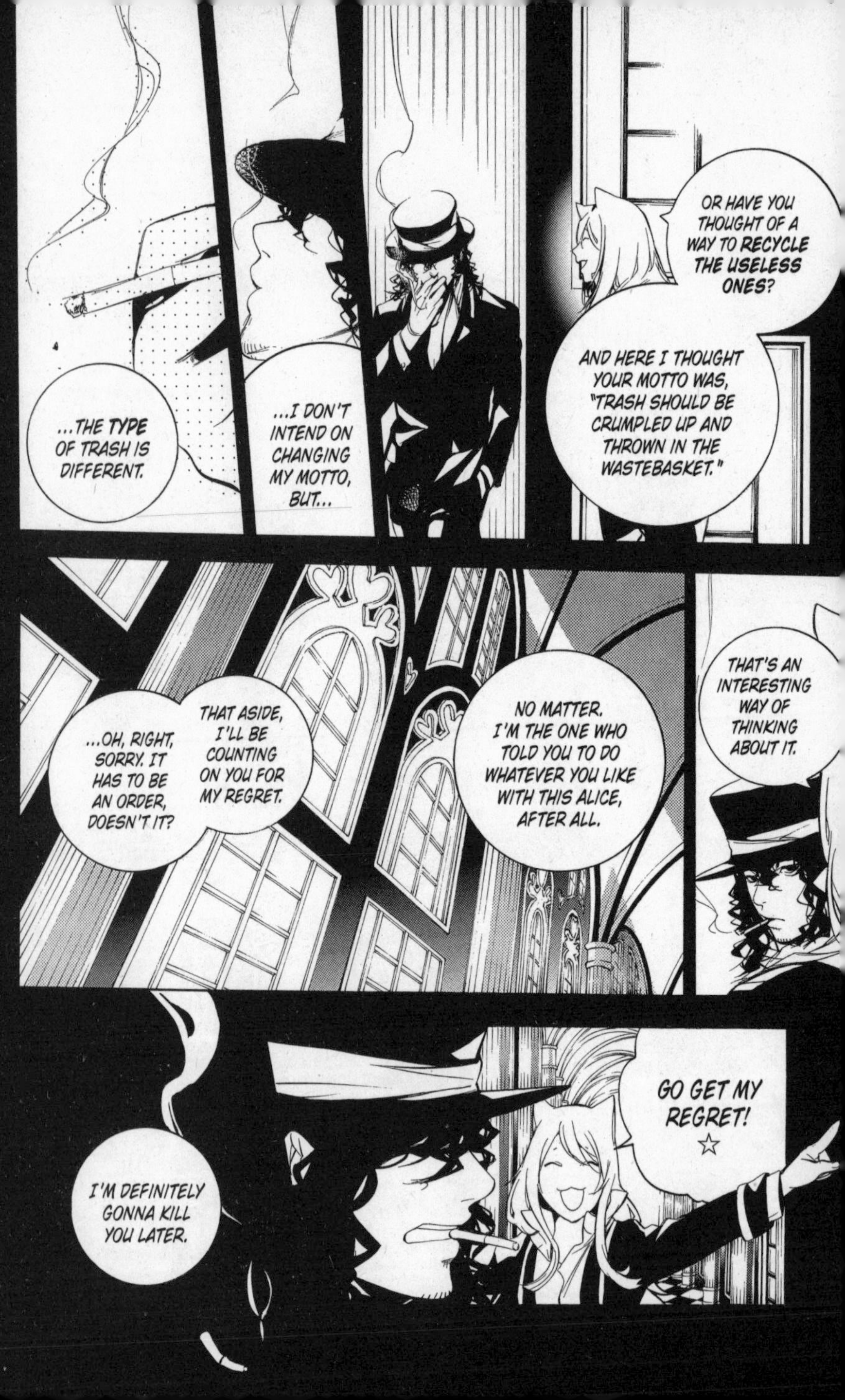
OR HAVE YOU THOUGHT OF A WAY TO RECYCLE THE USELESS ONES?
AND HERE I THOUGHT YOUR MOTTO WAS, "TRASH SHOULD BE CRUMPLED UP AND THROWN IN THE WASTEBASKET."
...I DON'T INTEND ON CHANGING MY MOTTO, BUT...
...THE TYPE OF TRASH IS DIFFERENT.
THAT'S AN INTERESTING WAY OF THINKING ABOUT IT.
NO MATTER. I'M THE ONE WHO TOLD YOU TO DO WHATEVER YOU LIKE WITH THIS ALICE, AFTER ALL.
THAT ASIDE, I'LL BE COUNTING ON YOU FOR MY REGRET.
...OH, RIGHT, SORRY. IT HAS TO BE AN ORDER, DOESN'T IT?
GO GET MY REGRET! ☆
I'M DEFINITELY GONNA KILL YOU LATER.

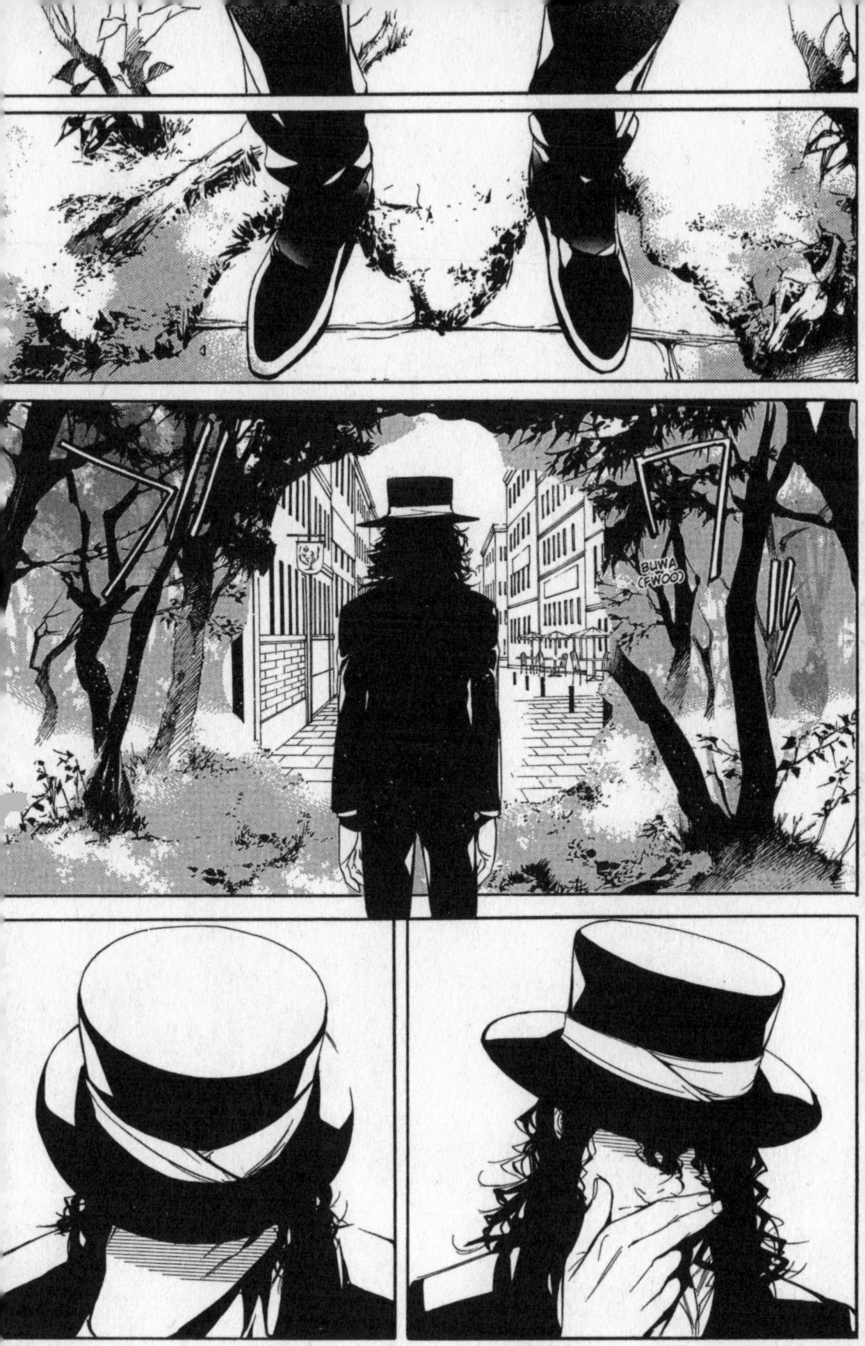
BUWA
(FWOO)

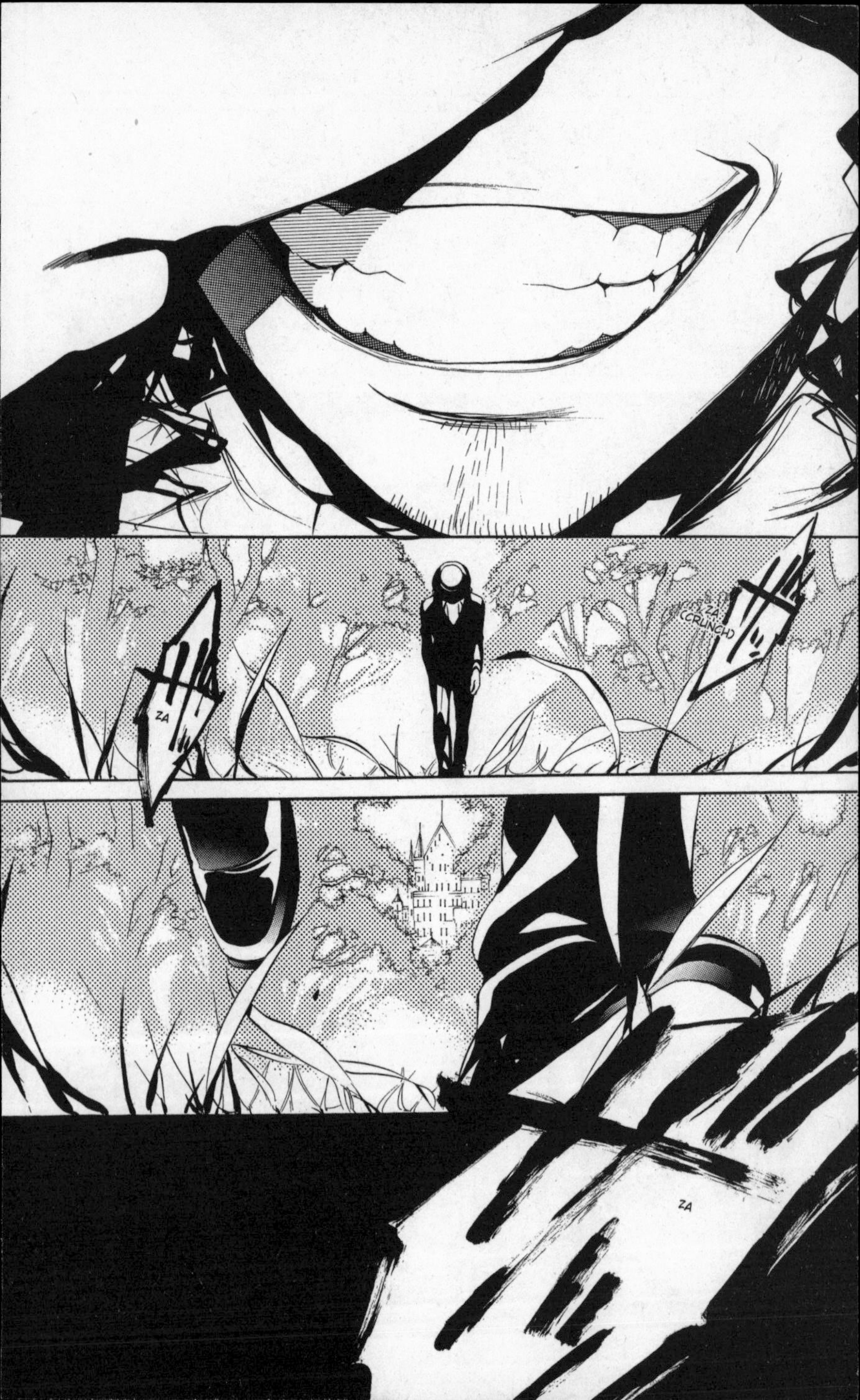
ZA (CRUNCH)
ZA
ZA

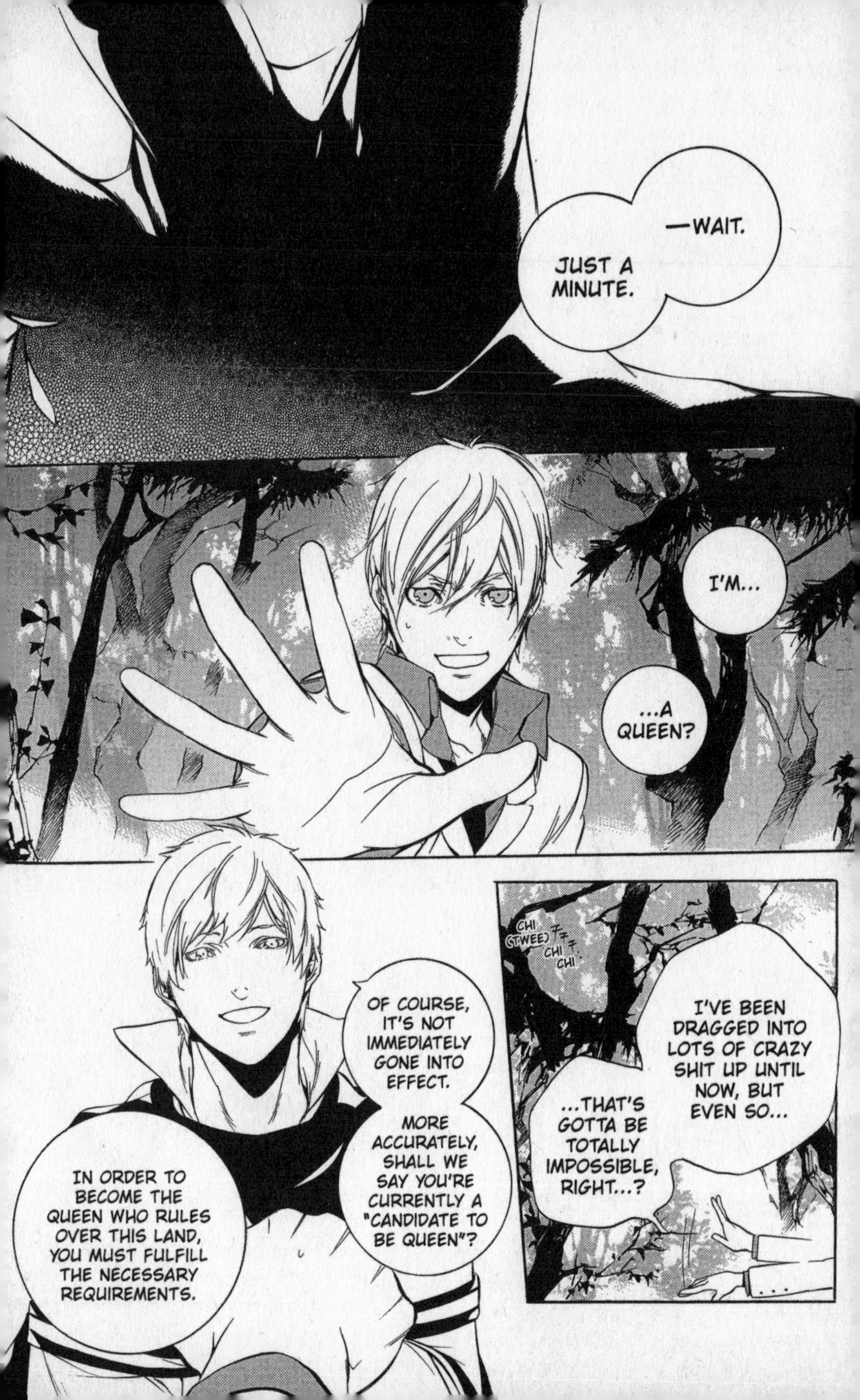
—WAIT.
JUST A MINUTE.
I'M...
...A QUEEN?
チチチ
CHI (TWEET) CHI CHI
I'VE BEEN DRAGGED INTO LOTS OF CRAZY SHIT UP UNTIL NOW, BUT EVEN SO...
...THAT'S GOTTA BE TOTALLY IMPOSSIBLE, RIGHT...?
OF COURSE, IT'S NOT IMMEDIATELY GONE INTO EFFECT.
MORE ACCURATELY, SHALL WE SAY YOU'RE CURRENTLY A "CANDIDATE TO BE QUEEN"?
IN ORDER TO BECOME THE QUEEN WHO RULES OVER THIS LAND, YOU MUST FULFILL THE NECESSARY REQUIREMENTS.

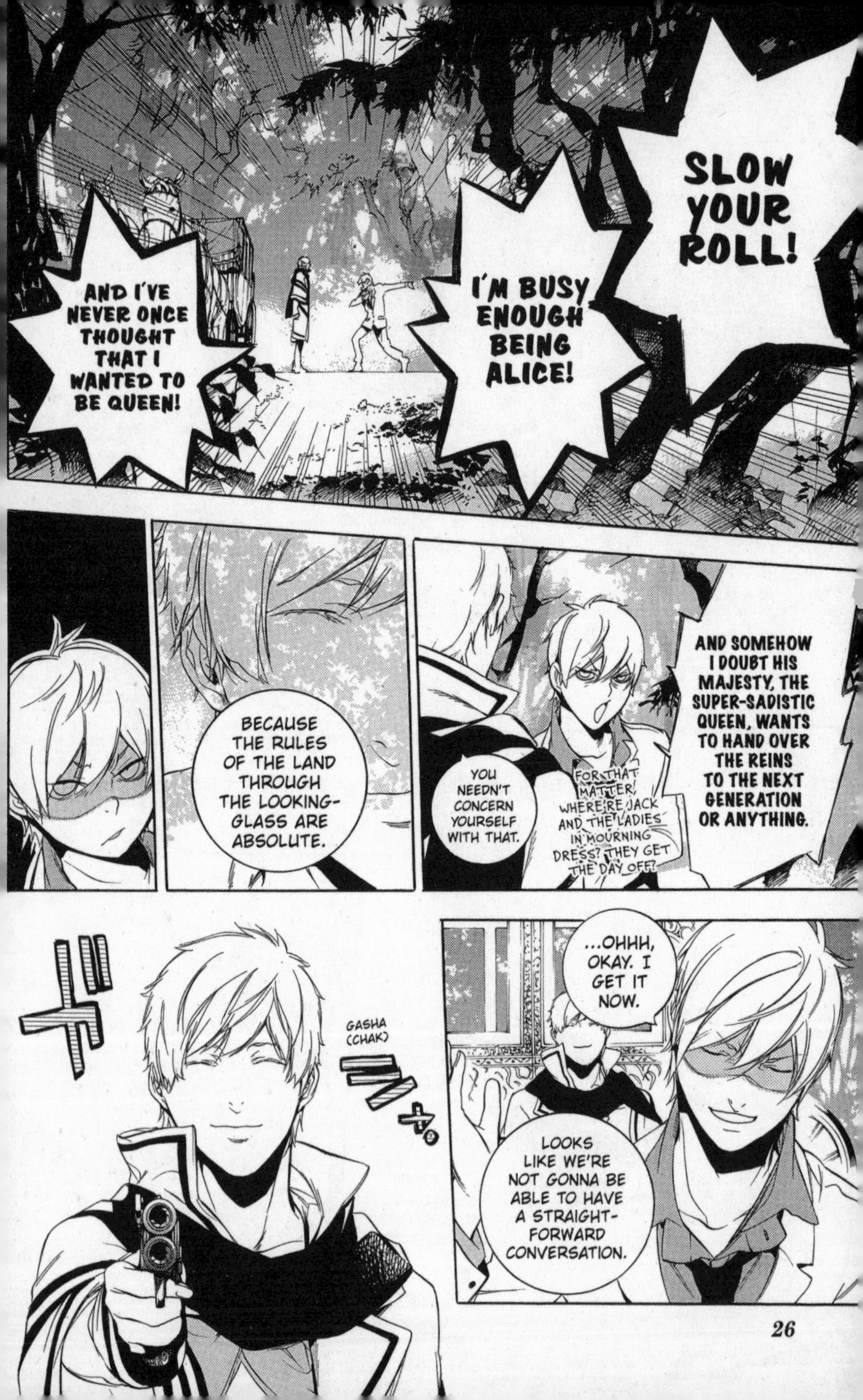
SLOW YOUR ROLL!
I'M BUSY ENOUGH BEING ALICE!
AND I'VE NEVER ONCE THOUGHT THAT I WANTED TO BE QUEEN!
AND SOMEHOW I DOUBT HIS MAJESTY, THE SUPER-SADISTIC QUEEN, WANTS TO HAND OVER THE REINS TO THE NEXT GENERATION OR ANYTHING.
FOR THAT MATTER, WHERE'RE JACK AND THE LADIES IN MOURNING DRESS? THEY GET THE DAY OFF?
YOU NEEDN'T CONCERN YOURSELF WITH THAT.
BECAUSE THE RULES OF THE LAND THROUGH THE LOOKING-GLASS ARE ABSOLUTE.
...OHHH, OKAY. I GET IT NOW.
LOOKS LIKE WE'RE NOT GONNA BE ABLE TO HAVE A STRAIGHT-FORWARD CONVERSATION.
GASHA (CHAK)

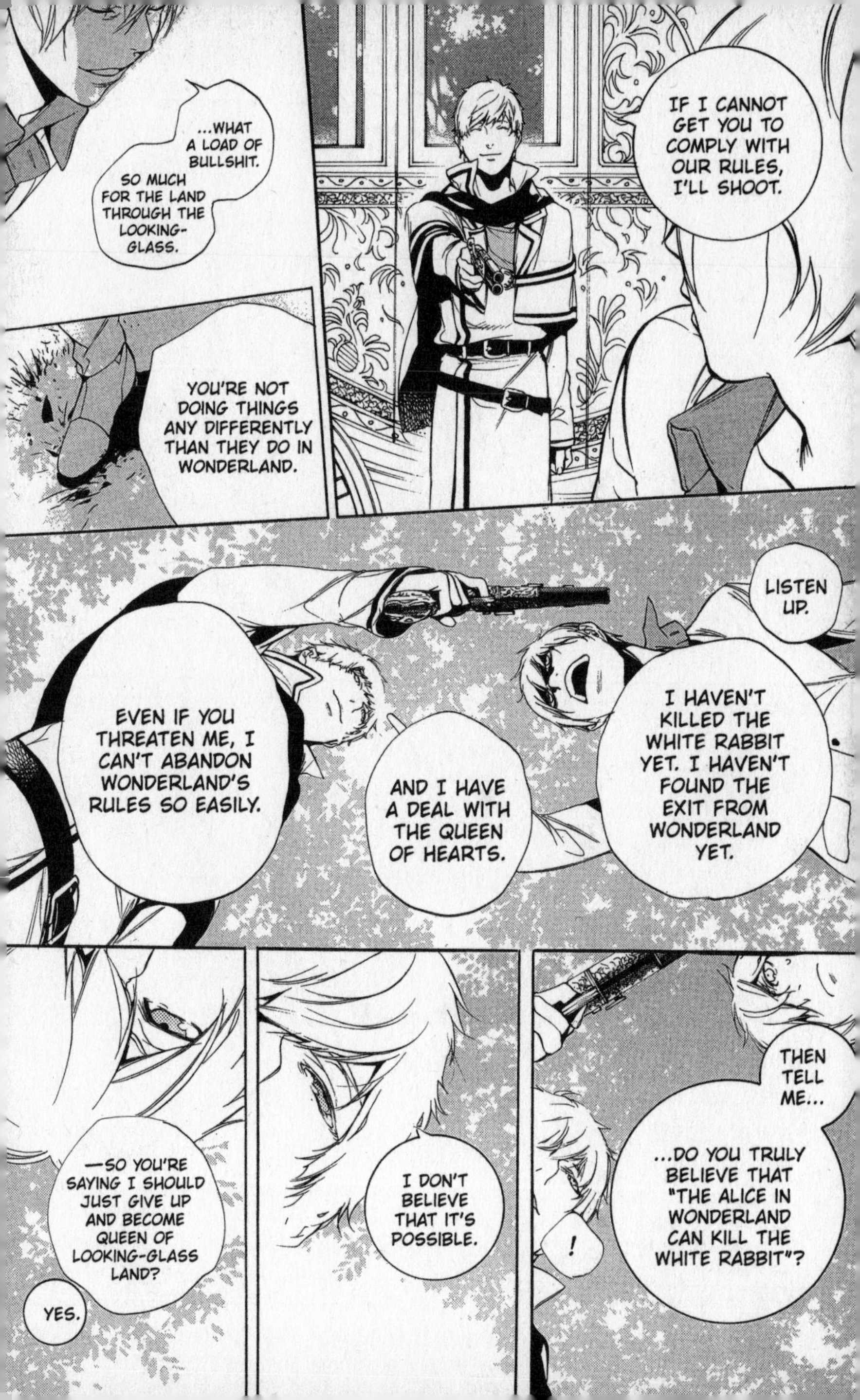
IF I CANNOT GET YOU TO COMPLY WITH OUR RULES, I'LL SHOOT.
...WHAT A LOAD OF BULLSHIT.
SO MUCH FOR THE LAND THROUGH THE LOOKING-GLASS.
YOU'RE NOT DOING THINGS ANY DIFFERENTLY THAN THEY DO IN WONDERLAND.
LISTEN UP.
I HAVEN'T KILLED THE WHITE RABBIT YET. I HAVEN'T FOUND THE EXIT FROM WONDERLAND YET.
AND I HAVE A DEAL WITH THE QUEEN OF HEARTS.
EVEN IF YOU THREATEN ME, I CAN'T ABANDON WONDERLAND'S RULES SO EASILY.
THEN TELL ME...
...DO YOU TRULY BELIEVE THAT "THE ALICE IN WONDERLAND CAN KILL THE WHITE RABBIT"?
!
I DON'T BELIEVE THAT IT'S POSSIBLE.
—SO YOU'RE SAYING I SHOULD JUST GIVE UP AND BECOME QUEEN OF LOOKING-GLASS LAND?
YES.

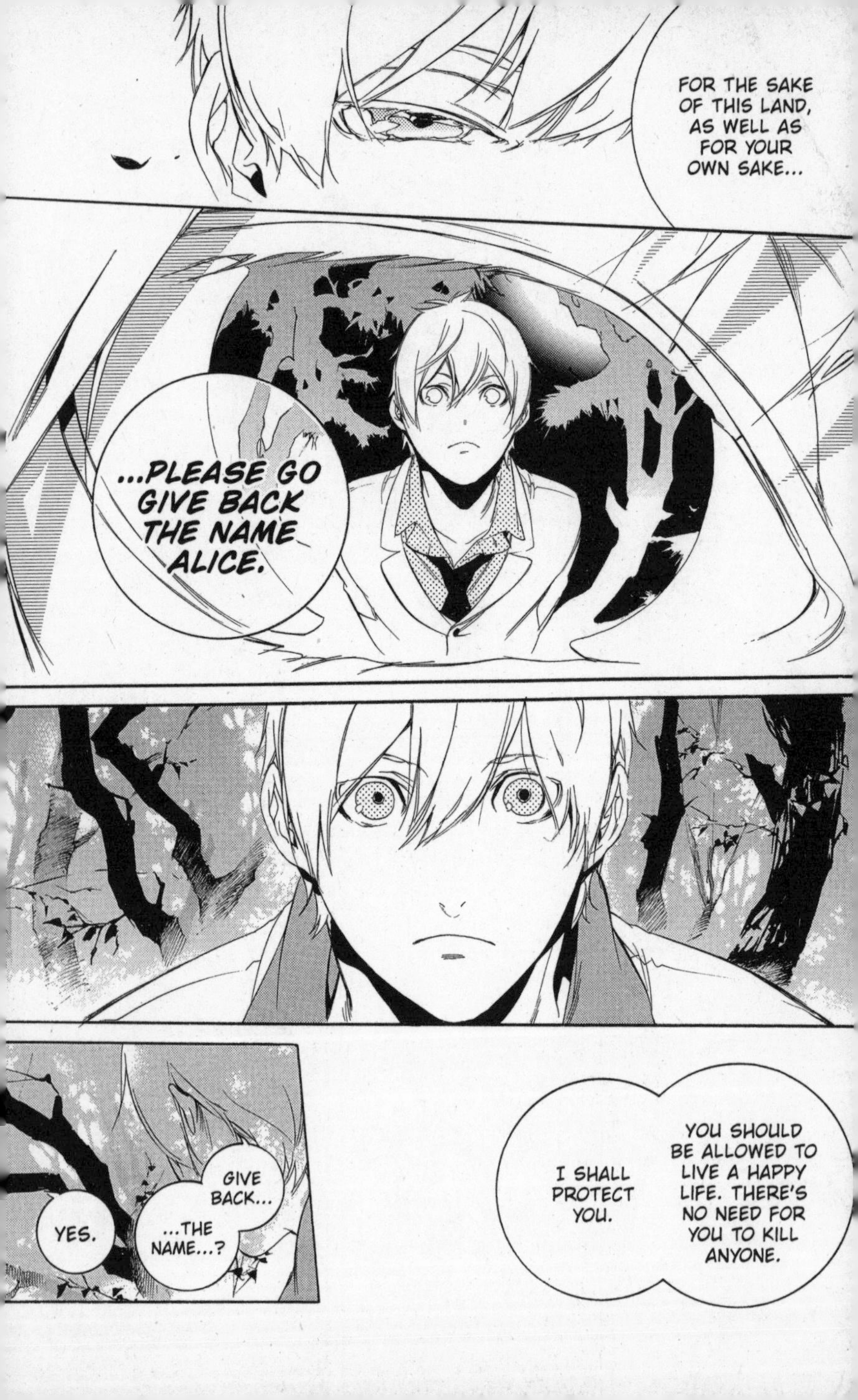
FOR THE SAKE OF THIS LAND, AS WELL AS FOR YOUR OWN SAKE...
...PLEASE GO GIVE BACK THE NAME ALICE.
YOU SHOULD BE ALLOWED TO LIVE A HAPPY LIFE. THERE'S NO NEED FOR YOU TO KILL ANYONE.
I SHALL PROTECT YOU.
GIVE BACK...
...THE NAME...?
YES.

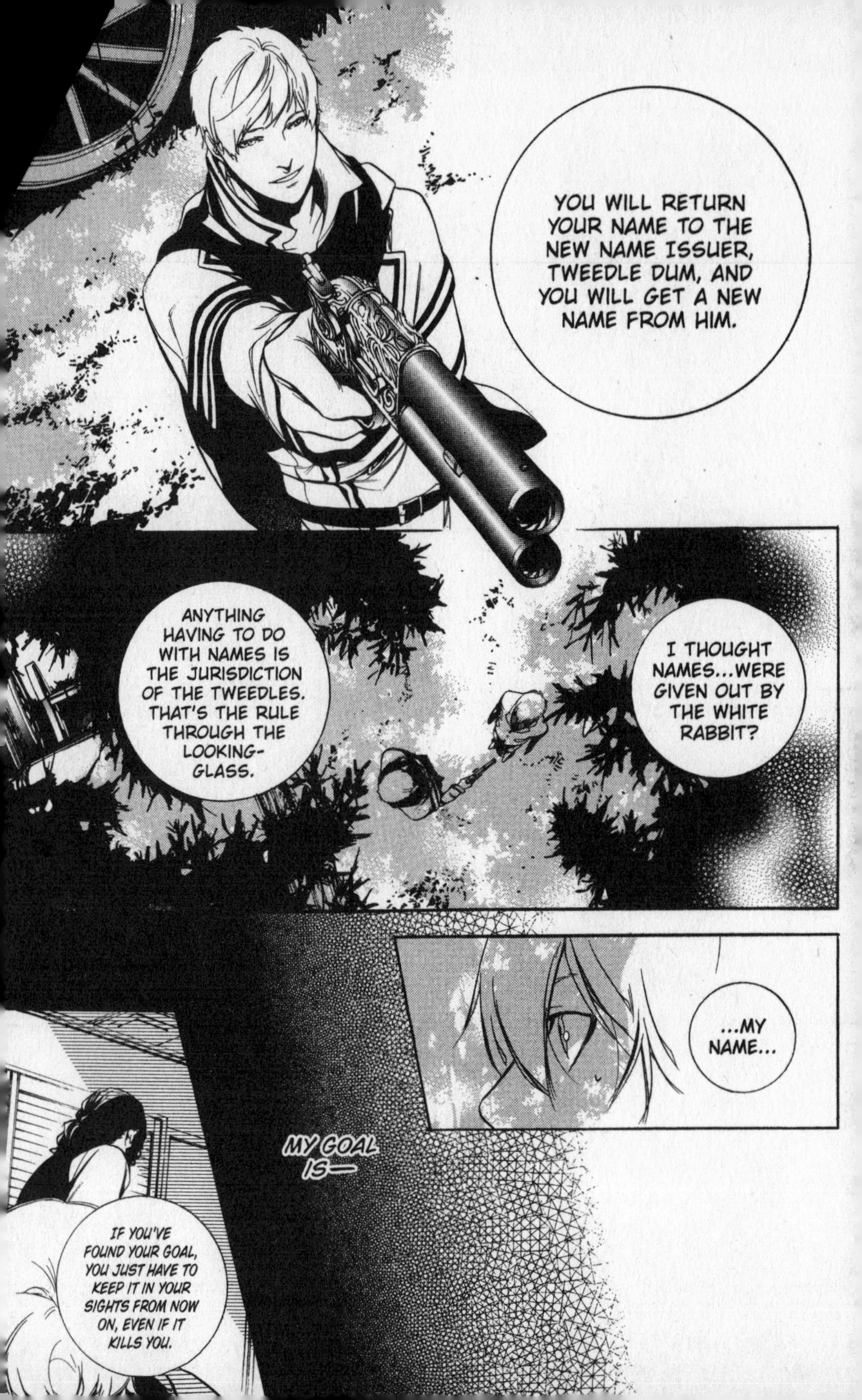
YOU WILL RETURN YOUR NAME TO THE NEW NAME ISSUER, TWEEDLE DUM, AND YOU WILL GET A NEW NAME FROM HIM.
I THOUGHT NAMES...WERE GIVEN OUT BY THE WHITE RABBIT?
ANYTHING HAVING TO DO WITH NAMES IS THE JURISDICTION OF THE TWEEDLES. THAT'S THE RULE THROUGH THE LOOKING-GLASS.
...MY NAME...
MY GOAL IS—
IF YOU'VE FOUND YOUR GOAL, YOU JUST HAVE TO KEEP IT IN YOUR SIGHTS FROM NOW ON, EVEN IF IT KILLS YOU.

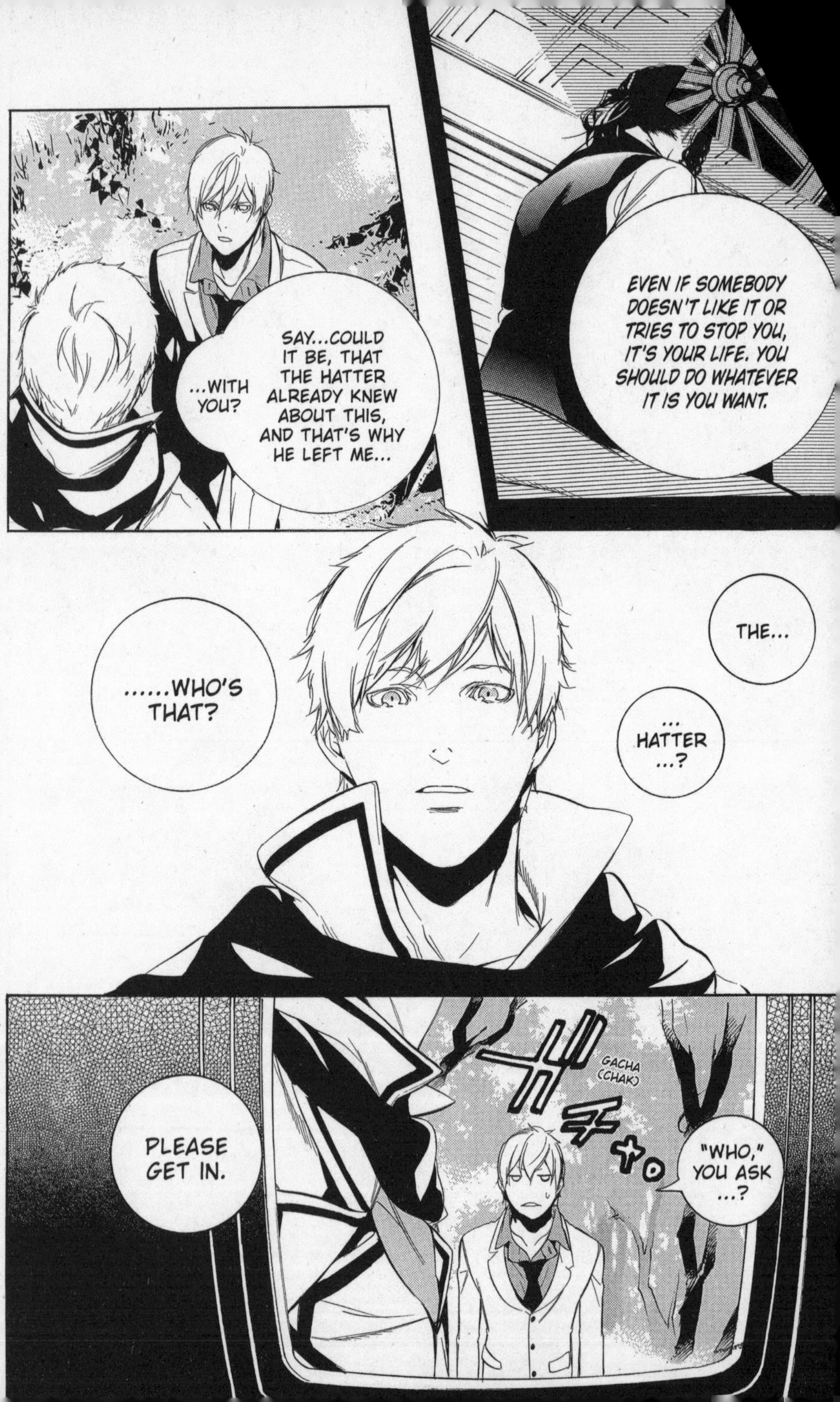
EVEN IF SOMEBODY DOESN'T LIKE IT OR TRIES TO STOP YOU, IT'S YOUR LIFE. YOU SHOULD DO WHATEVER IT IS YOU WANT.
SAY...COULD IT BE, THAT THE HATTER ALREADY KNEW ABOUT THIS, AND THAT'S WHY HE LEFT ME...
...WITH YOU?
THE...
...HATTER...?
......WHO'S THAT?
GACHA (CHAK)
"WHO," YOU ASK...?
PLEASE GET IN.

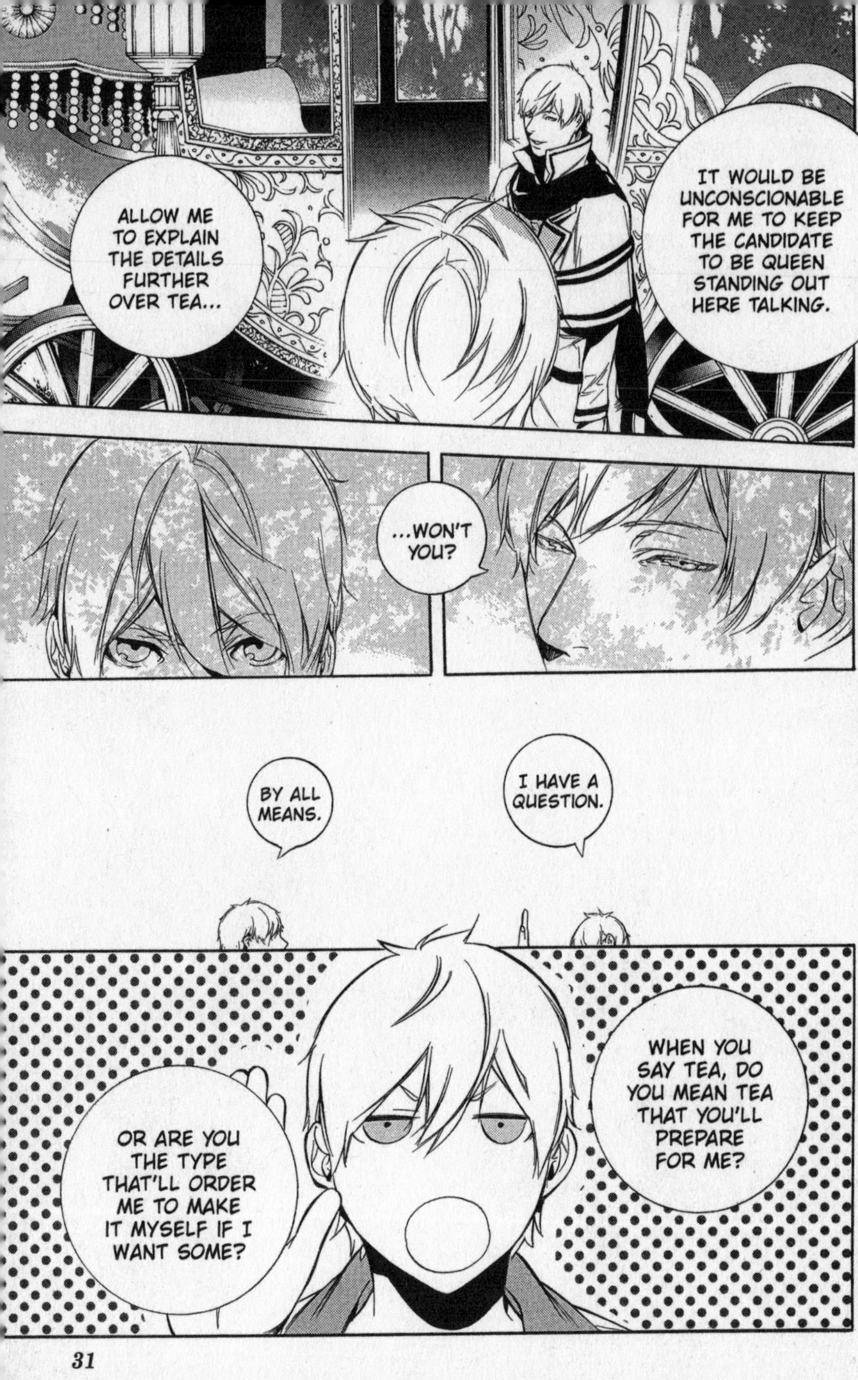
IT WOULD BE UNCONSCIONABLE FOR ME TO KEEP THE CANDIDATE TO BE QUEEN STANDING OUT HERE TALKING.
ALLOW ME TO EXPLAIN THE DETAILS FURTHER OVER TEA...
...WON'T YOU?
I HAVE A QUESTION.
BY ALL MEANS.
WHEN YOU SAY TEA, DO YOU MEAN TEA THAT YOU'LL PREPARE FOR ME?
OR ARE YOU THE TYPE THAT'LL ORDER ME TO MAKE IT MYSELF IF I WANT SOME?

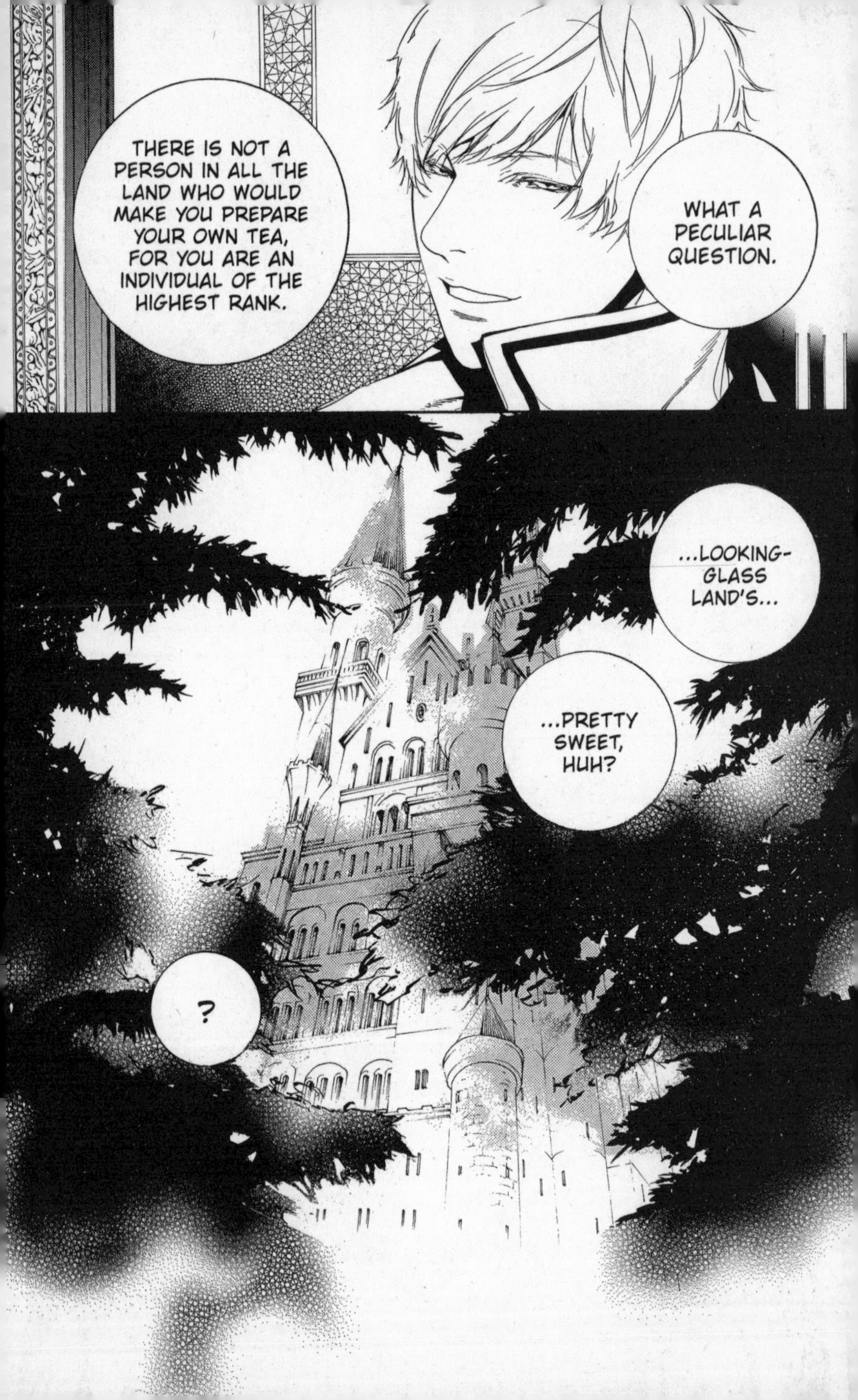
WHAT A PECULIAR QUESTION.
THERE IS NOT A PERSON IN ALL THE LAND WHO WOULD MAKE YOU PREPARE YOUR OWN TEA, FOR YOU ARE AN INDIVIDUAL OF THE HIGHEST RANK.
...LOOKING-GLASS LAND'S...
...PRETTY SWEET, HUH?
?

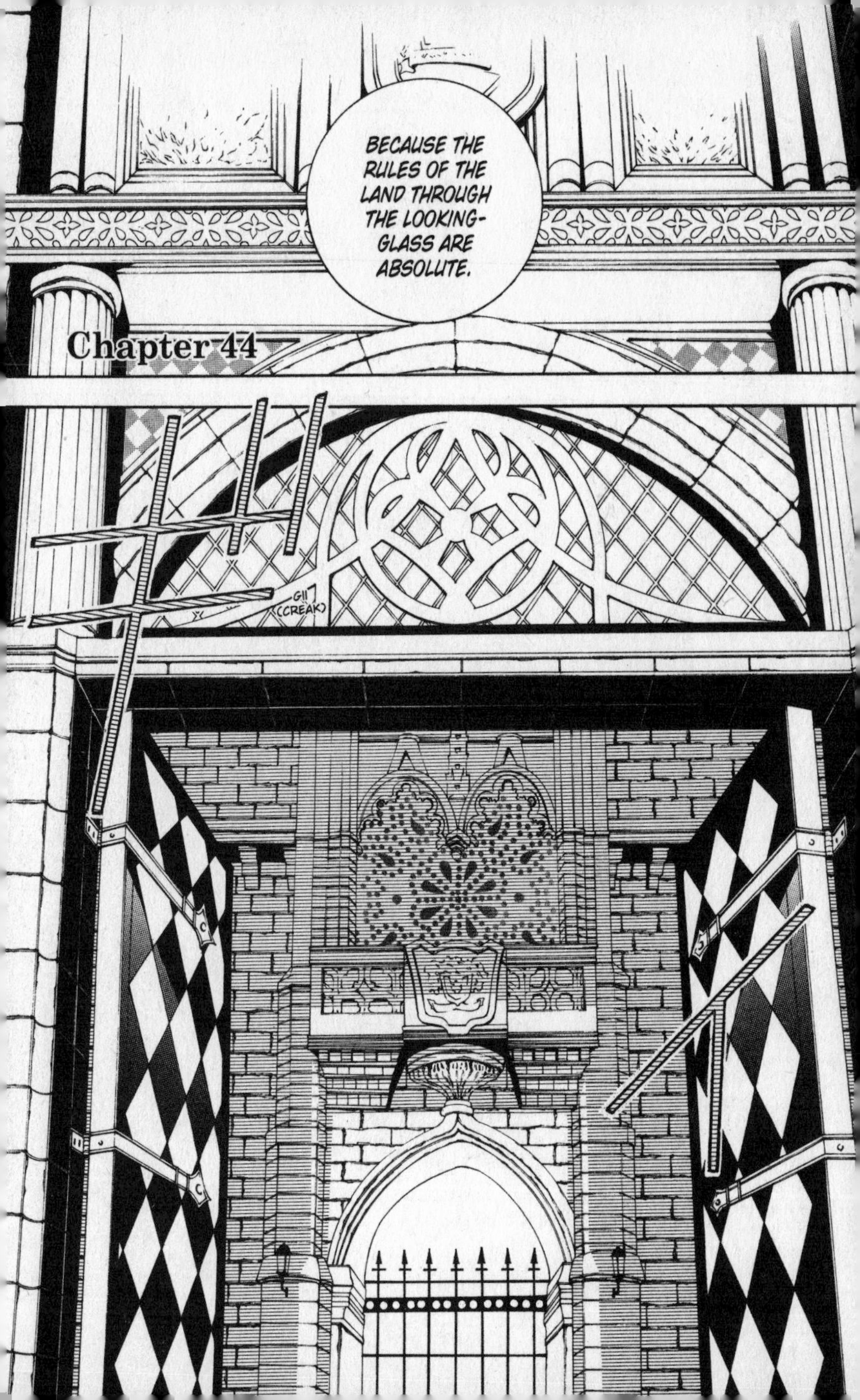
BECAUSE THE RULES OF THE LAND THROUGH THE LOOKING-GLASS ARE ABSOLUTE.
Chapter 44
GII (CREAK)

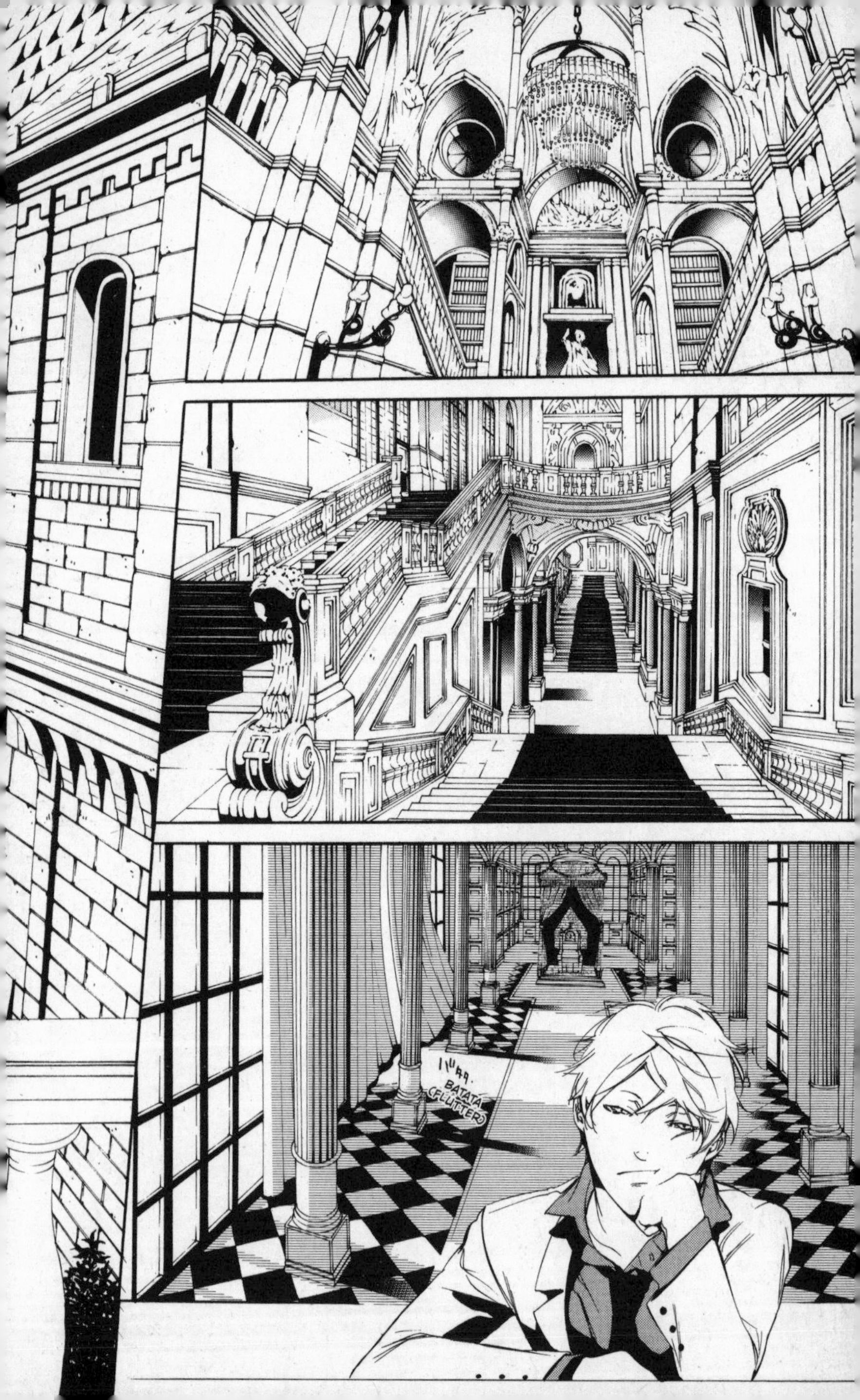
BATATA (FLUTTER)
...

Chapter 44
A Make-or-Break Moment.

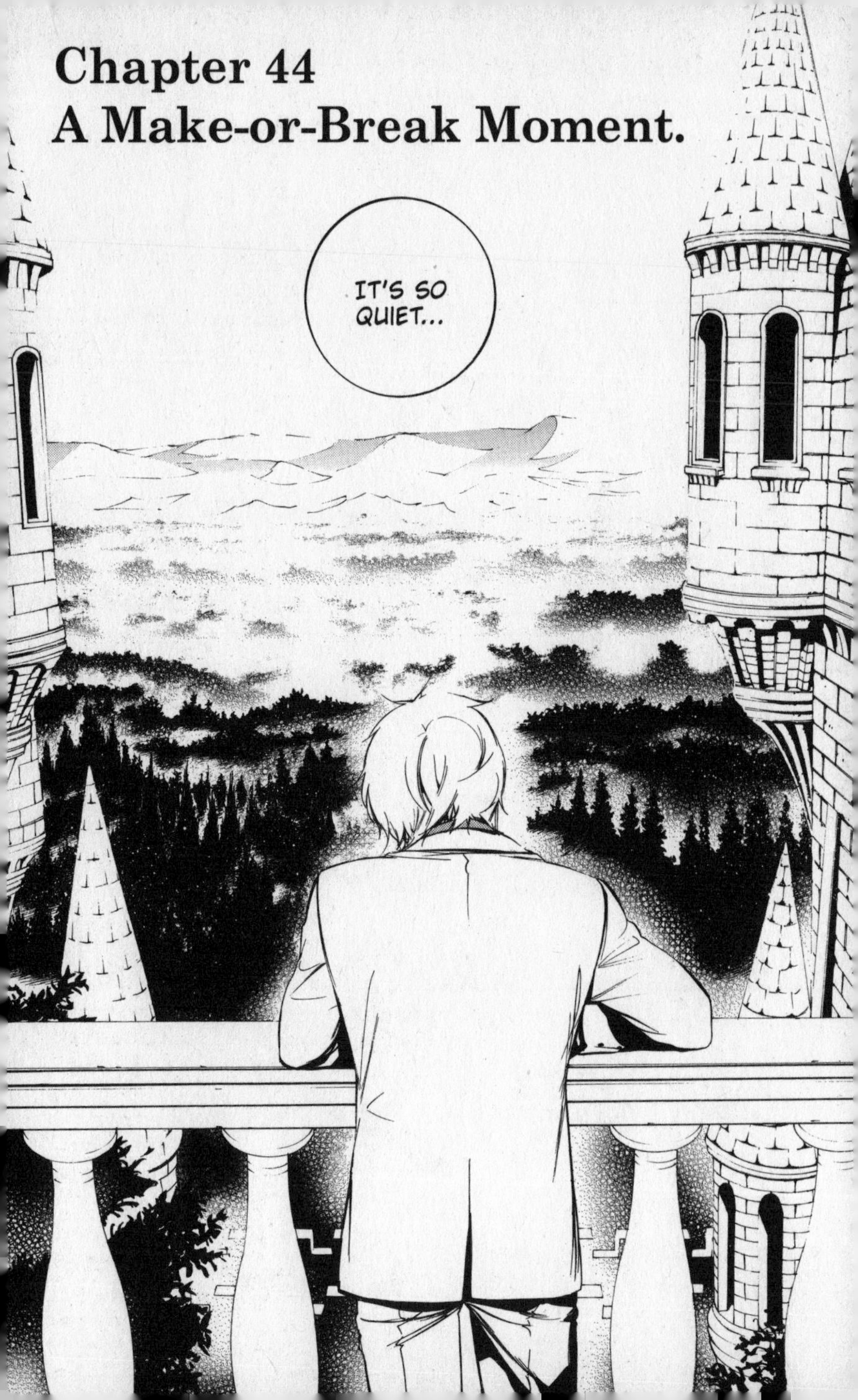
IT'S SO QUIET...

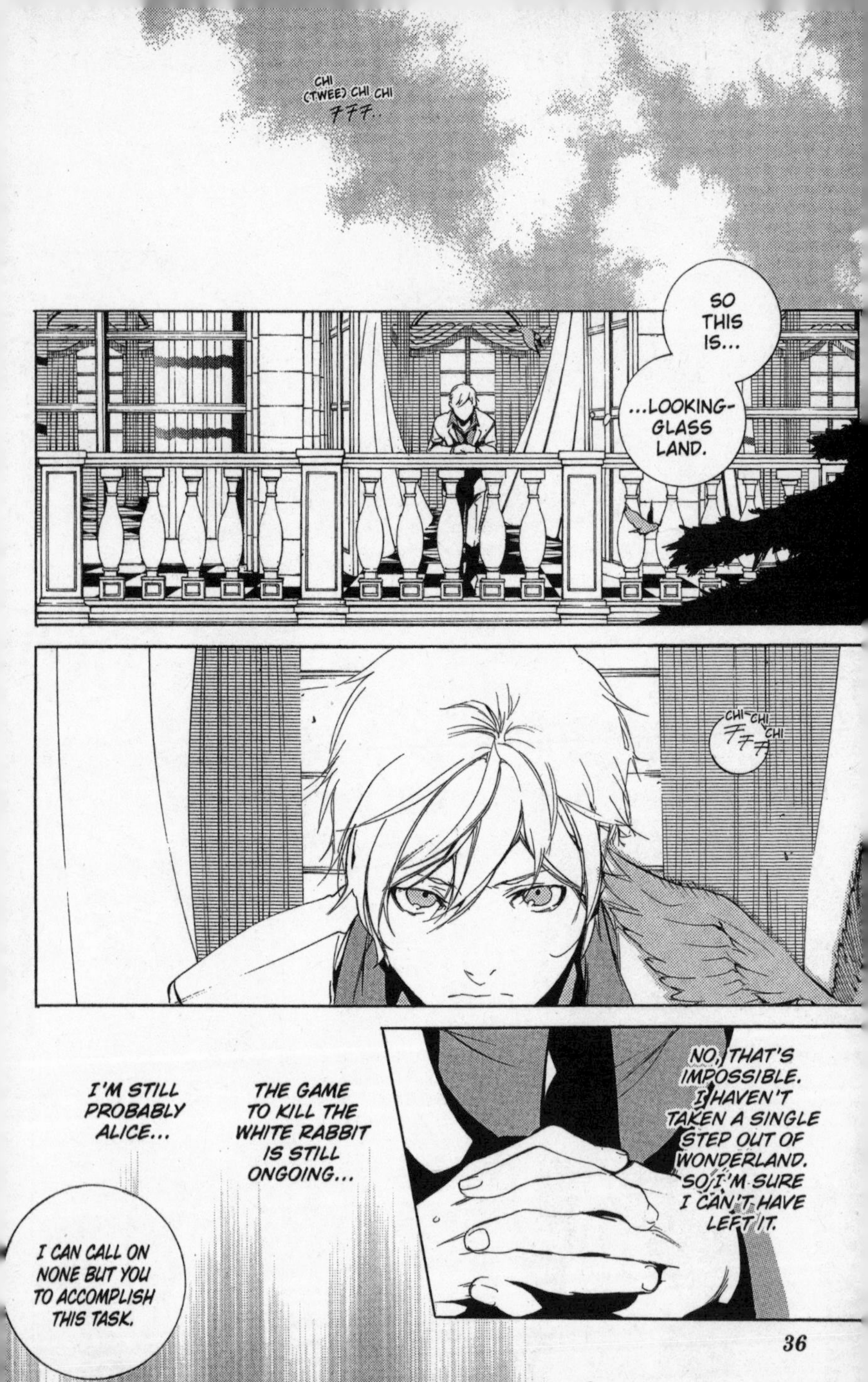
CHI (TWEE) CHI CHI
SO THIS IS...
...LOOKING-GLASS LAND.
CHI CHI CHI
NO, THAT'S IMPOSSIBLE. I HAVEN'T TAKEN A SINGLE STEP OUT OF WONDERLAND. SO I'M SURE I CAN'T HAVE LEFT IT.
THE GAME TO KILL THE WHITE RABBIT IS STILL ONGOING...
I'M STILL PROBABLY ALICE...
I CAN CALL ON NONE BUT YOU TO ACCOMPLISH THIS TASK.

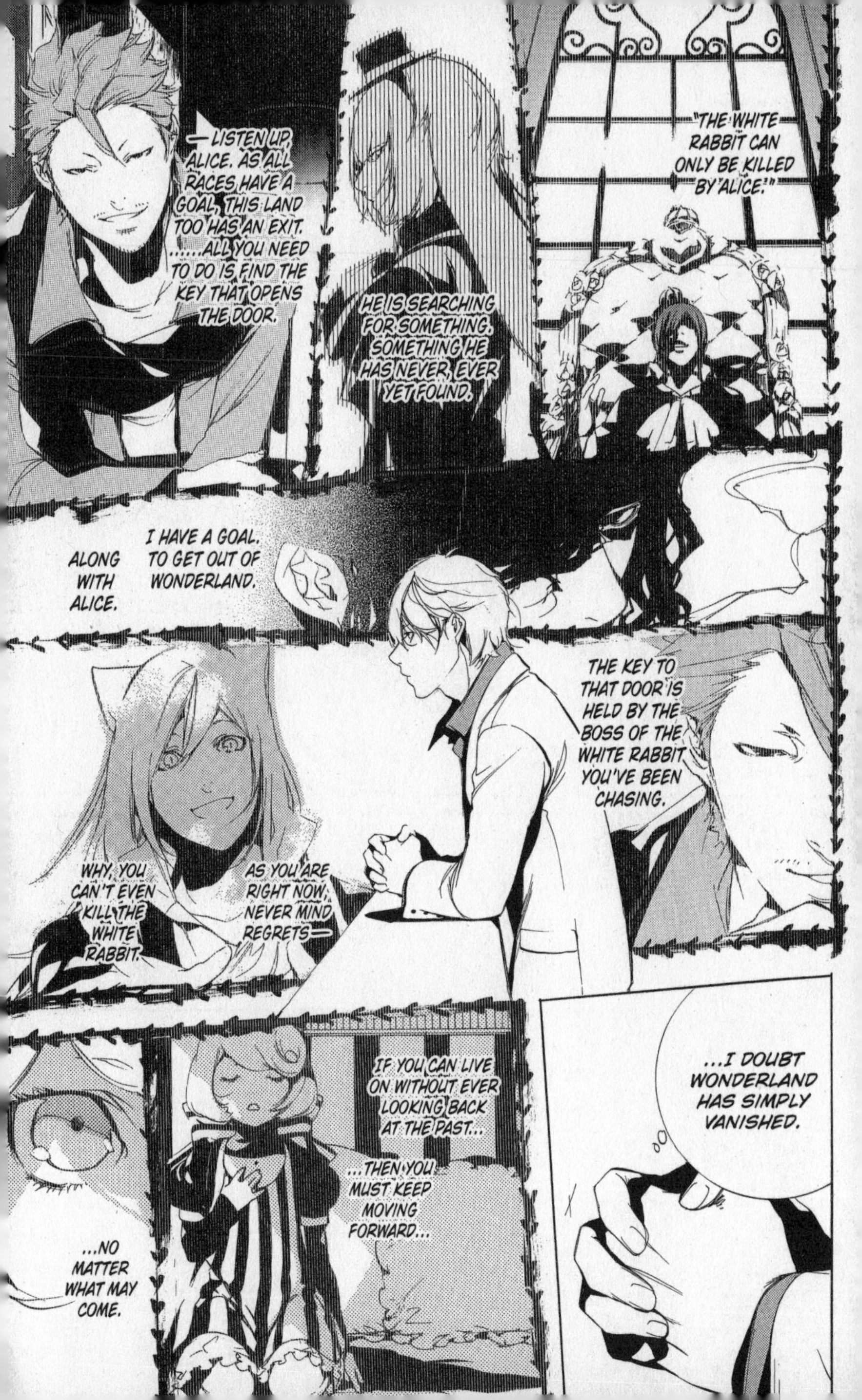
"THE WHITE RABBIT CAN ONLY BE KILLED BY ALICE."
HE IS SEARCHING FOR SOMETHING. SOMETHING HE HAS NEVER, EVER YET FOUND.
—LISTEN UP, ALICE. AS ALL RACES HAVE A GOAL, THIS LAND TOO HAS AN EXIT. ......ALL YOU NEED TO DO IS FIND THE KEY THAT OPENS THE DOOR.
I HAVE A GOAL. TO GET OUT OF WONDERLAND.
ALONG WITH ALICE.
THE KEY TO THAT DOOR IS HELD BY THE BOSS OF THE WHITE RABBIT YOU'VE BEEN CHASING.
AS YOU ARE RIGHT NOW, NEVER MIND REGRETS—
WHY, YOU CAN'T EVEN KILL THE WHITE RABBIT.
...I DOUBT WONDERLAND HAS SIMPLY VANISHED.
IF YOU CAN LIVE ON WITHOUT EVER LOOKING BACK AT THE PAST...
...THEN YOU MUST KEEP MOVING FORWARD...
...NO MATTER WHAT MAY COME.

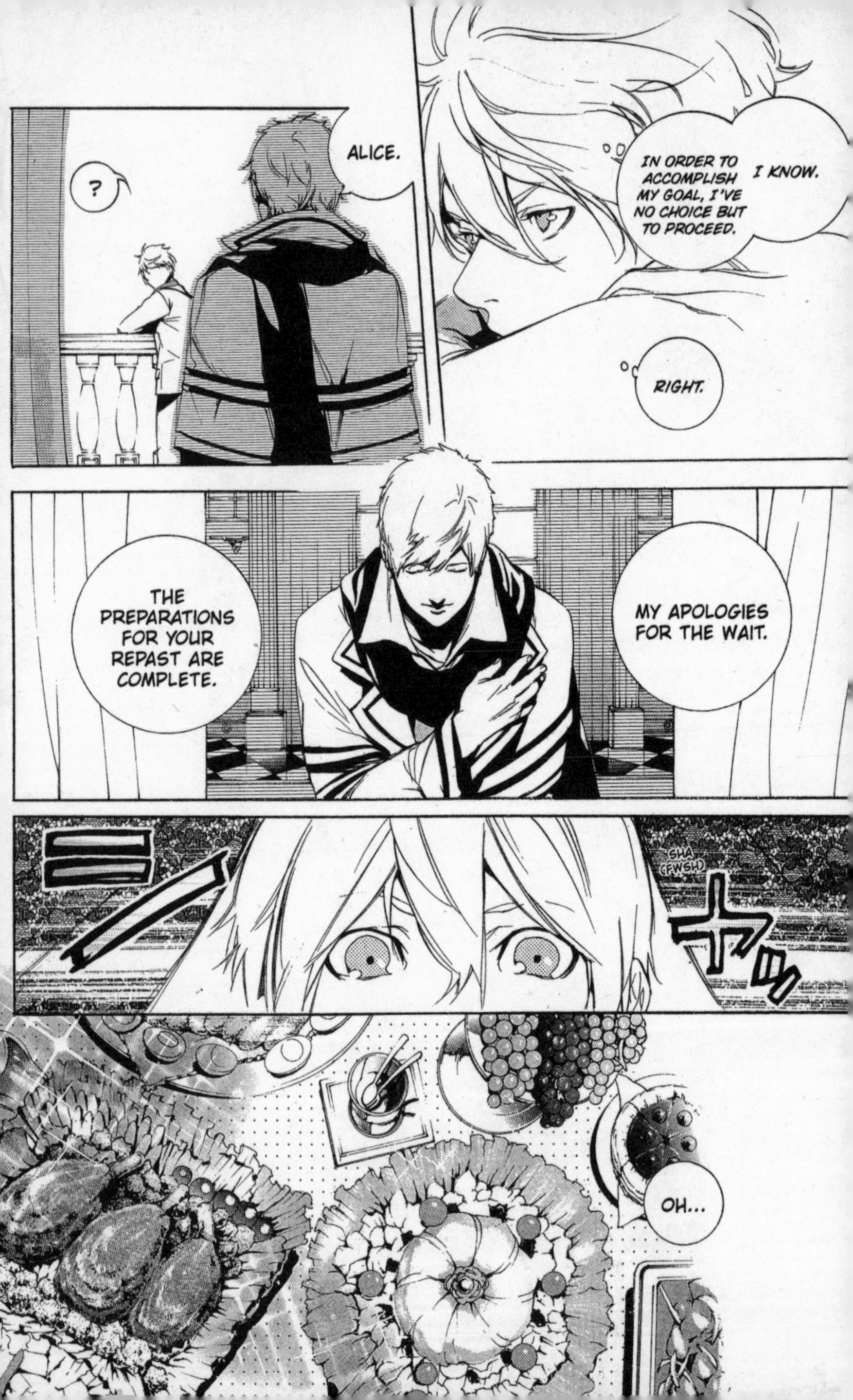
I KNOW.
IN ORDER TO ACCOMPLISH MY GOAL, I'VE NO CHOICE BUT TO PROCEED.
RIGHT.
ALICE.
?
MY APOLOGIES FOR THE WAIT.
THE PREPARATIONS FOR YOUR REPAST ARE COMPLETE.
SHA (FWSH)
OH...

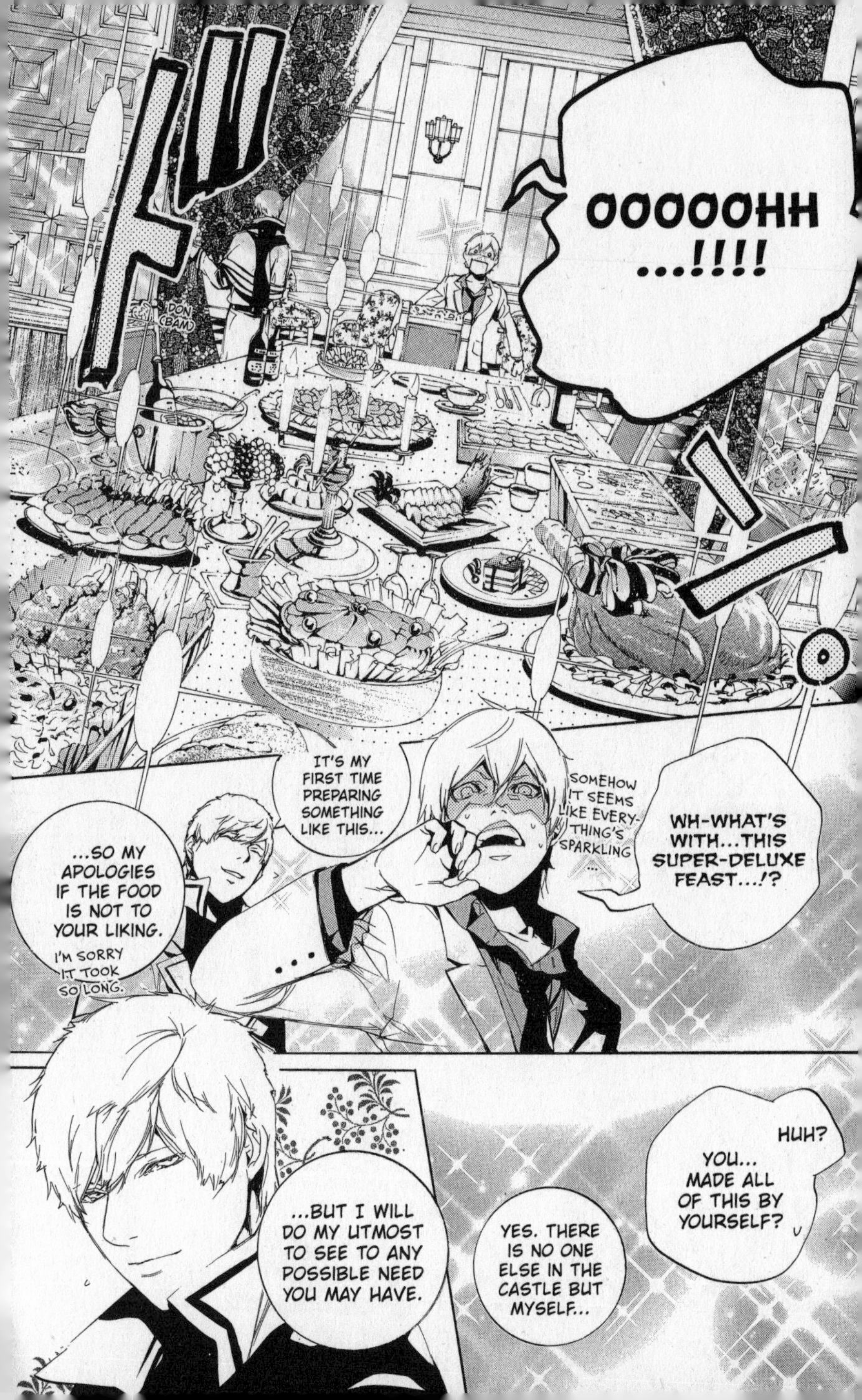
OOOOOHH ...!!!!
DON (BAM)
WH-WHAT'S WITH...THIS SUPER-DELUXE FEAST...!?
SOMEHOW IT SEEMS LIKE EVERY-THING'S SPARKLING ...
IT'S MY FIRST TIME PREPARING SOMETHING LIKE THIS...
...SO MY APOLOGIES IF THE FOOD IS NOT TO YOUR LIKING.
I'M SORRY IT TOOK SO LONG.
...
HUH?
YOU... MADE ALL OF THIS BY YOURSELF?
YES. THERE IS NO ONE ELSE IN THE CASTLE BUT MYSELF...
...BUT I WILL DO MY UTMOST TO SEE TO ANY POSSIBLE NEED YOU MAY HAVE.

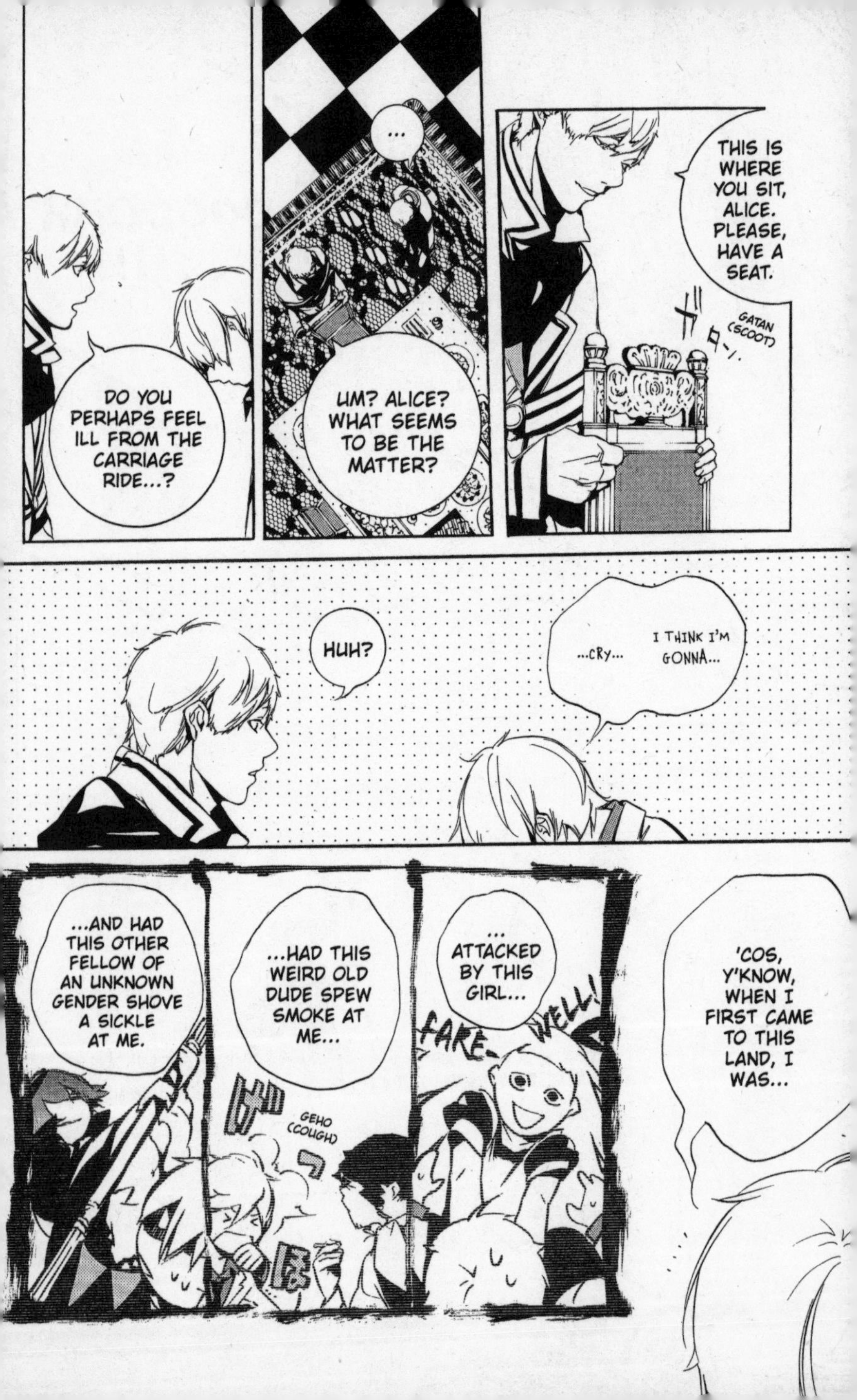
THIS IS WHERE YOU SIT, ALICE. PLEASE, HAVE A SEAT.
GATAN (SCOOT)
...
UM? ALICE? WHAT SEEMS TO BE THE MATTER?
DO YOU PERHAPS FEEL ILL FROM THE CARRIAGE RIDE...?
I THINK I'M GONNA... ...CRY...
HUH?
'COS, Y'KNOW, WHEN I FIRST CAME TO THIS LAND, I WAS...
...ATTACKED BY THIS GIRL...
FARE-WELL!
...HAD THIS WEIRD OLD DUDE SPEW SMOKE AT ME...
GEHO (COUGH)
...AND HAD THIS OTHER FELLOW OF AN UNKNOWN GENDER SHOVE A SICKLE AT ME.

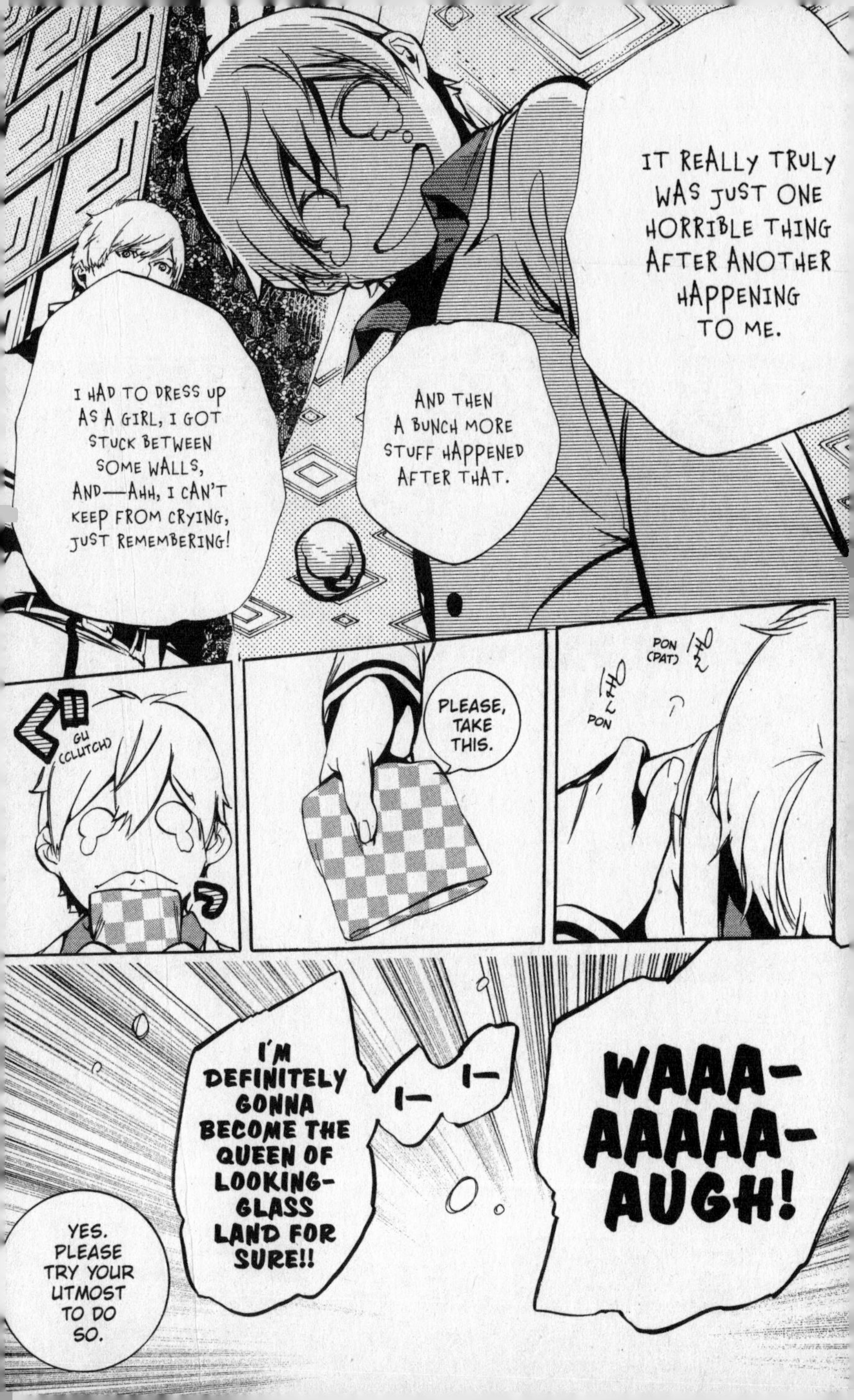
IT REALLY TRULY WAS JUST ONE HORRIBLE THING AFTER ANOTHER HAPPENING TO ME.
AND THEN A BUNCH MORE STUFF HAPPENED AFTER THAT.
I HAD TO DRESS UP AS A GIRL, I GOT STUCK BETWEEN SOME WALLS, AND—AHH, I CAN'T KEEP FROM CRYING, JUST REMEMBERING!
PON (PAT)
PON
PLEASE, TAKE THIS.
GU (CLUTCH)
WAAA-AAAAA-AUGH!
I— I—
I'M DEFINITELY GONNA BECOME THE QUEEN OF LOOKING-GLASS LAND FOR SURE!!
YES. PLEASE TRY YOUR UTMOST TO DO SO.

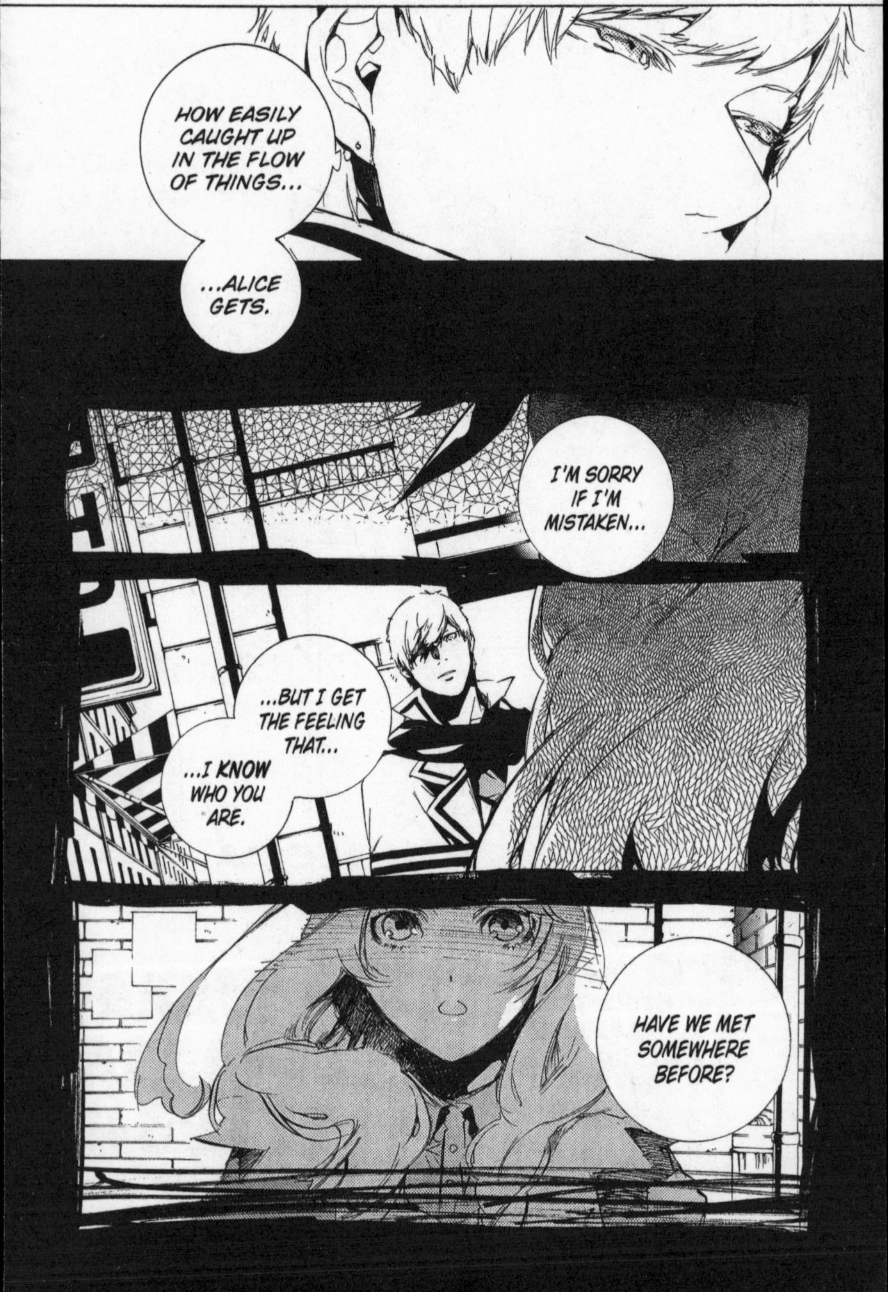
HOW EASILY CAUGHT UP IN THE FLOW OF THINGS...
...ALICE GETS.
I'M SORRY IF I'M MISTAKEN...
...BUT I GET THE FEELING THAT...
...I KNOW WHO YOU ARE.
HAVE WE MET SOMEWHERE BEFORE?

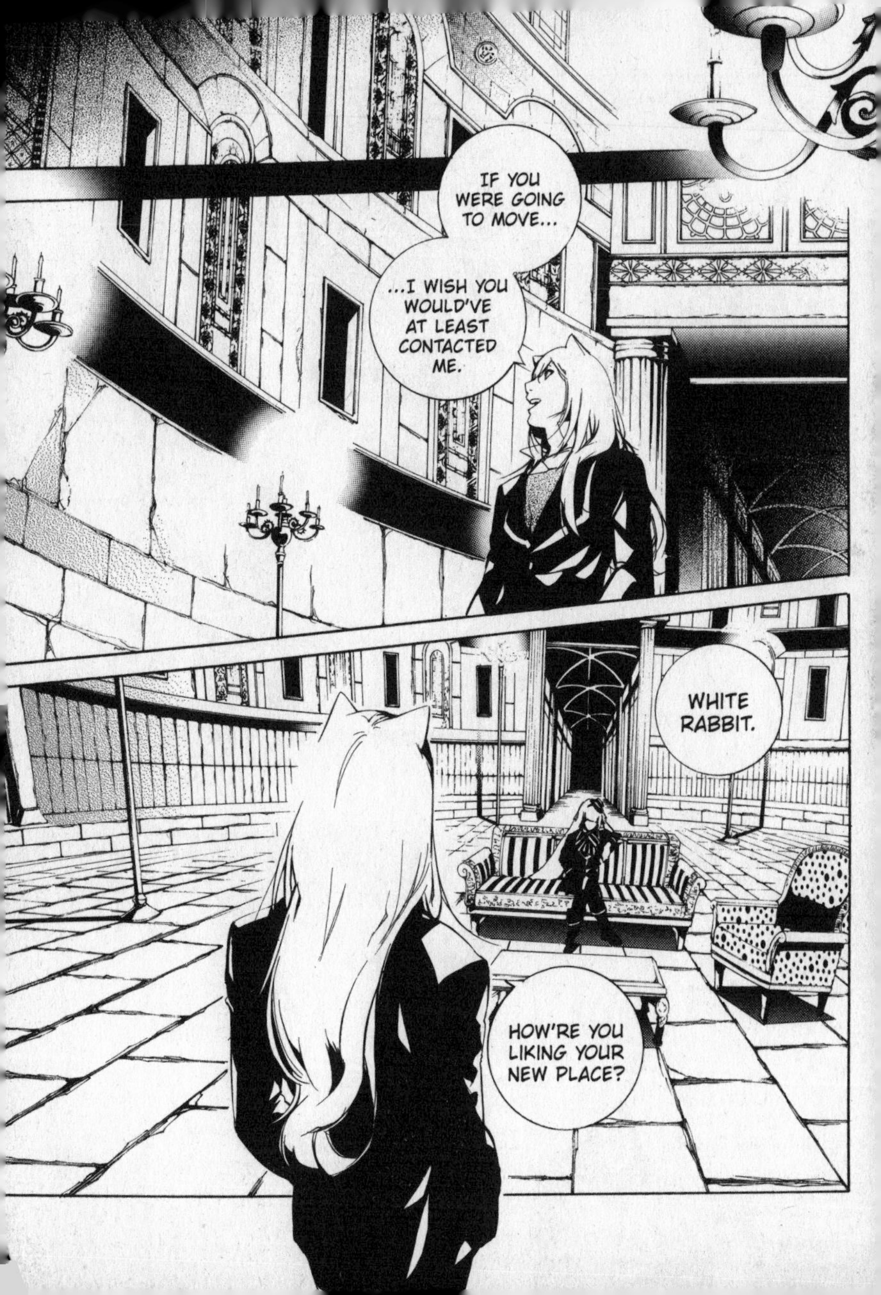
IF YOU WERE GOING TO MOVE...
...I WISH YOU WOULD'VE AT LEAST CONTACTED ME.
WHITE RABBIT.
HOW'RE YOU LIKING YOUR NEW PLACE?

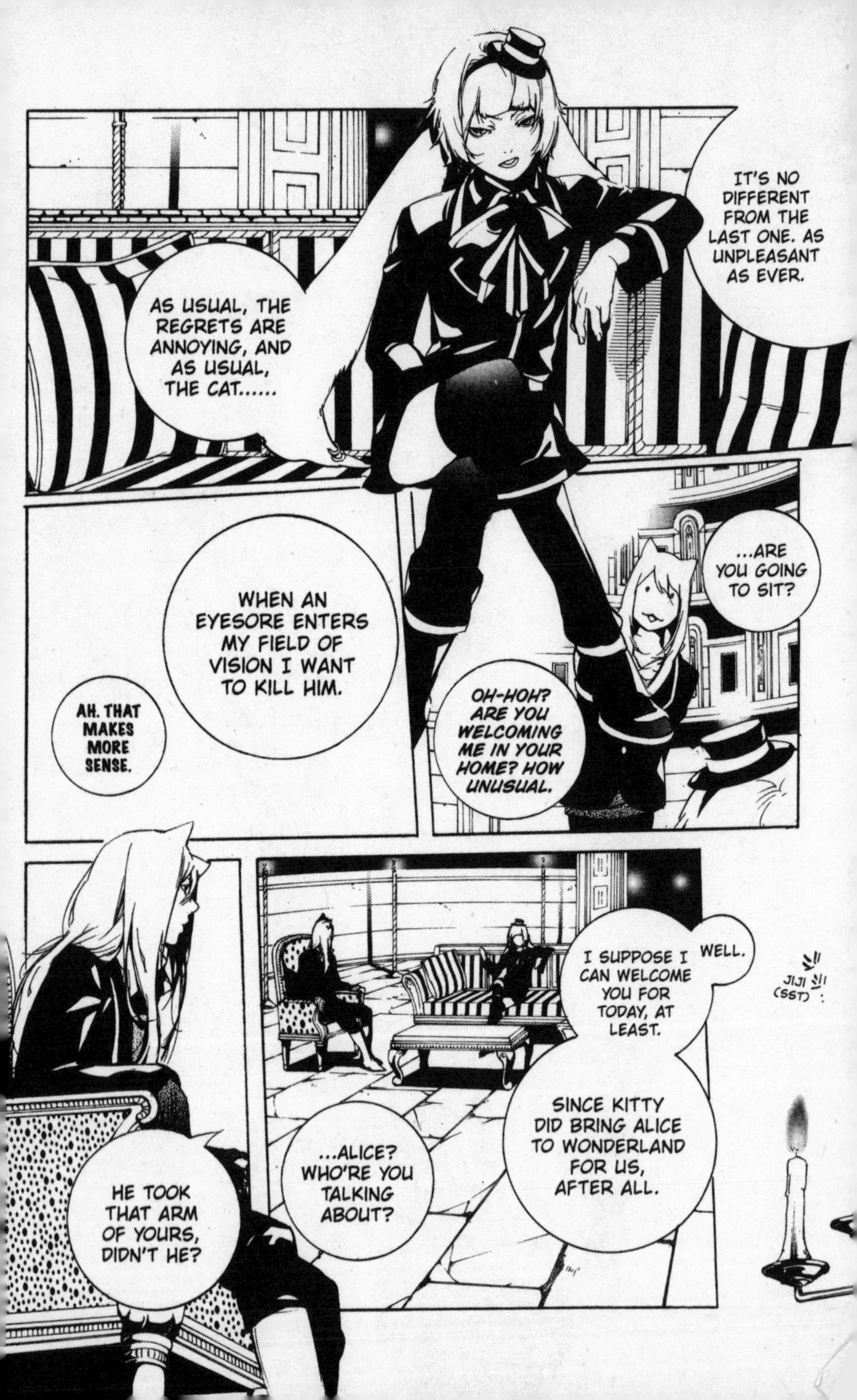
IT'S NO DIFFERENT FROM THE LAST ONE. AS UNPLEASANT AS EVER.
AS USUAL, THE REGRETS ARE ANNOYING, AND AS USUAL, THE CAT......
...ARE YOU GOING TO SIT?
OH-HOH? ARE YOU WELCOMING ME IN YOUR HOME? HOW UNUSUAL.
WHEN AN EYESORE ENTERS MY FIELD OF VISION I WANT TO KILL HIM.
AH. THAT MAKES MORE SENSE.
JIJI (SST)
WELL.
I SUPPOSE I CAN WELCOME YOU FOR TODAY, AT LEAST.
SINCE KITTY DID BRING ALICE TO WONDERLAND FOR US, AFTER ALL.
...ALICE? WHO'RE YOU TALKING ABOUT?
HE TOOK THAT ARM OF YOURS, DIDN'T HE?

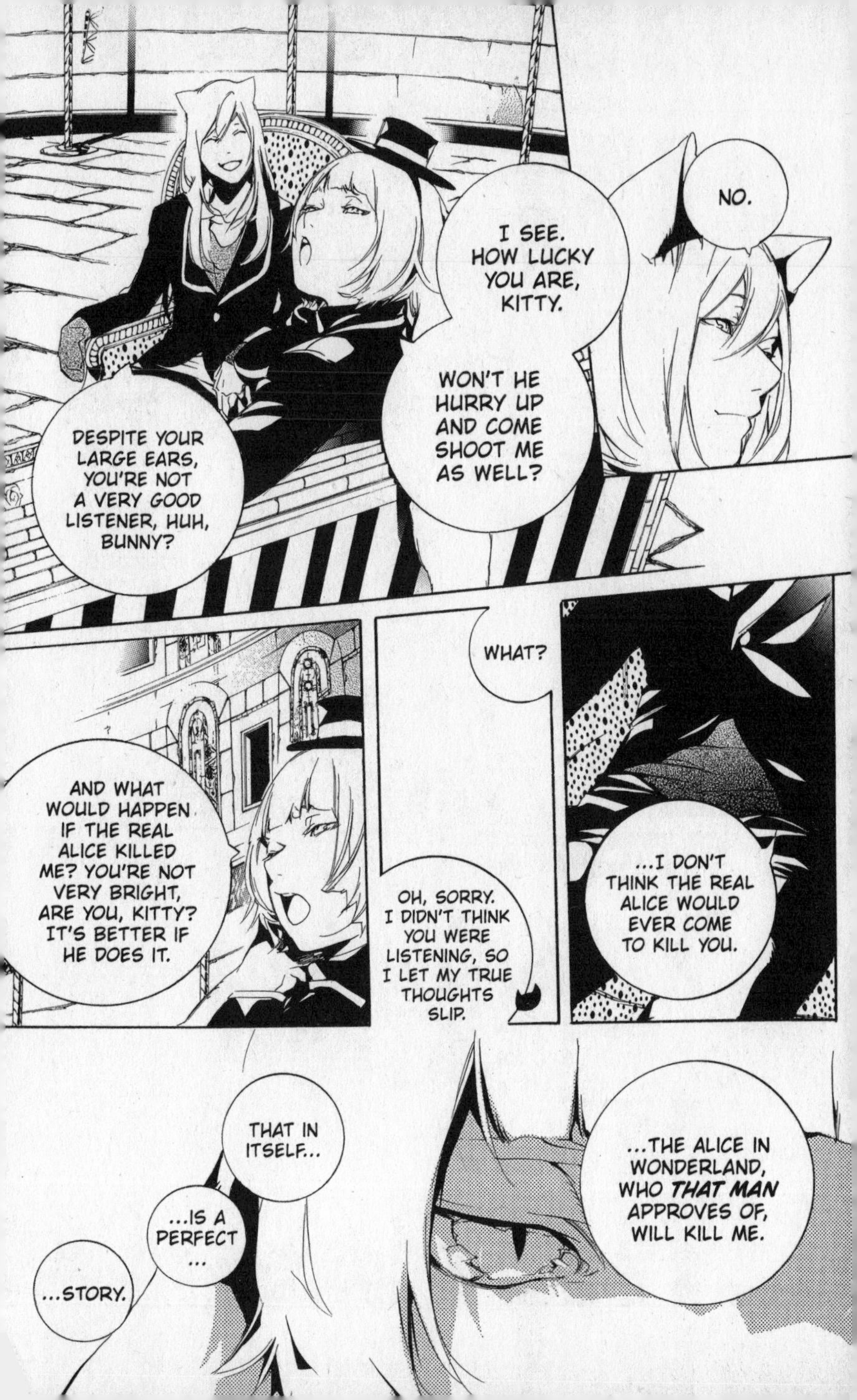
NO.
I SEE. HOW LUCKY YOU ARE, KITTY.
WON'T HE HURRY UP AND COME SHOOT ME AS WELL?
DESPITE YOUR LARGE EARS, YOU'RE NOT A VERY GOOD LISTENER, HUH, BUNNY?
...I DON'T THINK THE REAL ALICE WOULD EVER COME TO KILL YOU.
WHAT?
OH, SORRY. I DIDN'T THINK YOU WERE LISTENING, SO I LET MY TRUE THOUGHTS SLIP.
AND WHAT WOULD HAPPEN IF THE REAL ALICE KILLED ME? YOU'RE NOT VERY BRIGHT, ARE YOU, KITTY? IT'S BETTER IF HE DOES IT.
...THE ALICE IN WONDERLAND, WHO *THAT MAN* APPROVES OF, WILL KILL ME.
THAT IN ITSELF...
...IS A PERFECT ...
...STORY.

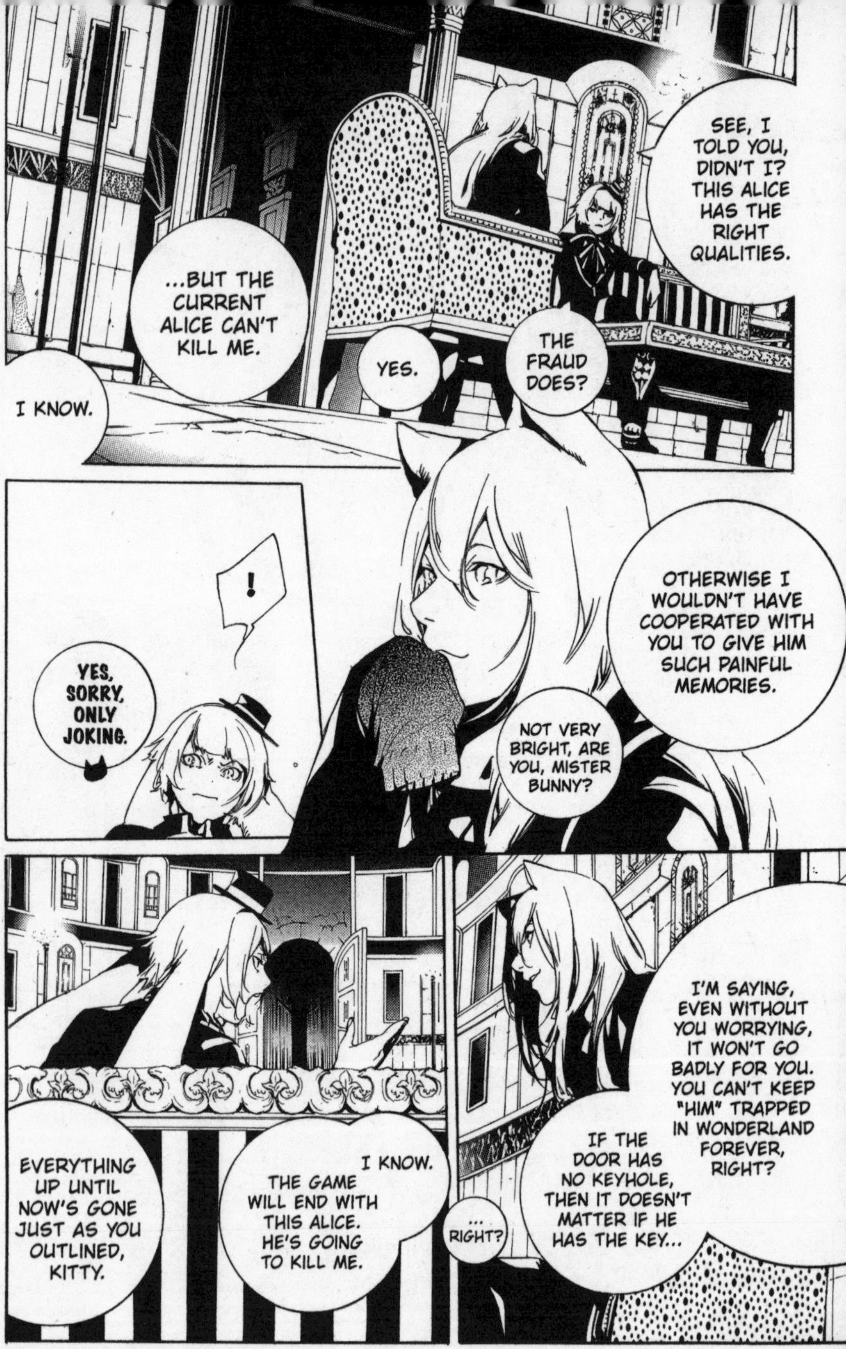
SEE, I TOLD YOU, DIDN'T I? THIS ALICE HAS THE RIGHT QUALITIES.
THE FRAUD DOES?
YES.
...BUT THE CURRENT ALICE CAN'T KILL ME.
I KNOW.
OTHERWISE I WOULDN'T HAVE COOPERATED WITH YOU TO GIVE HIM SUCH PAINFUL MEMORIES.
NOT VERY BRIGHT, ARE YOU, MISTER BUNNY?
!
YES, SORRY, ONLY JOKING.
I'M SAYING, EVEN WITHOUT YOU WORRYING, IT WON'T GO BADLY FOR YOU. YOU CAN'T KEEP "HIM" TRAPPED IN WONDERLAND FOREVER, RIGHT?
IF THE DOOR HAS NO KEYHOLE, THEN IT DOESN'T MATTER IF HE HAS THE KEY...
...RIGHT?
I KNOW. THE GAME WILL END WITH THIS ALICE. HE'S GOING TO KILL ME.
EVERYTHING UP UNTIL NOW'S GONE JUST AS YOU OUTLINED, KITTY.

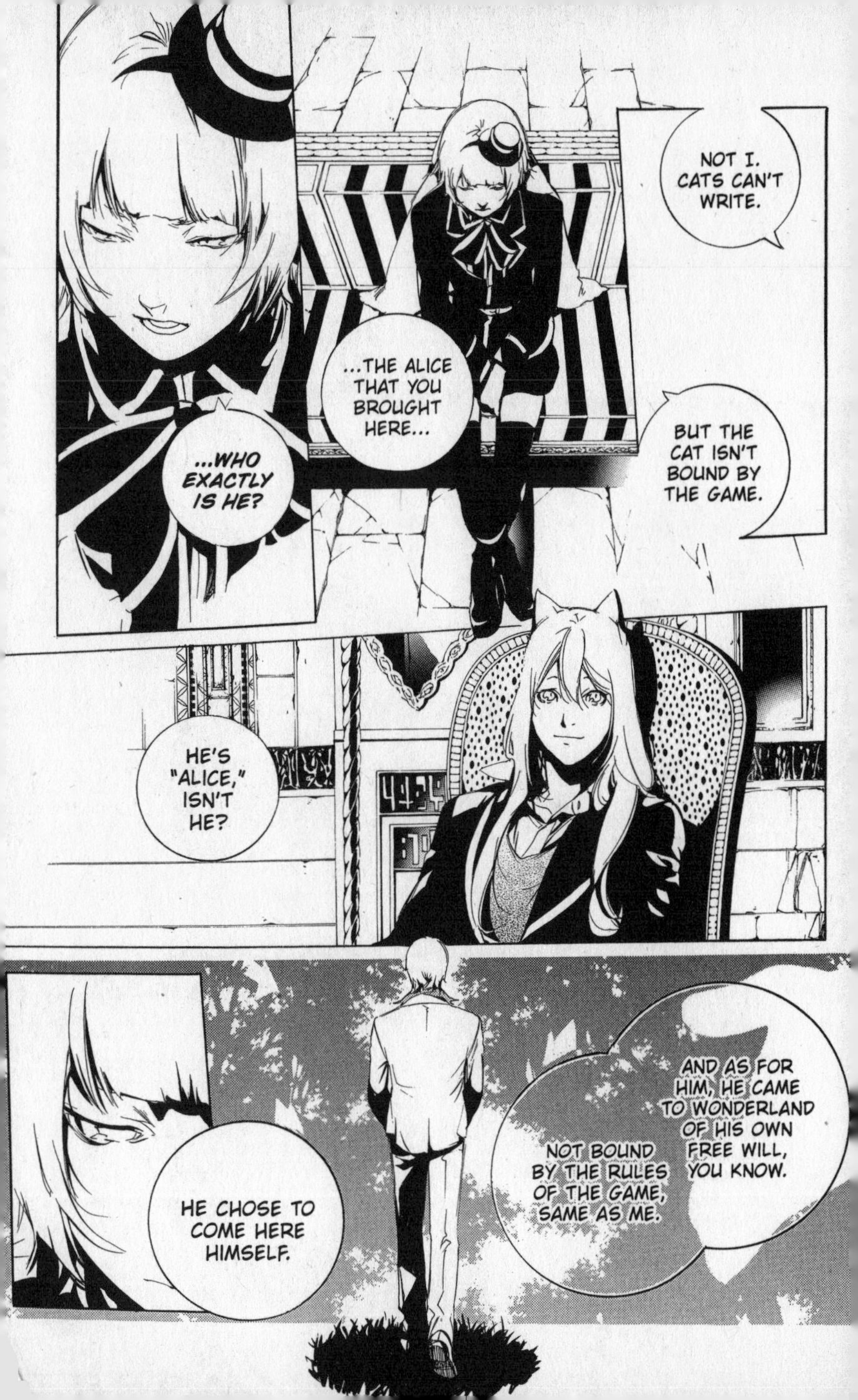
NOT I. CATS CAN'T WRITE.
BUT THE CAT ISN'T BOUND BY THE GAME.
...THE ALICE THAT YOU BROUGHT HERE...
...WHO EXACTLY IS HE?
HE'S "ALICE," ISN'T HE?
AND AS FOR HIM, HE CAME TO WONDERLAND OF HIS OWN FREE WILL, YOU KNOW.
NOT BOUND BY THE RULES OF THE GAME, SAME AS ME.
HE CHOSE TO COME HERE HIMSELF.

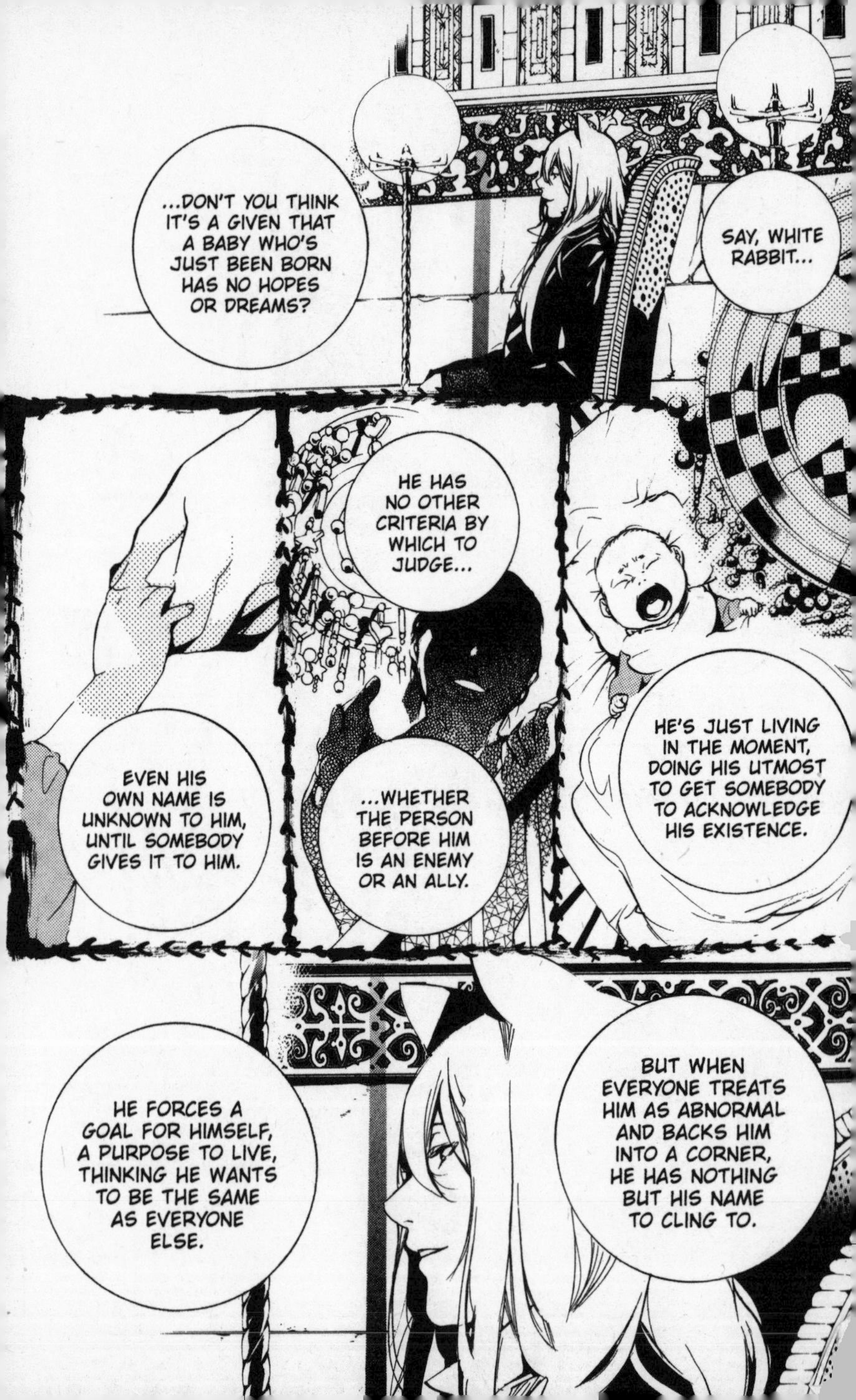
SAY, WHITE RABBIT...
...DON'T YOU THINK IT'S A GIVEN THAT A BABY WHO'S JUST BEEN BORN HAS NO HOPES OR DREAMS?
HE'S JUST LIVING IN THE MOMENT, DOING HIS UTMOST TO GET SOMEBODY TO ACKNOWLEDGE HIS EXISTENCE.
HE HAS NO OTHER CRITERIA BY WHICH TO JUDGE...
...WHETHER THE PERSON BEFORE HIM IS AN ENEMY OR AN ALLY.
EVEN HIS OWN NAME IS UNKNOWN TO HIM, UNTIL SOMEBODY GIVES IT TO HIM.
BUT WHEN EVERYONE TREATS HIM AS ABNORMAL AND BACKS HIM INTO A CORNER, HE HAS NOTHING BUT HIS NAME TO CLING TO.
HE FORCES A GOAL FOR HIMSELF, A PURPOSE TO LIVE, THINKING HE WANTS TO BE THE SAME AS EVERYONE ELSE.

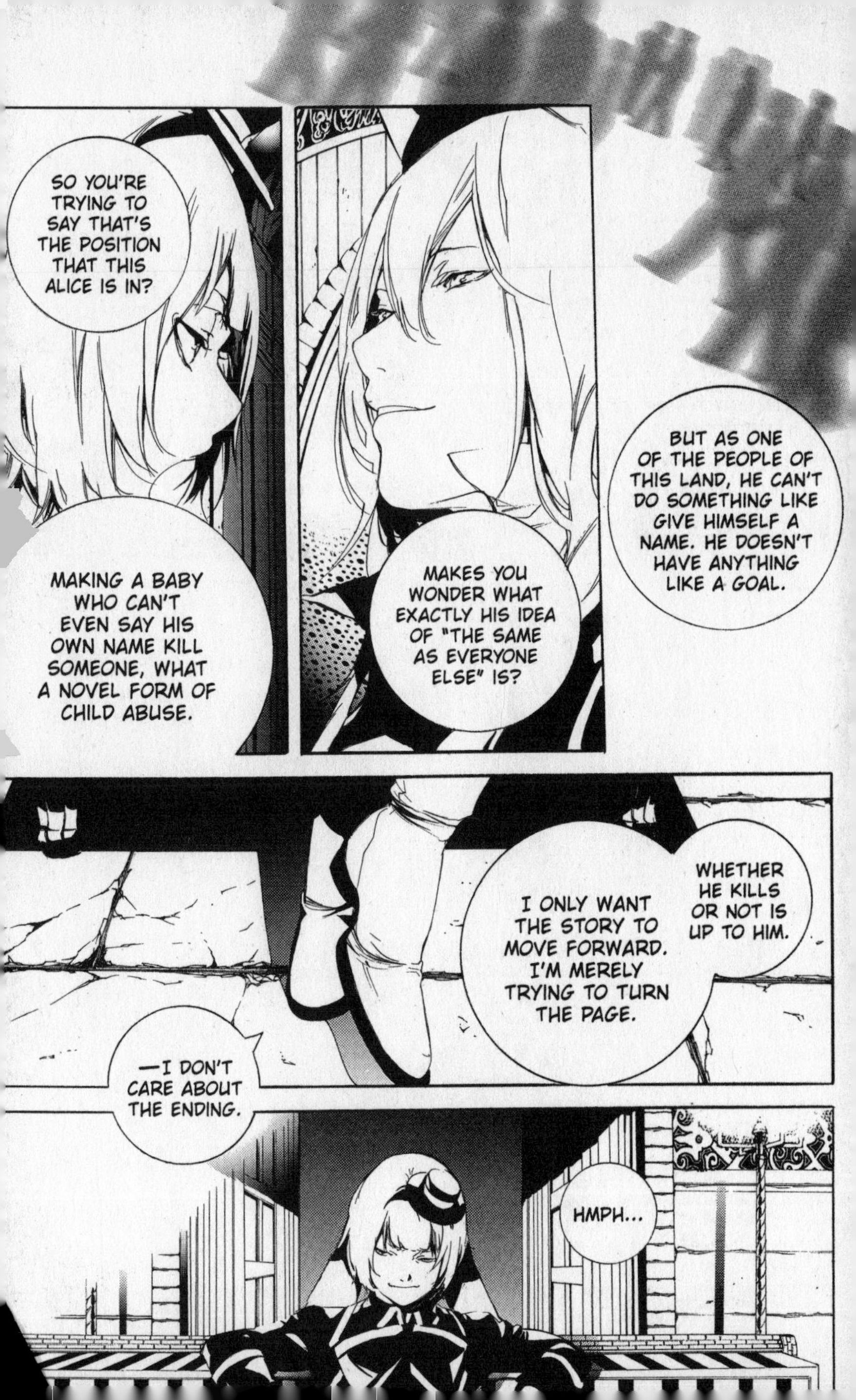
BUT AS ONE OF THE PEOPLE OF THIS LAND, HE CAN'T DO SOMETHING LIKE GIVE HIMSELF A NAME. HE DOESN'T HAVE ANYTHING LIKE A GOAL.
MAKES YOU WONDER WHAT EXACTLY HIS IDEA OF "THE SAME AS EVERYONE ELSE" IS?
SO YOU'RE TRYING TO SAY THAT'S THE POSITION THAT THIS ALICE IS IN?
MAKING A BABY WHO CAN'T EVEN SAY HIS OWN NAME KILL SOMEONE, WHAT A NOVEL FORM OF CHILD ABUSE.
WHETHER HE KILLS OR NOT IS UP TO HIM.
I ONLY WANT THE STORY TO MOVE FORWARD. I'M MERELY TRYING TO TURN THE PAGE.
—I DON'T CARE ABOUT THE ENDING.
HMPH...

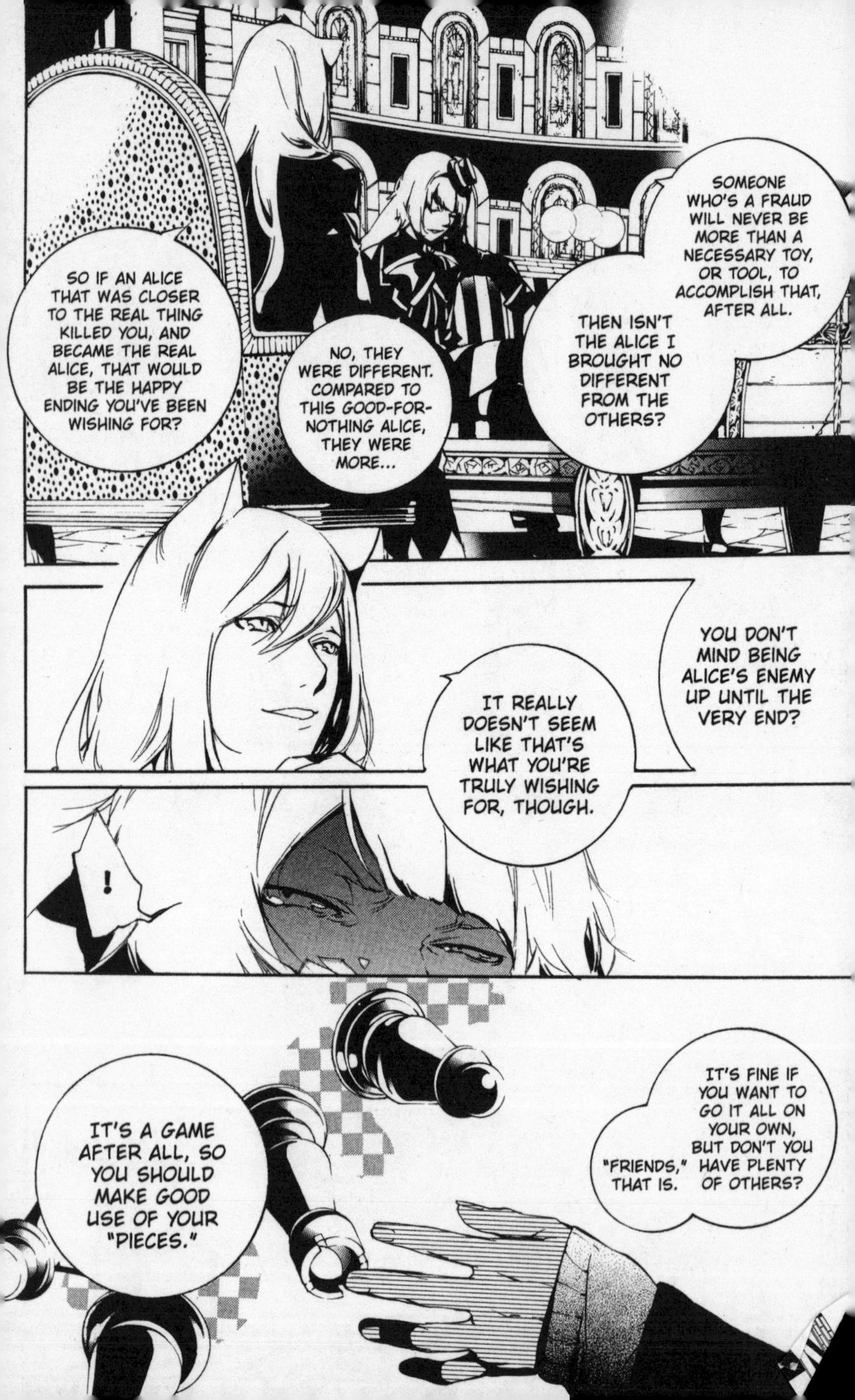
SOMEONE WHO'S A FRAUD WILL NEVER BE MORE THAN A NECESSARY TOY, OR TOOL, TO ACCOMPLISH THAT, AFTER ALL.
THEN ISN'T THE ALICE I BROUGHT NO DIFFERENT FROM THE OTHERS?
NO, THEY WERE DIFFERENT. COMPARED TO THIS GOOD-FOR-NOTHING ALICE, THEY WERE MORE...
SO IF AN ALICE THAT WAS CLOSER TO THE REAL THING KILLED YOU, AND BECAME THE REAL ALICE, THAT WOULD BE THE HAPPY ENDING YOU'VE BEEN WISHING FOR?
YOU DON'T MIND BEING ALICE'S ENEMY UP UNTIL THE VERY END?
IT REALLY DOESN'T SEEM LIKE THAT'S WHAT YOU'RE TRULY WISHING FOR, THOUGH.
!
IT'S FINE IF YOU WANT TO GO IT ALL ON YOUR OWN, BUT DON'T YOU HAVE PLENTY OF OTHERS?
"FRIENDS," THAT IS.
IT'S A GAME AFTER ALL, SO YOU SHOULD MAKE GOOD USE OF YOUR "PIECES."

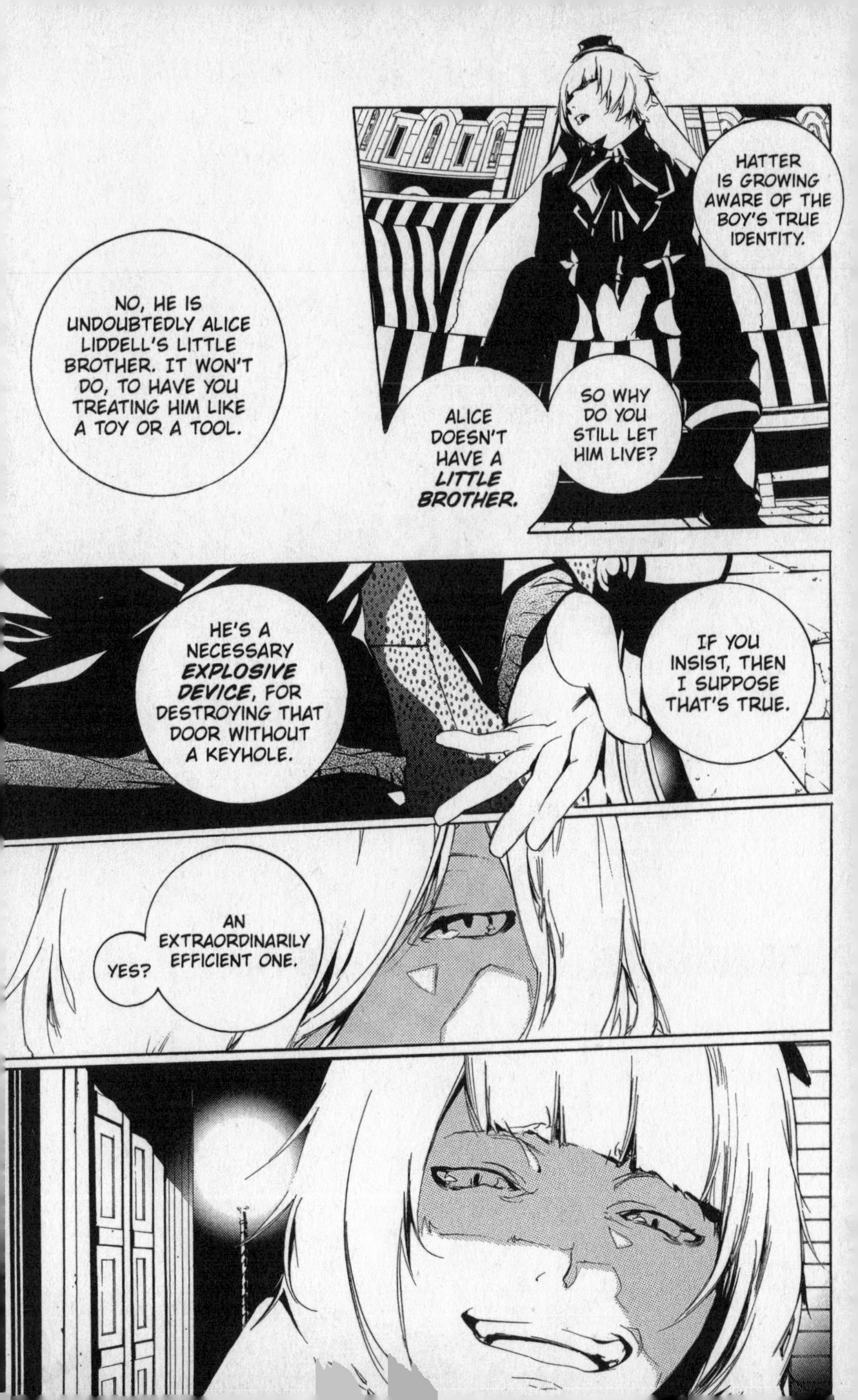
HATTER IS GROWING AWARE OF THE BOY'S TRUE IDENTITY.
NO, HE IS UNDOUBTEDLY ALICE LIDDELL'S LITTLE BROTHER. IT WON'T DO, TO HAVE YOU TREATING HIM LIKE A TOY OR A TOOL.
ALICE DOESN'T HAVE A *LITTLE BROTHER.*
SO WHY DO YOU STILL LET HIM LIVE?
HE'S A NECESSARY *EXPLOSIVE DEVICE*, FOR DESTROYING THAT DOOR WITHOUT A KEYHOLE.
IF YOU INSIST, THEN I SUPPOSE THAT'S TRUE.
AN EXTRAORDINARILY EFFICIENT ONE.
YES?

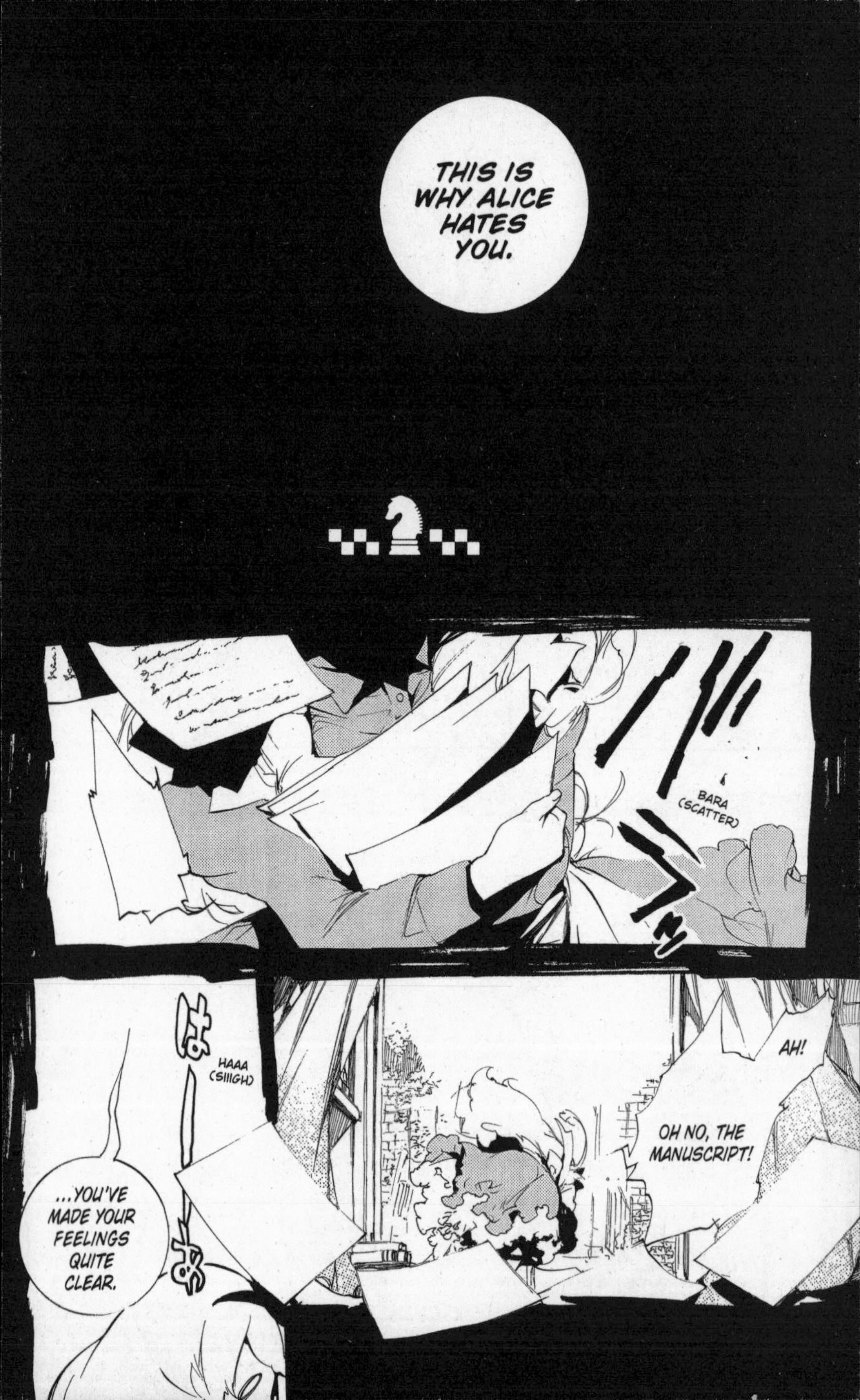
THIS IS WHY ALICE HATES YOU.
BARA (SCATTER)
AH!
OH NO, THE MANUSCRIPT!
は
HAAA (SIIIGH)
...YOU'VE MADE YOUR FEELINGS QUITE CLEAR.

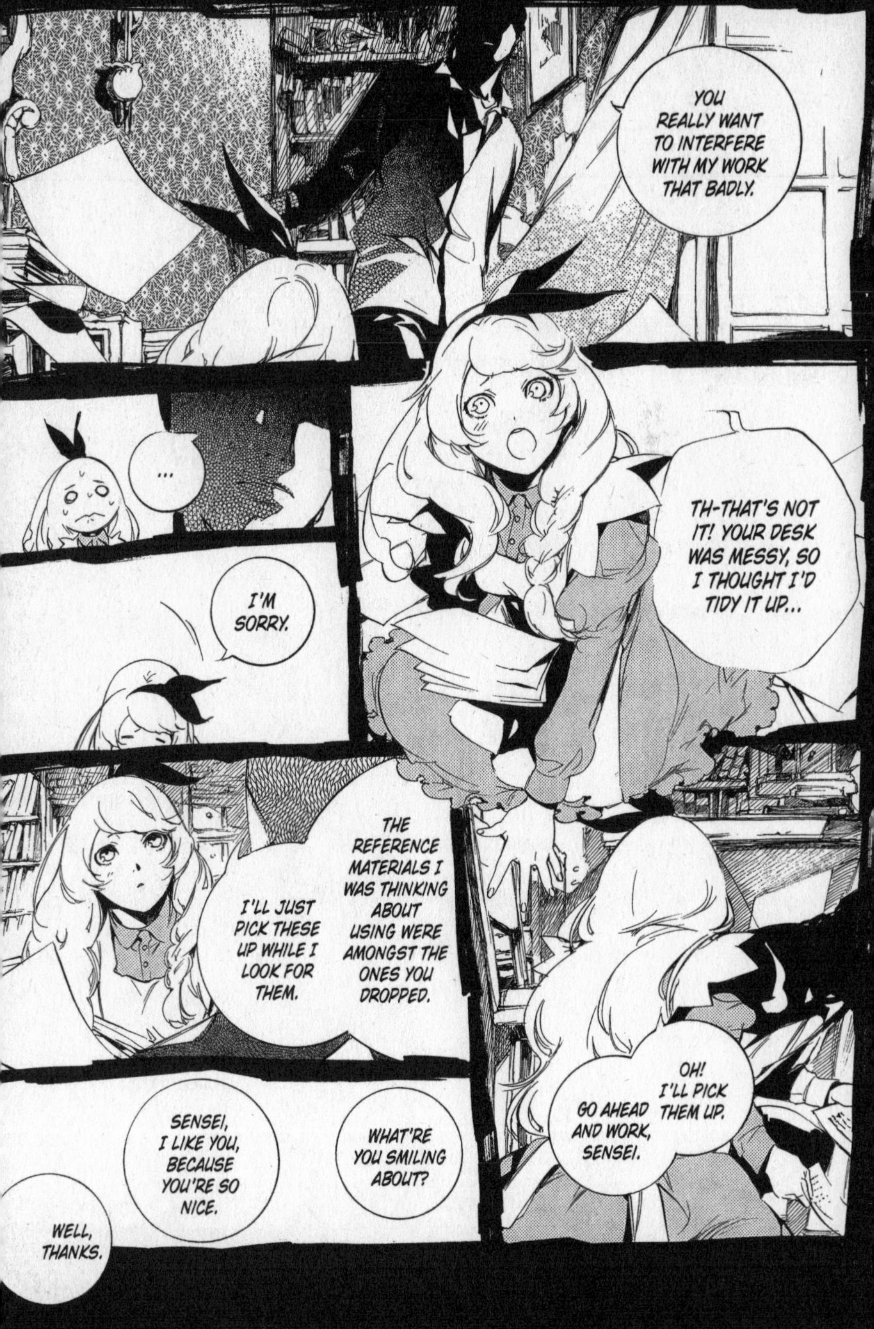
YOU REALLY WANT TO INTERFERE WITH MY WORK THAT BADLY.
TH-THAT'S NOT IT! YOUR DESK WAS MESSY, SO I THOUGHT I'D TIDY IT UP...
...
I'M SORRY.
OH! I'LL PICK THEM UP.
GO AHEAD AND WORK, SENSEI.
THE REFERENCE MATERIALS I WAS THINKING ABOUT USING WERE AMONGST THE ONES YOU DROPPED.
I'LL JUST PICK THESE UP WHILE I LOOK FOR THEM.
WHAT'RE YOU SMILING ABOUT?
SENSEI, I LIKE YOU, BECAUSE YOU'RE SO NICE.
WELL, THANKS.

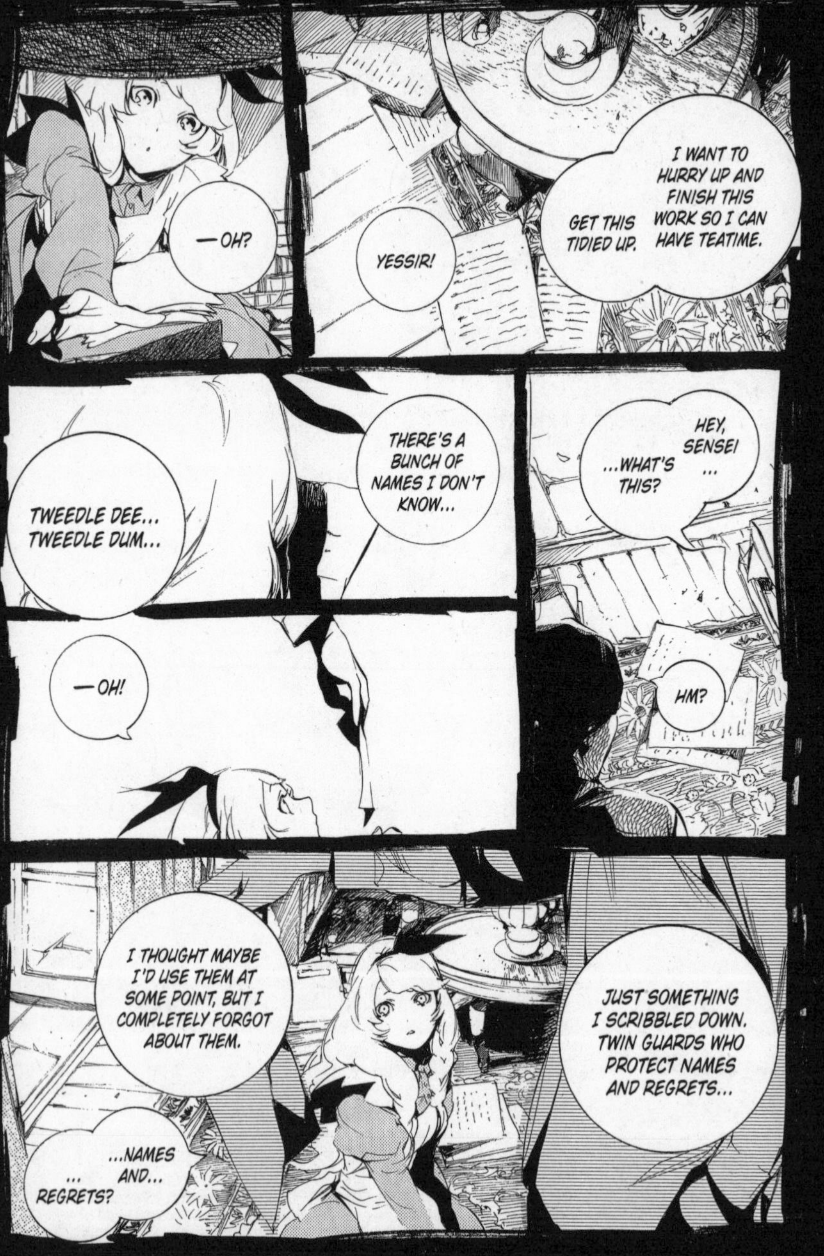
I WANT TO HURRY UP AND FINISH THIS WORK SO I CAN HAVE TEATIME.
GET THIS TIDIED UP.
YESSIR!
—OH?
HEY, SENSEI ...
...WHAT'S THIS?
HM?
THERE'S A BUNCH OF NAMES I DON'T KNOW...
TWEEDLE DEE... TWEEDLE DUM...
—OH!
JUST SOMETHING I SCRIBBLED DOWN. TWIN GUARDS WHO PROTECT NAMES AND REGRETS...
I THOUGHT MAYBE I'D USE THEM AT SOME POINT, BUT I COMPLETELY FORGOT ABOUT THEM.
...NAMES AND... ...REGRETS?

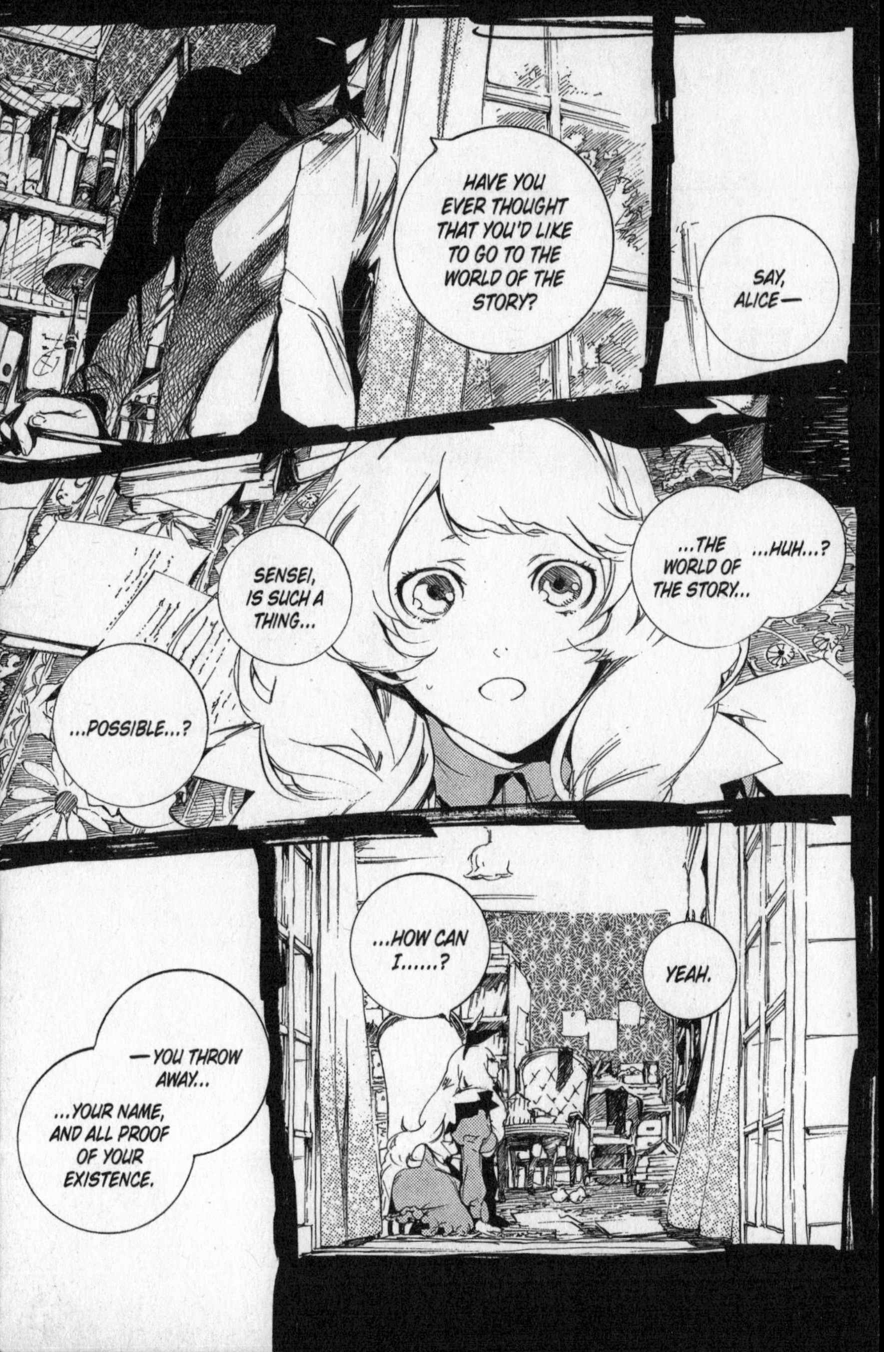
SAY, ALICE—
HAVE YOU EVER THOUGHT THAT YOU'D LIKE TO GO TO THE WORLD OF THE STORY?
...HUH...?
...THE WORLD OF THE STORY...
SENSEI, IS SUCH A THING...
...POSSIBLE...?
YEAH.
...HOW CAN I......?
—YOU THROW AWAY...
...YOUR NAME, AND ALL PROOF OF YOUR EXISTENCE.

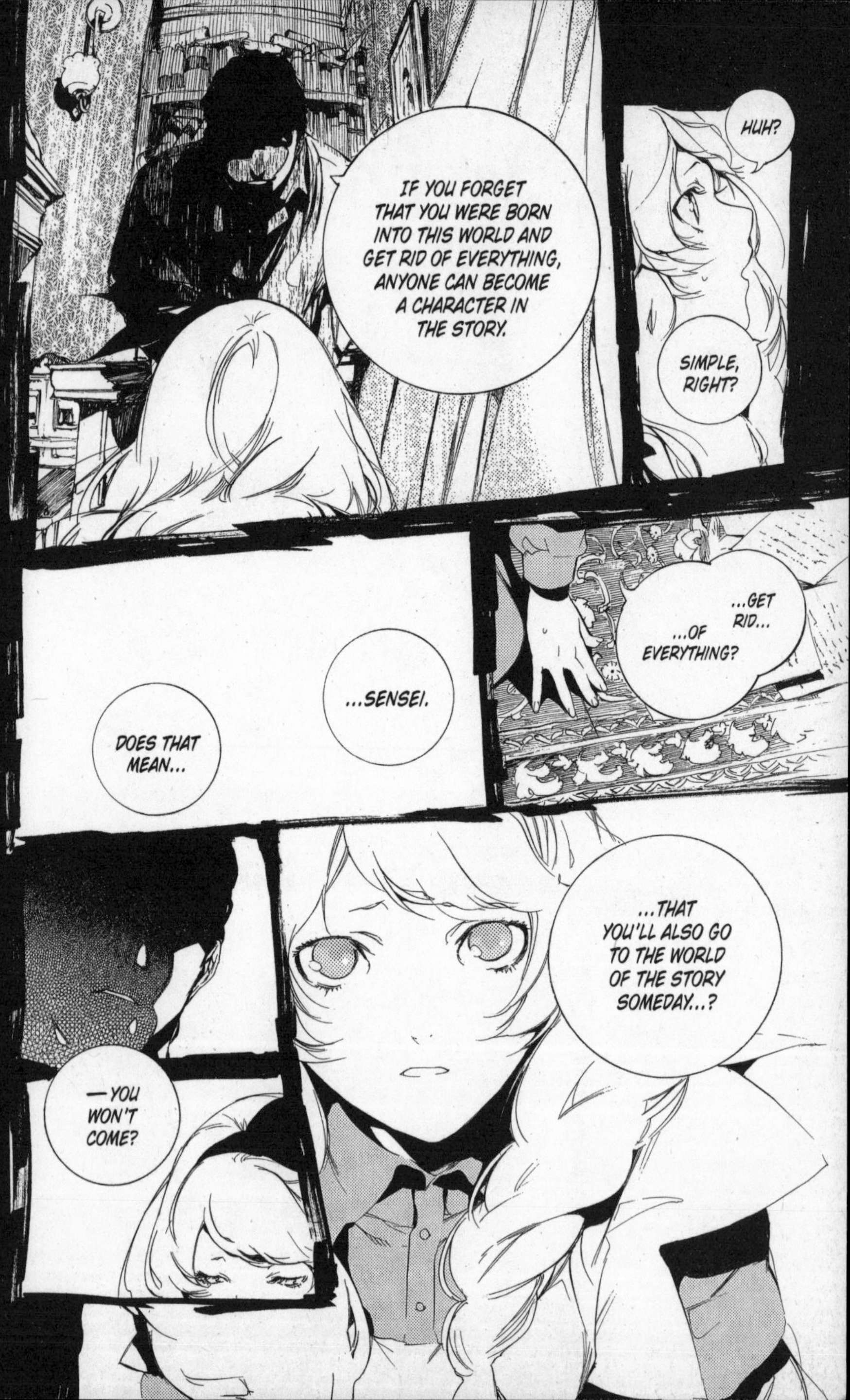
HUH?
SIMPLE, RIGHT?
IF YOU FORGET THAT YOU WERE BORN INTO THIS WORLD AND GET RID OF EVERYTHING, ANYONE CAN BECOME A CHARACTER IN THE STORY.
...GET RID...
...OF EVERYTHING?
...SENSEI.
DOES THAT MEAN...
...THAT YOU'LL ALSO GO TO THE WORLD OF THE STORY SOMEDAY...?
—YOU WON'T COME?

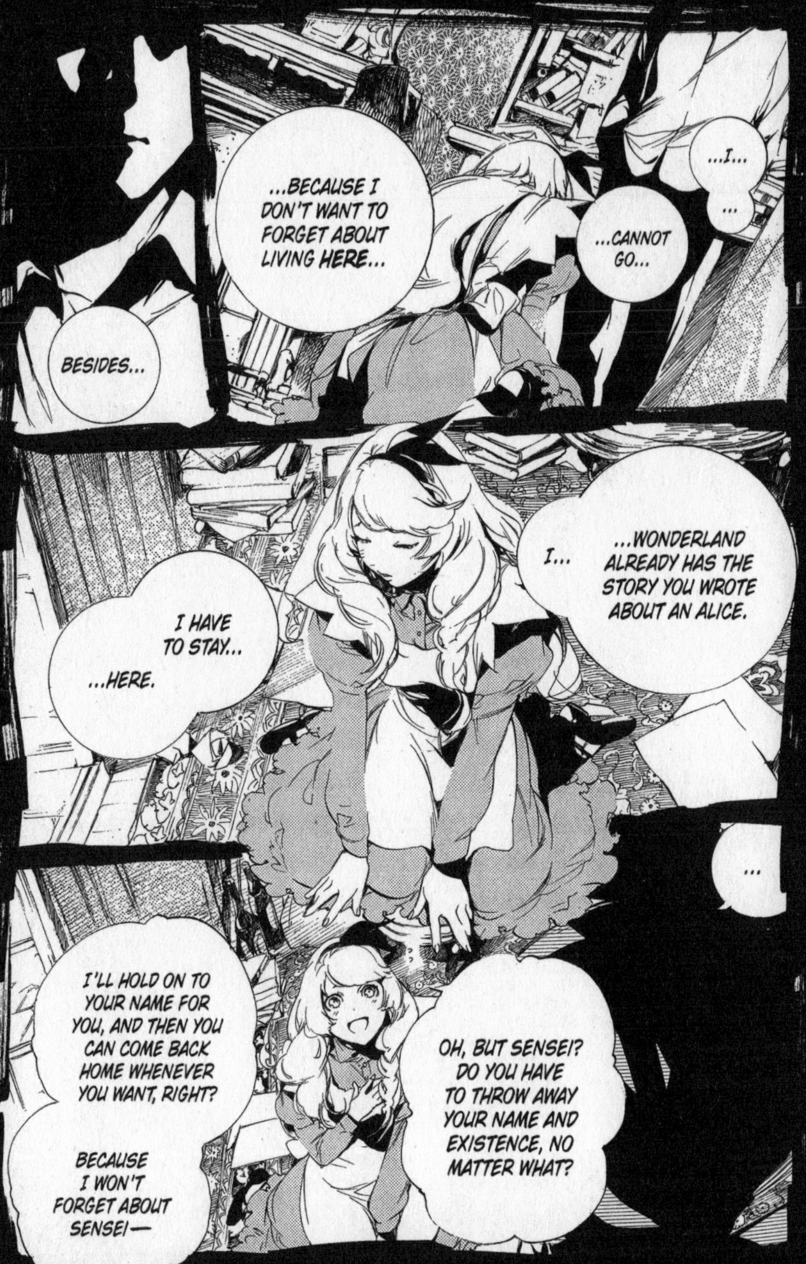
...I...
...
...CANNOT GO...
...BECAUSE I DON'T WANT TO FORGET ABOUT LIVING HERE...
BESIDES...
I...
...WONDERLAND ALREADY HAS THE STORY YOU WROTE ABOUT AN ALICE.
I HAVE TO STAY...
...HERE.
...
OH, BUT SENSEI? DO YOU HAVE TO THROW AWAY YOUR NAME AND EXISTENCE, NO MATTER WHAT?
I'LL HOLD ON TO YOUR NAME FOR YOU, AND THEN YOU CAN COME BACK HOME WHENEVER YOU WANT, RIGHT?
BECAUSE I WON'T FORGET ABOUT SENSEI—

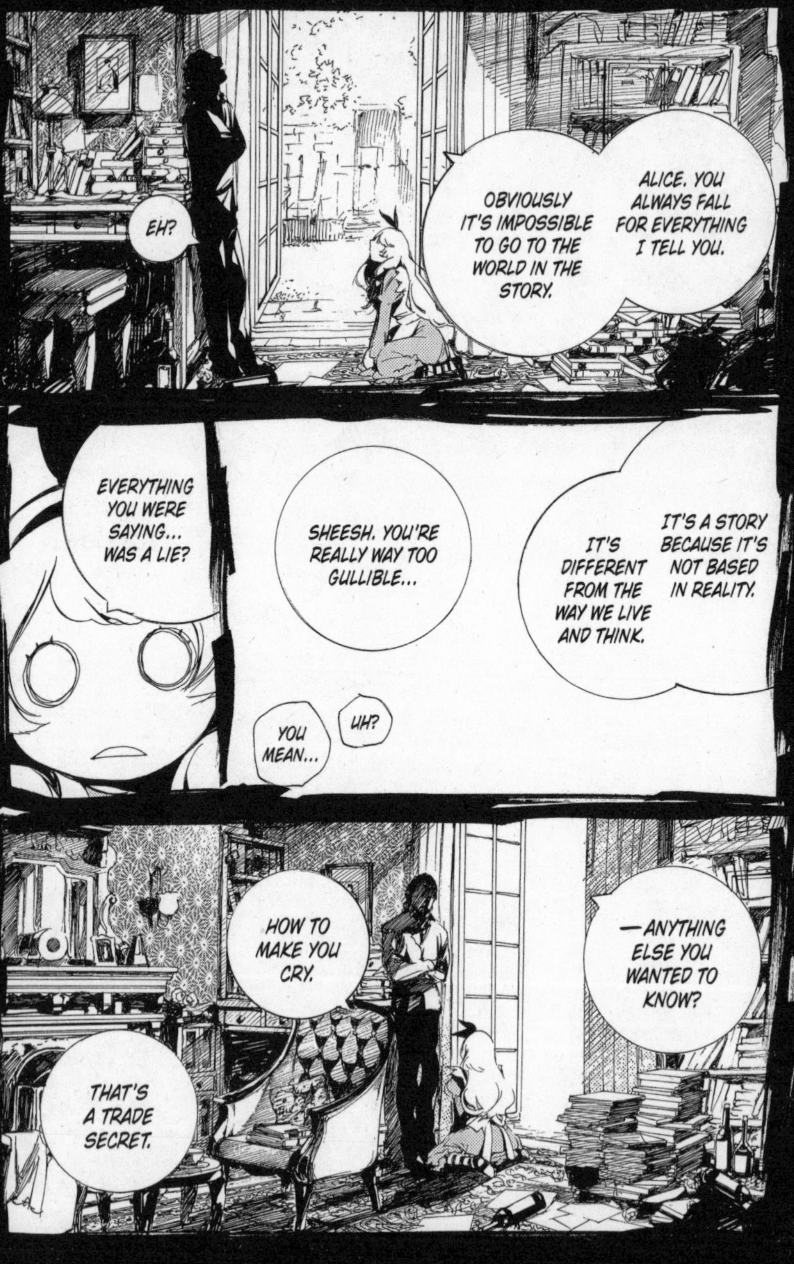
ALICE. YOU ALWAYS FALL FOR EVERYTHING I TELL YOU.
OBVIOUSLY IT'S IMPOSSIBLE TO GO TO THE WORLD IN THE STORY.
EH?
IT'S A STORY BECAUSE IT'S NOT BASED IN REALITY.
IT'S DIFFERENT FROM THE WAY WE LIVE AND THINK.
SHEESH. YOU'RE REALLY WAY TOO GULLIBLE...
UH?
YOU MEAN...
EVERYTHING YOU WERE SAYING... WAS A LIE?
—ANYTHING ELSE YOU WANTED TO KNOW?
HOW TO MAKE YOU CRY.
THAT'S A TRADE SECRET.

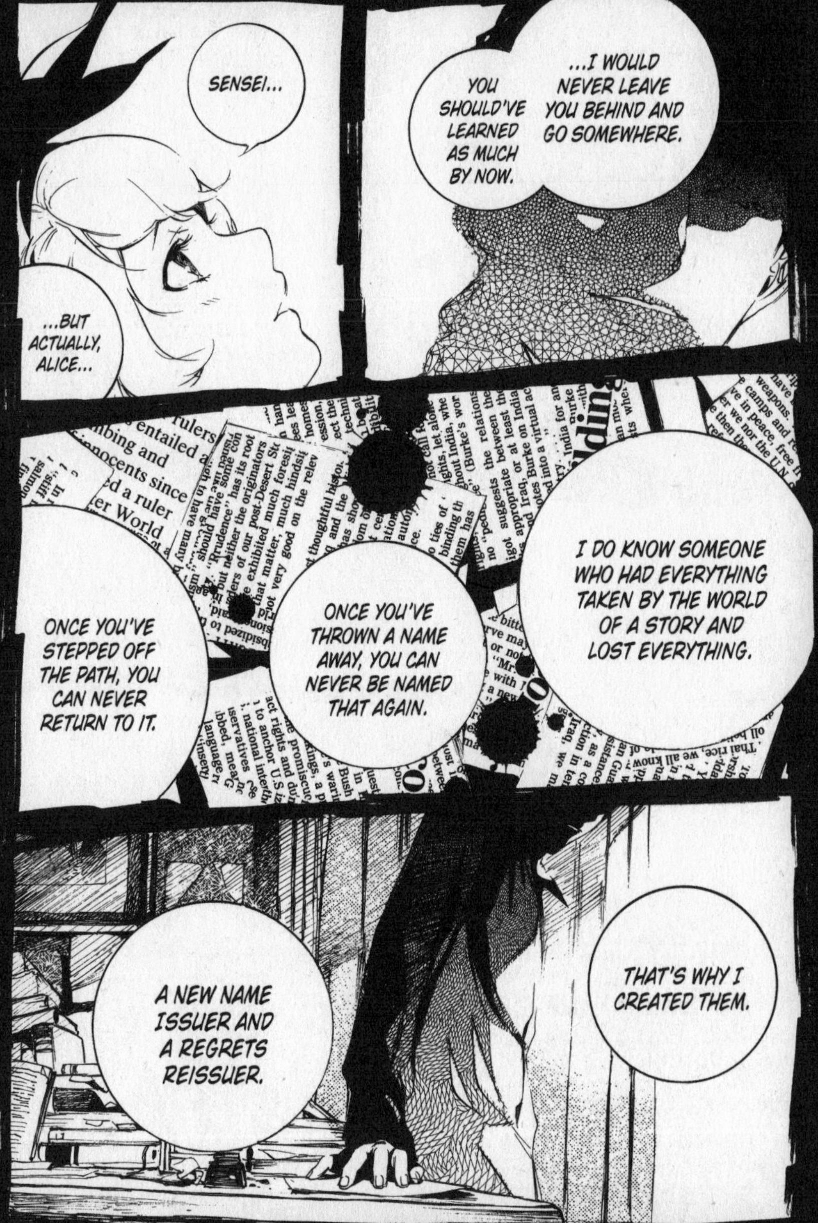
...I WOULD NEVER LEAVE YOU BEHIND AND GO SOMEWHERE.
YOU SHOULD'VE LEARNED AS MUCH BY NOW.
SENSEI...
...BUT ACTUALLY, ALICE...
I DO KNOW SOMEONE WHO HAD EVERYTHING TAKEN BY THE WORLD OF A STORY AND LOST EVERYTHING.
ONCE YOU'VE THROWN A NAME AWAY, YOU CAN NEVER BE NAMED THAT AGAIN.
ONCE YOU'VE STEPPED OFF THE PATH, YOU CAN NEVER RETURN TO IT.
THAT'S WHY I CREATED THEM.
A NEW NAME ISSUER AND A REGRETS REISSUER.

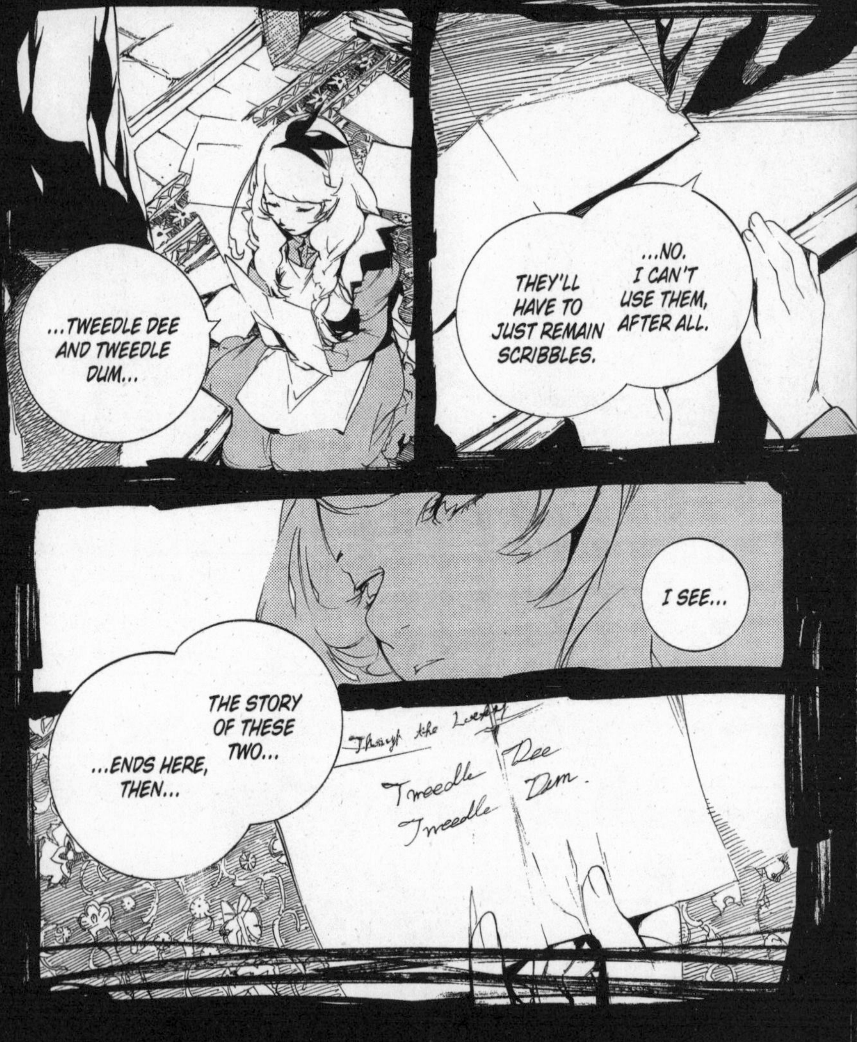
...NO. I CAN'T USE THEM, AFTER ALL.
THEY'LL HAVE TO JUST REMAIN SCRIBBLES.
...TWEEDLE DEE AND TWEEDLE DUM...
I SEE...
THE STORY OF THESE TWO...
...ENDS HERE, THEN...
Tweedle Dee
Tweedle Dum.

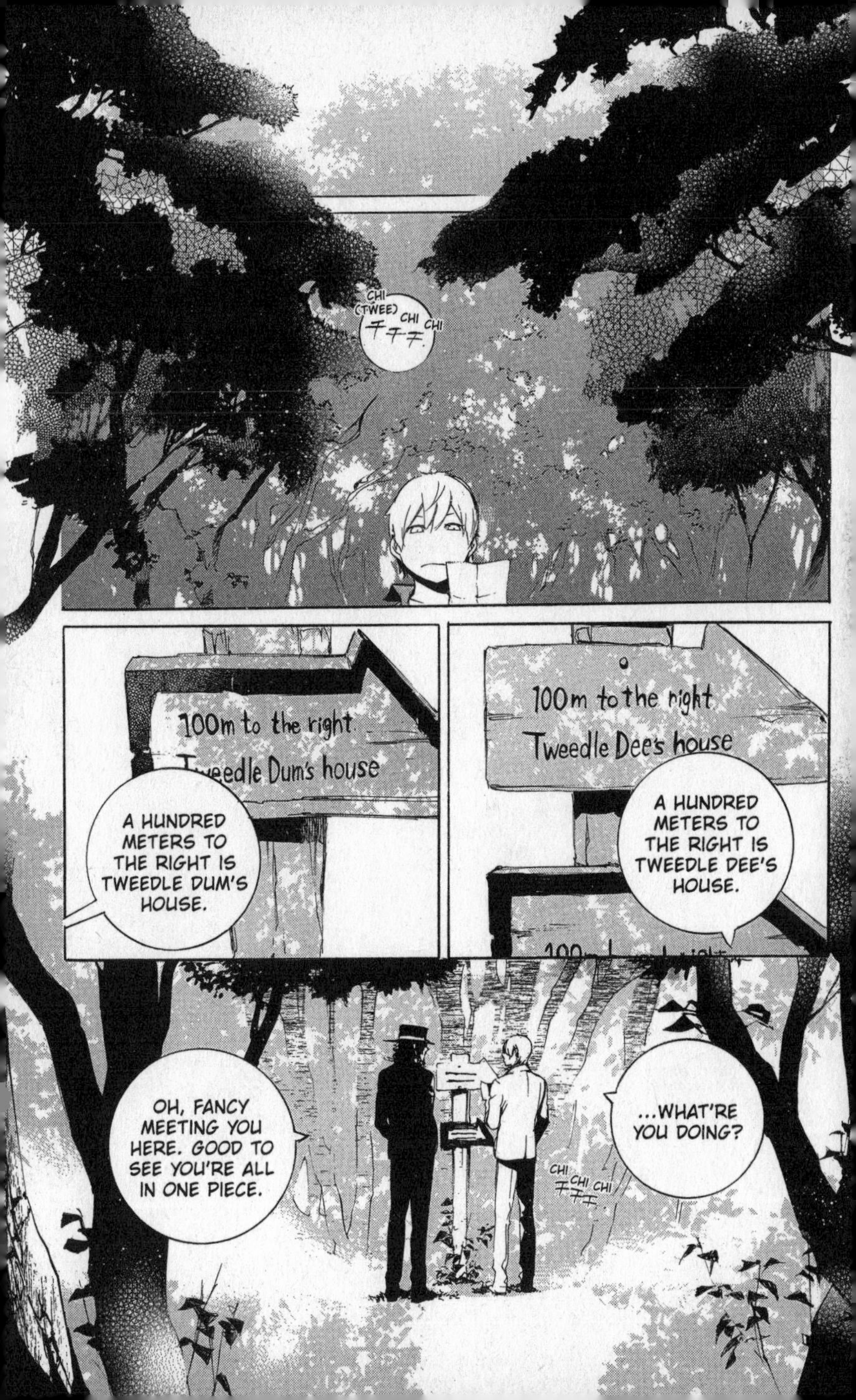
CHI (TWEE) CHI CHI
チチチ
100m to the right
Tweedle Dee's house
A HUNDRED METERS TO THE RIGHT IS TWEEDLE DEE'S HOUSE.
100m to the right
Tweedle Dum's house
A HUNDRED METERS TO THE RIGHT IS TWEEDLE DUM'S HOUSE.
...WHAT'RE YOU DOING?
CHI CHI CHI
チチチ
OH, FANCY MEETING YOU HERE. GOOD TO SEE YOU'RE ALL IN ONE PIECE.

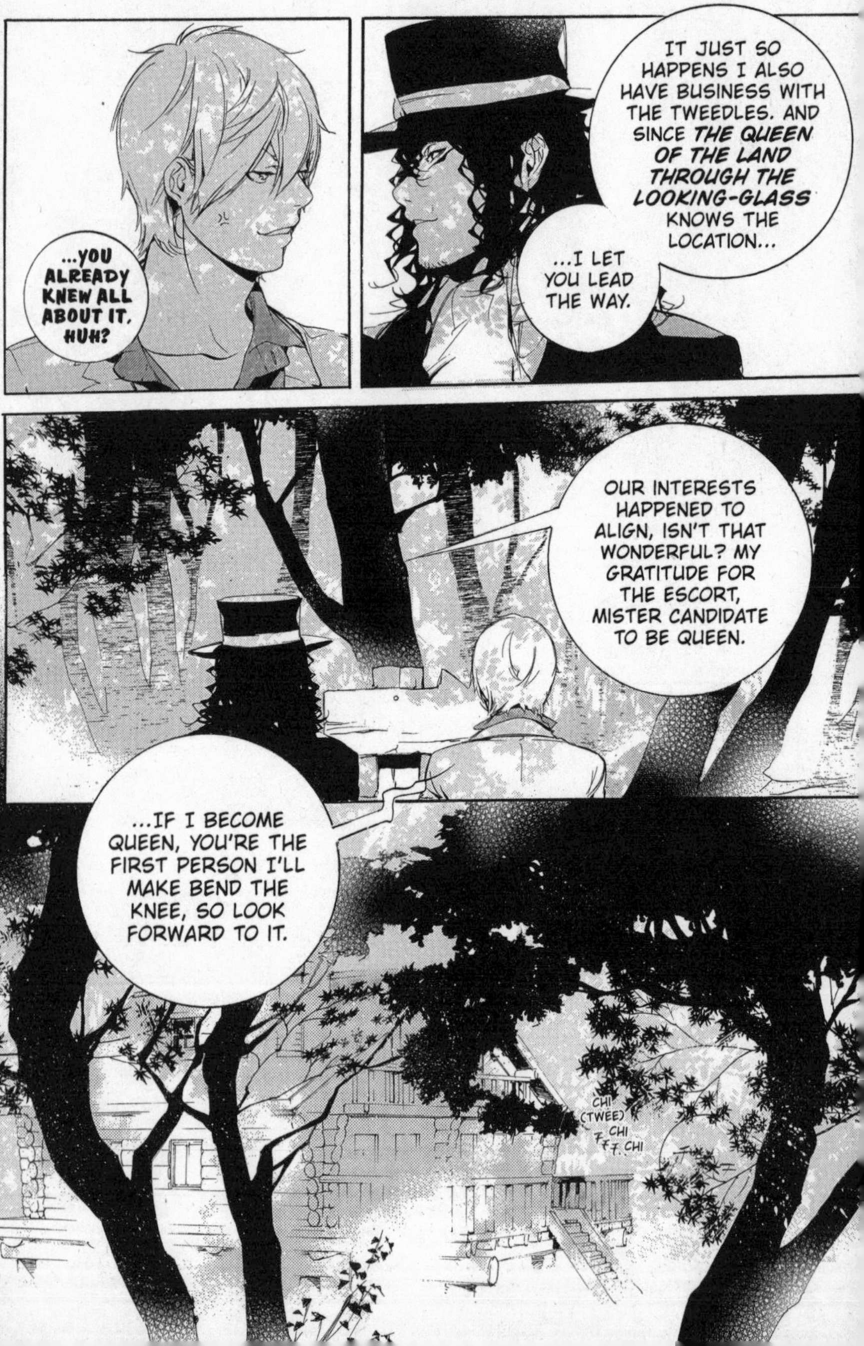
IT JUST SO HAPPENS I ALSO HAVE BUSINESS WITH THE TWEEDLES. AND SINCE *THE QUEEN OF THE LAND THROUGH THE LOOKING-GLASS* KNOWS THE LOCATION...
...I LET YOU LEAD THE WAY.
...YOU ALREADY KNEW ALL ABOUT IT, HUH?
OUR INTERESTS HAPPENED TO ALIGN, ISN'T THAT WONDERFUL? MY GRATITUDE FOR THE ESCORT, MISTER CANDIDATE TO BE QUEEN.
...IF I BECOME QUEEN, YOU'RE THE FIRST PERSON I'LL MAKE BEND THE KNEE, SO LOOK FORWARD TO IT.
CHI (TWEE) CHI CHI

Chapter 45 Double Barrel.

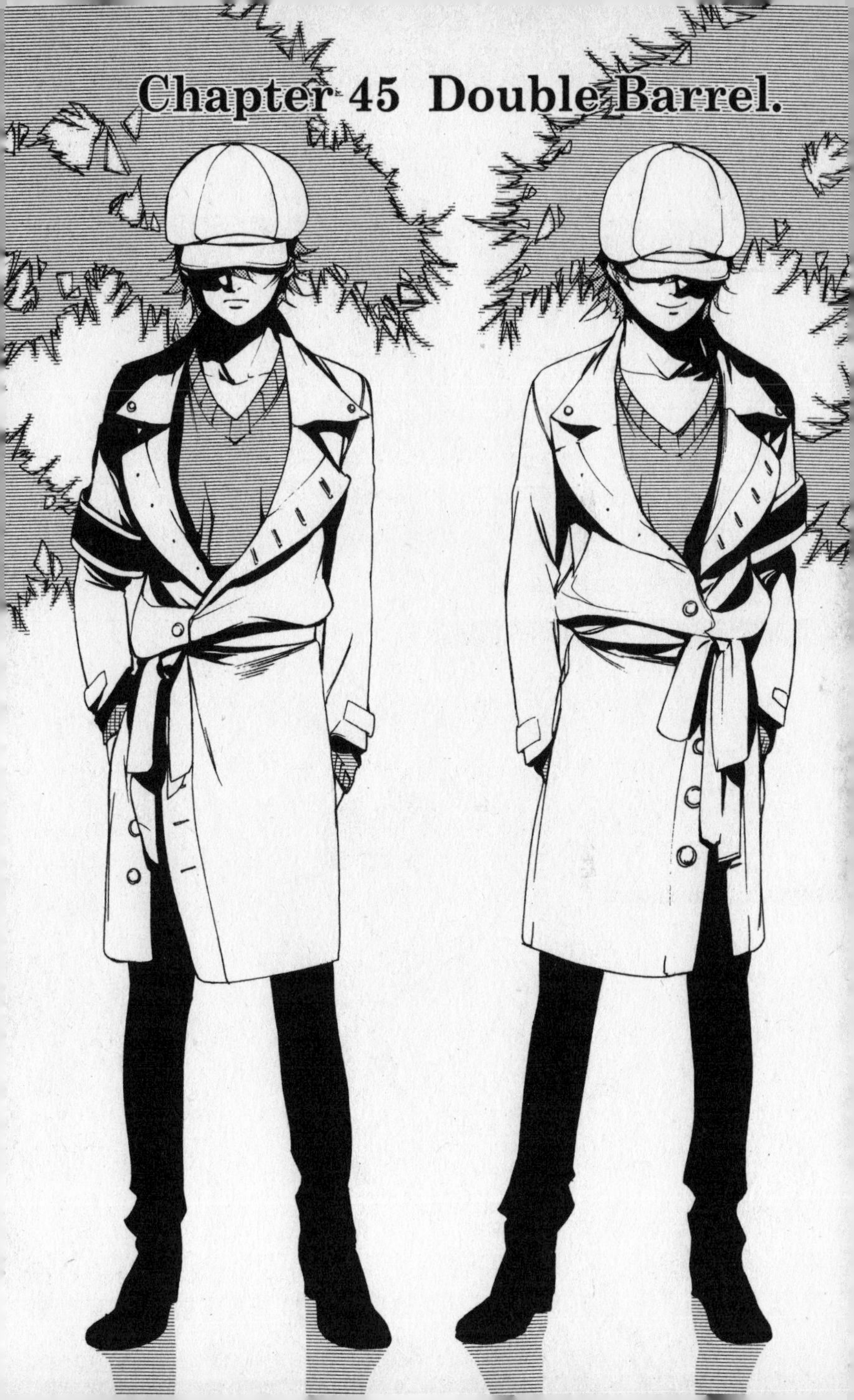

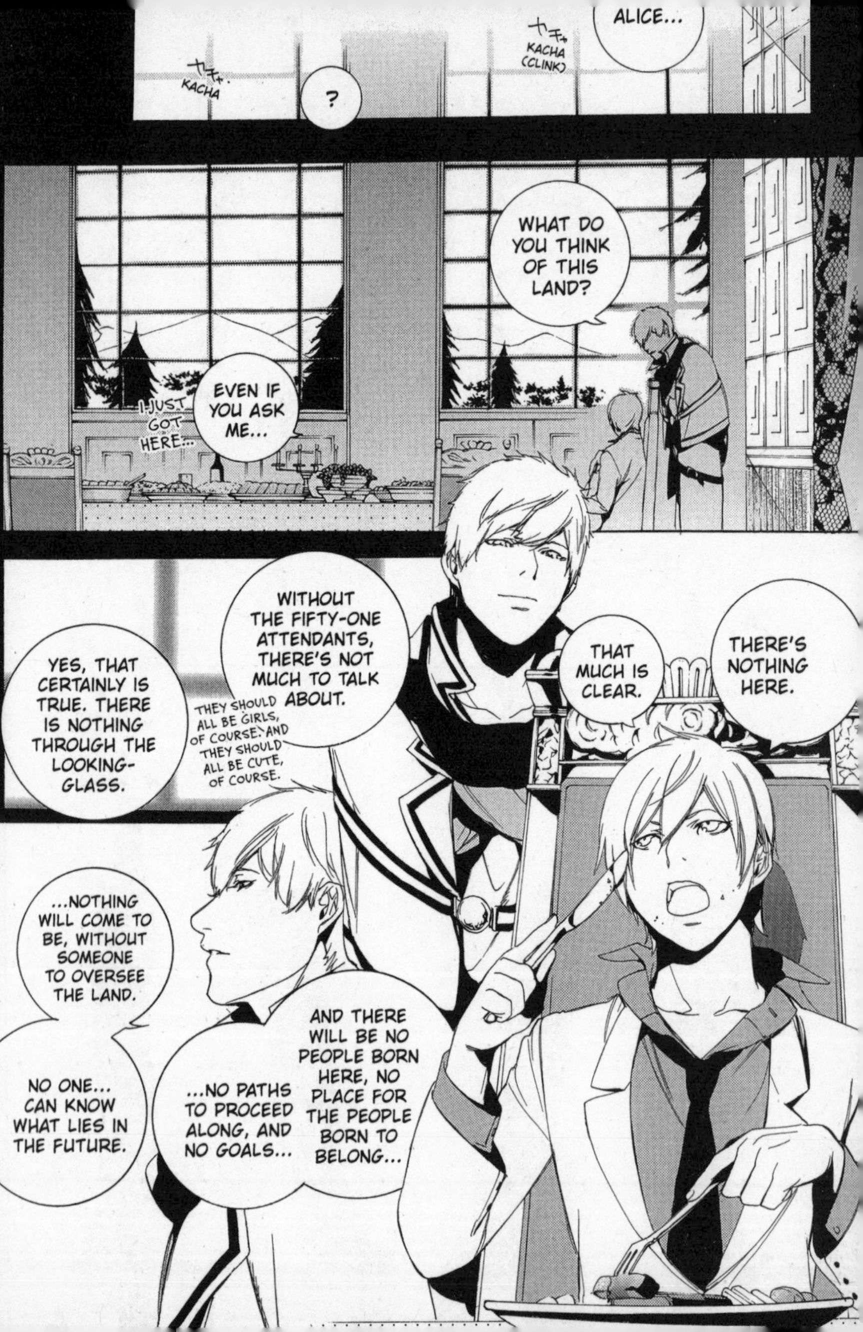
ALICE...
カチャ
KACHA (CLINK)
?
カチャ
KACHA
WHAT DO YOU THINK OF THIS LAND?
EVEN IF YOU ASK ME...
I JUST GOT HERE...
THERE'S NOTHING HERE.
THAT MUCH IS CLEAR.
WITHOUT THE FIFTY-ONE ATTENDANTS, THERE'S NOT MUCH TO TALK ABOUT.
THEY SHOULD ALL BE GIRLS, OF COURSE. AND THEY SHOULD ALL BE CUTE, OF COURSE.
YES, THAT CERTAINLY IS TRUE. THERE IS NOTHING THROUGH THE LOOKING-GLASS.
...NOTHING WILL COME TO BE, WITHOUT SOMEONE TO OVERSEE THE LAND.
...NO PATHS TO PROCEED ALONG, AND NO GOALS...
AND THERE WILL BE NO PEOPLE BORN HERE, NO PLACE FOR THE PEOPLE BORN TO BELONG...
NO ONE... CAN KNOW WHAT LIES IN THE FUTURE.

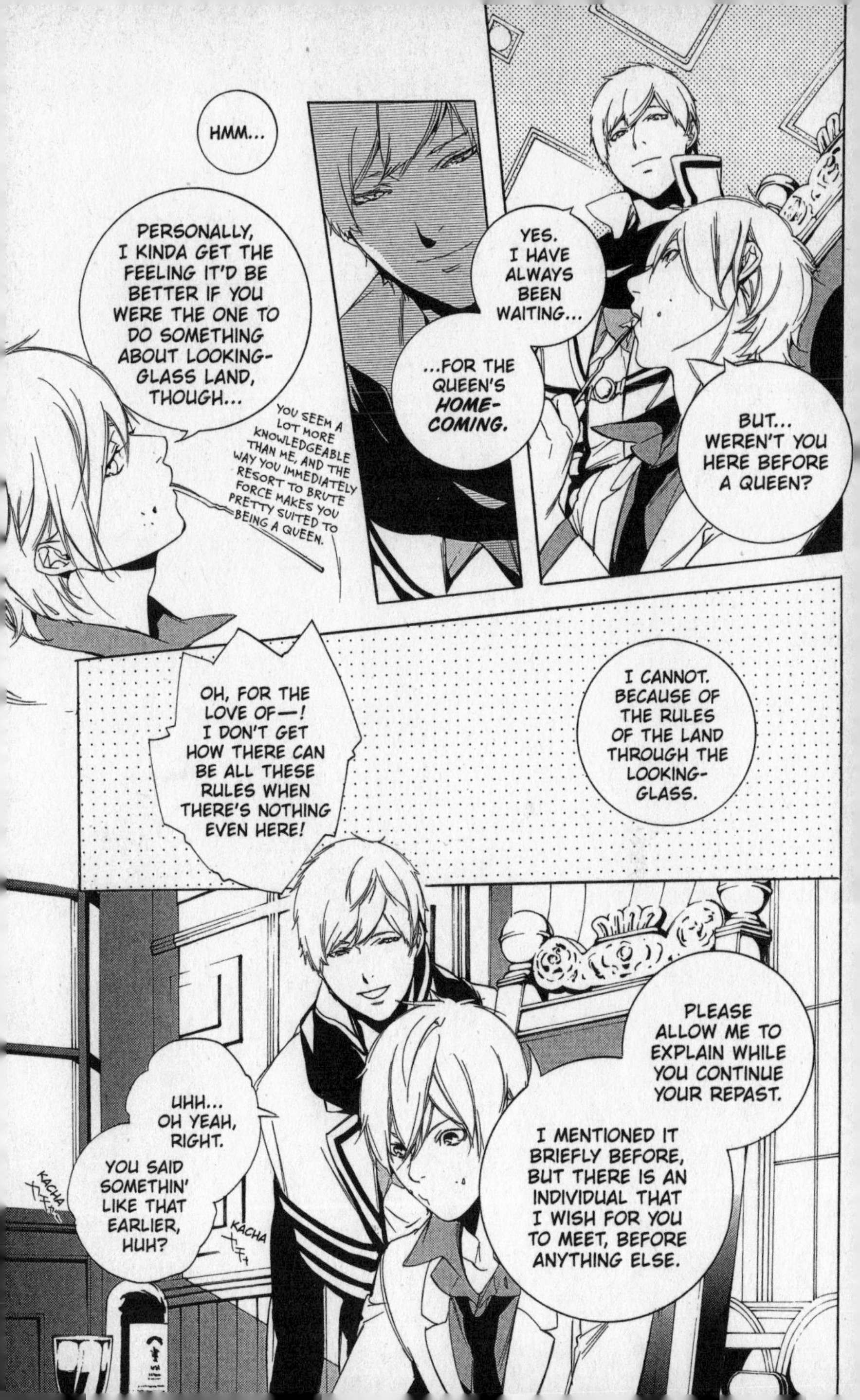
YES. I HAVE ALWAYS BEEN WAITING...
...FOR THE QUEEN'S *HOMECOMING.*
BUT... WEREN'T YOU HERE BEFORE A QUEEN?
HMM...
PERSONALLY, I KINDA GET THE FEELING IT'D BE BETTER IF YOU WERE THE ONE TO DO SOMETHING ABOUT LOOKING-GLASS LAND, THOUGH...
YOU SEEM A LOT MORE KNOWLEDGEABLE THAN ME, AND THE WAY YOU IMMEDIATELY RESORT TO BRUTE FORCE MAKES YOU PRETTY SUITED TO BEING A QUEEN.
I CANNOT. BECAUSE OF THE RULES OF THE LAND THROUGH THE LOOKING-GLASS.
OH, FOR THE LOVE OF—! I DON'T GET HOW THERE CAN BE ALL THESE RULES WHEN THERE'S NOTHING EVEN HERE!
PLEASE ALLOW ME TO EXPLAIN WHILE YOU CONTINUE YOUR REPAST.
I MENTIONED IT BRIEFLY BEFORE, BUT THERE IS AN INDIVIDUAL THAT I WISH FOR YOU TO MEET, BEFORE ANYTHING ELSE.
KACHA
UHH... OH YEAH, RIGHT.
YOU SAID SOMETHIN' LIKE THAT EARLIER, HUH?
KACHA

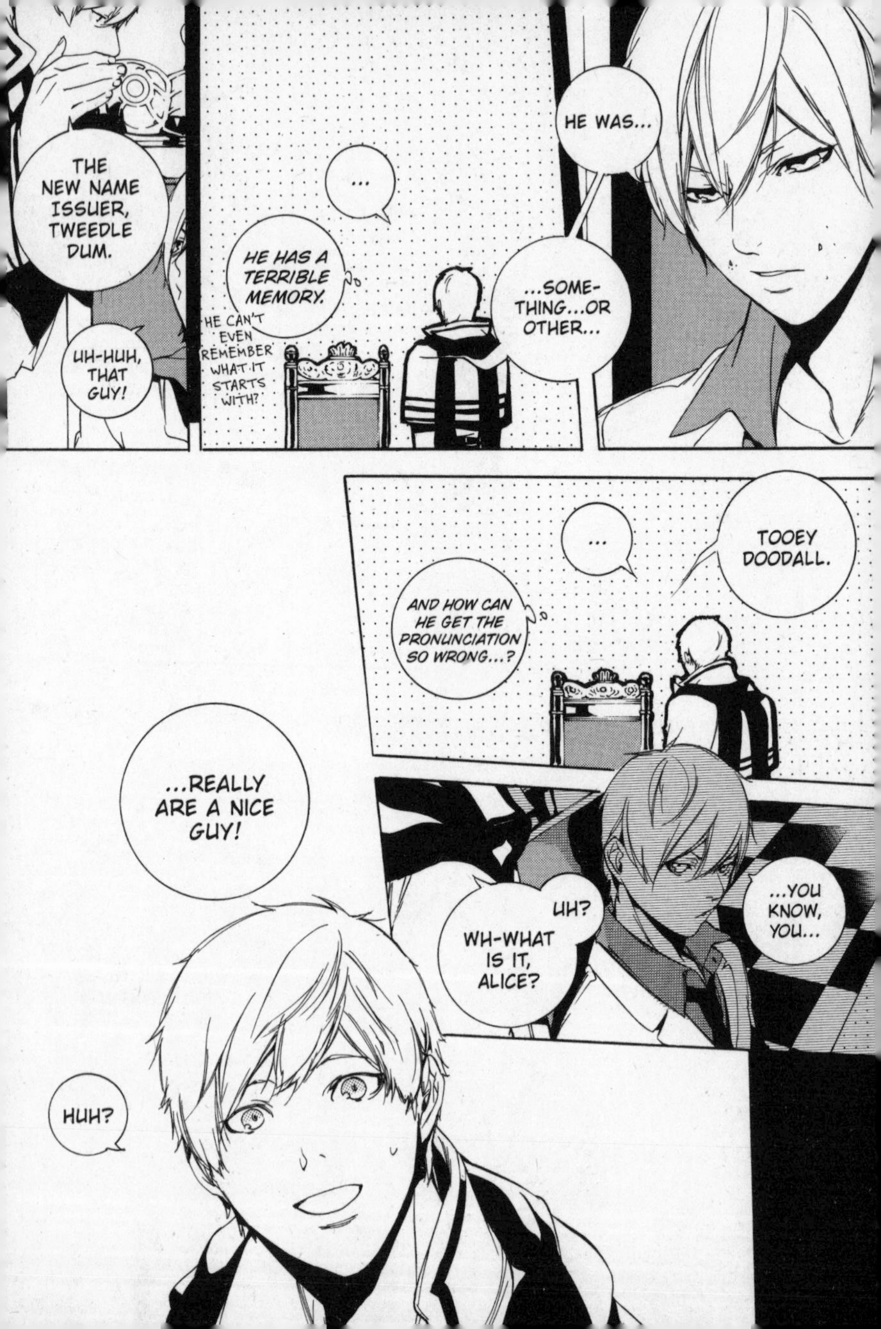
HE WAS...
...SOME-THING...OR OTHER...
...
HE HAS A TERRIBLE MEMORY.
HE CAN'T EVEN REMEMBER WHAT IT STARTS WITH?
THE NEW NAME ISSUER, TWEEDLE DUM.
UH-HUH, THAT GUY!
TOOEY DOODALL.
...
AND HOW CAN HE GET THE PRONUNCIATION SO WRONG...?
...YOU KNOW, YOU...
UH? WH-WHAT IS IT, ALICE?
...REALLY ARE A NICE GUY!
HUH?

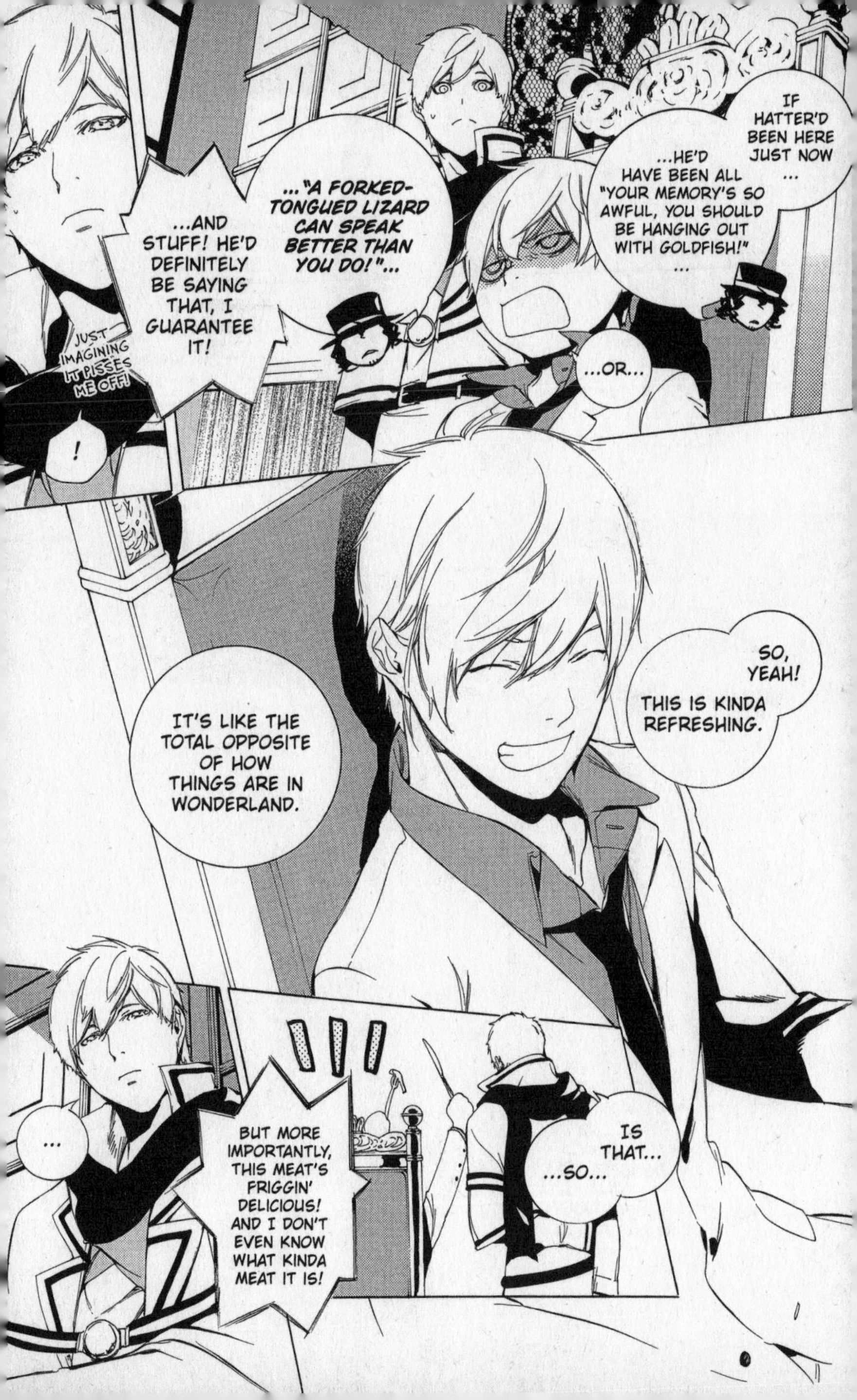
IF HATTER'D BEEN HERE JUST NOW ...
...HE'D HAVE BEEN ALL "YOUR MEMORY'S SO AWFUL, YOU SHOULD BE HANGING OUT WITH GOLDFISH!" ...
...OR...
..."A FORKED-TONGUED LIZARD CAN SPEAK BETTER THAN YOU DO!"...
...AND STUFF! HE'D DEFINITELY BE SAYING THAT, I GUARANTEE IT!
JUST IMAGINING IT PISSES ME OFF!
!
SO, YEAH!
THIS IS KINDA REFRESHING.
IT'S LIKE THE TOTAL OPPOSITE OF HOW THINGS ARE IN WONDERLAND.
IS THAT...
...SO...
BUT MORE IMPORTANTLY, THIS MEAT'S FRIGGIN' DELICIOUS! AND I DON'T EVEN KNOW WHAT KINDA MEAT IT IS!
...

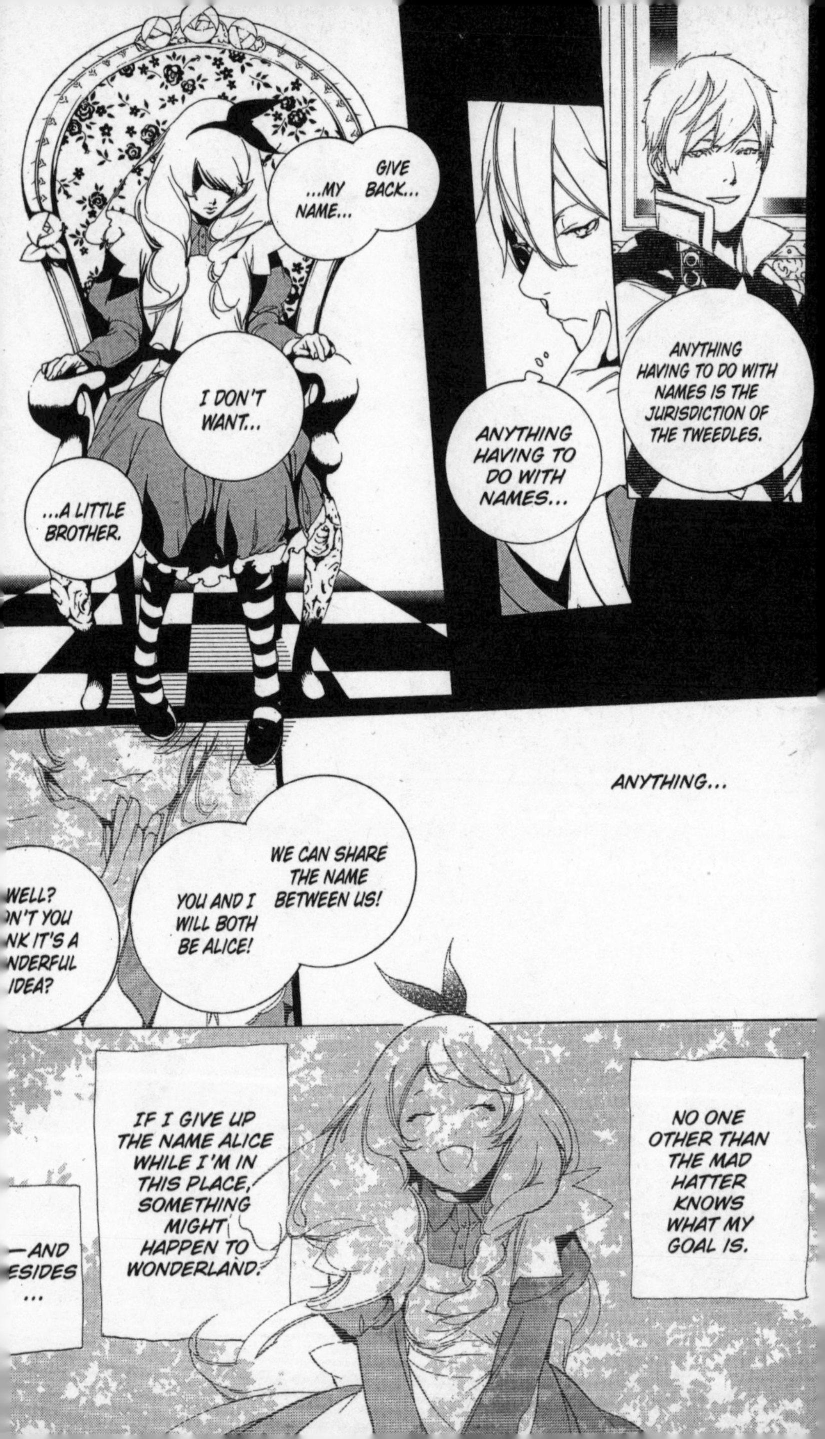
ANYTHING HAVING TO DO WITH NAMES IS THE JURISDICTION OF THE TWEEDLES.
ANYTHING HAVING TO DO WITH NAMES...
...MY NAME... GIVE BACK...
I DON'T WANT...
...A LITTLE BROTHER.
ANYTHING...
WE CAN SHARE THE NAME BETWEEN US! YOU AND I WILL BOTH BE ALICE!
WELL? N'T YOU NK IT'S A NDERFUL IDEA?
NO ONE OTHER THAN THE MAD HATTER KNOWS WHAT MY GOAL IS.
IF I GIVE UP THE NAME ALICE WHILE I'M IN THIS PLACE, SOMETHING MIGHT HAPPEN TO WONDERLAND.
—AND ESIDES ...

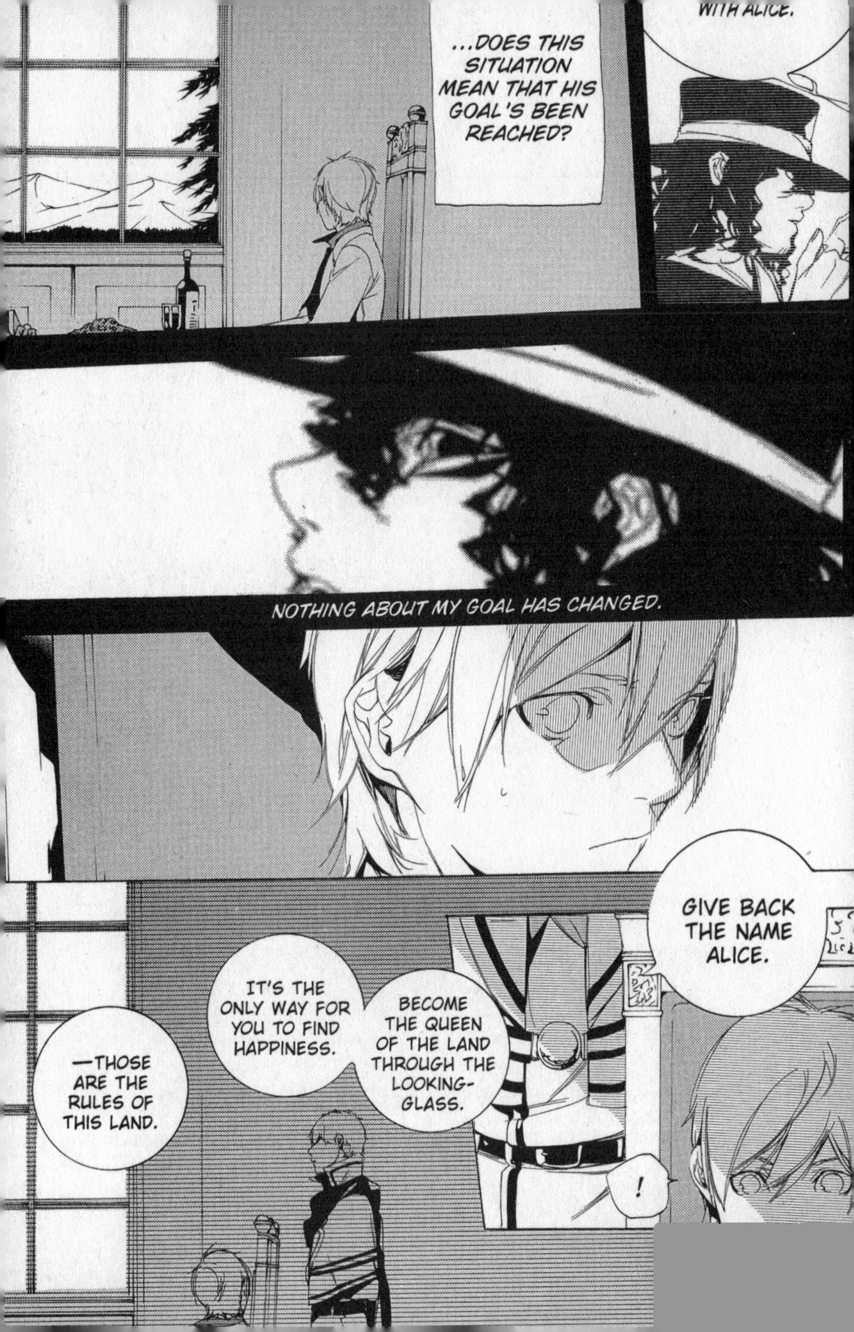
WITH ALICE.
...DOES THIS SITUATION MEAN THAT HIS GOAL'S BEEN REACHED?
NOTHING ABOUT MY GOAL HAS CHANGED.
GIVE BACK THE NAME ALICE.
BECOME THE QUEEN OF THE LAND THROUGH THE LOOKING-GLASS.
IT'S THE ONLY WAY FOR YOU TO FIND HAPPINESS.
—THOSE ARE THE RULES OF THIS LAND.
!

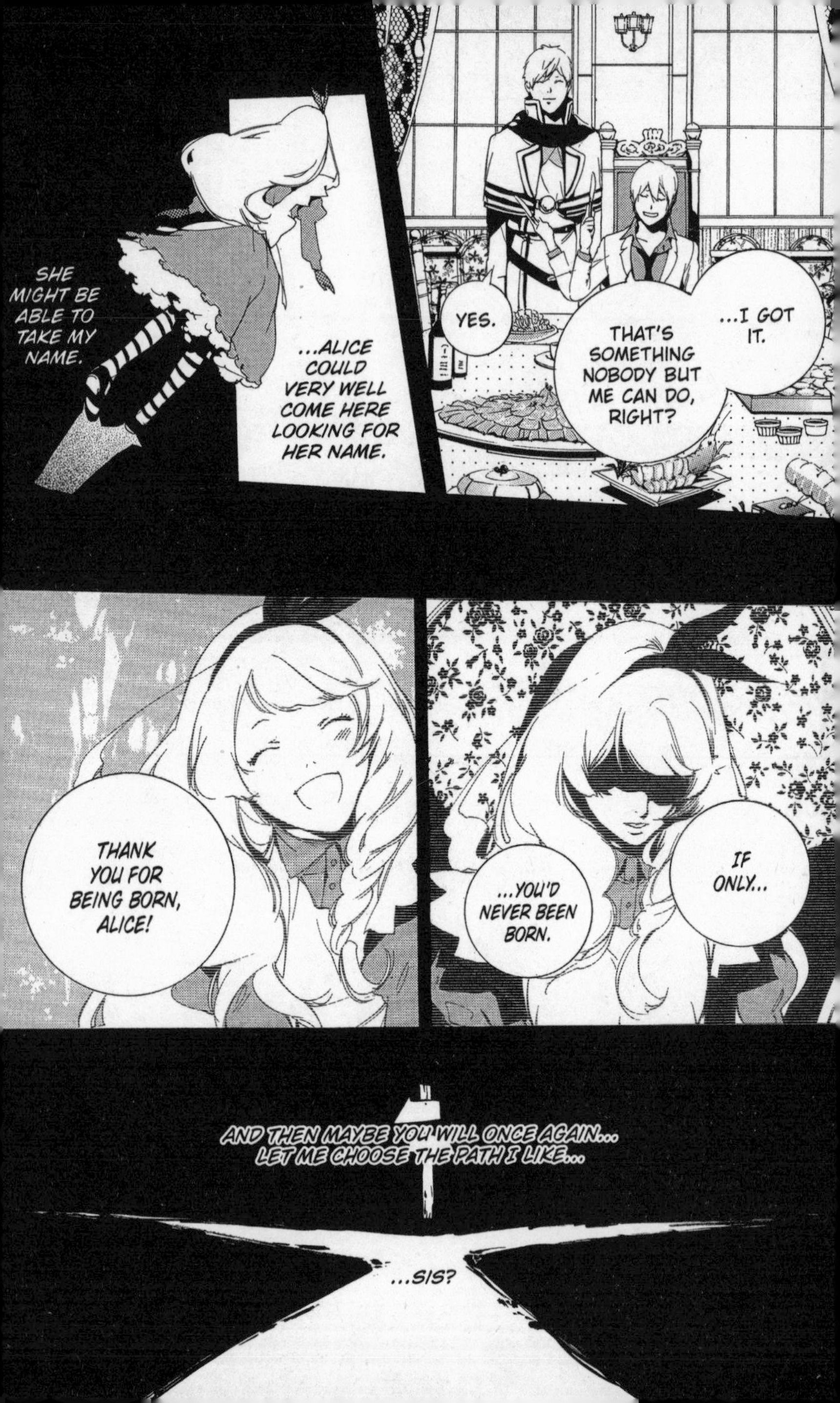
...I GOT IT.
THAT'S SOMETHING NOBODY BUT ME CAN DO, RIGHT?
YES.
...ALICE COULD VERY WELL COME HERE LOOKING FOR HER NAME.
SHE MIGHT BE ABLE TO TAKE MY NAME.
IF ONLY...
...YOU'D NEVER BEEN BORN.
THANK YOU FOR BEING BORN, ALICE!
AND THEN MAYBE YOU WILL ONCE AGAIN...
LET ME CHOOSE THE PATH I LIKE...
...SIS?

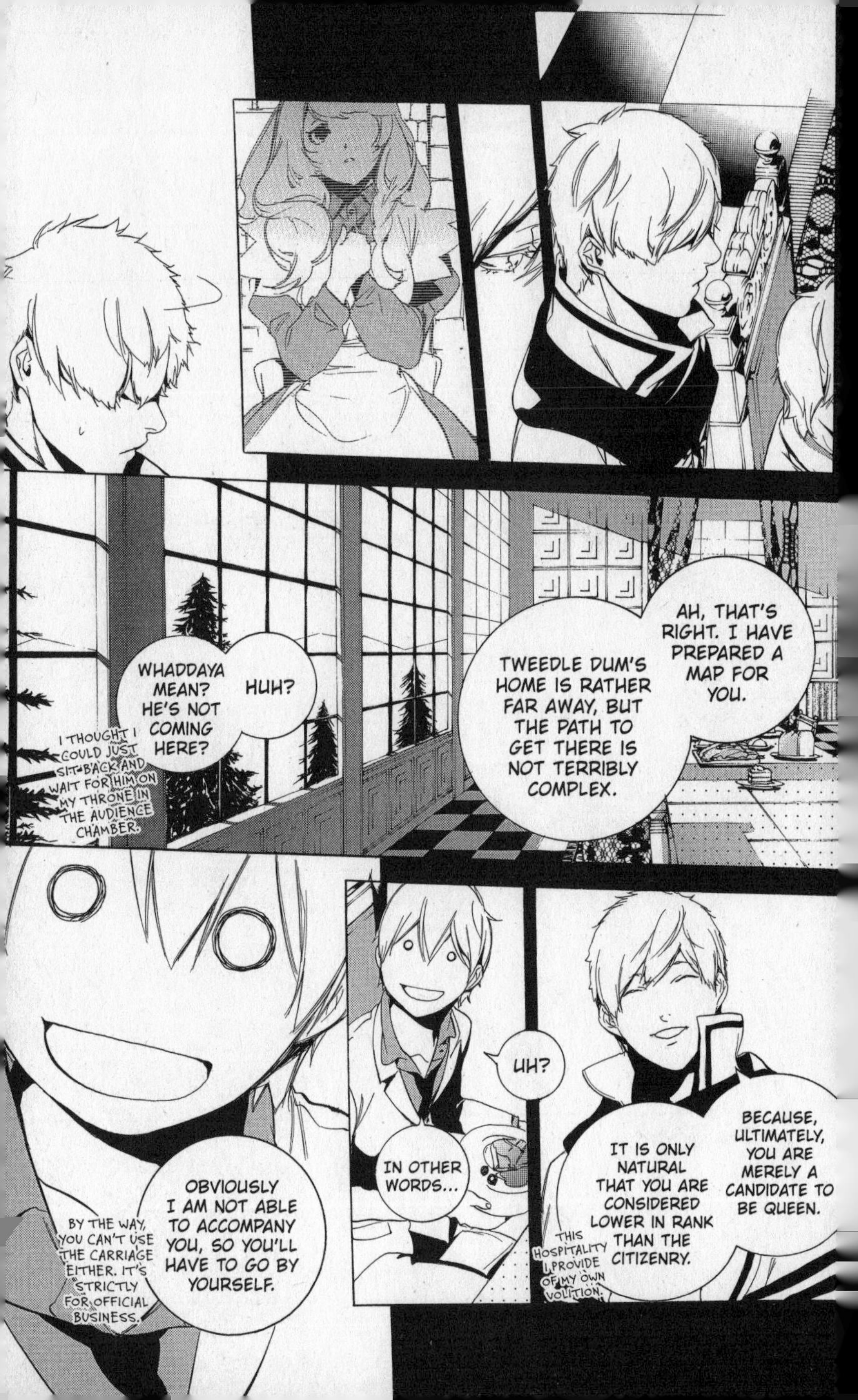
AH, THAT'S RIGHT. I HAVE PREPARED A MAP FOR YOU.
TWEEDLE DUM'S HOME IS RATHER FAR AWAY, BUT THE PATH TO GET THERE IS NOT TERRIBLY COMPLEX.
HUH?
WHADDAYA MEAN? HE'S NOT COMING HERE?
I THOUGHT I COULD JUST SIT BACK AND WAIT FOR HIM ON MY THRONE IN THE AUDIENCE CHAMBER.
BECAUSE, ULTIMATELY, YOU ARE MERELY A CANDIDATE TO BE QUEEN.
IT IS ONLY NATURAL THAT YOU ARE CONSIDERED LOWER IN RANK THAN THE CITIZENRY.
THIS HOSPITALITY I PROVIDE OF MY OWN VOLITION.
UH?
IN OTHER WORDS...
OBVIOUSLY I AM NOT ABLE TO ACCOMPANY YOU, SO YOU'LL HAVE TO GO BY YOURSELF.
BY THE WAY, YOU CAN'T USE THE CARRIAGE EITHER. IT'S STRICTLY FOR OFFICIAL BUSINESS.

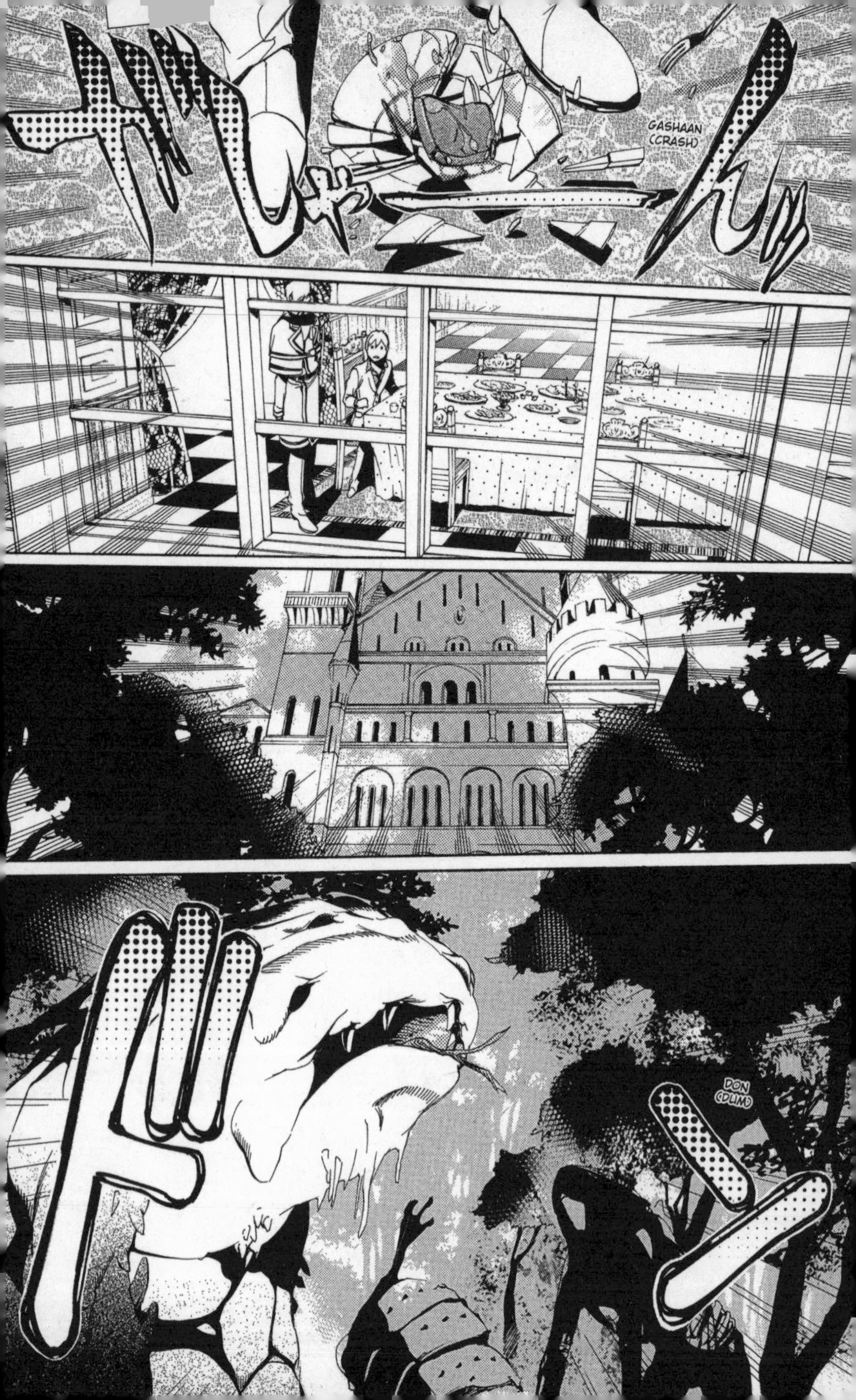
GASHAAN
(CRASH)
DON
(DUM)

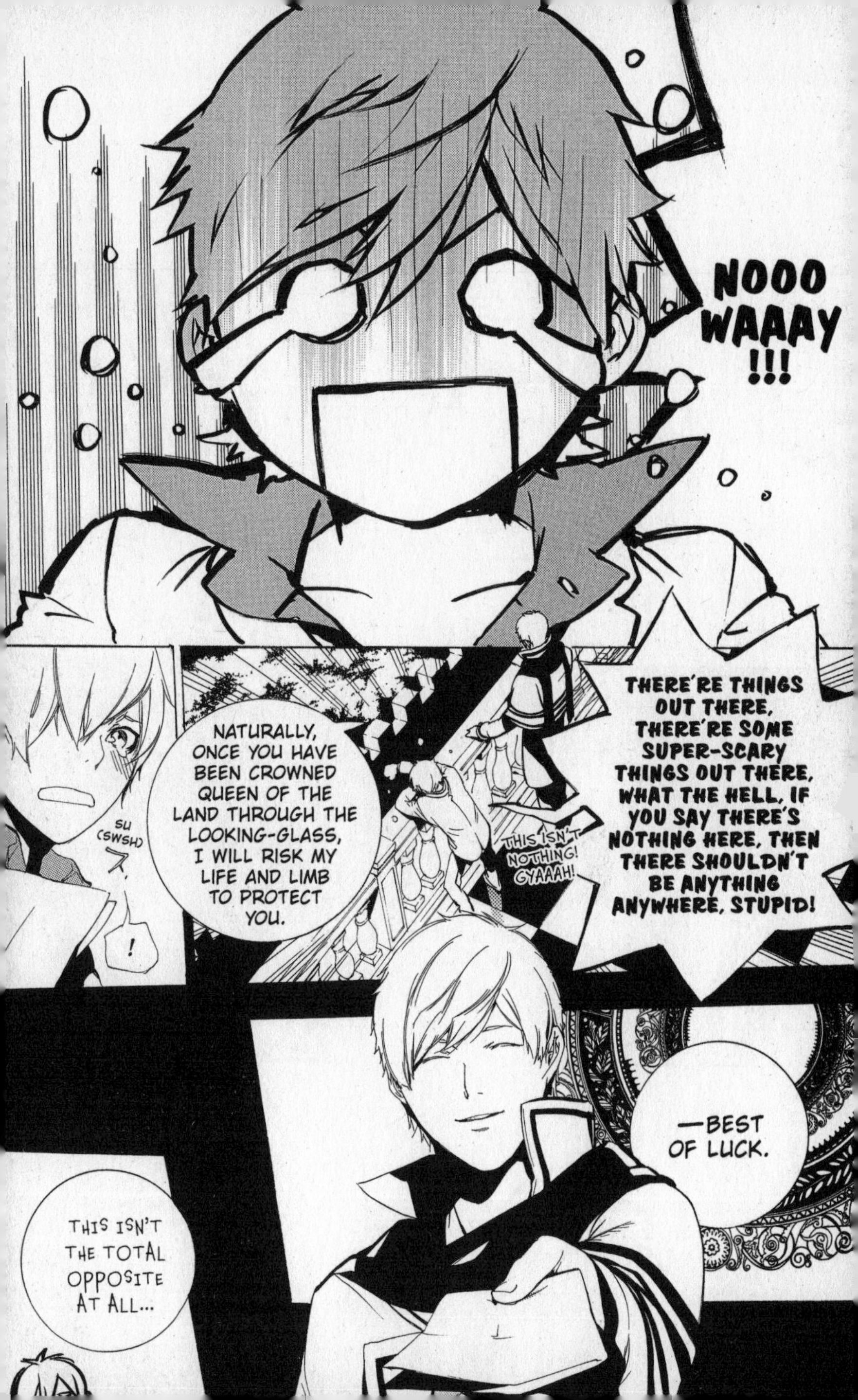
NOOO WAAAY !!!
THERE'RE THINGS OUT THERE, THERE'RE SOME SUPER-SCARY THINGS OUT THERE, WHAT THE HELL, IF YOU SAY THERE'S NOTHING HERE, THEN THERE SHOULDN'T BE ANYTHING ANYWHERE, STUPID!
THIS ISN'T NOTHING! GYAAAH!
NATURALLY, ONCE YOU HAVE BEEN CROWNED QUEEN OF THE LAND THROUGH THE LOOKING-GLASS, I WILL RISK MY LIFE AND LIMB TO PROTECT YOU.
SU (SWSH)
ス
!
—BEST OF LUCK.
THIS ISN'T THE TOTAL OPPOSITE AT ALL...

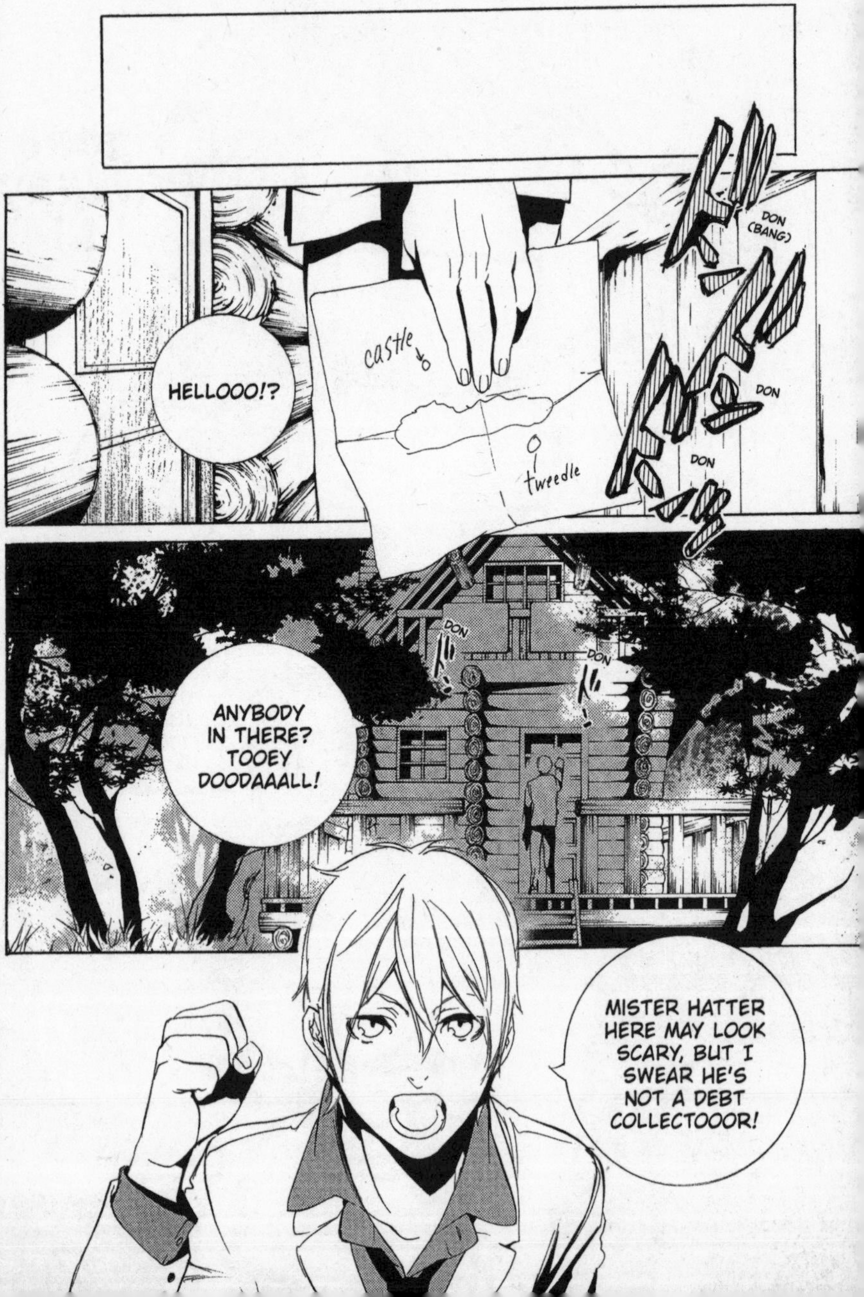
DON (BANG)
DON
DON
castle
tweedle
HELLOOO!?
DON
DON
ANYBODY IN THERE? TOOEY DOODAAALL!
MISTER HATTER HERE MAY LOOK SCARY, BUT I SWEAR HE'S NOT A DEBT COLLECTOOOR!

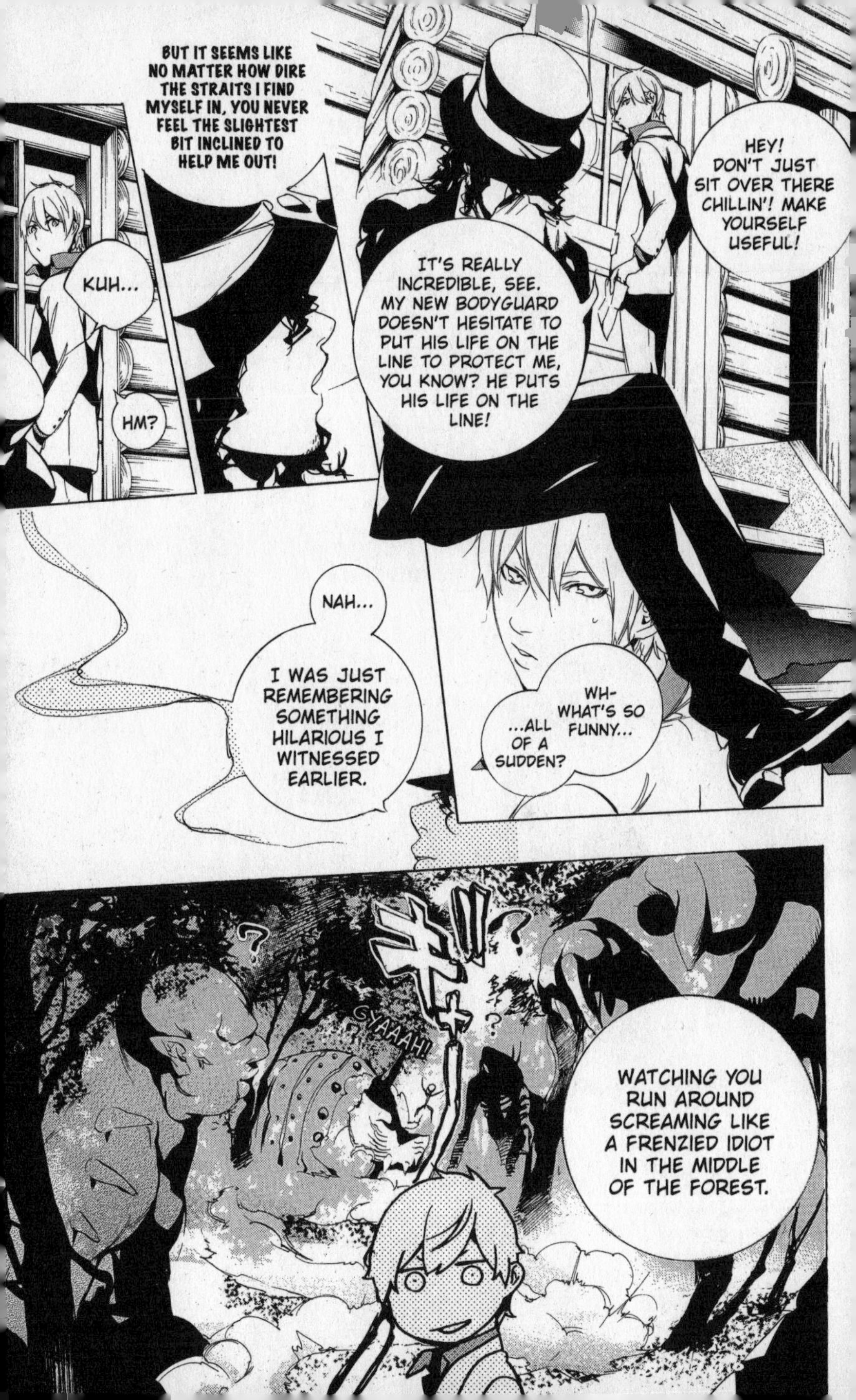
HEY! DON'T JUST SIT OVER THERE CHILLIN'! MAKE YOURSELF USEFUL!
IT'S REALLY INCREDIBLE, SEE. MY NEW BODYGUARD DOESN'T HESITATE TO PUT HIS LIFE ON THE LINE TO PROTECT ME, YOU KNOW? HE PUTS HIS LIFE ON THE LINE!
BUT IT SEEMS LIKE NO MATTER HOW DIRE THE STRAITS I FIND MYSELF IN, YOU NEVER FEEL THE SLIGHTEST BIT INCLINED TO HELP ME OUT!
KUH...
HM?
WH- WHAT'S SO FUNNY...
...ALL OF A SUDDEN?
NAH...
I WAS JUST REMEMBERING SOMETHING HILARIOUS I WITNESSED EARLIER.
GYAAAH!
WATCHING YOU RUN AROUND SCREAMING LIKE A FRENZIED IDIOT IN THE MIDDLE OF THE FOREST.

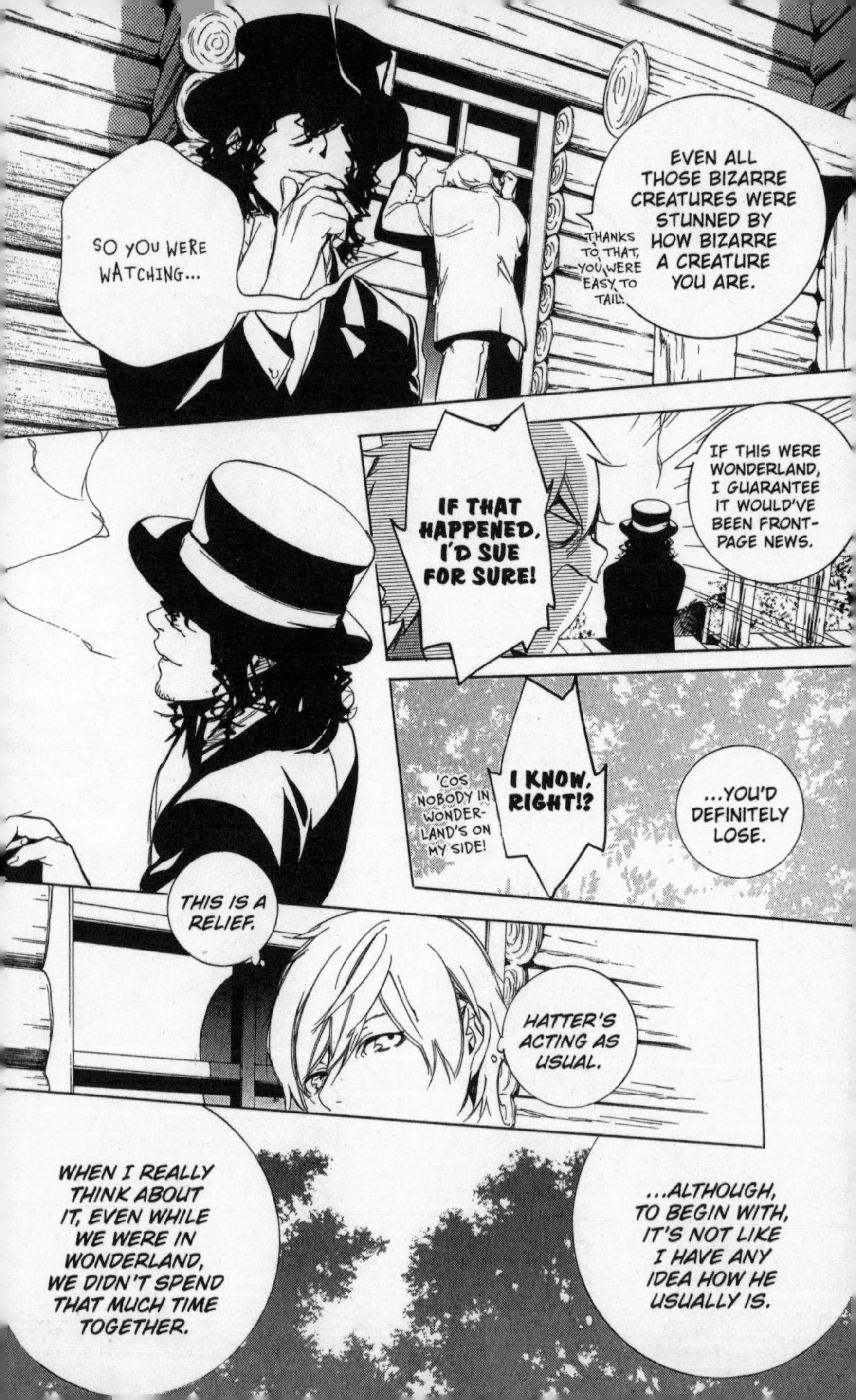

EVEN ALL THOSE BIZARRE CREATURES WERE STUNNED BY HOW BIZARRE A CREATURE YOU ARE.
THANKS TO THAT, YOU WERE EASY TO TAIL!
SO YOU WERE WATCHING...
IF THIS WERE WONDERLAND, I GUARANTEE IT WOULD'VE BEEN FRONT-PAGE NEWS.
IF THAT HAPPENED, I'D SUE FOR SURE!
...YOU'D DEFINITELY LOSE.
I KNOW, RIGHT!?
'COS NOBODY IN WONDERLAND'S ON MY SIDE!
HATTER'S ACTING AS USUAL.
THIS IS A RELIEF.
...ALTHOUGH, TO BEGIN WITH, IT'S NOT LIKE I HAVE ANY IDEA HOW HE USUALLY IS.
WHEN I REALLY THINK ABOUT IT, EVEN WHILE WE WERE IN WONDERLAND, WE DIDN'T SPEND THAT MUCH TIME TOGETHER.

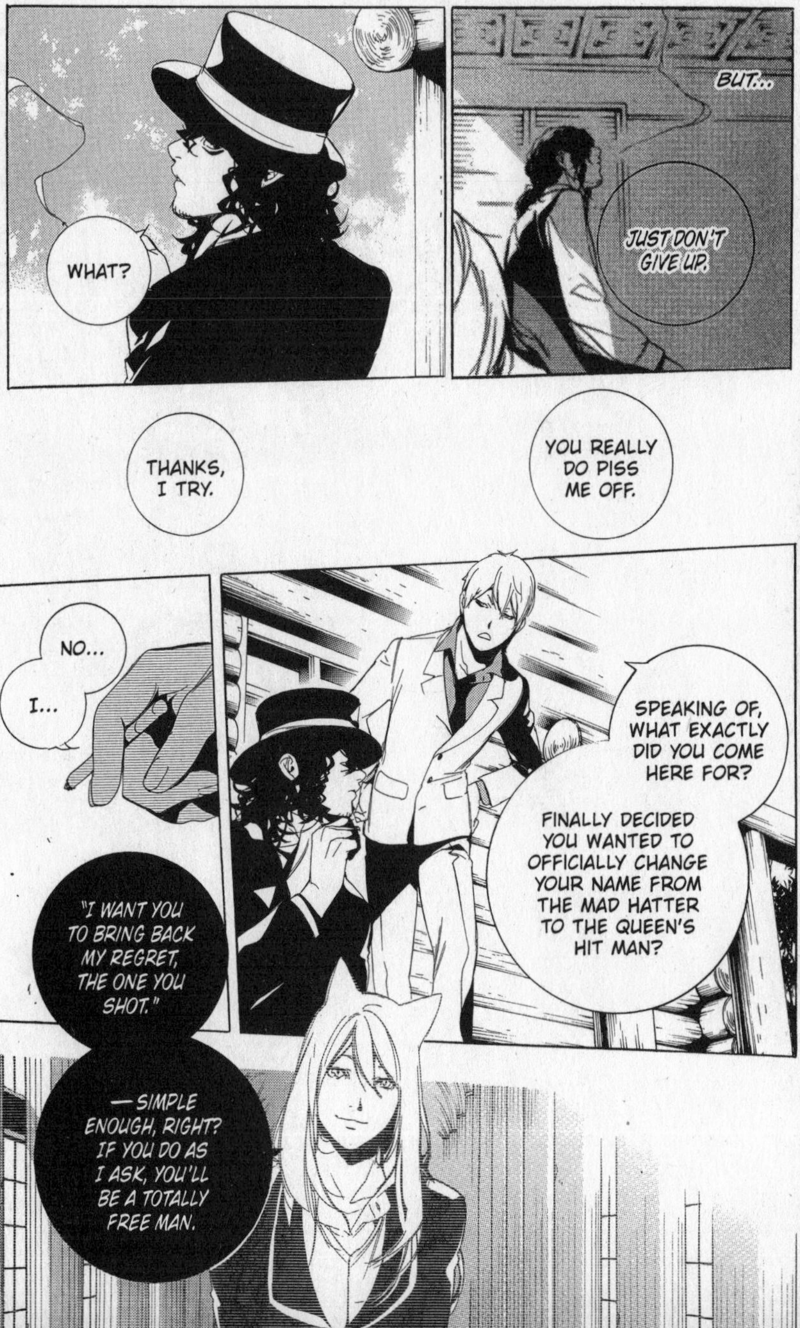
BUT...
JUST DON'T GIVE UP.
WHAT?
YOU REALLY DO PISS ME OFF.
THANKS, I TRY.
SPEAKING OF, WHAT EXACTLY DID YOU COME HERE FOR?
FINALLY DECIDED YOU WANTED TO OFFICIALLY CHANGE YOUR NAME FROM THE MAD HATTER TO THE QUEEN'S HIT MAN?
NO...
I...
"I WANT YOU TO BRING BACK MY REGRET, THE ONE YOU SHOT."
—SIMPLE ENOUGH, RIGHT? IF YOU DO AS I ASK, YOU'LL BE A TOTALLY FREE MAN.

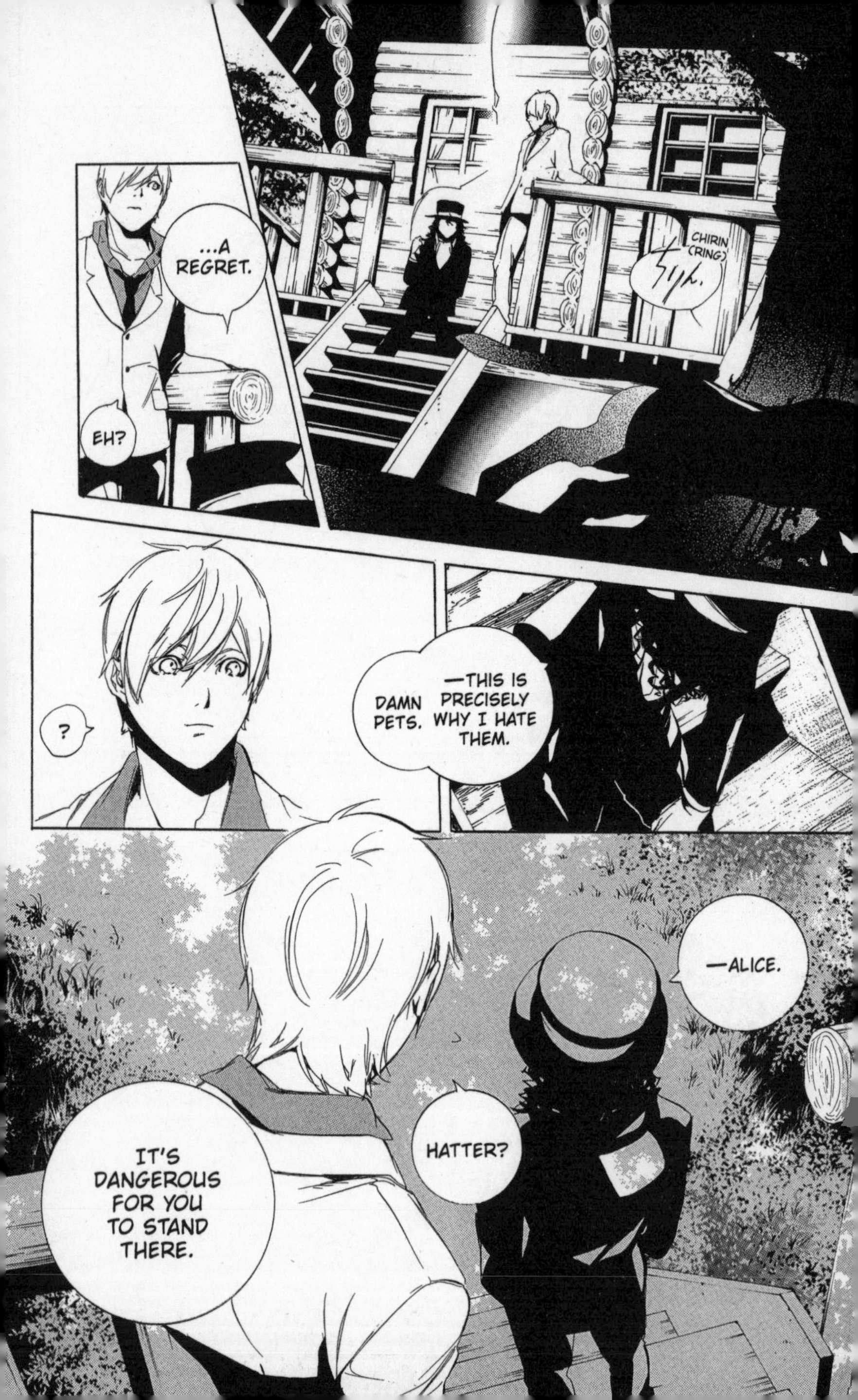
CHIRIN (RING)
ちりん
...A REGRET.
EH?
—THIS IS PRECISELY WHY I HATE THEM. DAMN PETS.
?
—ALICE.
HATTER?
IT'S DANGEROUS FOR YOU TO STAND THERE.

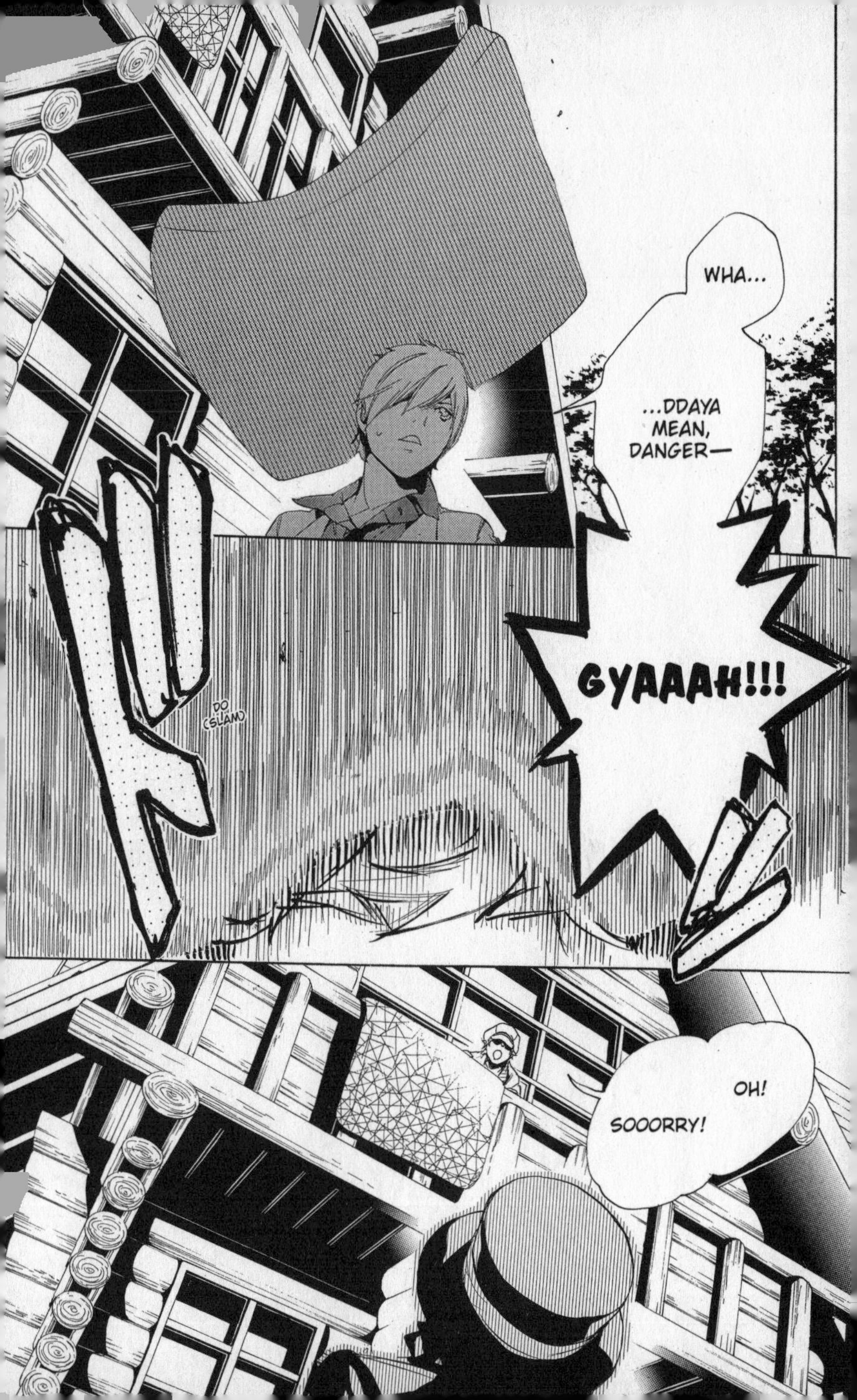
WHA...
...DDAYA MEAN, DANGER—
GYAAAH!!!
DO (SLAM)
OH!
SOOORRY!

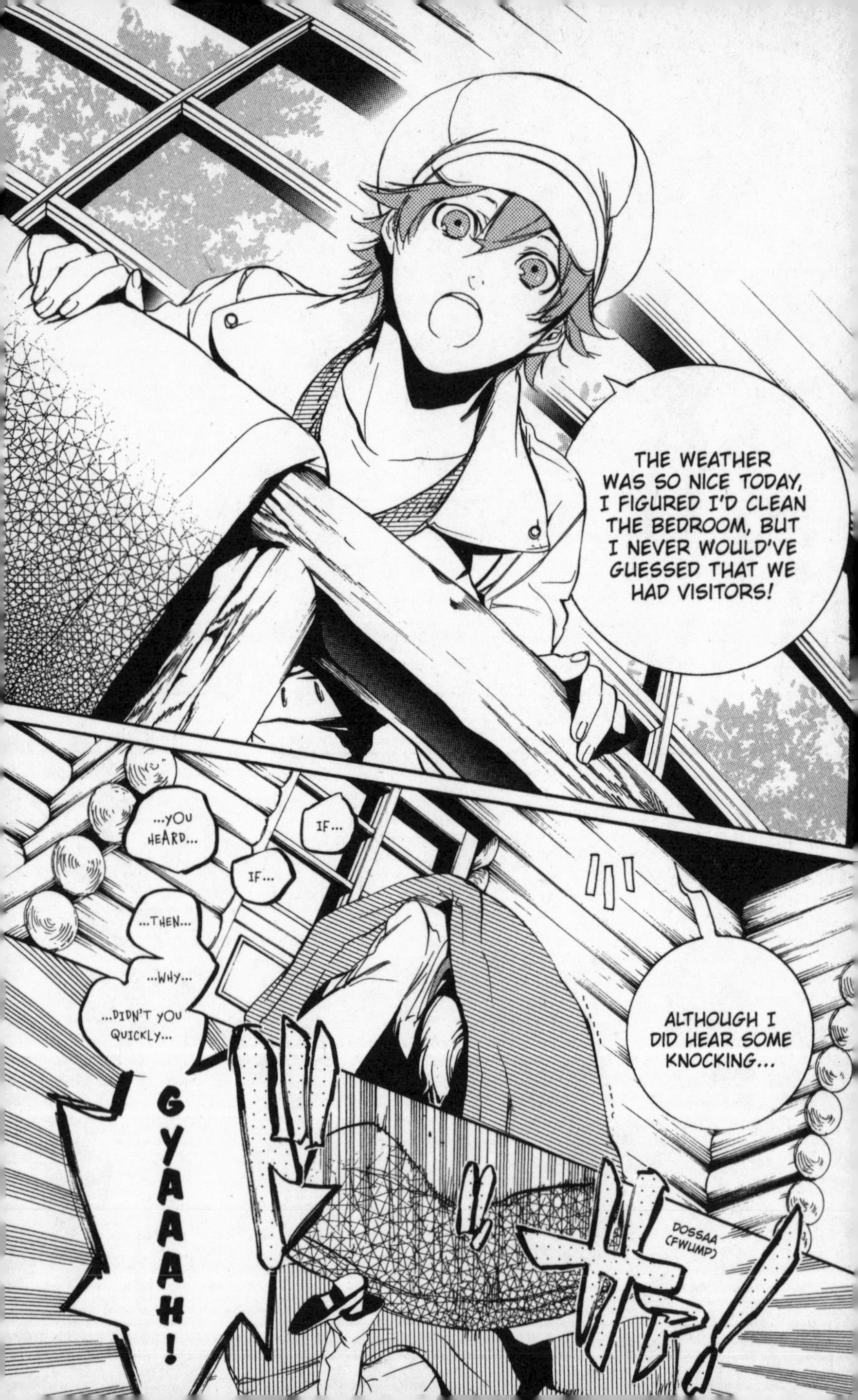
THE WEATHER WAS SO NICE TODAY, I FIGURED I'D CLEAN THE BEDROOM, BUT I NEVER WOULD'VE GUESSED THAT WE HAD VISITORS!
ALTHOUGH I DID HEAR SOME KNOCKING...
...YOU HEARD...
IF...
IF...
...THEN...
...WHY...
...DIDN'T YOU QUICKLY...
DOSSAA (FWUMP)
GYAAAH!

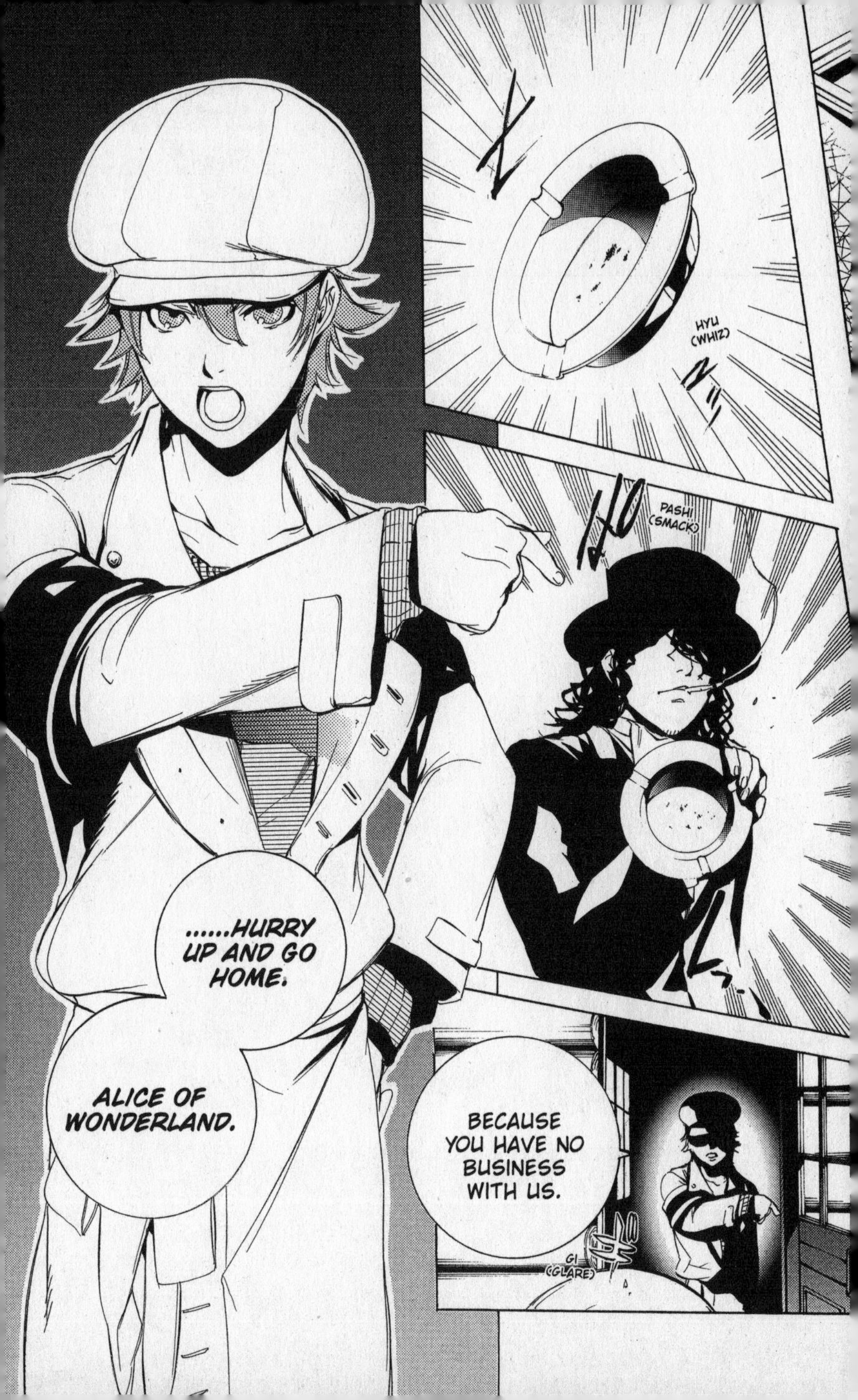
HYU
(WHIZ)
PASHI
(SMACK)
BECAUSE YOU HAVE NO BUSINESS WITH US.
GI
(GLARE)
......HURRY UP AND GO HOME.
ALICE OF WONDERLAND.

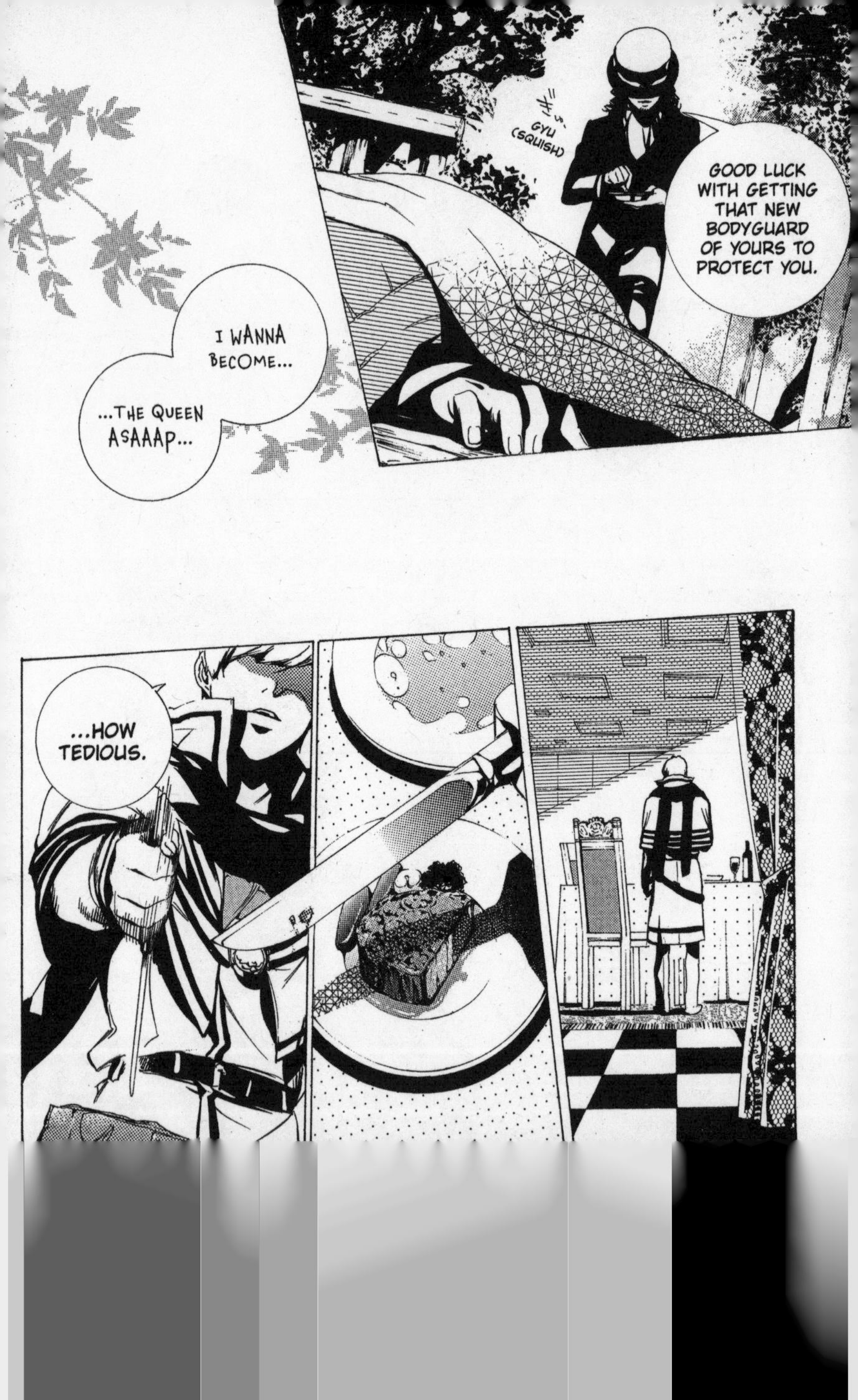
GOOD LUCK WITH GETTING THAT NEW BODYGUARD OF YOURS TO PROTECT YOU.
GYU (SQUISH)
I WANNA BECOME...
...THE QUEEN ASAAAP...
...HOW TEDIOUS.

Chapter 46

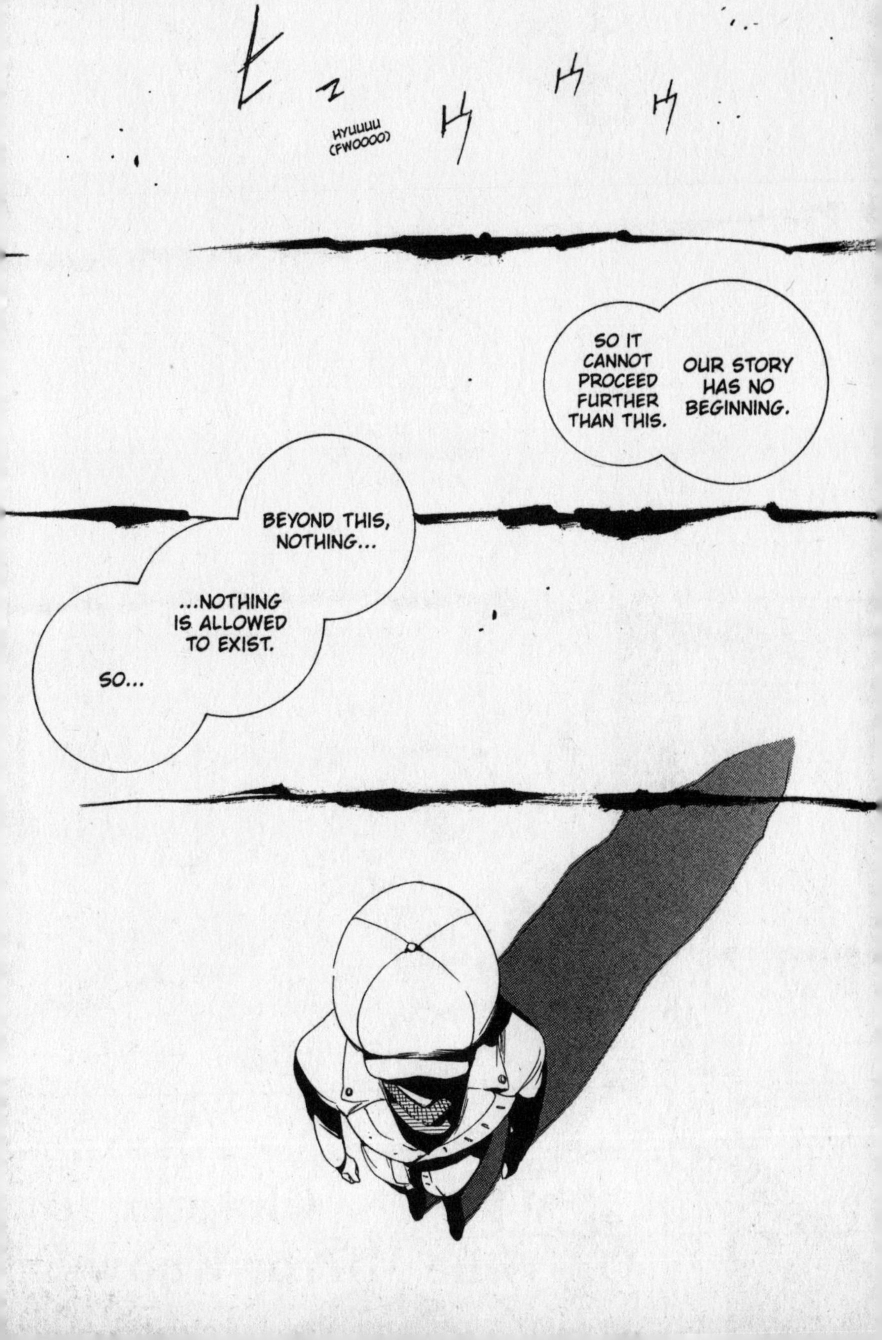
HYUUUU
(FWOOOO)
OUR STORY HAS NO BEGINNING.
SO IT CANNOT PROCEED FURTHER THAN THIS.
BEYOND THIS, NOTHING...
...NOTHING IS ALLOWED TO EXIST.
SO...

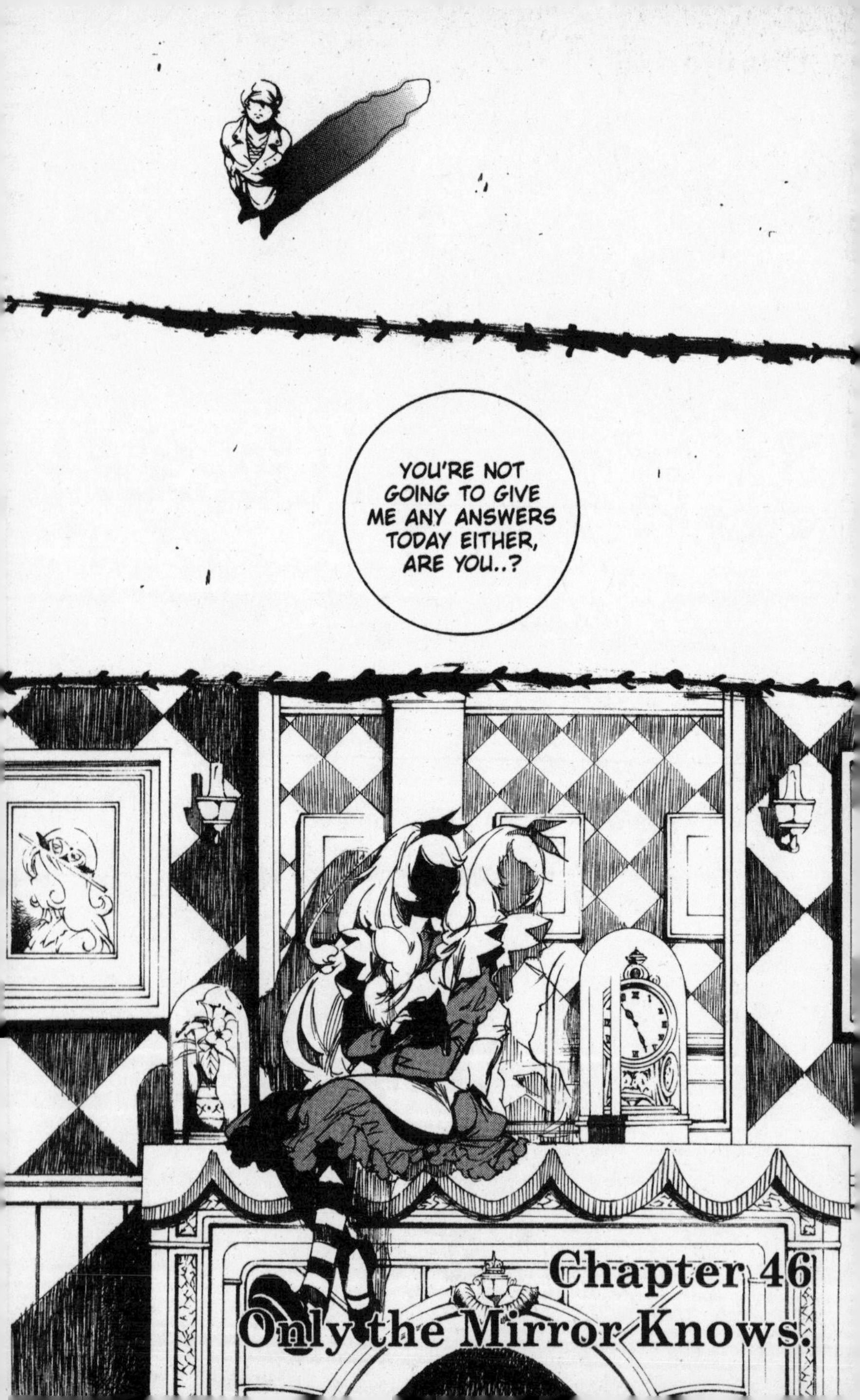
YOU'RE NOT GOING TO GIVE ME ANY ANSWERS TODAY EITHER, ARE YOU..?
Chapter 46
Only the Mirror Knows.

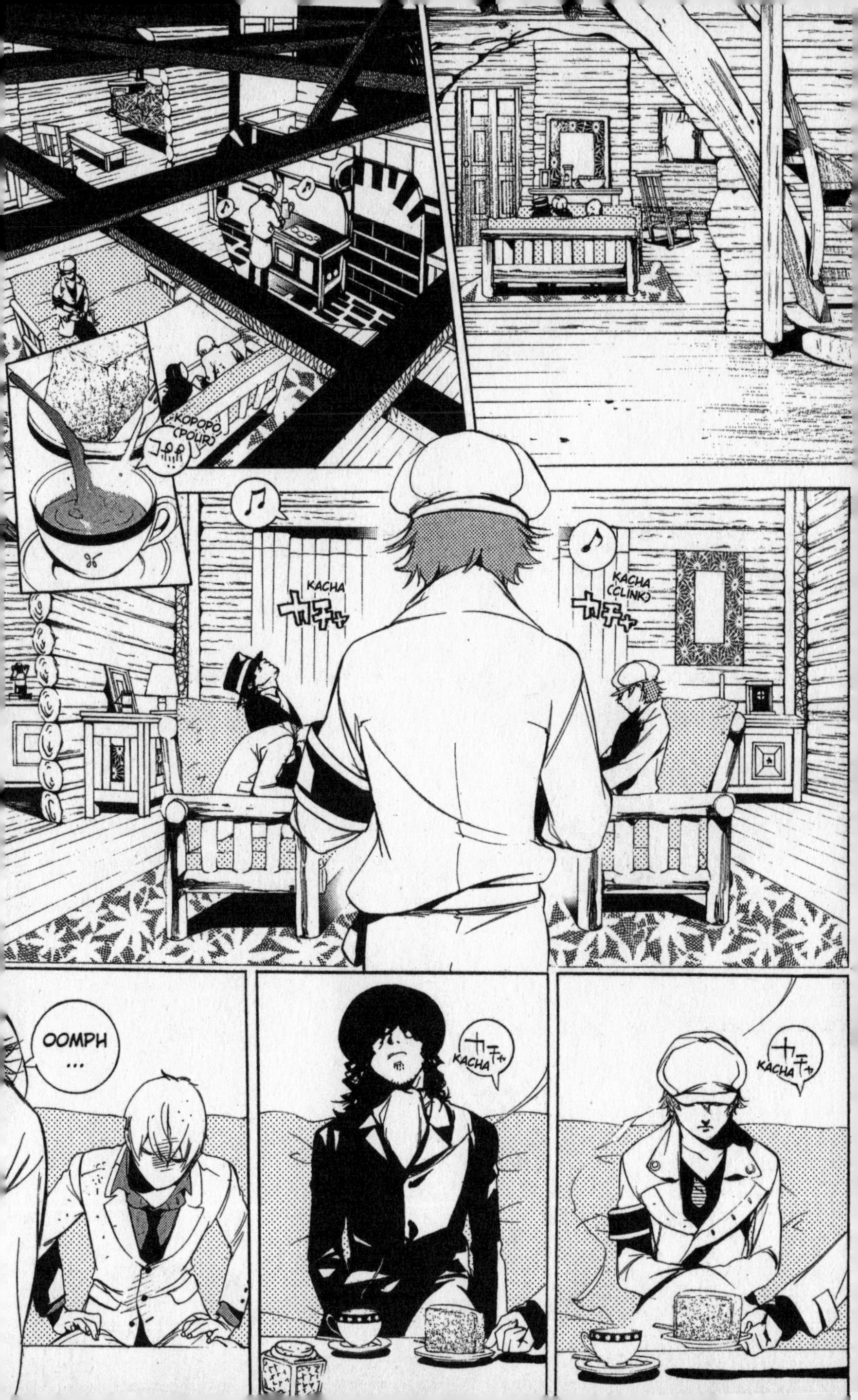

KOPOPO (POUR)
コポポ
KACHA (CLINK)
カチャ
KACHA
カチャ
カチャ
KACHA
カチャ
KACHA
OOMPH ...

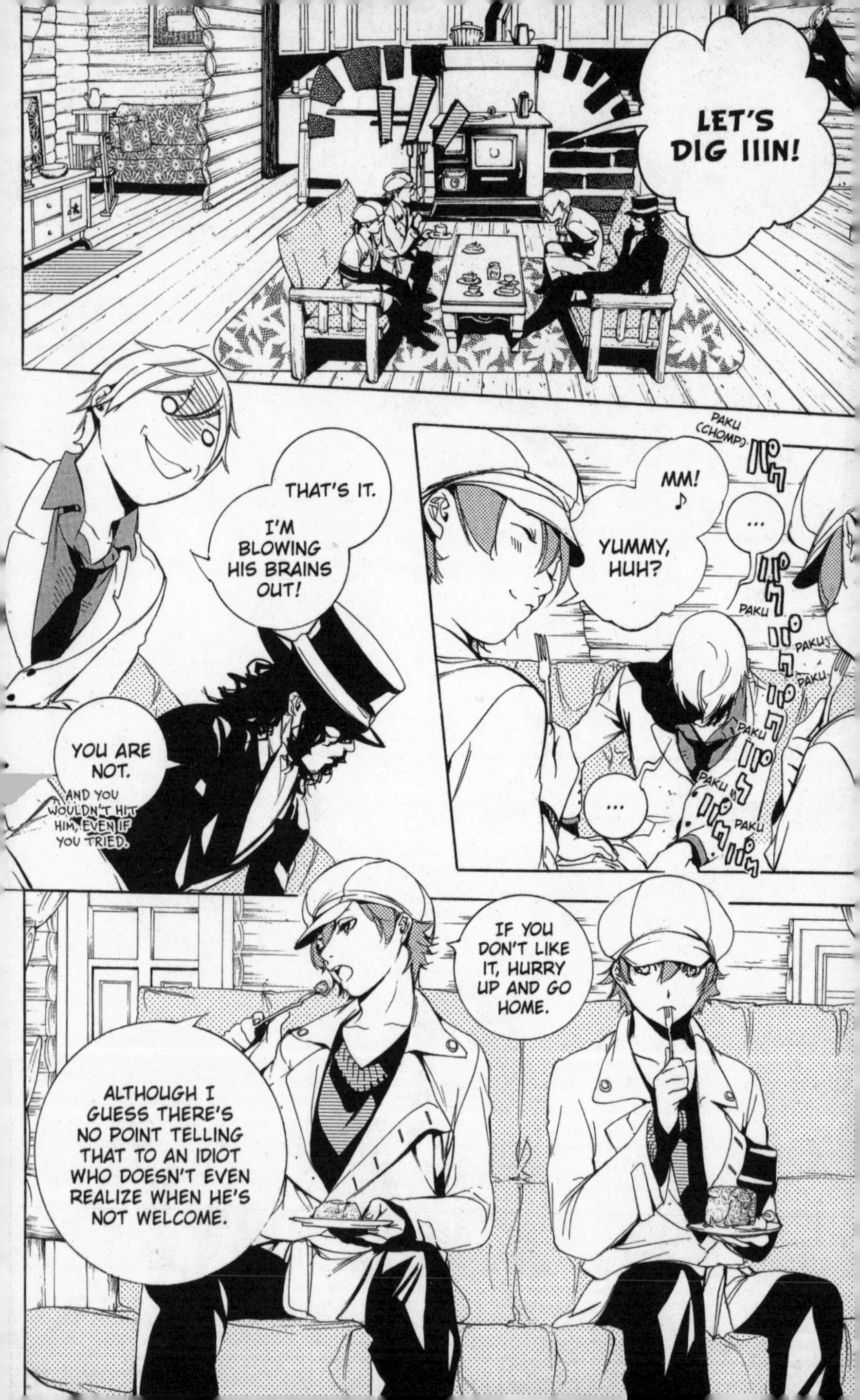
LET'S DIG IIIN!
PAKU (CHOMP)
MM! ♪
YUMMY, HUH?
...
PAKU
PAKU
PAKU
PAKU
PAKU
PAKU
...
THAT'S IT.
I'M BLOWING HIS BRAINS OUT!
YOU ARE NOT.
AND YOU WOULDN'T HIT HIM, EVEN IF YOU TRIED.
IF YOU DON'T LIKE IT, HURRY UP AND GO HOME.
ALTHOUGH I GUESS THERE'S NO POINT TELLING THAT TO AN IDIOT WHO DOESN'T EVEN REALIZE WHEN HE'S NOT WELCOME.

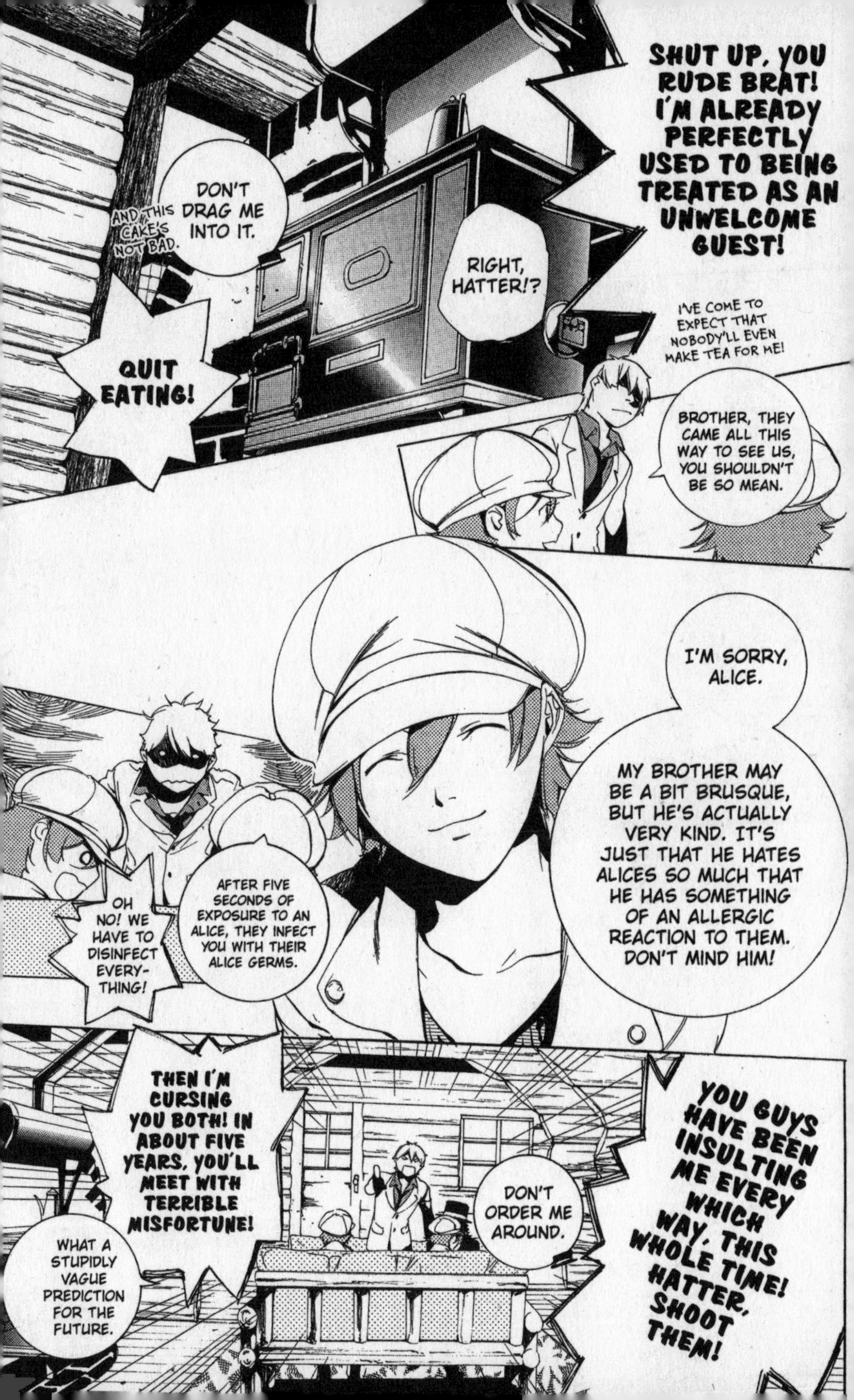
SHUT UP, YOU RUDE BRAT! I'M ALREADY PERFECTLY USED TO BEING TREATED AS AN UNWELCOME GUEST!
I'VE COME TO EXPECT THAT NOBODY'LL EVEN MAKE TEA FOR ME!
RIGHT, HATTER!?
DON'T DRAG ME INTO IT.
AND THIS CAKE'S NOT BAD.
QUIT EATING!
BROTHER, THEY CAME ALL THIS WAY TO SEE US, YOU SHOULDN'T BE SO MEAN.
I'M SORRY, ALICE.
MY BROTHER MAY BE A BIT BRUSQUE, BUT HE'S ACTUALLY VERY KIND. IT'S JUST THAT HE HATES ALICES SO MUCH THAT HE HAS SOMETHING OF AN ALLERGIC REACTION TO THEM. DON'T MIND HIM!
AFTER FIVE SECONDS OF EXPOSURE TO AN ALICE, THEY INFECT YOU WITH THEIR ALICE GERMS.
OH NO! WE HAVE TO DISINFECT EVERY-THING!
YOU GUYS HAVE BEEN INSULTING ME EVERY WHICH WAY, THIS WHOLE TIME! HATTER, SHOOT THEM!
DON'T ORDER ME AROUND.
THEN I'M CURSING YOU BOTH! IN ABOUT FIVE YEARS, YOU'LL MEET WITH TERRIBLE MISFORTUNE!
WHAT A STUPIDLY VAGUE PREDICTION FOR THE FUTURE.

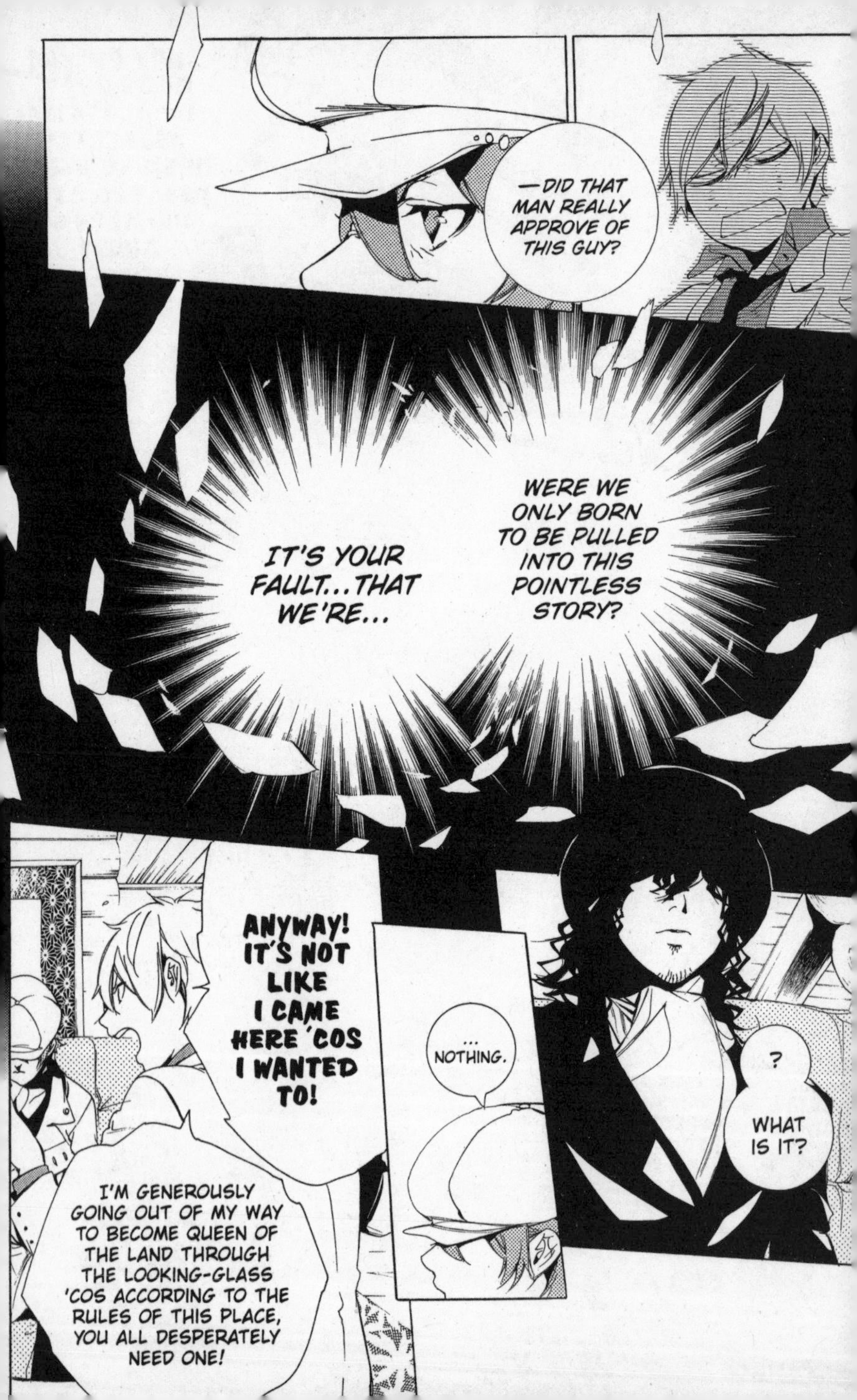
—DID THAT MAN REALLY APPROVE OF THIS GUY?
WERE WE ONLY BORN TO BE PULLED INTO THIS POINTLESS STORY?
IT'S YOUR FAULT...THAT WE'RE...
?
WHAT IS IT?
... NOTHING.
ANYWAY! IT'S NOT LIKE I CAME HERE 'COS I WANTED TO!
I'M GENEROUSLY GOING OUT OF MY WAY TO BECOME QUEEN OF THE LAND THROUGH THE LOOKING-GLASS 'COS ACCORDING TO THE RULES OF THIS PLACE, YOU ALL DESPERATELY NEED ONE!

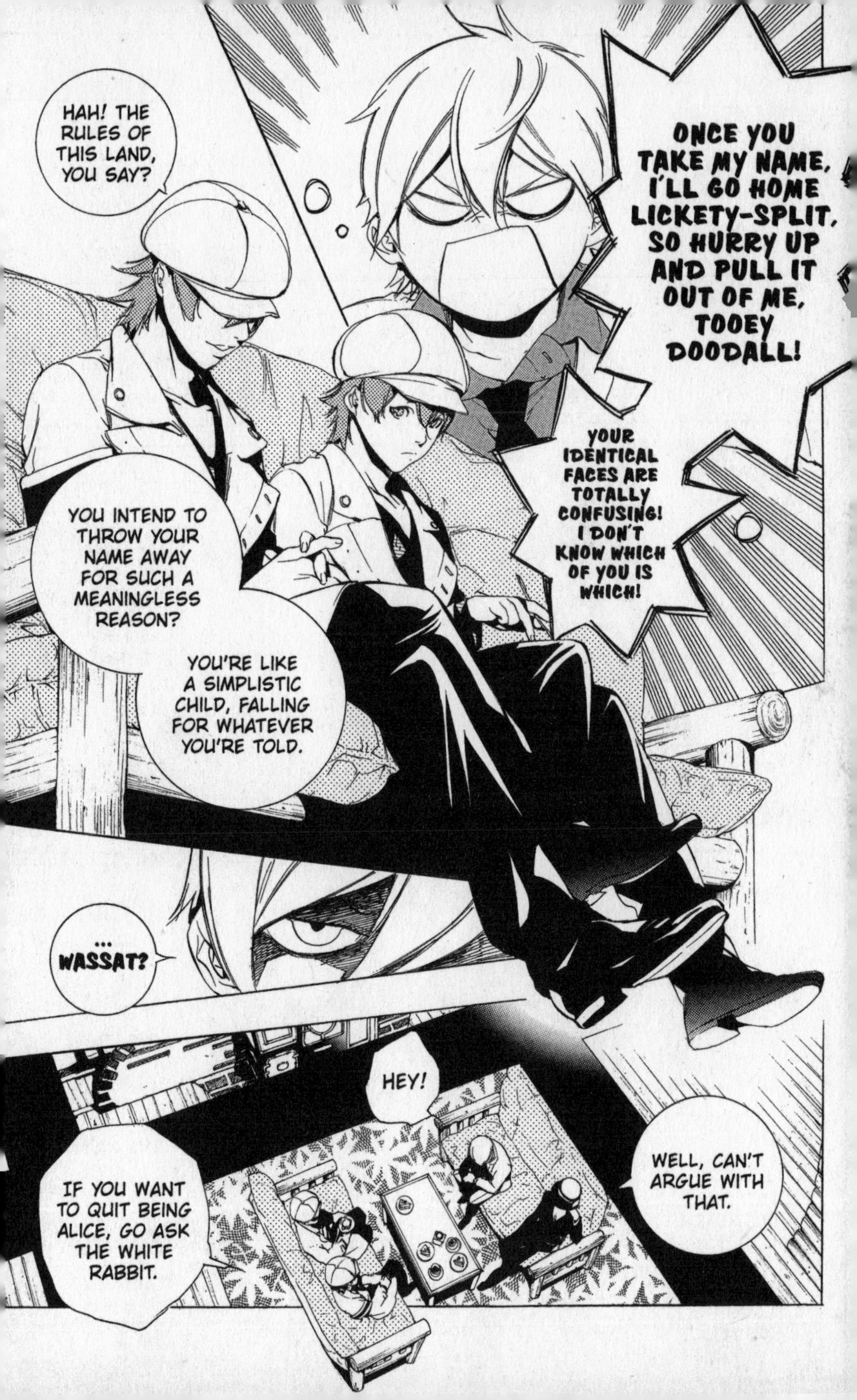
ONCE YOU TAKE MY NAME, I'LL GO HOME LICKETY-SPLIT, SO HURRY UP AND PULL IT OUT OF ME, TOOEY DOODALL!
YOUR IDENTICAL FACES ARE TOTALLY CONFUSING! I DON'T KNOW WHICH OF YOU IS WHICH!
HAH! THE RULES OF THIS LAND, YOU SAY?
YOU INTEND TO THROW YOUR NAME AWAY FOR SUCH A MEANINGLESS REASON?
YOU'RE LIKE A SIMPLISTIC CHILD, FALLING FOR WHATEVER YOU'RE TOLD.
... WASSAT?
HEY!
IF YOU WANT TO QUIT BEING ALICE, GO ASK THE WHITE RABBIT.
WELL, CAN'T ARGUE WITH THAT.

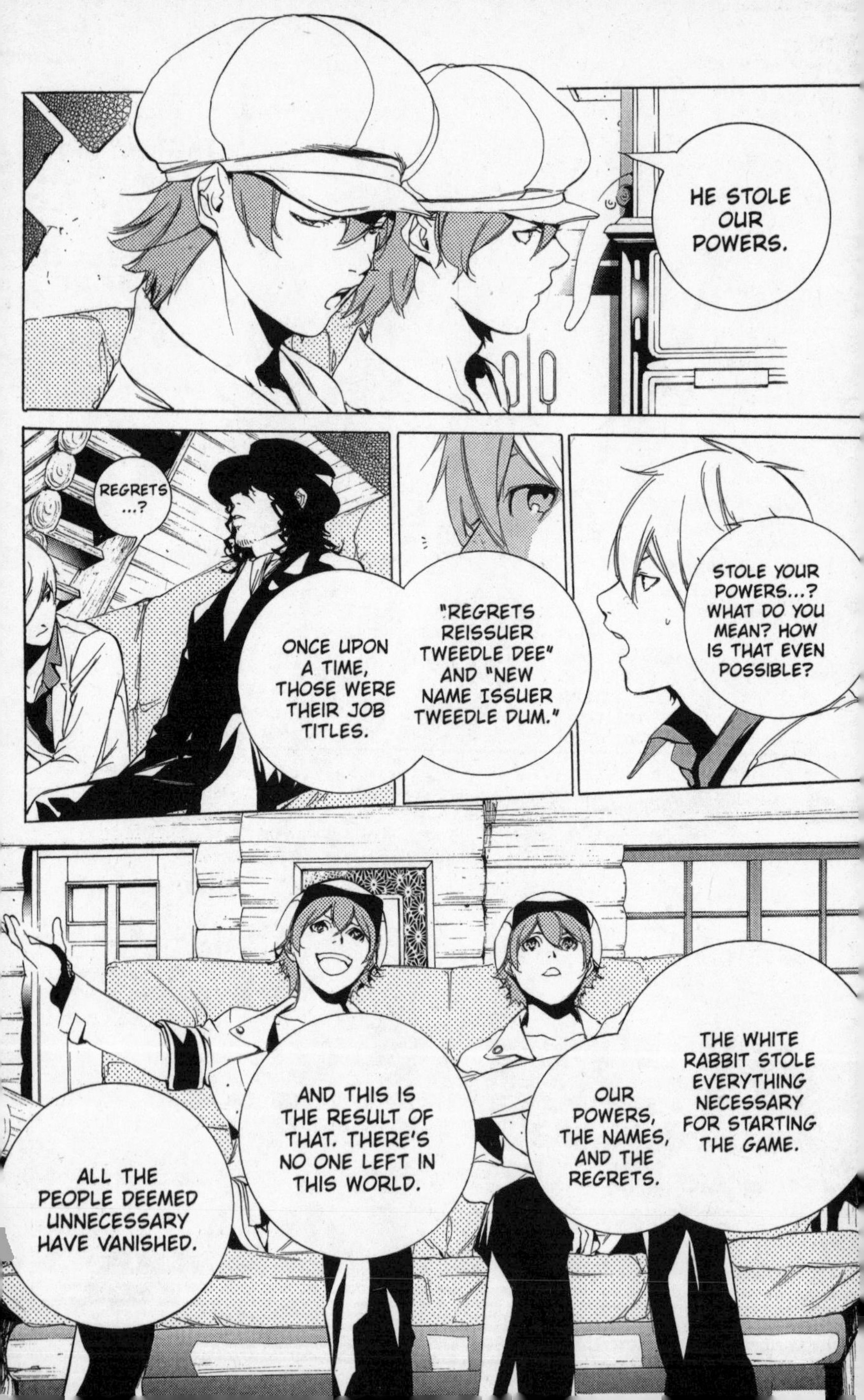
HE STOLE OUR POWERS.
STOLE YOUR POWERS...? WHAT DO YOU MEAN? HOW IS THAT EVEN POSSIBLE?
"REGRETS REISSUER TWEEDLE DEE" AND "NEW NAME ISSUER TWEEDLE DUM."
REGRETS ...?
ONCE UPON A TIME, THOSE WERE THEIR JOB TITLES.
THE WHITE RABBIT STOLE EVERYTHING NECESSARY FOR STARTING THE GAME.
OUR POWERS, THE NAMES, AND THE REGRETS.
AND THIS IS THE RESULT OF THAT. THERE'S NO ONE LEFT IN THIS WORLD.
ALL THE PEOPLE DEEMED UNNECESSARY HAVE VANISHED.

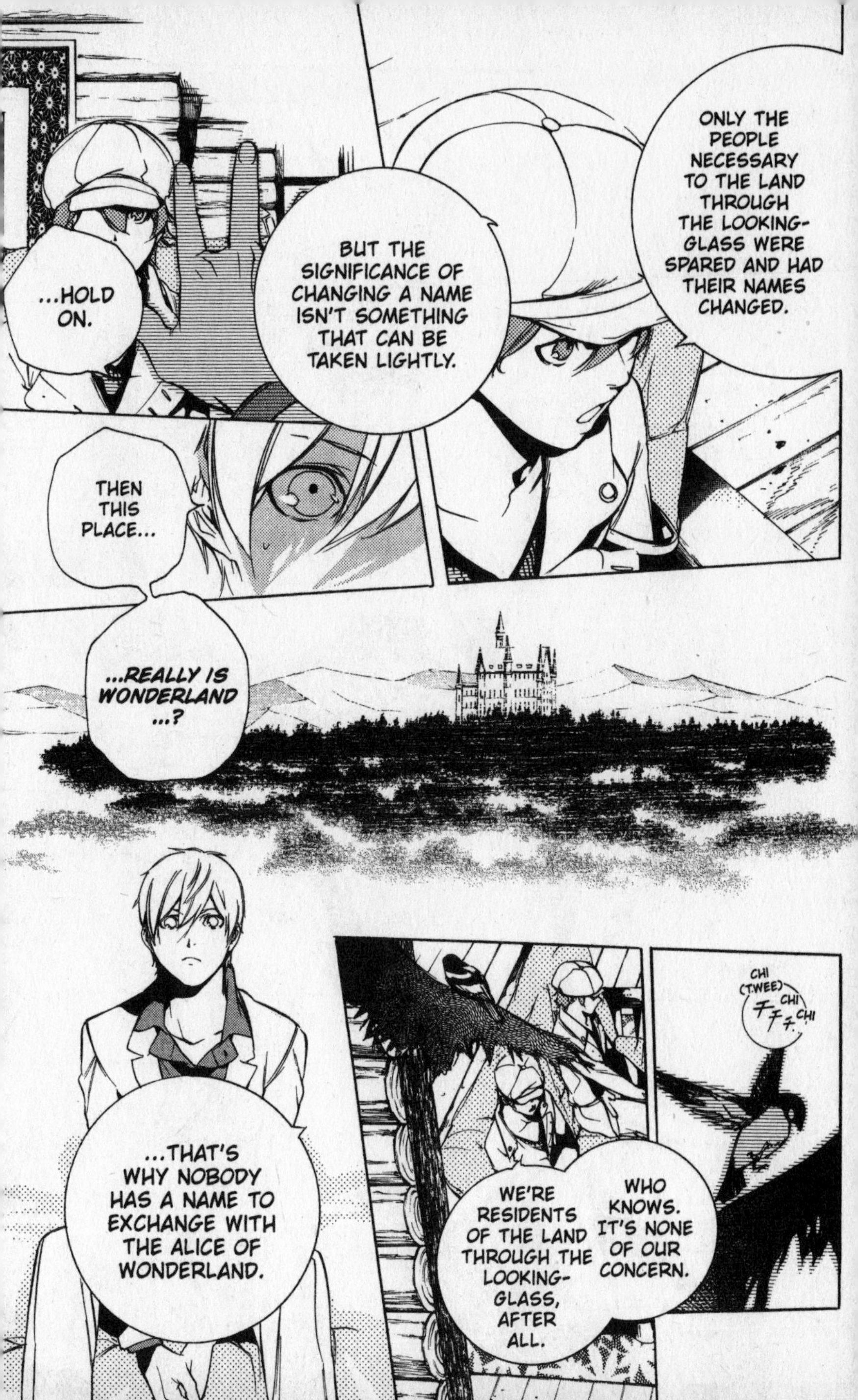
ONLY THE PEOPLE NECESSARY TO THE LAND THROUGH THE LOOKING-GLASS WERE SPARED AND HAD THEIR NAMES CHANGED.
BUT THE SIGNIFICANCE OF CHANGING A NAME ISN'T SOMETHING THAT CAN BE TAKEN LIGHTLY.
...HOLD ON.
THEN THIS PLACE...
...REALLY IS WONDERLAND ...?
CHI (TWEE) CHI CHI
WHO KNOWS. IT'S NONE OF OUR CONCERN.
WE'RE RESIDENTS OF THE LAND THROUGH THE LOOKING-GLASS, AFTER ALL.
...THAT'S WHY NOBODY HAS A NAME TO EXCHANGE WITH THE ALICE OF WONDERLAND.

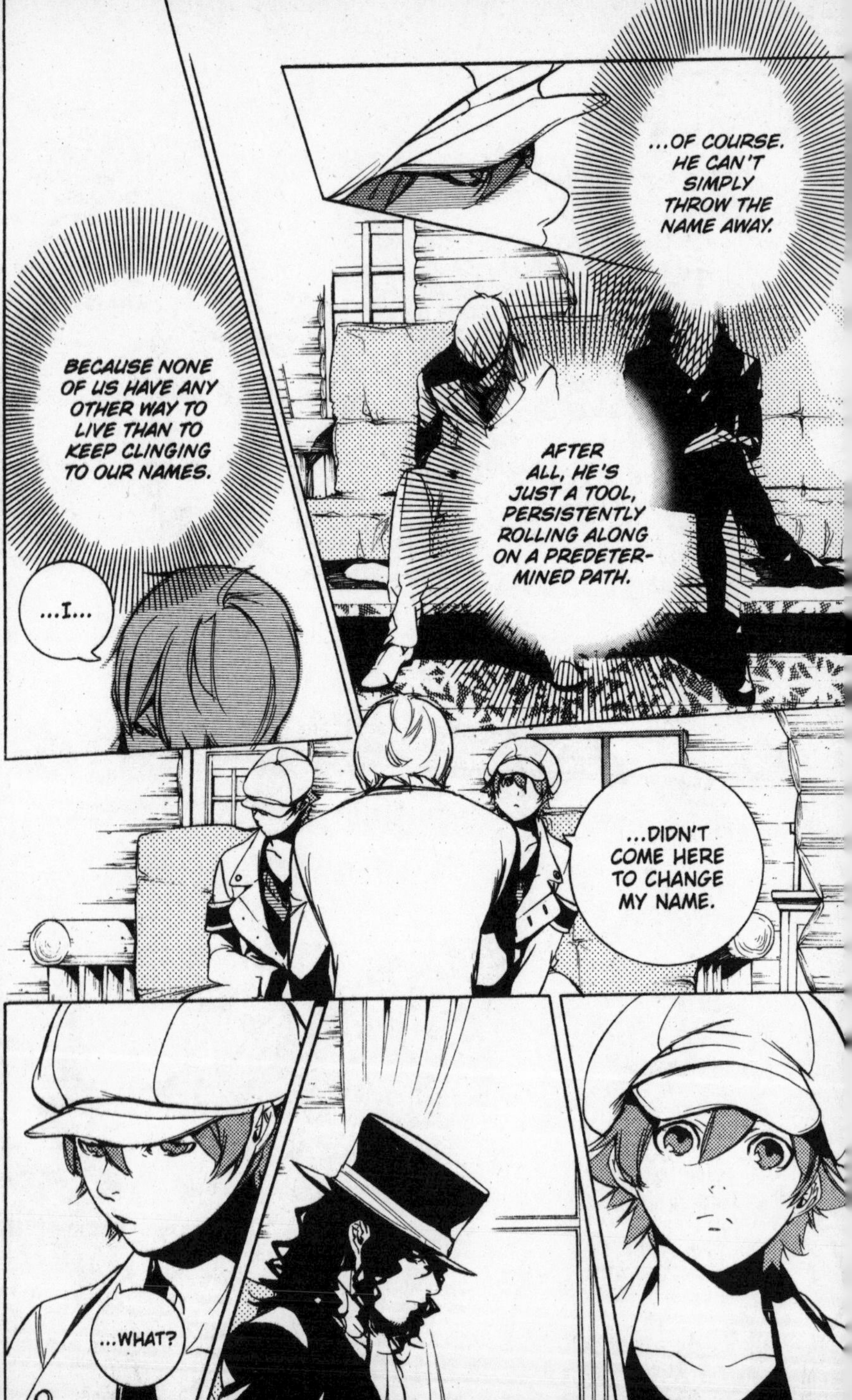
...OF COURSE. HE CAN'T SIMPLY THROW THE NAME AWAY.
AFTER ALL, HE'S JUST A TOOL, PERSISTENTLY ROLLING ALONG ON A PREDETERMINED PATH.
BECAUSE NONE OF US HAVE ANY OTHER WAY TO LIVE THAN TO KEEP CLINGING TO OUR NAMES.
...I...
...DIDN'T COME HERE TO CHANGE MY NAME.
...WHAT?

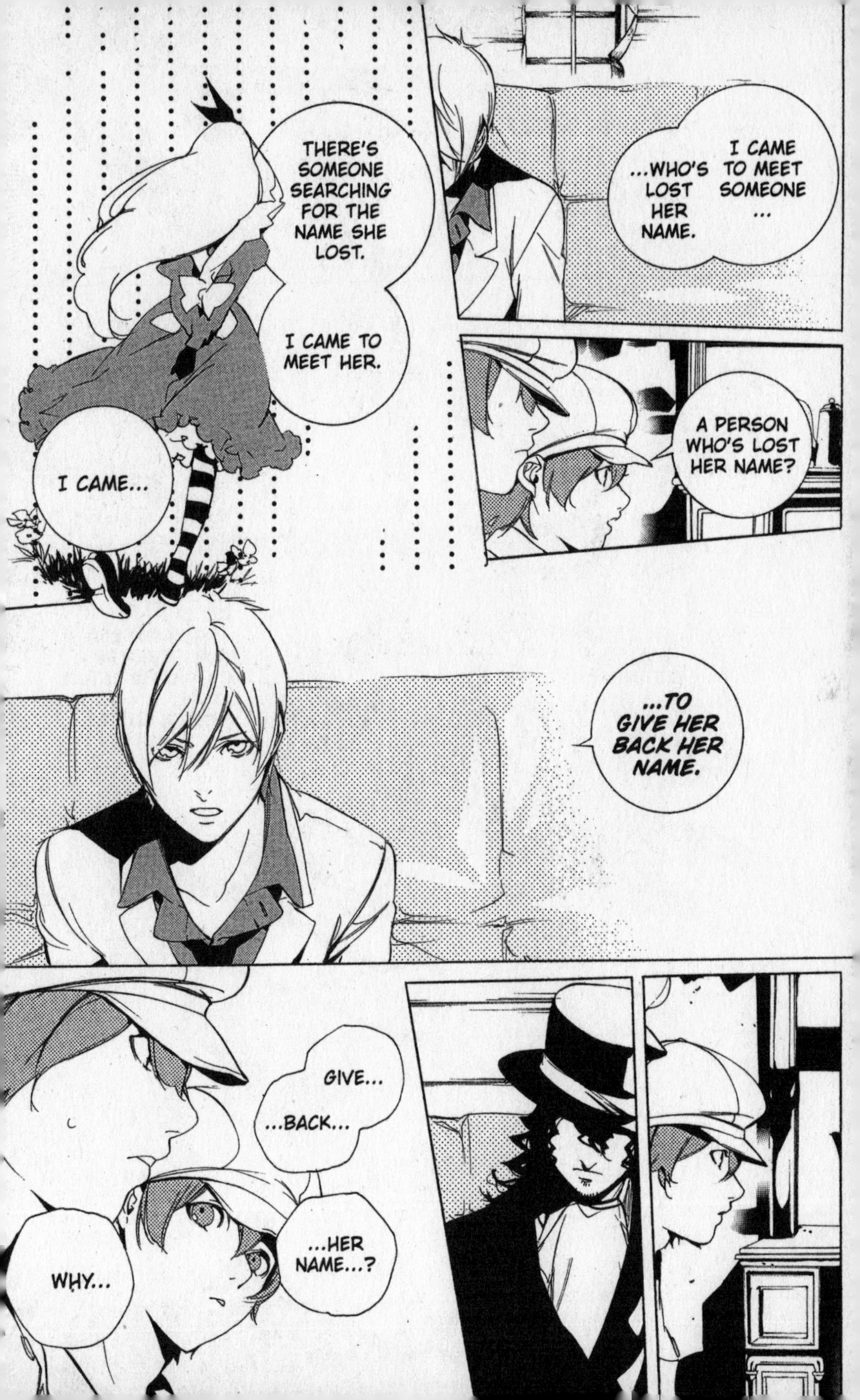
I CAME TO MEET SOMEONE ...
...WHO'S LOST HER NAME.
A PERSON WHO'S LOST HER NAME?
THERE'S SOMEONE SEARCHING FOR THE NAME SHE LOST.
I CAME TO MEET HER.
I CAME...
...TO GIVE HER BACK HER NAME.
GIVE...
...BACK...
...HER NAME...?
WHY...

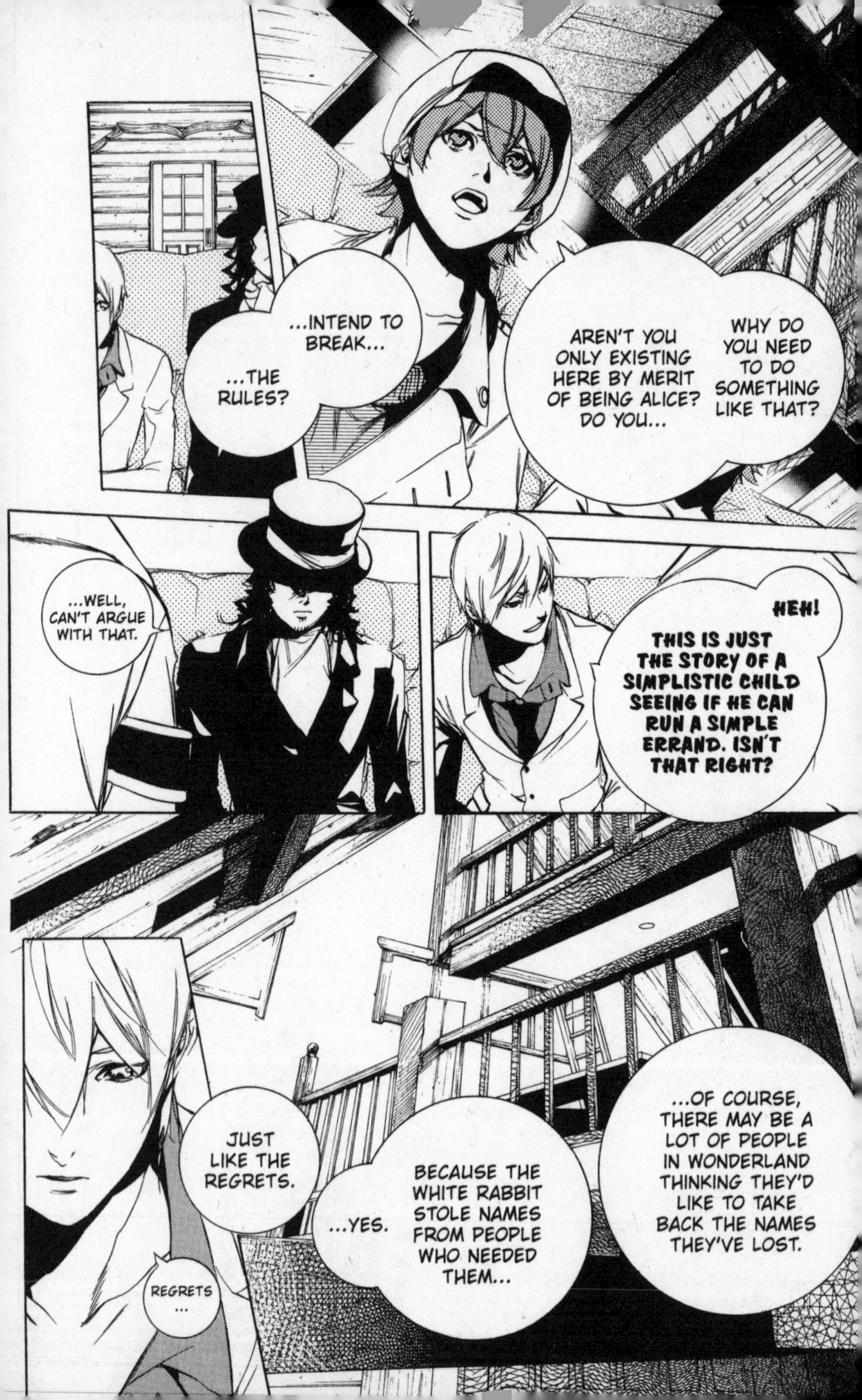
WHY DO YOU NEED TO DO SOMETHING LIKE THAT?
AREN'T YOU ONLY EXISTING HERE BY MERIT OF BEING ALICE? DO YOU...
...INTEND TO BREAK...
...THE RULES?
HEH!
THIS IS JUST THE STORY OF A SIMPLISTIC CHILD SEEING IF HE CAN RUN A SIMPLE ERRAND. ISN'T THAT RIGHT?
...WELL, CAN'T ARGUE WITH THAT.
...OF COURSE, THERE MAY BE A LOT OF PEOPLE IN WONDERLAND THINKING THEY'D LIKE TO TAKE BACK THE NAMES THEY'VE LOST.
BECAUSE THE WHITE RABBIT STOLE NAMES FROM PEOPLE WHO NEEDED THEM...
...YES.
JUST LIKE THE REGRETS.
REGRETS ...

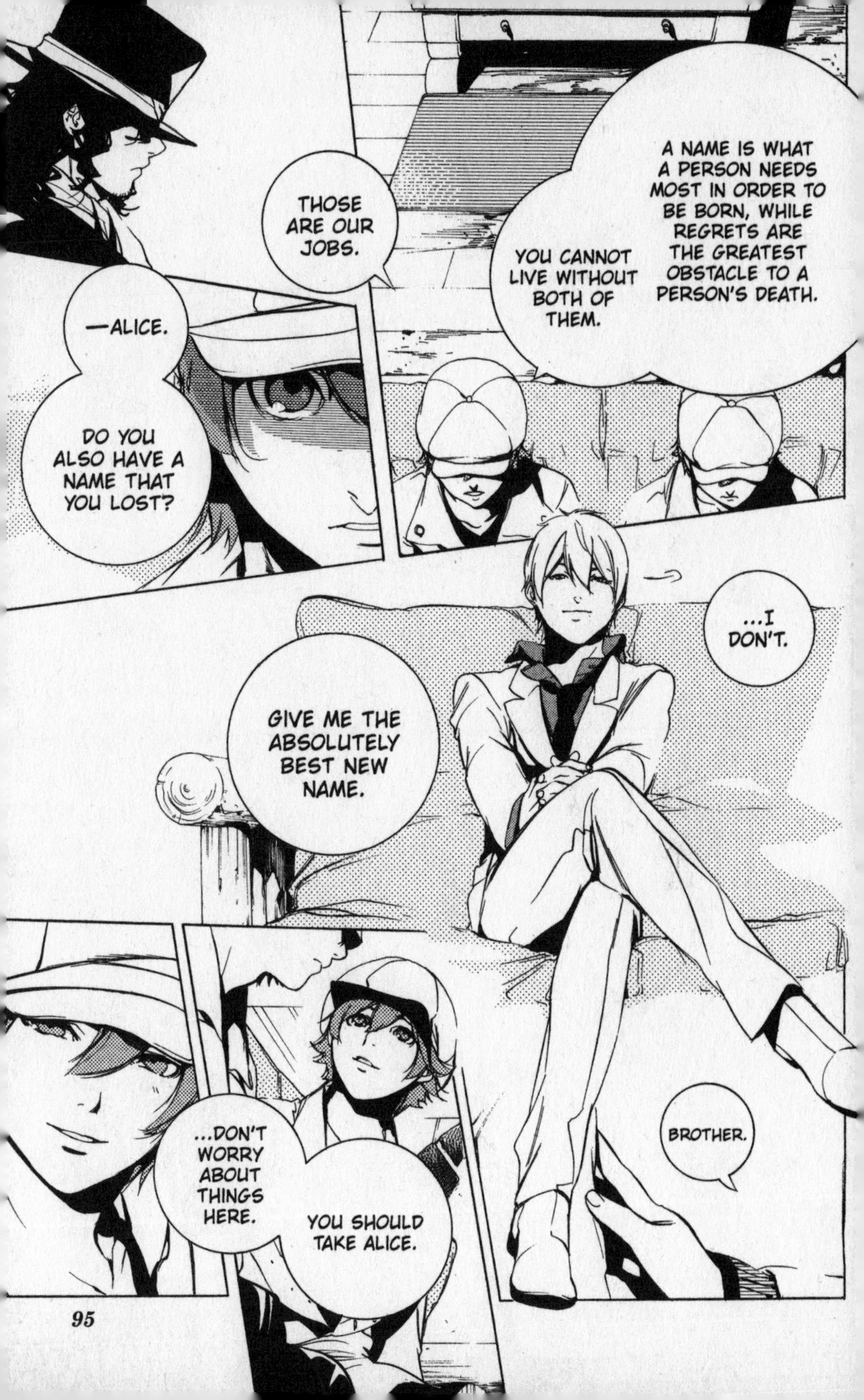
A NAME IS WHAT A PERSON NEEDS MOST IN ORDER TO BE BORN, WHILE REGRETS ARE THE GREATEST OBSTACLE TO A PERSON'S DEATH.
YOU CANNOT LIVE WITHOUT BOTH OF THEM.
THOSE ARE OUR JOBS.
—ALICE.
DO YOU ALSO HAVE A NAME THAT YOU LOST?
...I DON'T.
GIVE ME THE ABSOLUTELY BEST NEW NAME.
BROTHER.
...DON'T WORRY ABOUT THINGS HERE.
YOU SHOULD TAKE ALICE.

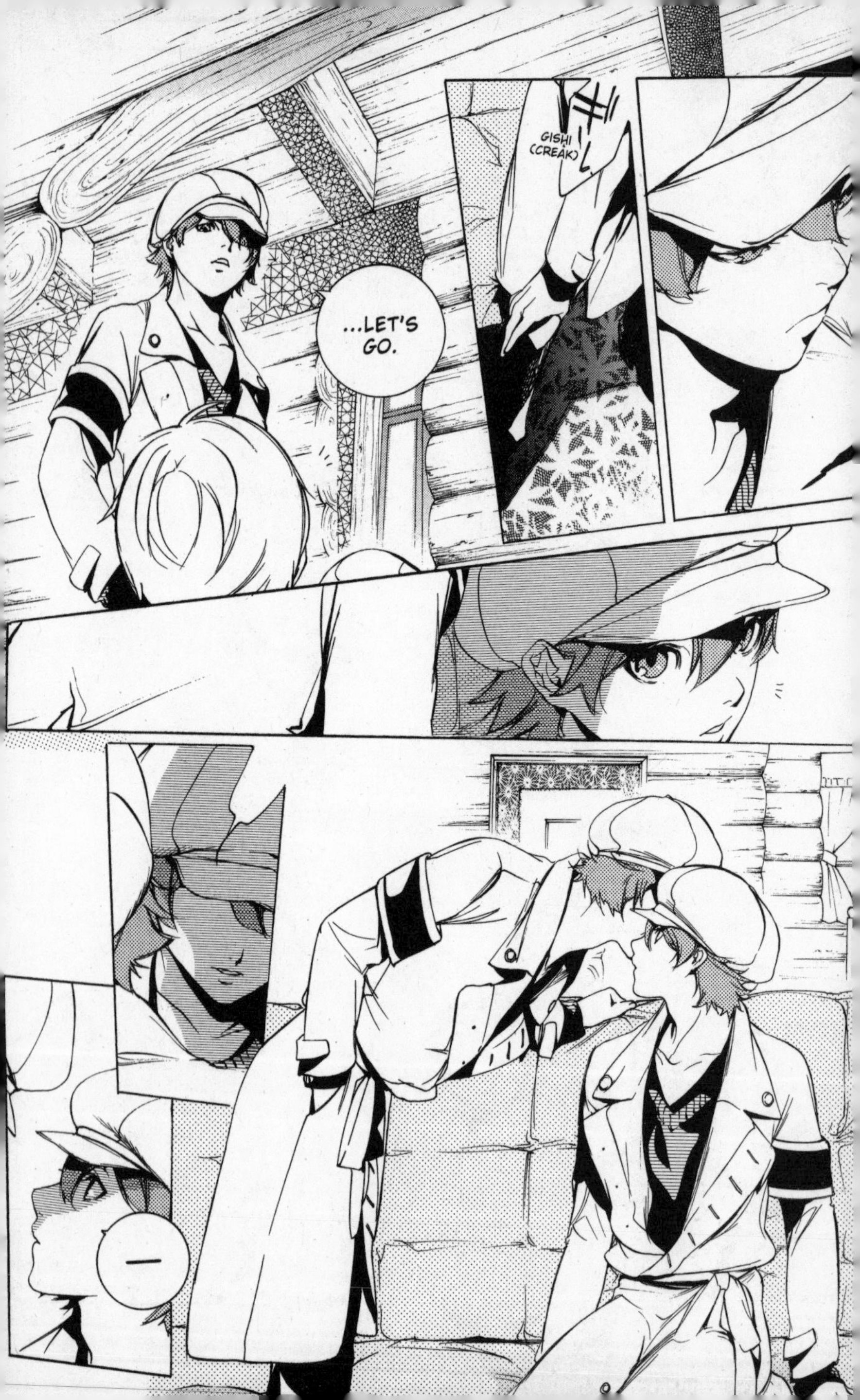
GISHI (CREAK)
...LET'S GO.
—

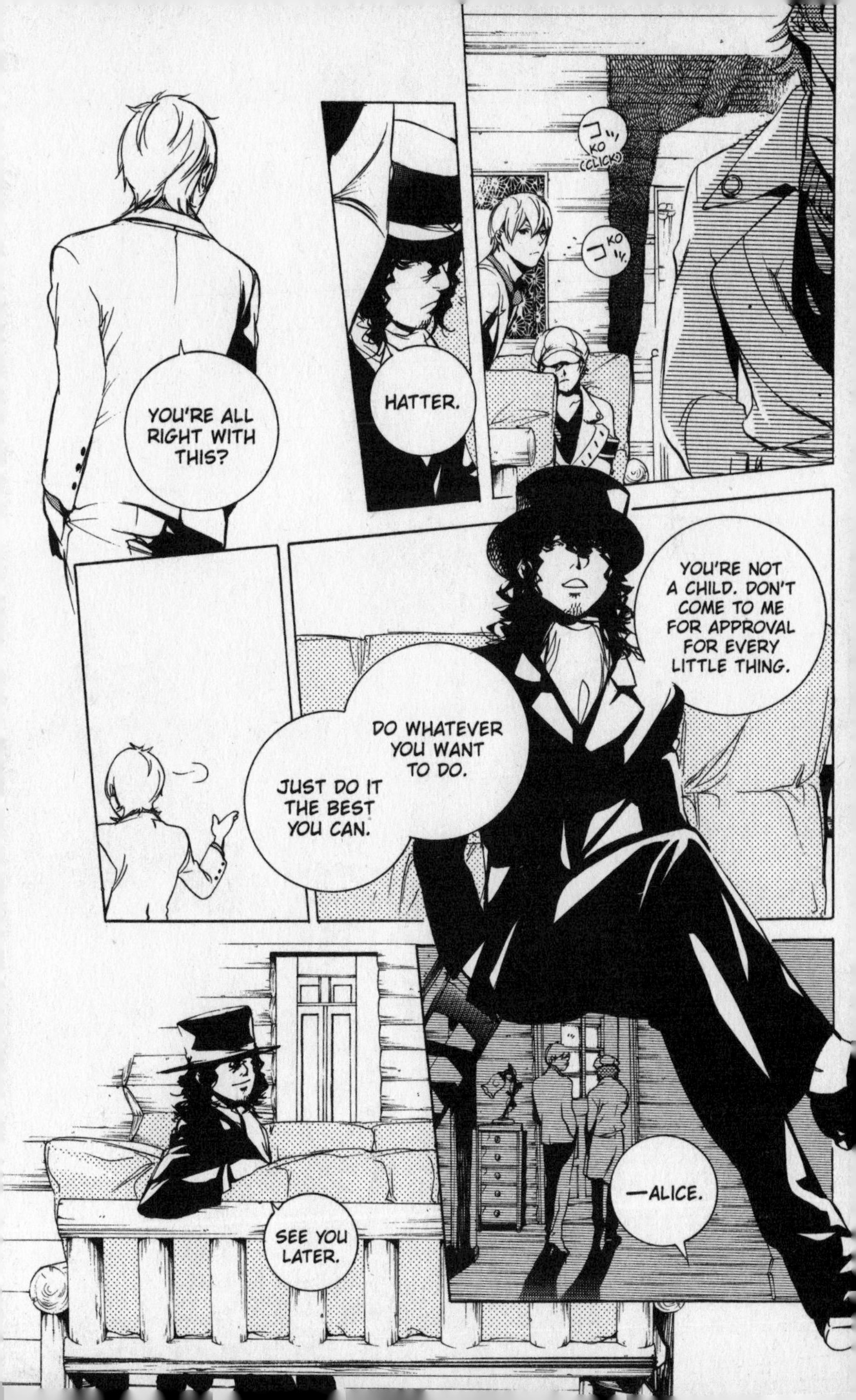
コッ
KO
(CLICK)
コッ
KO
HATTER.
YOU'RE ALL RIGHT WITH THIS?
YOU'RE NOT A CHILD. DON'T COME TO ME FOR APPROVAL FOR EVERY LITTLE THING.
DO WHATEVER YOU WANT TO DO.
JUST DO IT THE BEST YOU CAN.
—ALICE.
SEE YOU LATER.

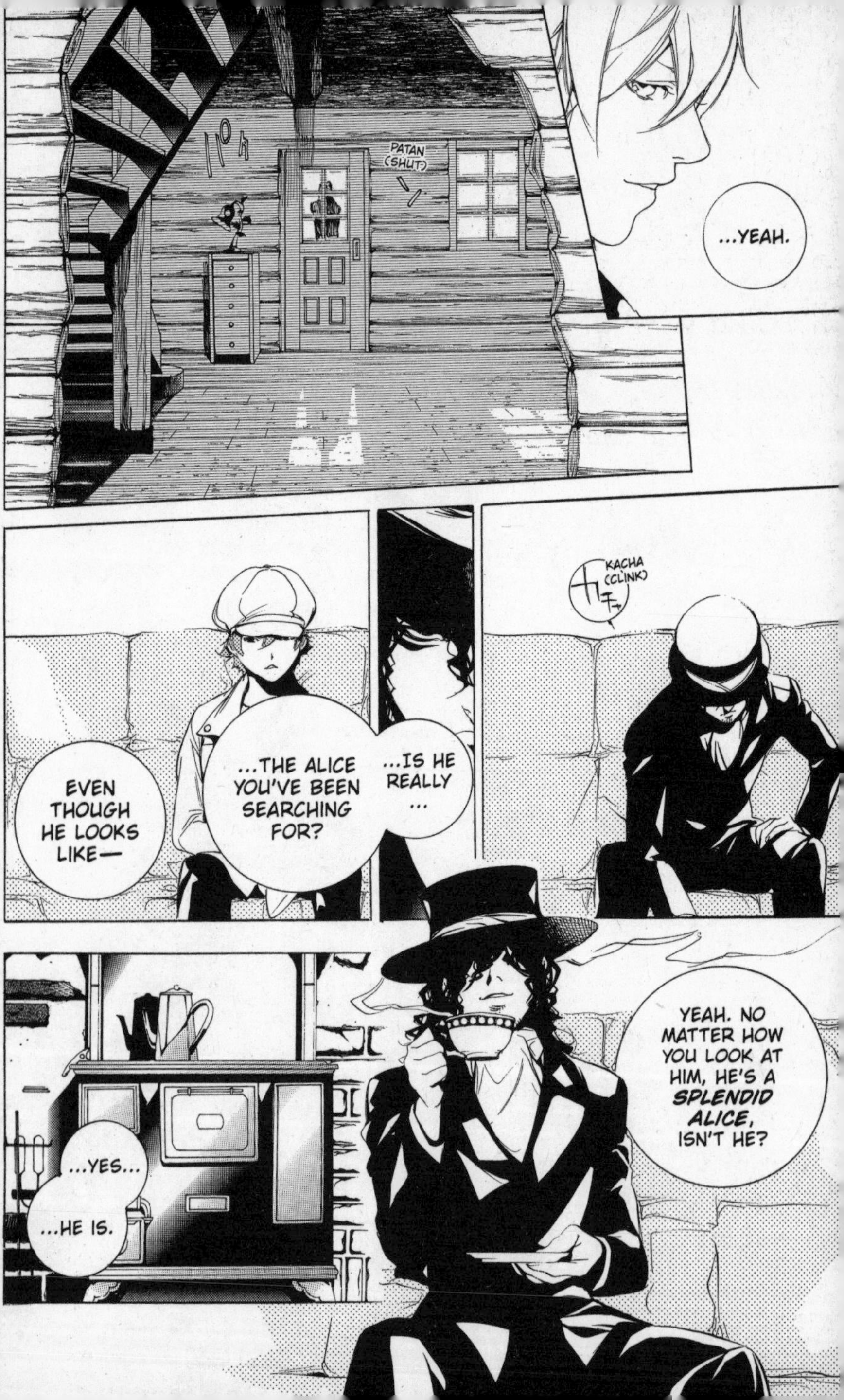
...YEAH.
PATAN (SHUT)
KACHA (CLINK)
...IS HE REALLY ...
...THE ALICE YOU'VE BEEN SEARCHING FOR?
EVEN THOUGH HE LOOKS LIKE—
YEAH. NO MATTER HOW YOU LOOK AT HIM, HE'S A *SPLENDID ALICE*, ISN'T HE?
...YES...
...HE IS.

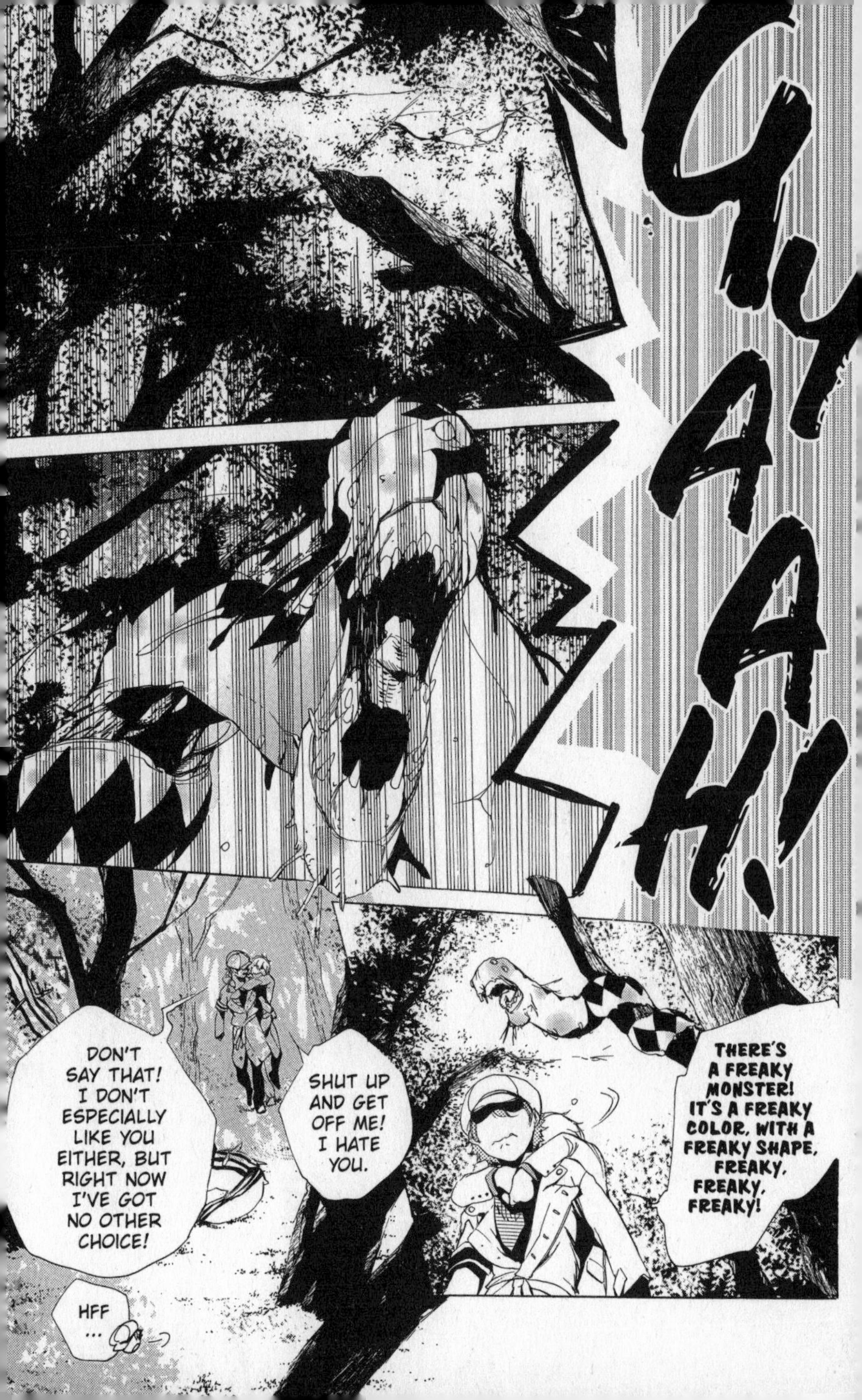
GYAAH!!
THERE'S A FREAKY MONSTER! IT'S A FREAKY COLOR, WITH A FREAKY SHAPE, FREAKY, FREAKY, FREAKY!
SHUT UP AND GET OFF ME! I HATE YOU.
DON'T SAY THAT! I DON'T ESPECIALLY LIKE YOU EITHER, BUT RIGHT NOW I'VE GOT NO OTHER CHOICE!
HFF ...

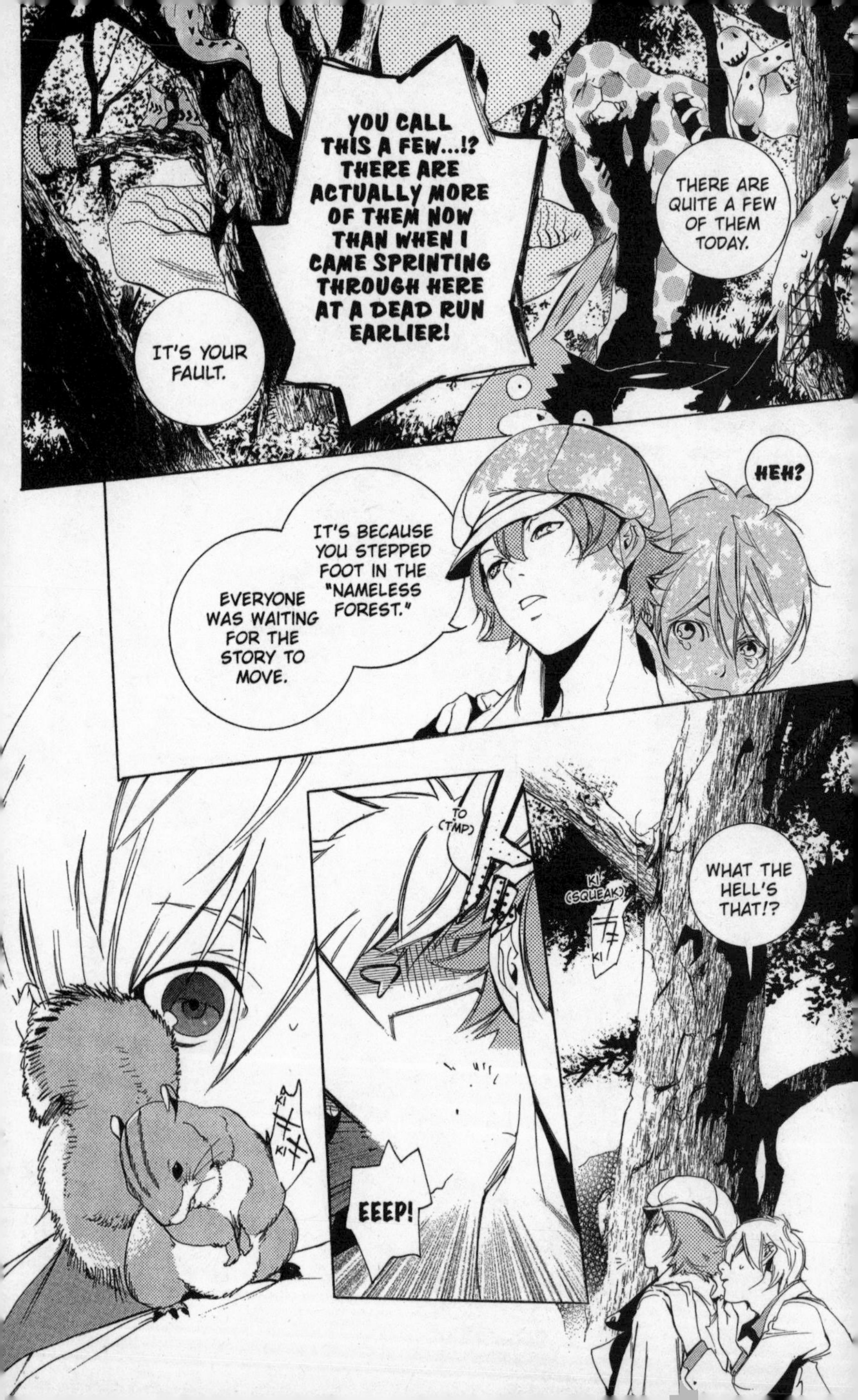
THERE ARE QUITE A FEW OF THEM TODAY.
YOU CALL THIS A FEW...!? THERE ARE ACTUALLY MORE OF THEM NOW THAN WHEN I CAME SPRINTING THROUGH HERE AT A DEAD RUN EARLIER!
IT'S YOUR FAULT.
HEH?
IT'S BECAUSE YOU STEPPED FOOT IN THE "NAMELESS FOREST."
EVERYONE WAS WAITING FOR THE STORY TO MOVE.
WHAT THE HELL'S THAT!?
KI (SQUEAK)
KI
TO (TMP)
EEEP!
KI
KI

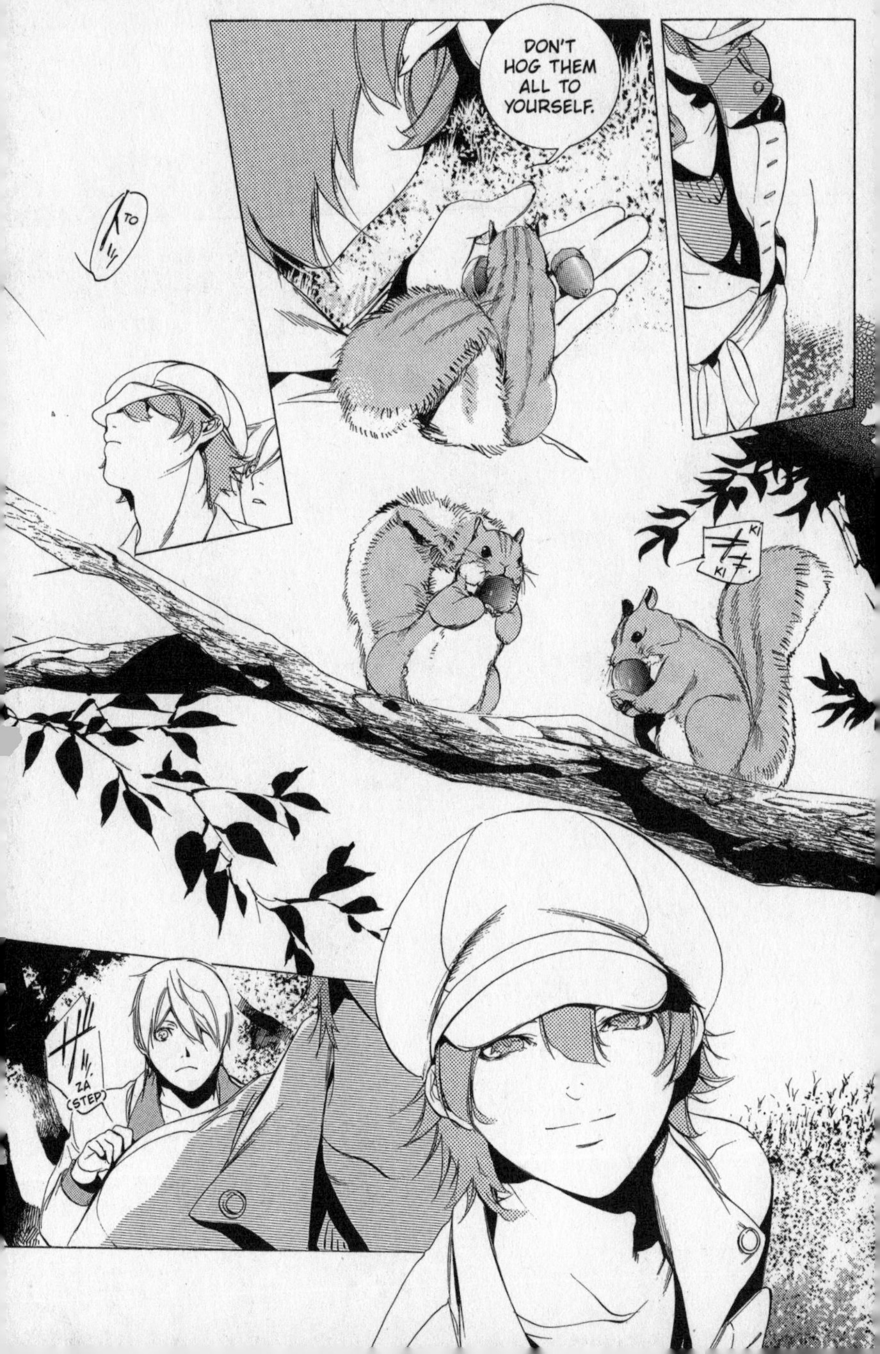
DON'T HOG THEM ALL TO YOURSELF.
TO
KI KI
ZA (STEP)

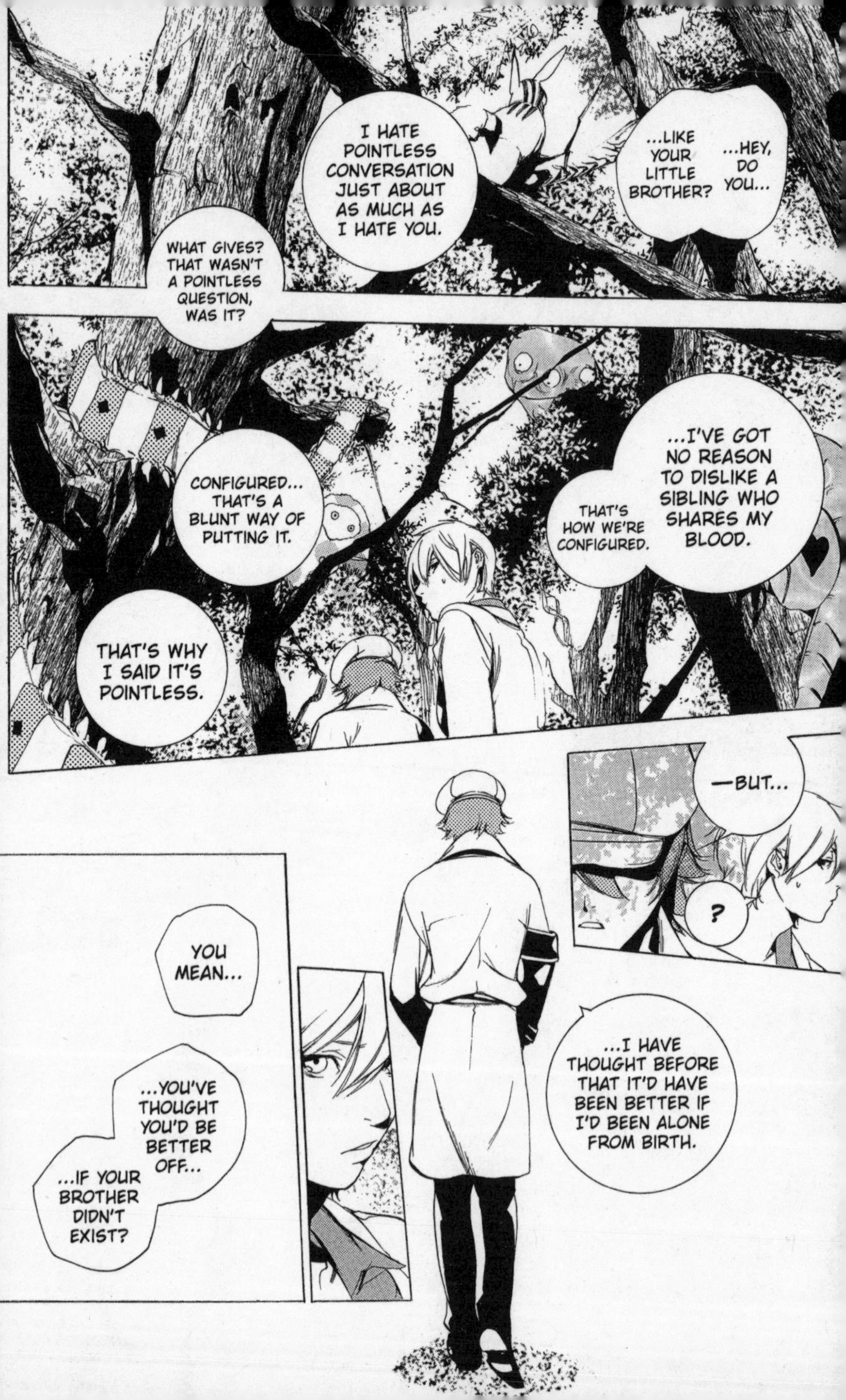
...HEY, DO YOU...
...LIKE YOUR LITTLE BROTHER?
I HATE POINTLESS CONVERSATION JUST ABOUT AS MUCH AS I HATE YOU.
WHAT GIVES? THAT WASN'T A POINTLESS QUESTION, WAS IT?
...I'VE GOT NO REASON TO DISLIKE A SIBLING WHO SHARES MY BLOOD.
THAT'S HOW WE'RE CONFIGURED.
CONFIGURED... THAT'S A BLUNT WAY OF PUTTING IT.
THAT'S WHY I SAID IT'S POINTLESS.
—BUT...
?
...I HAVE THOUGHT BEFORE THAT IT'D HAVE BEEN BETTER IF I'D BEEN ALONE FROM BIRTH.
YOU MEAN...
...YOU'VE THOUGHT YOU'D BE BETTER OFF...
...IF YOUR BROTHER DIDN'T EXIST?

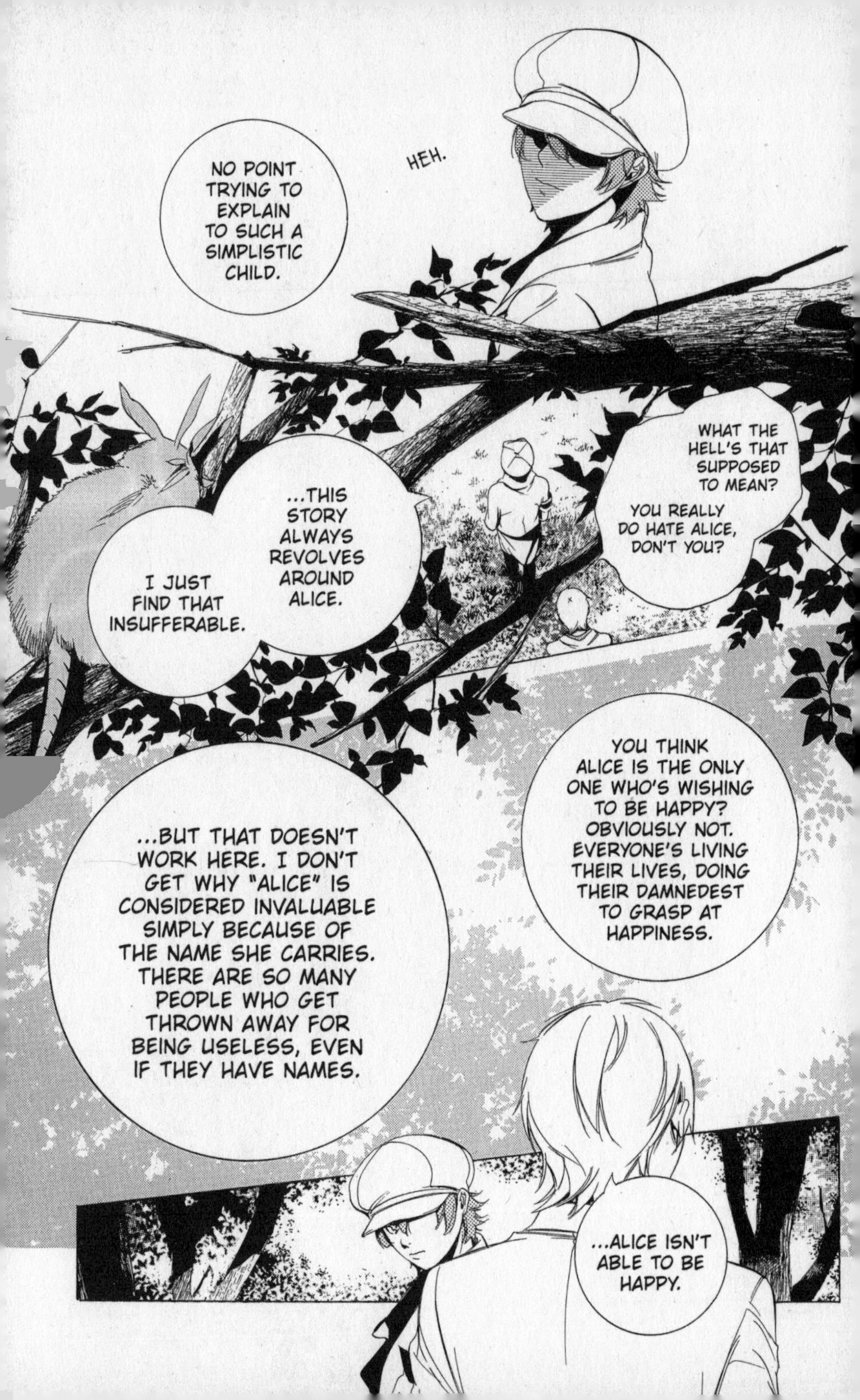
HEH.
NO POINT TRYING TO EXPLAIN TO SUCH A SIMPLISTIC CHILD.
WHAT THE HELL'S THAT SUPPOSED TO MEAN?
YOU REALLY DO HATE ALICE, DON'T YOU?
...THIS STORY ALWAYS REVOLVES AROUND ALICE.
I JUST FIND THAT INSUFFERABLE.
YOU THINK ALICE IS THE ONLY ONE WHO'S WISHING TO BE HAPPY? OBVIOUSLY NOT. EVERYONE'S LIVING THEIR LIVES, DOING THEIR DAMNEDEST TO GRASP AT HAPPINESS.
...BUT THAT DOESN'T WORK HERE. I DON'T GET WHY "ALICE" IS CONSIDERED INVALUABLE SIMPLY BECAUSE OF THE NAME SHE CARRIES. THERE ARE SO MANY PEOPLE WHO GET THROWN AWAY FOR BEING USELESS, EVEN IF THEY HAVE NAMES.
...ALICE ISN'T ABLE TO BE HAPPY.

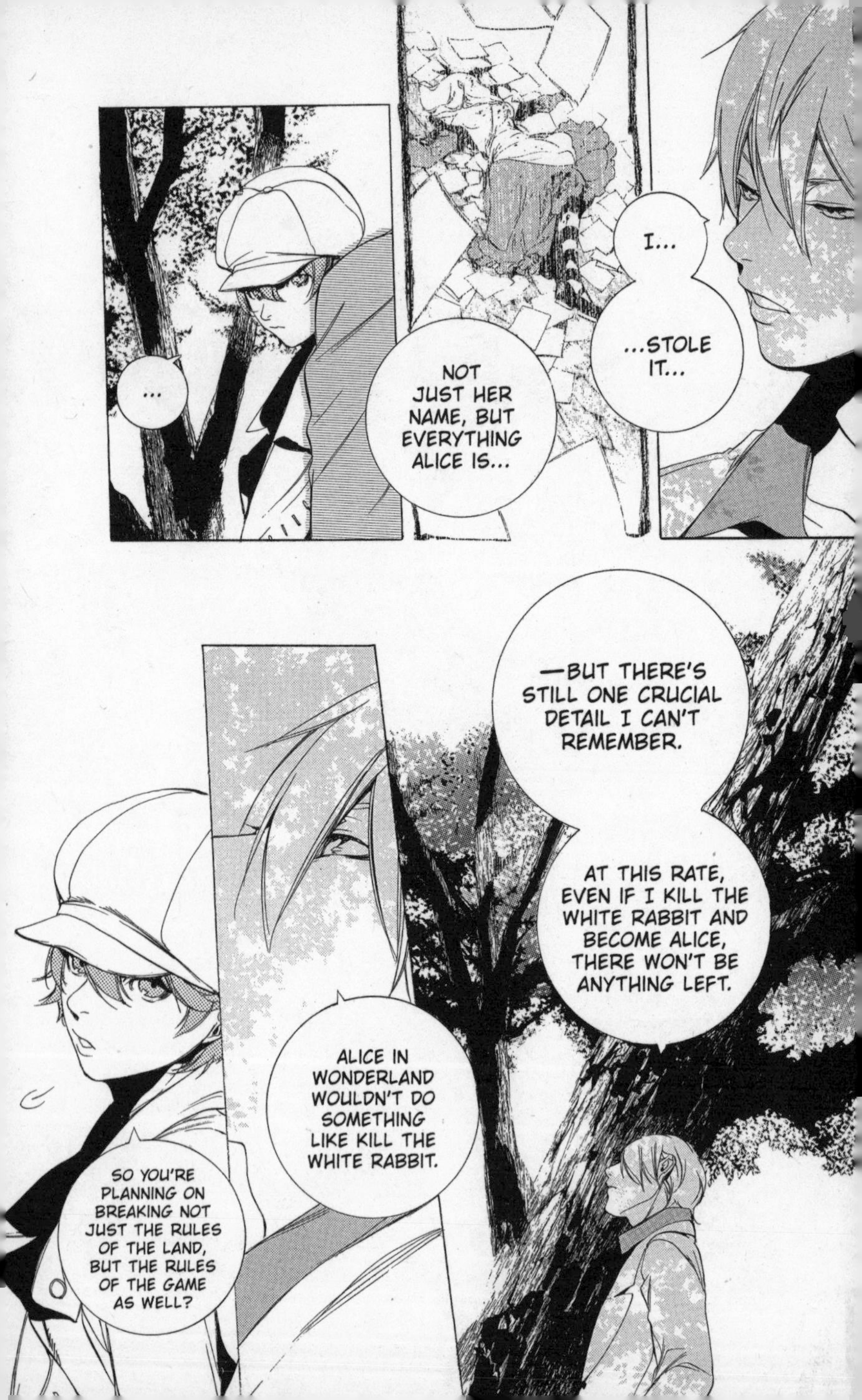
I...
...STOLE IT...
NOT JUST HER NAME, BUT EVERYTHING ALICE IS...
...
—BUT THERE'S STILL ONE CRUCIAL DETAIL I CAN'T REMEMBER.
AT THIS RATE, EVEN IF I KILL THE WHITE RABBIT AND BECOME ALICE, THERE WON'T BE ANYTHING LEFT.
ALICE IN WONDERLAND WOULDN'T DO SOMETHING LIKE KILL THE WHITE RABBIT.
SO YOU'RE PLANNING ON BREAKING NOT JUST THE RULES OF THE LAND, BUT THE RULES OF THE GAME AS WELL?

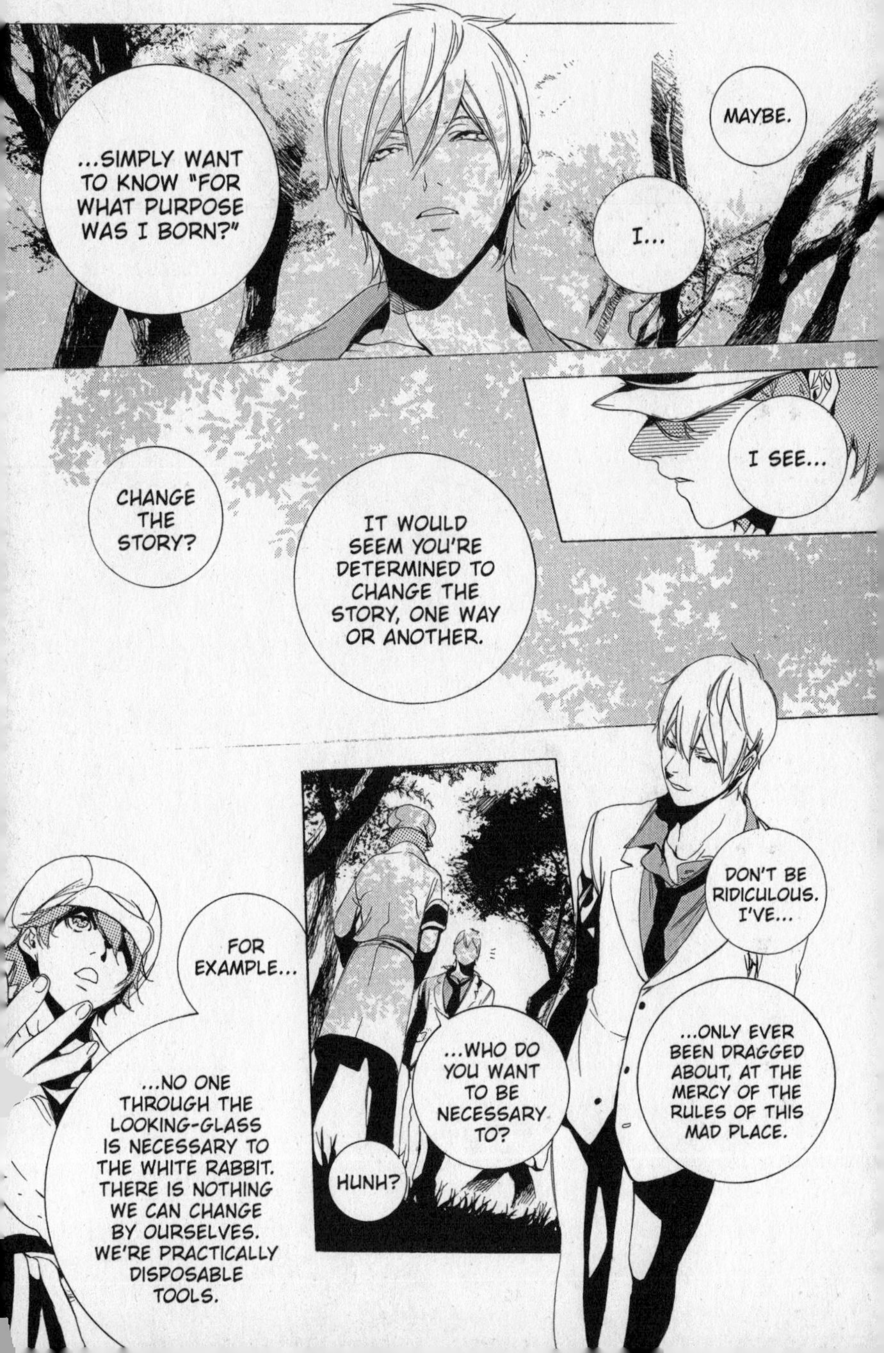
MAYBE.
I...
...SIMPLY WANT TO KNOW "FOR WHAT PURPOSE WAS I BORN?"
I SEE...
IT WOULD SEEM YOU'RE DETERMINED TO CHANGE THE STORY, ONE WAY OR ANOTHER.
CHANGE THE STORY?
DON'T BE RIDICULOUS. I'VE...
...ONLY EVER BEEN DRAGGED ABOUT, AT THE MERCY OF THE RULES OF THIS MAD PLACE.
...WHO DO YOU WANT TO BE NECESSARY TO?
HUNH?
FOR EXAMPLE...
...NO ONE THROUGH THE LOOKING-GLASS IS NECESSARY TO THE WHITE RABBIT. THERE IS NOTHING WE CAN CHANGE BY OURSELVES. WE'RE PRACTICALLY DISPOSABLE TOOLS.

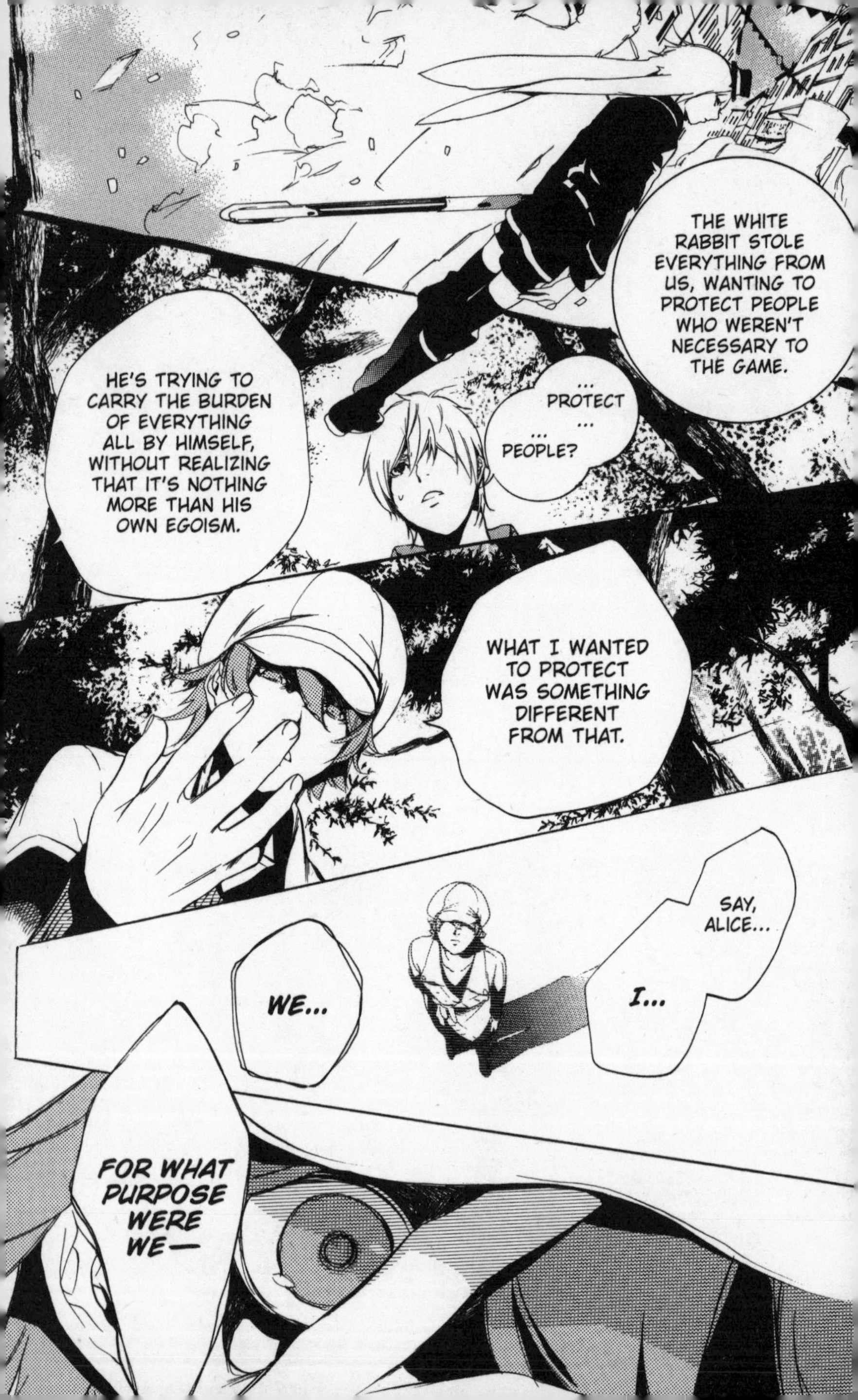
THE WHITE RABBIT STOLE EVERYTHING FROM US, WANTING TO PROTECT PEOPLE WHO WEREN'T NECESSARY TO THE GAME.
... PROTECT ... ... PEOPLE?
HE'S TRYING TO CARRY THE BURDEN OF EVERYTHING ALL BY HIMSELF, WITHOUT REALIZING THAT IT'S NOTHING MORE THAN HIS OWN EGOISM.
WHAT I WANTED TO PROTECT WAS SOMETHING DIFFERENT FROM THAT.
SAY, ALICE...
I...
WE...
FOR WHAT PURPOSE WERE WE—

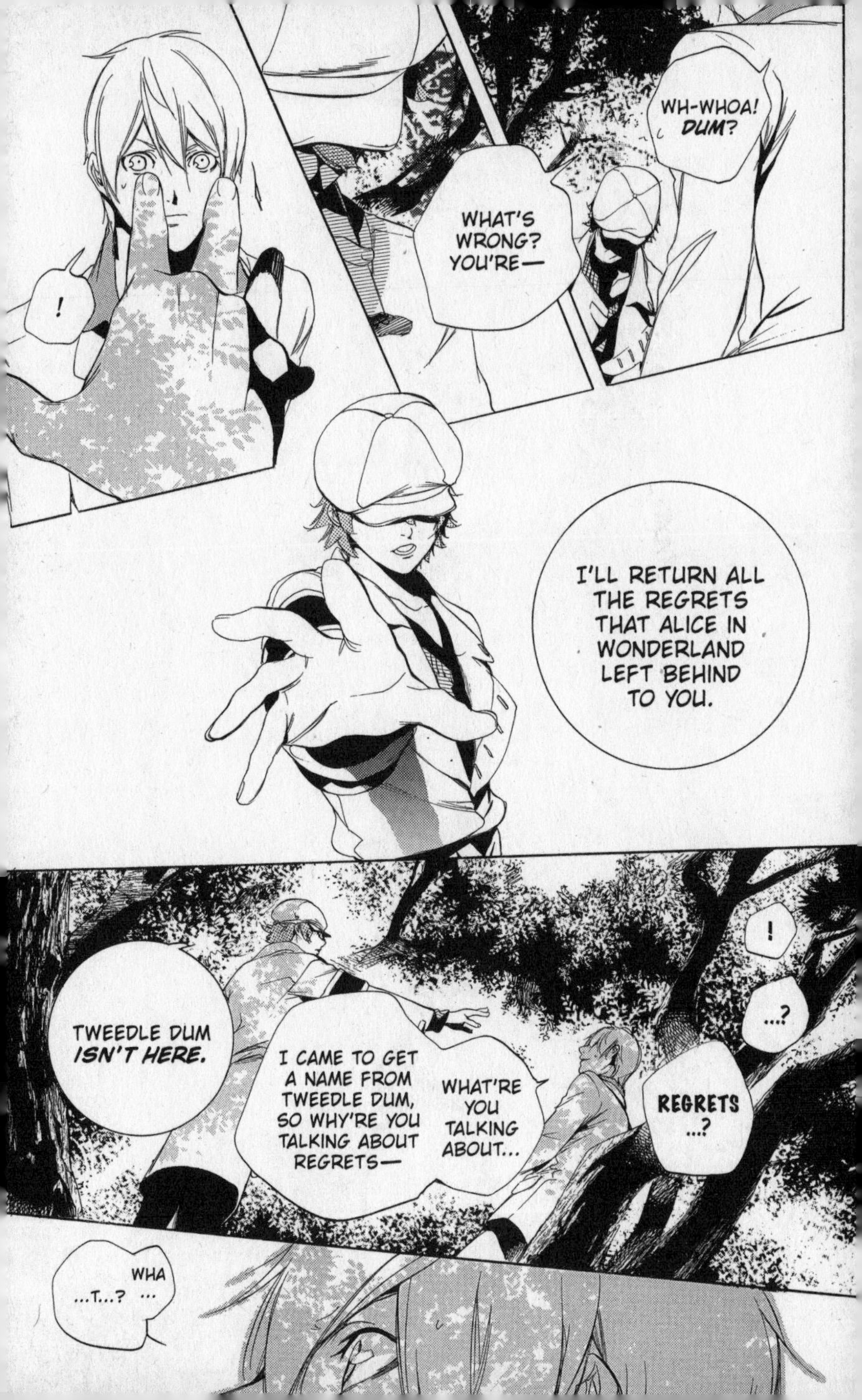
WH-WHOA! *DUM?*
WHAT'S WRONG? YOU'RE—
!
I'LL RETURN ALL THE REGRETS THAT ALICE IN WONDERLAND LEFT BEHIND TO YOU.
!
...?
REGRETS ...?
WHAT'RE YOU TALKING ABOUT...
I CAME TO GET A NAME FROM TWEEDLE DUM, SO WHY'RE YOU TALKING ABOUT REGRETS—
TWEEDLE DUM *ISN'T HERE.*
WHA ...T...? ...

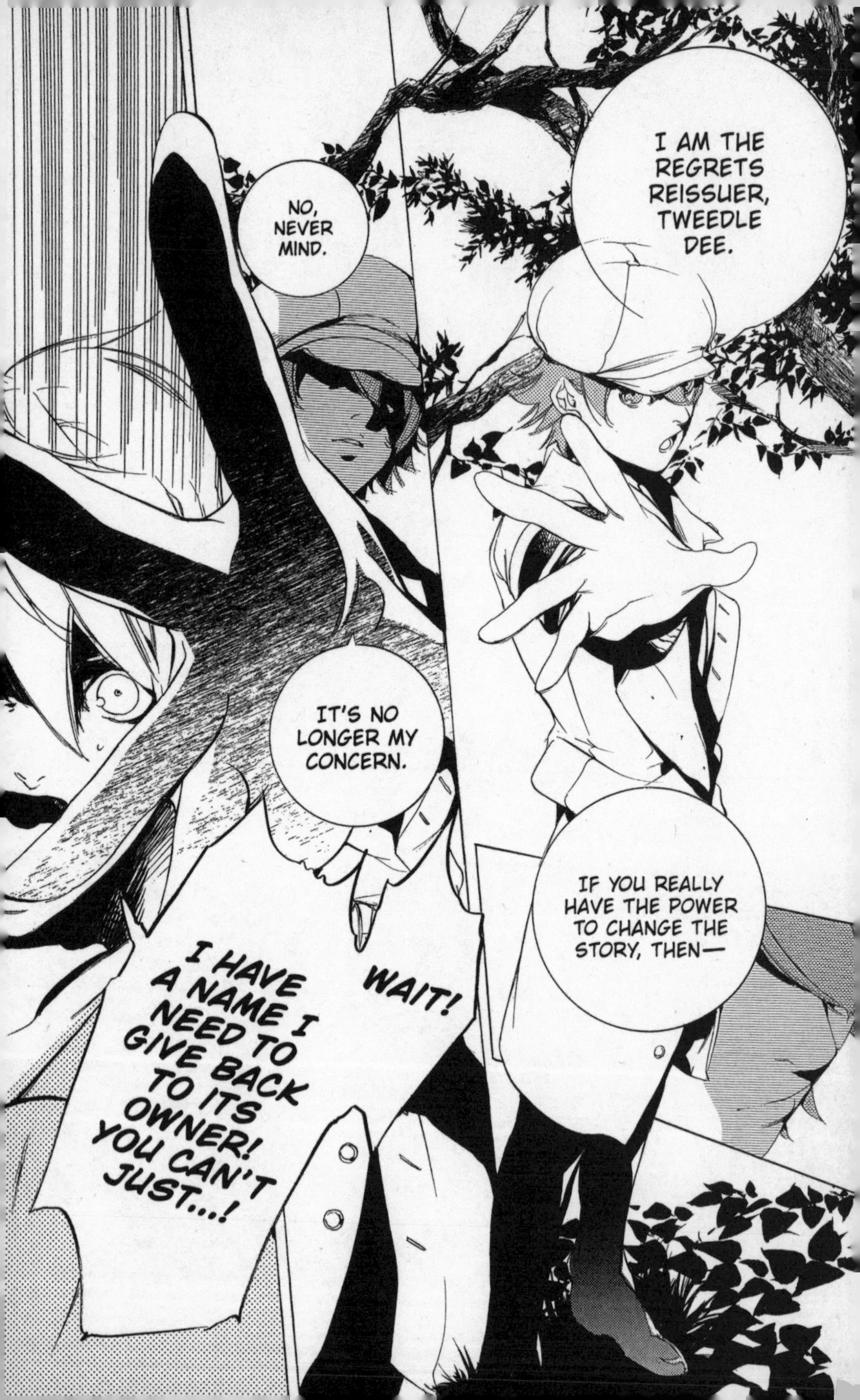
I AM THE REGRETS REISSUER, TWEEDLE DEE.
IF YOU REALLY HAVE THE POWER TO CHANGE THE STORY, THEN—
NO, NEVER MIND.
IT'S NO LONGER MY CONCERN.
WAIT!
I HAVE A NAME I NEED TO GIVE BACK TO ITS OWNER! YOU CAN'T JUST...!

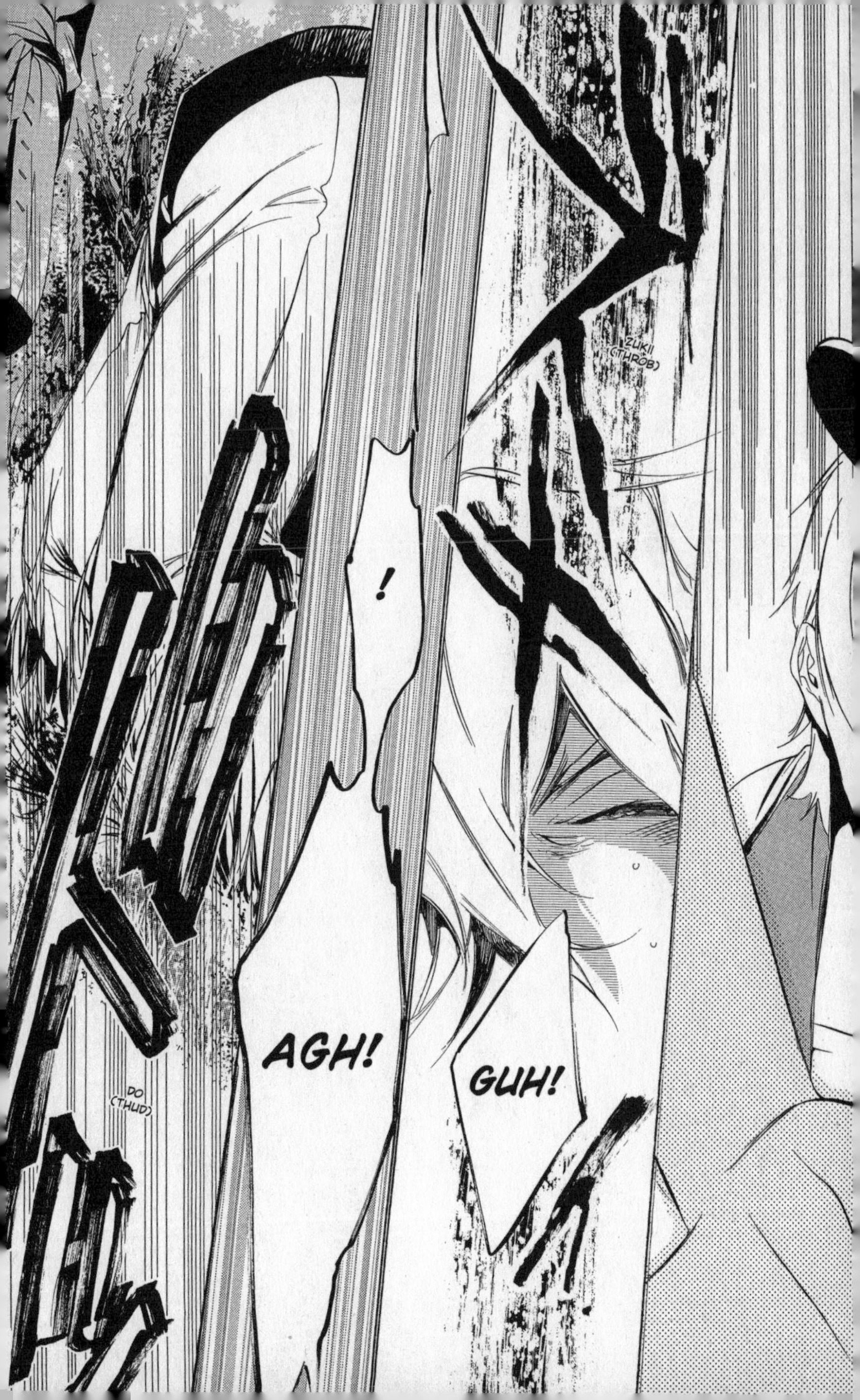
ZUKII (THROB)
GUH!
!
AGH!
DO (THUD)

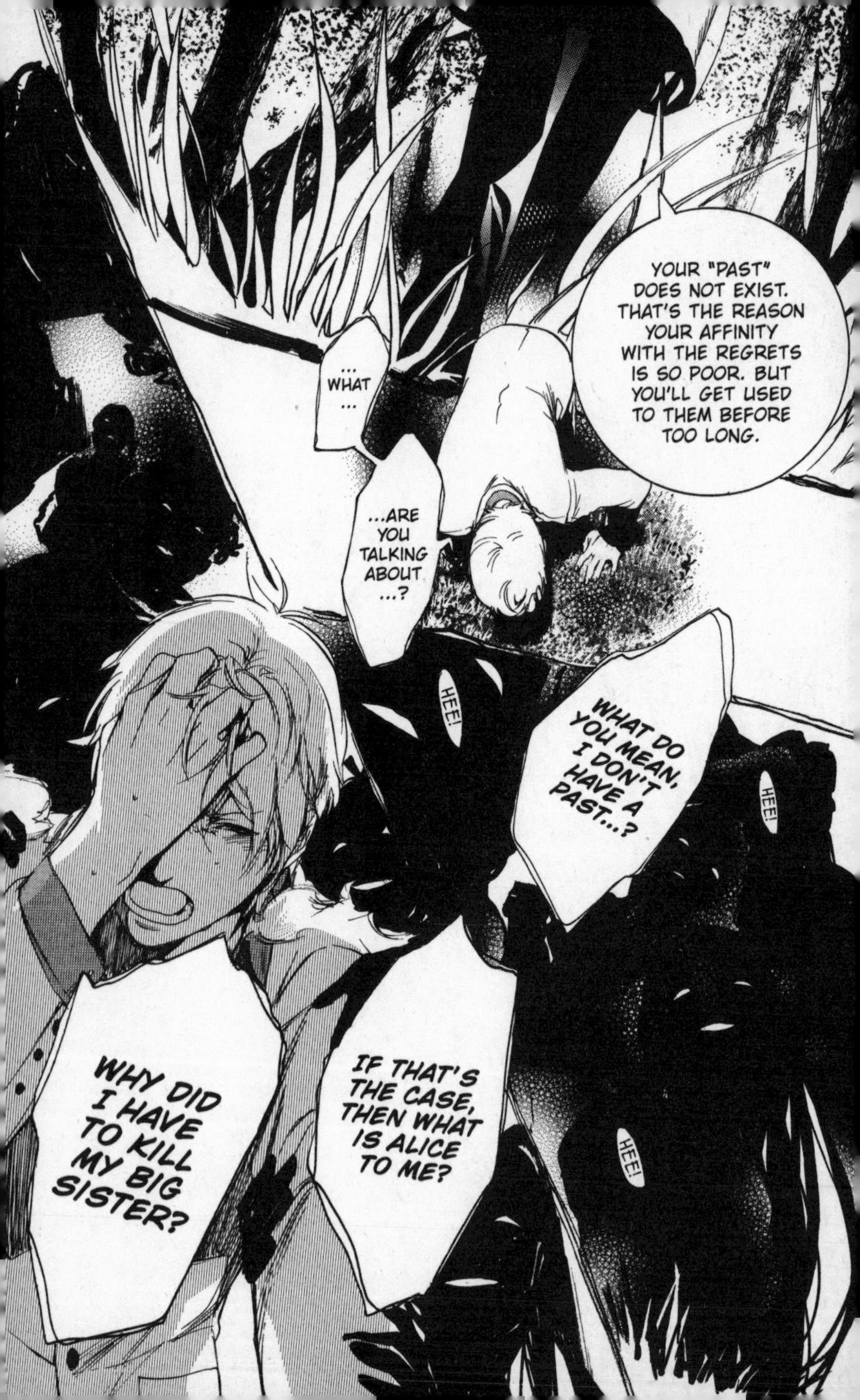

YOUR "PAST" DOES NOT EXIST. THAT'S THE REASON YOUR AFFINITY WITH THE REGRETS IS SO POOR. BUT YOU'LL GET USED TO THEM BEFORE TOO LONG.
...WHAT...
...ARE YOU TALKING ABOUT...?
WHAT DO YOU MEAN, I DON'T HAVE A PAST...?
HEE!
HEE!
HEE!
IF THAT'S THE CASE, THEN WHAT IS ALICE TO ME?
WHY DID I HAVE TO KILL MY BIG SISTER?

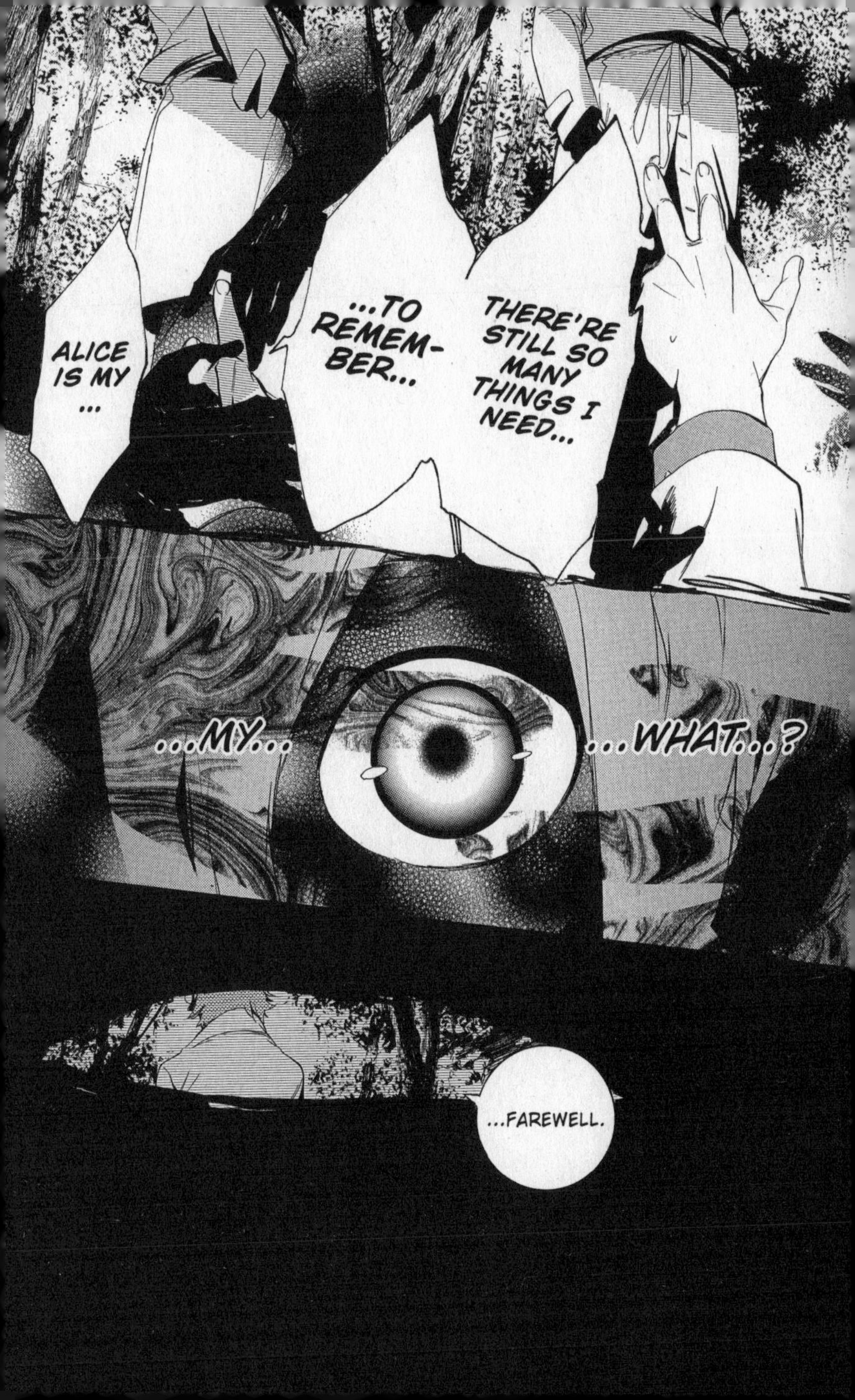
THERE'RE STILL SO MANY THINGS I NEED...
...TO REMEMBER...
ALICE IS MY ...
...WHAT...?
...MY...
...FAREWELL.

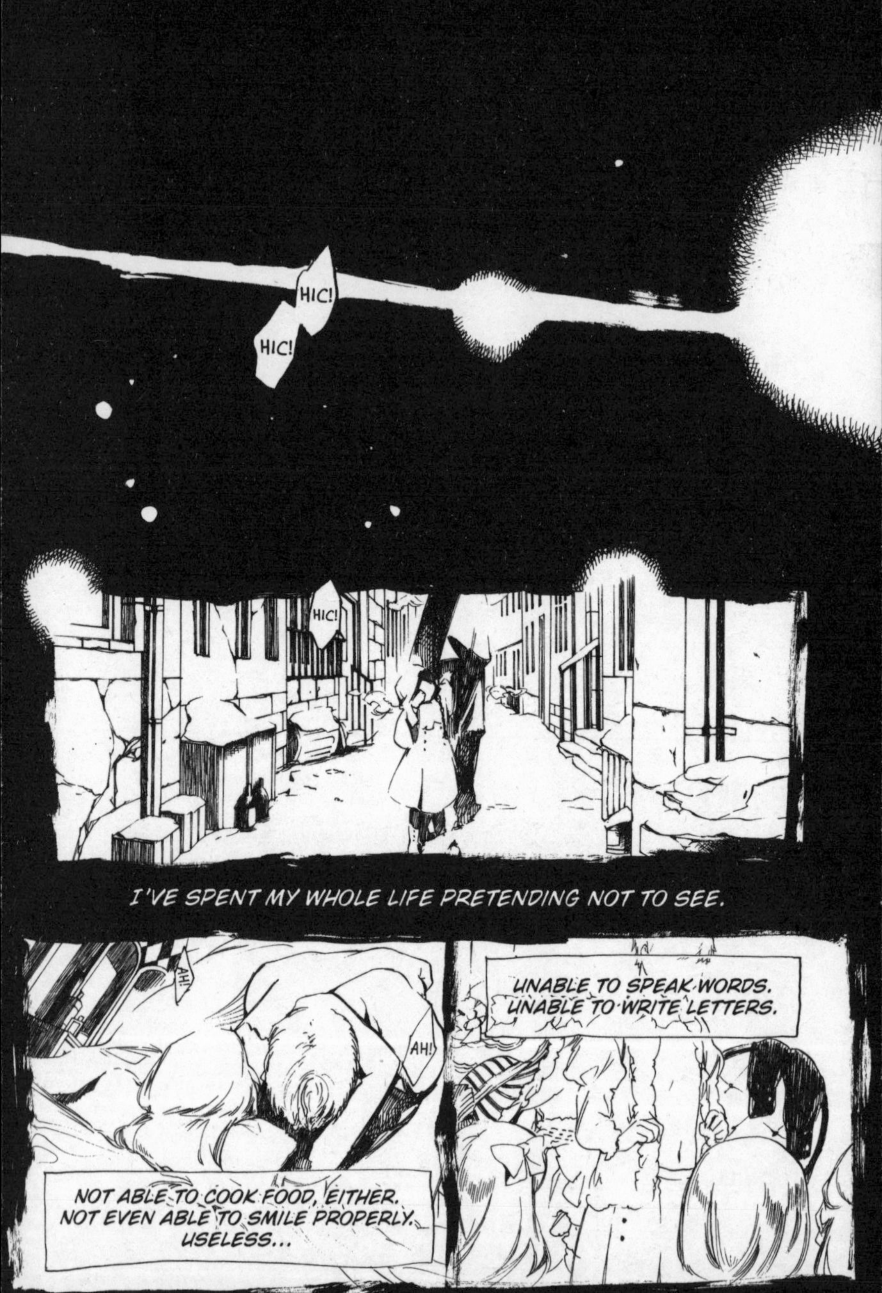
HIC!
HIC!
HIC!
I'VE SPENT MY WHOLE LIFE PRETENDING NOT TO SEE.
UNABLE TO SPEAK WORDS. UNABLE TO WRITE LETTERS.
AH!
AH!
NOT ABLE TO COOK FOOD, EITHER. NOT EVEN ABLE TO SMILE PROPERLY. USELESS...

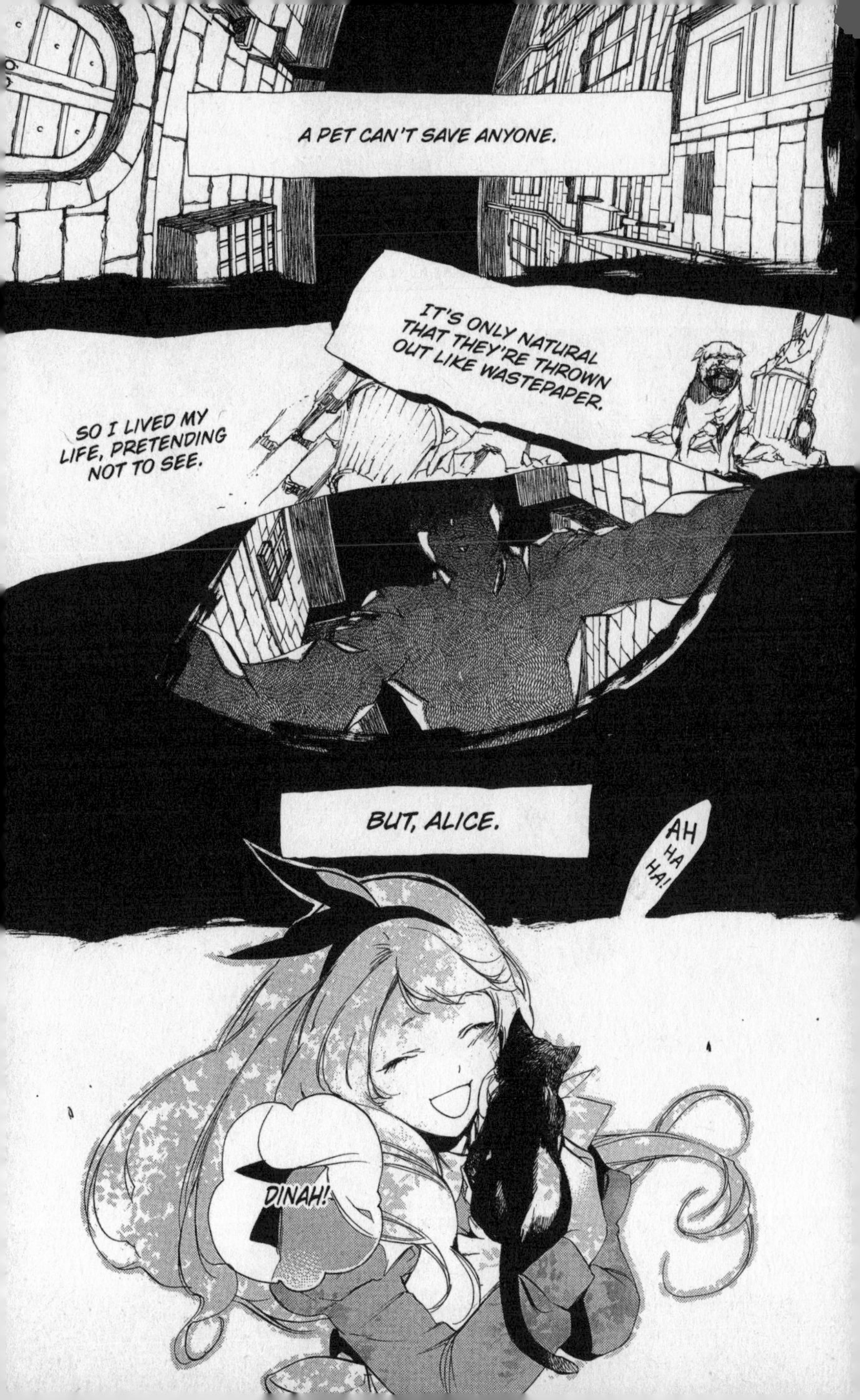
A PET CAN'T SAVE ANYONE.
IT'S ONLY NATURAL THAT THEY'RE THROWN OUT LIKE WASTEPAPER.
SO I LIVED MY LIFE, PRETENDING NOT TO SEE.
BUT, ALICE.
AH HA HA!
DINAH!

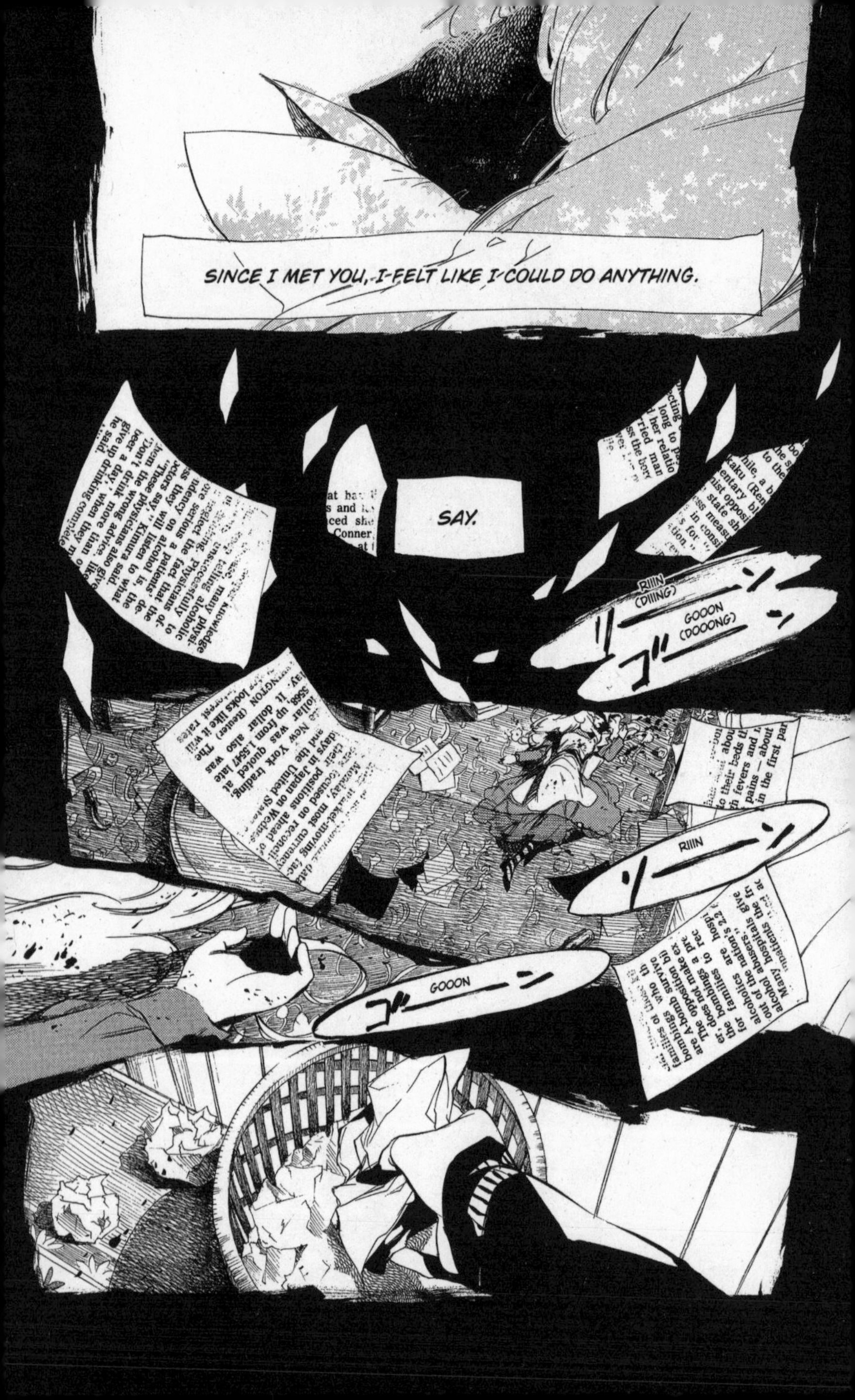
SINCE I MET YOU, I FELT LIKE I COULD DO ANYTHING.
SAY.
RIIIN (DIIING)
GOOON (DOOONG)
RIIIN
GOOON

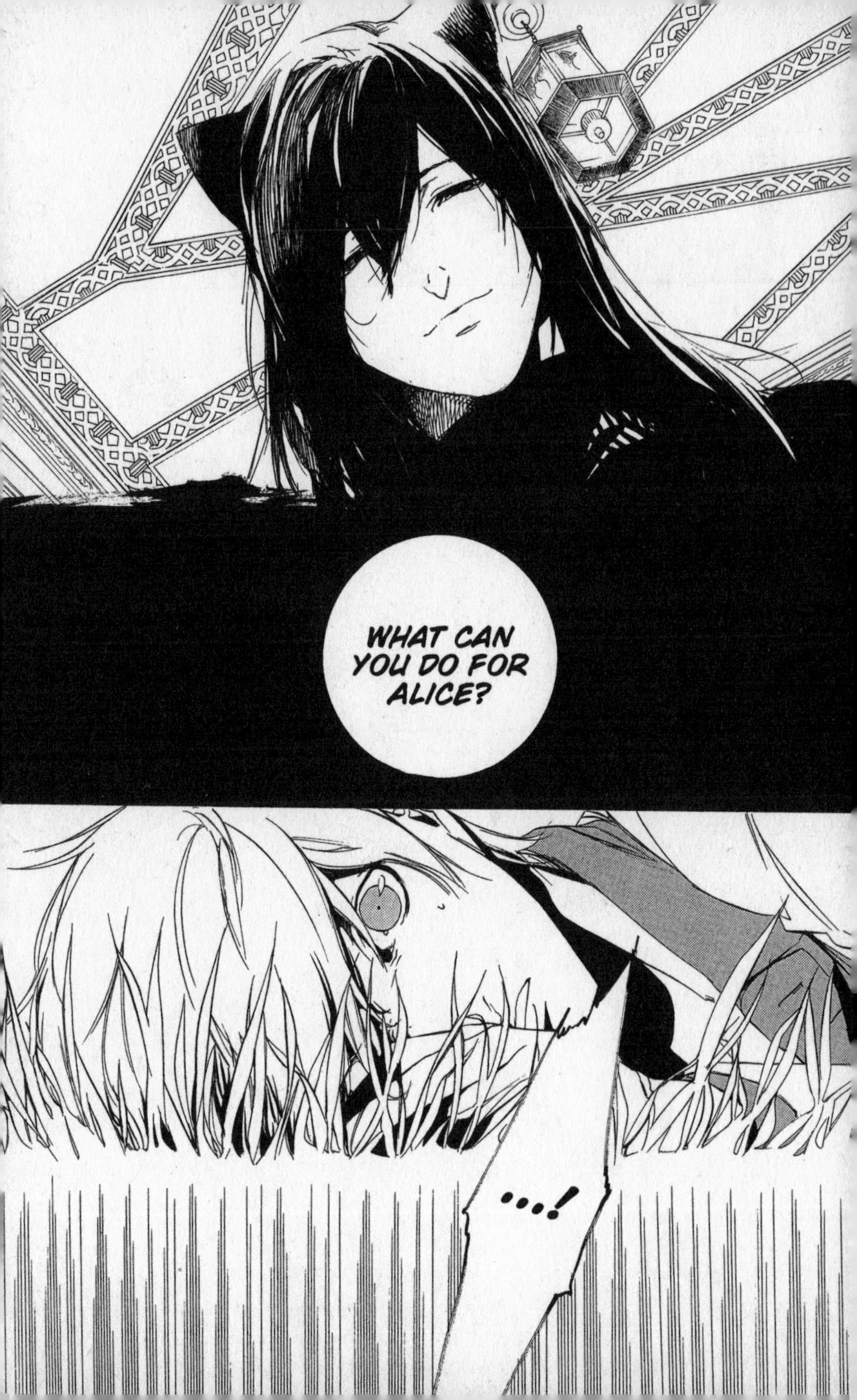
WHAT CAN YOU DO FOR ALICE?
...!

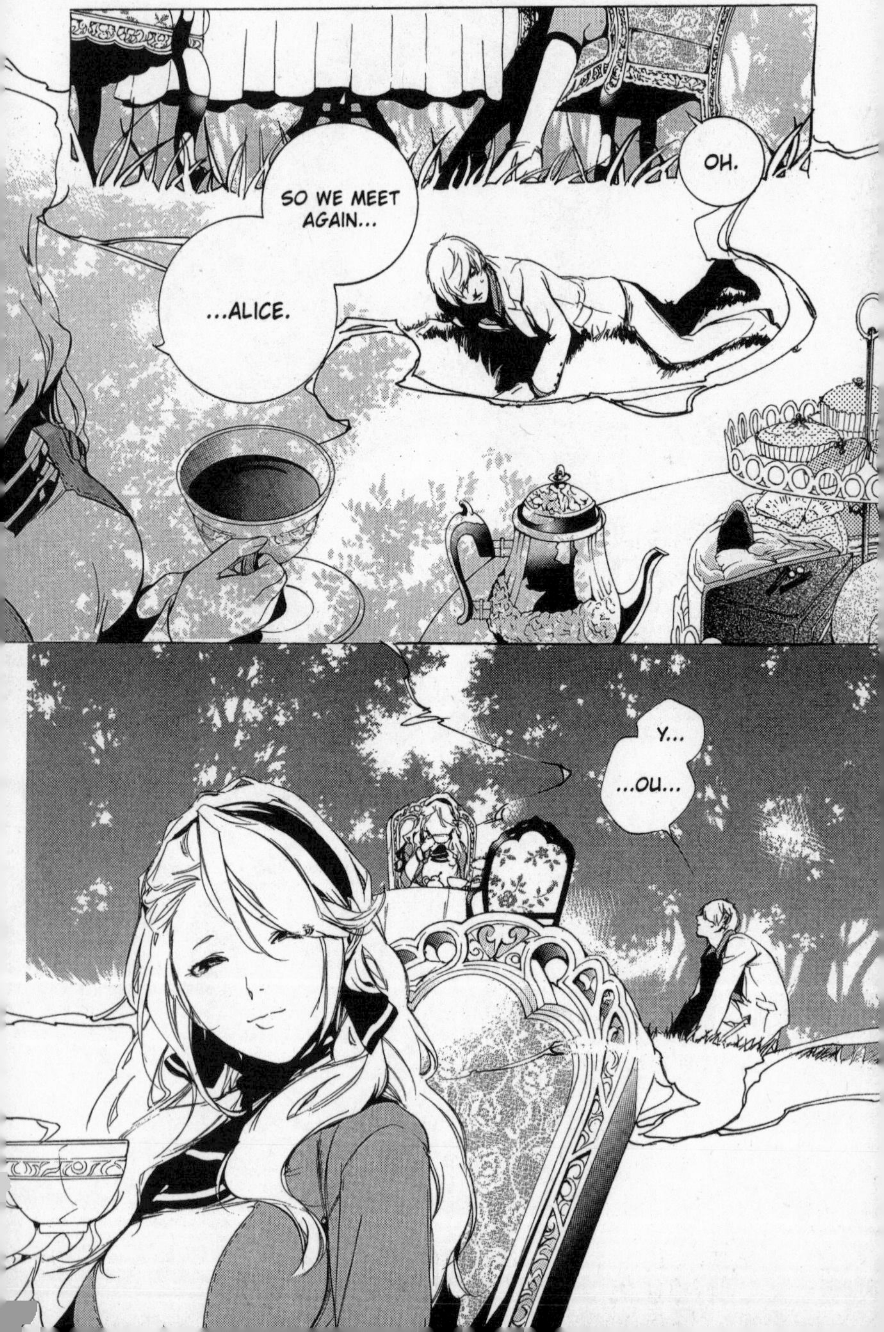
OH.
SO WE MEET AGAIN...
...ALICE.
Y...
...OU...

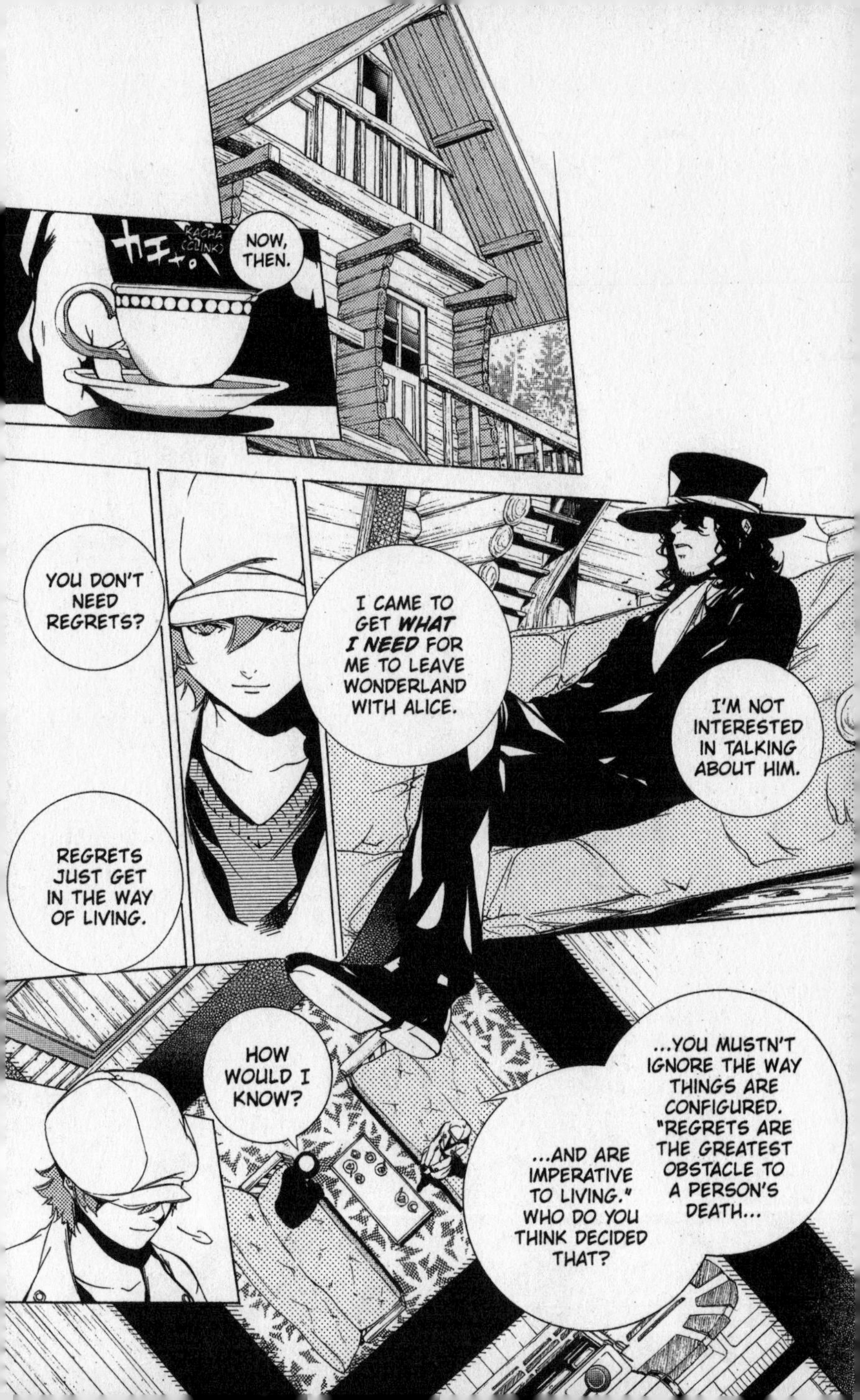
カチャ
KACHA (CLINK)
NOW, THEN.
I'M NOT INTERESTED IN TALKING ABOUT HIM.
I CAME TO GET ***WHAT I NEED*** FOR ME TO LEAVE WONDERLAND WITH ALICE.
YOU DON'T NEED REGRETS?
REGRETS JUST GET IN THE WAY OF LIVING.
...YOU MUSTN'T IGNORE THE WAY THINGS ARE CONFIGURED. "REGRETS ARE THE GREATEST OBSTACLE TO A PERSON'S DEATH...
...AND ARE IMPERATIVE TO LIVING." WHO DO YOU THINK DECIDED THAT?
HOW WOULD I KNOW?

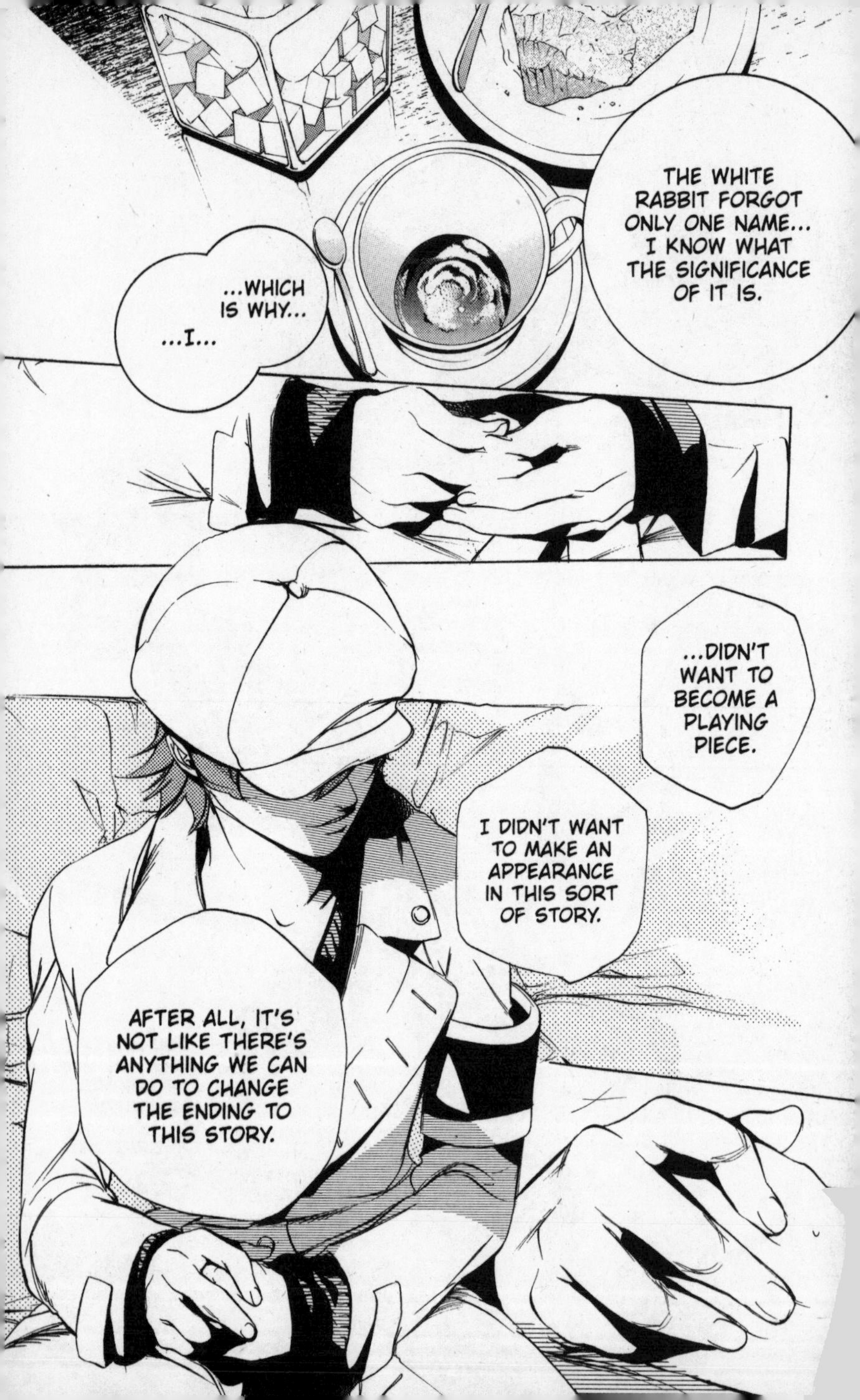
THE WHITE RABBIT FORGOT ONLY ONE NAME... I KNOW WHAT THE SIGNIFICANCE OF IT IS.
...WHICH IS WHY...
...I...
...DIDN'T WANT TO BECOME A PLAYING PIECE.
I DIDN'T WANT TO MAKE AN APPEARANCE IN THIS SORT OF STORY.
AFTER ALL, IT'S NOT LIKE THERE'S ANYTHING WE CAN DO TO CHANGE THE ENDING TO THIS STORY.

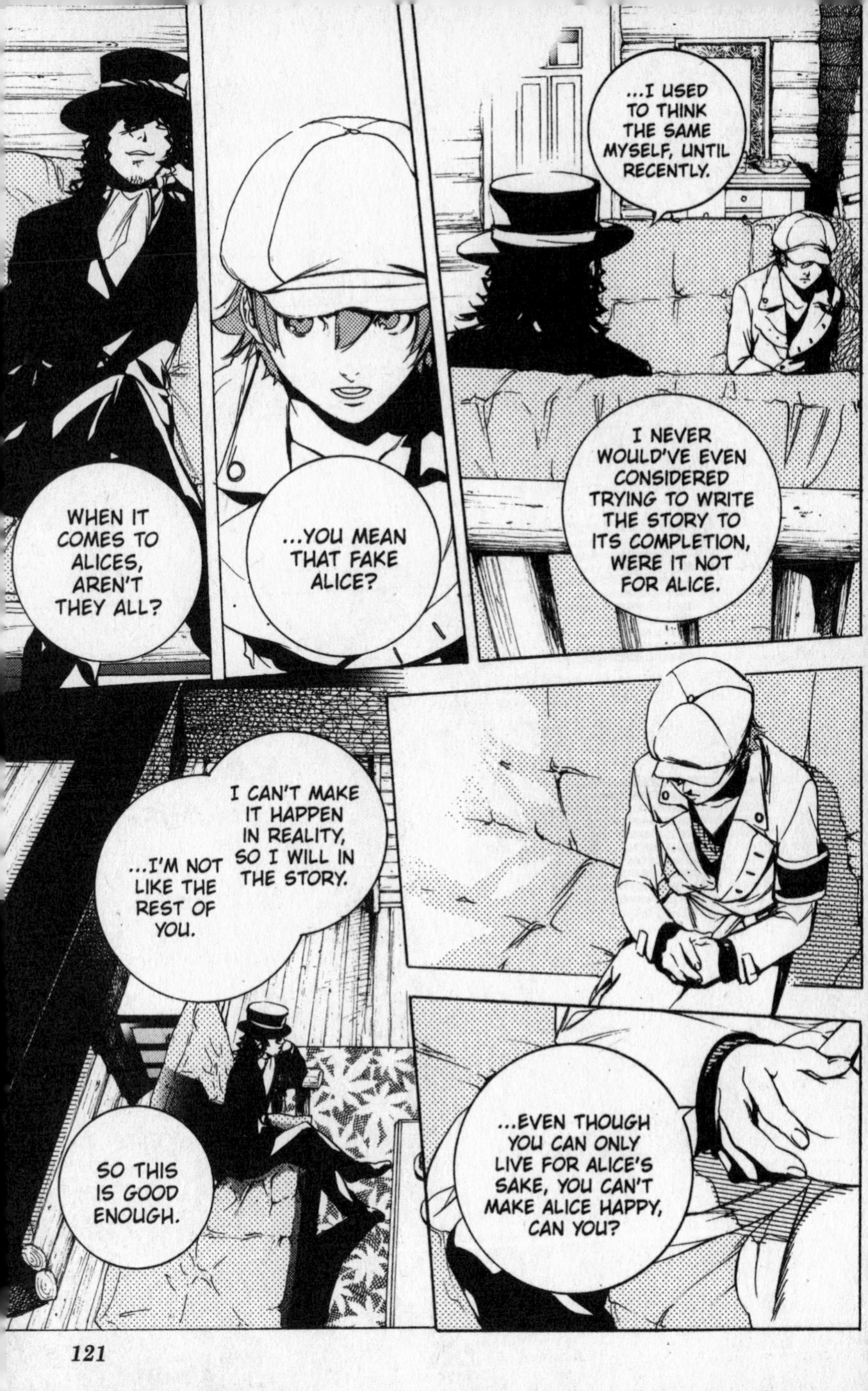
...I USED TO THINK THE SAME MYSELF, UNTIL RECENTLY.
I NEVER WOULD'VE EVEN CONSIDERED TRYING TO WRITE THE STORY TO ITS COMPLETION, WERE IT NOT FOR ALICE.
...YOU MEAN THAT FAKE ALICE?
WHEN IT COMES TO ALICES, AREN'T THEY ALL?
I CAN'T MAKE IT HAPPEN IN REALITY, SO I WILL IN THE STORY.
...I'M NOT LIKE THE REST OF YOU.
...EVEN THOUGH YOU CAN ONLY LIVE FOR ALICE'S SAKE, YOU CAN'T MAKE ALICE HAPPY, CAN YOU?
SO THIS IS GOOD ENOUGH.

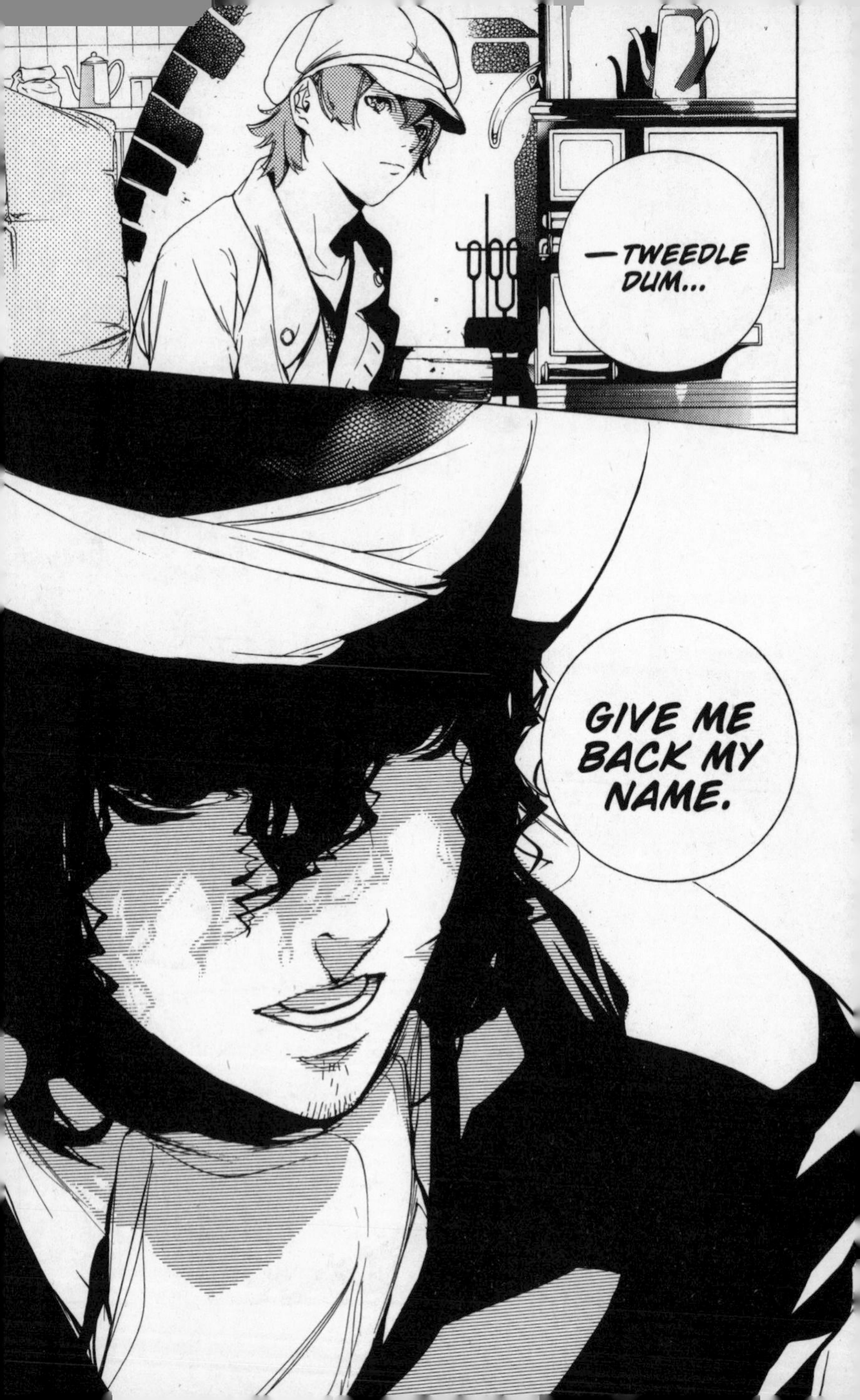
—TWEEDLE DUM...
GIVE ME BACK MY NAME.

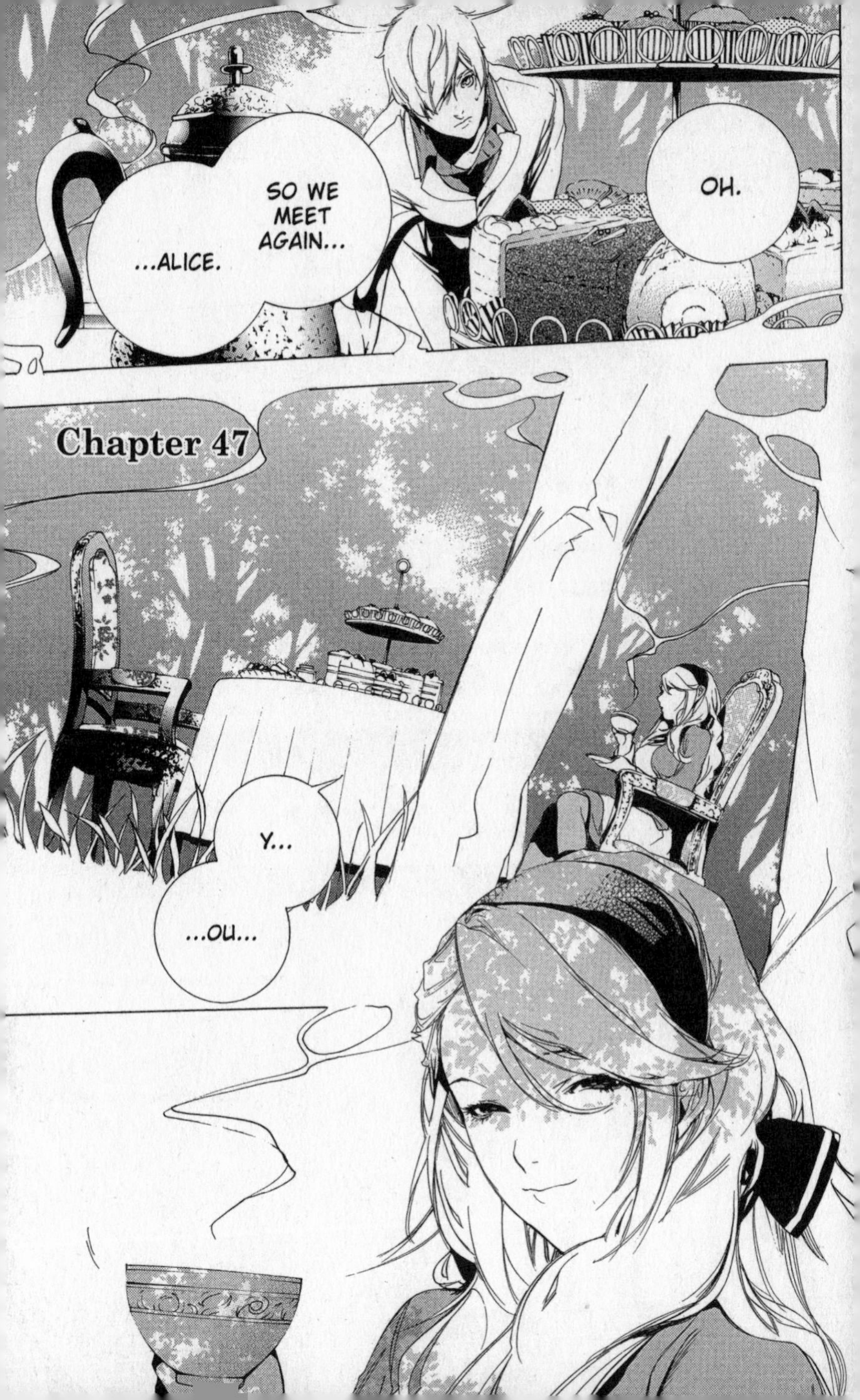
OH.
SO WE MEET AGAIN...
...ALICE.
Chapter 47
Y...
...OU...

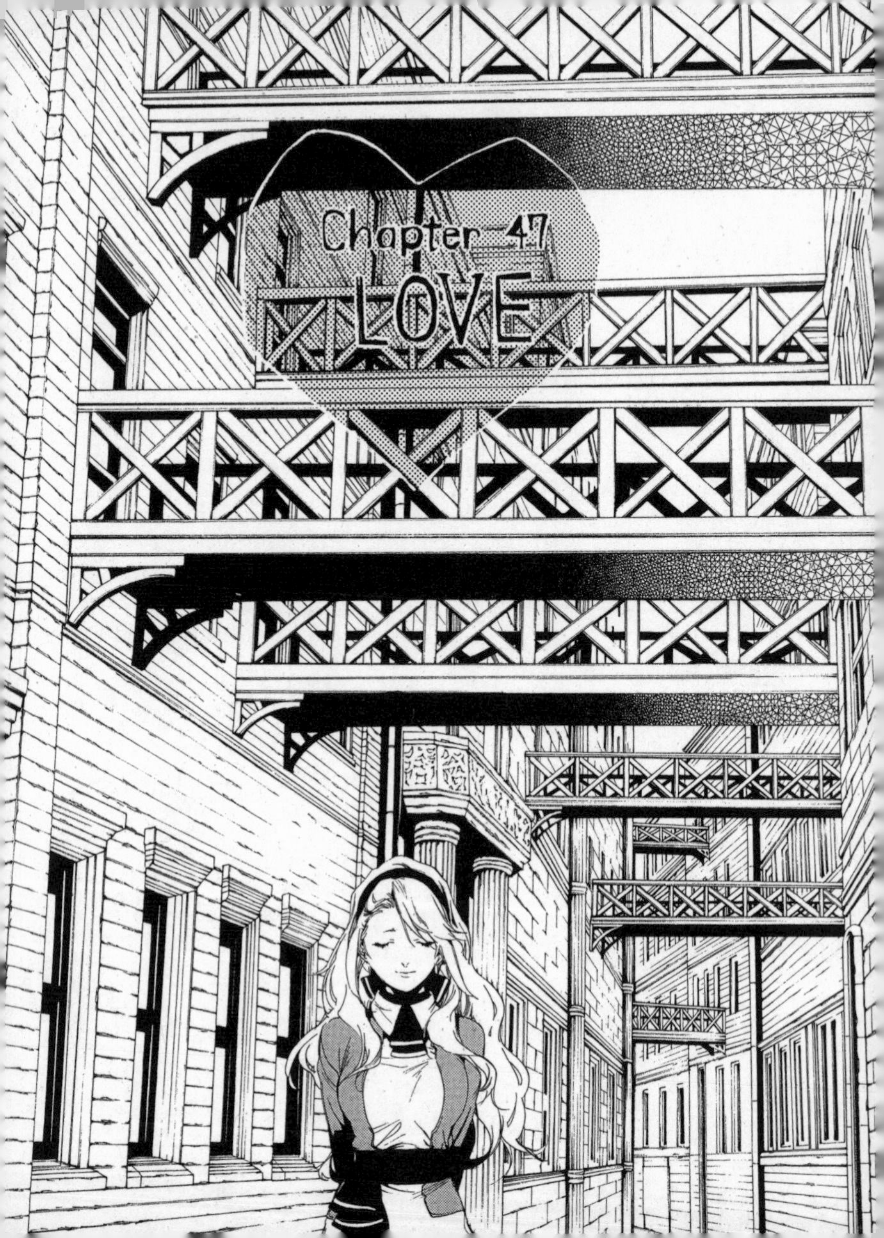
Chapter 47
LOVE

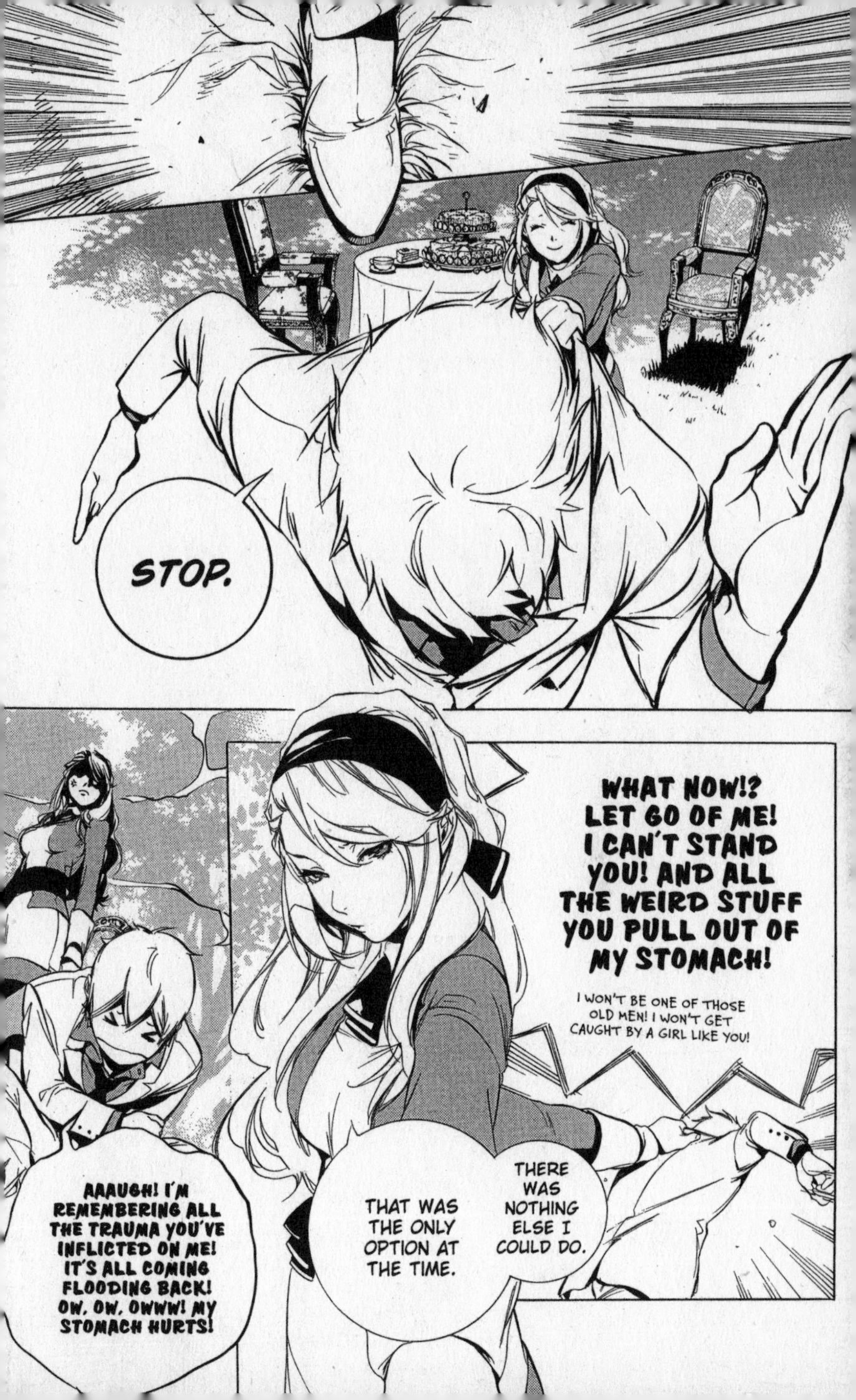
STOP.
WHAT NOW!? LET GO OF ME! I CAN'T STAND YOU! AND ALL THE WEIRD STUFF YOU PULL OUT OF MY STOMACH!
I WON'T BE ONE OF THOSE OLD MEN! I WON'T GET CAUGHT BY A GIRL LIKE YOU!
THERE WAS NOTHING ELSE I COULD DO.
THAT WAS THE ONLY OPTION AT THE TIME.
AAAUGH! I'M REMEMBERING ALL THE TRAUMA YOU'VE INFLICTED ON ME! IT'S ALL COMING FLOODING BACK! OW, OW, OWWW! MY STOMACH HURTS!

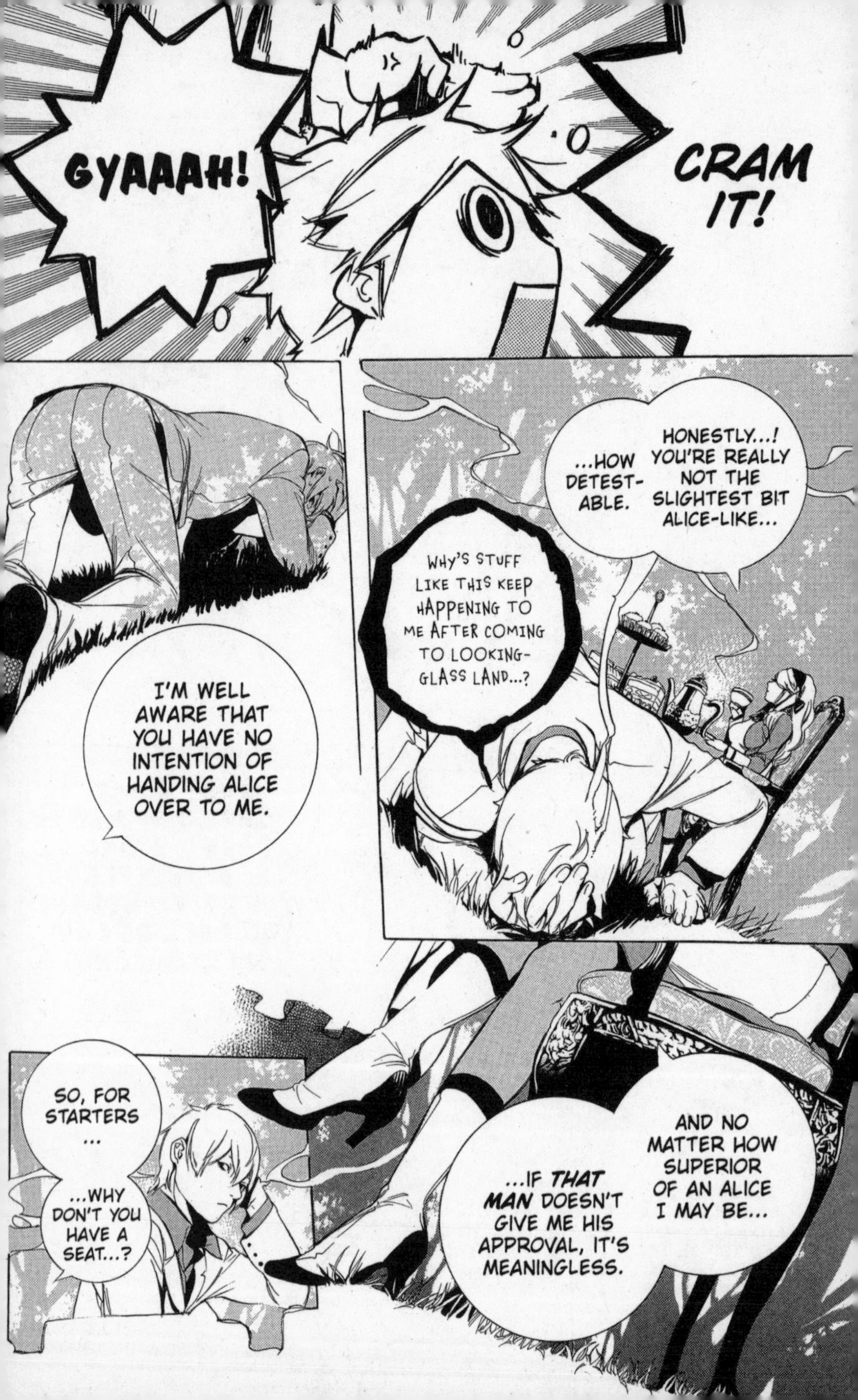
CRAM IT!
GYAAAH!
HONESTLY...! YOU'RE REALLY NOT THE SLIGHTEST BIT ALICE-LIKE...
...HOW DETEST-ABLE.
WHY'S STUFF LIKE THIS KEEP HAPPENING TO ME AFTER COMING TO LOOKING-GLASS LAND...?
I'M WELL AWARE THAT YOU HAVE NO INTENTION OF HANDING ALICE OVER TO ME.
AND NO MATTER HOW SUPERIOR OF AN ALICE I MAY BE...
...IF *THAT MAN* DOESN'T GIVE ME HIS APPROVAL, IT'S MEANINGLESS.
SO, FOR STARTERS ...
...WHY DON'T YOU HAVE A SEAT...?

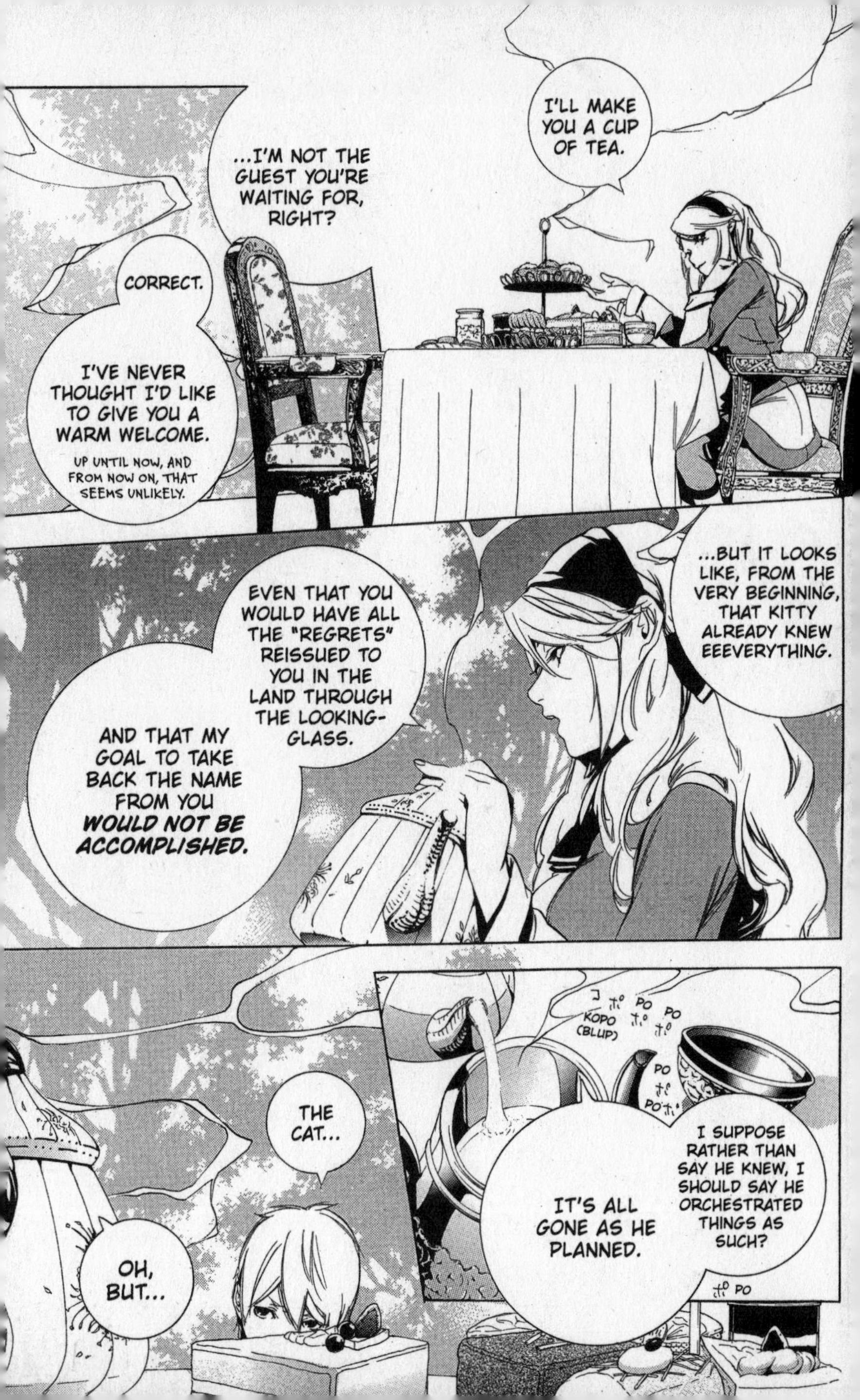
I'LL MAKE YOU A CUP OF TEA.
...I'M NOT THE GUEST YOU'RE WAITING FOR, RIGHT?
CORRECT.
I'VE NEVER THOUGHT I'D LIKE TO GIVE YOU A WARM WELCOME.
UP UNTIL NOW, AND FROM NOW ON, THAT SEEMS UNLIKELY.
...BUT IT LOOKS LIKE, FROM THE VERY BEGINNING, THAT KITTY ALREADY KNEW EEEVERYTHING.
EVEN THAT YOU WOULD HAVE ALL THE "REGRETS" REISSUED TO YOU IN THE LAND THROUGH THE LOOKING-GLASS.
AND THAT MY GOAL TO TAKE BACK THE NAME FROM YOU ***WOULD NOT BE ACCOMPLISHED.***
コポ KOPO (BLUP)
ポポ PO PO
ポポ PO PO
I SUPPOSE RATHER THAN SAY HE KNEW, I SHOULD SAY HE ORCHESTRATED THINGS AS SUCH?
IT'S ALL GONE AS HE PLANNED.
ポ PO
THE CAT...
OH, BUT...

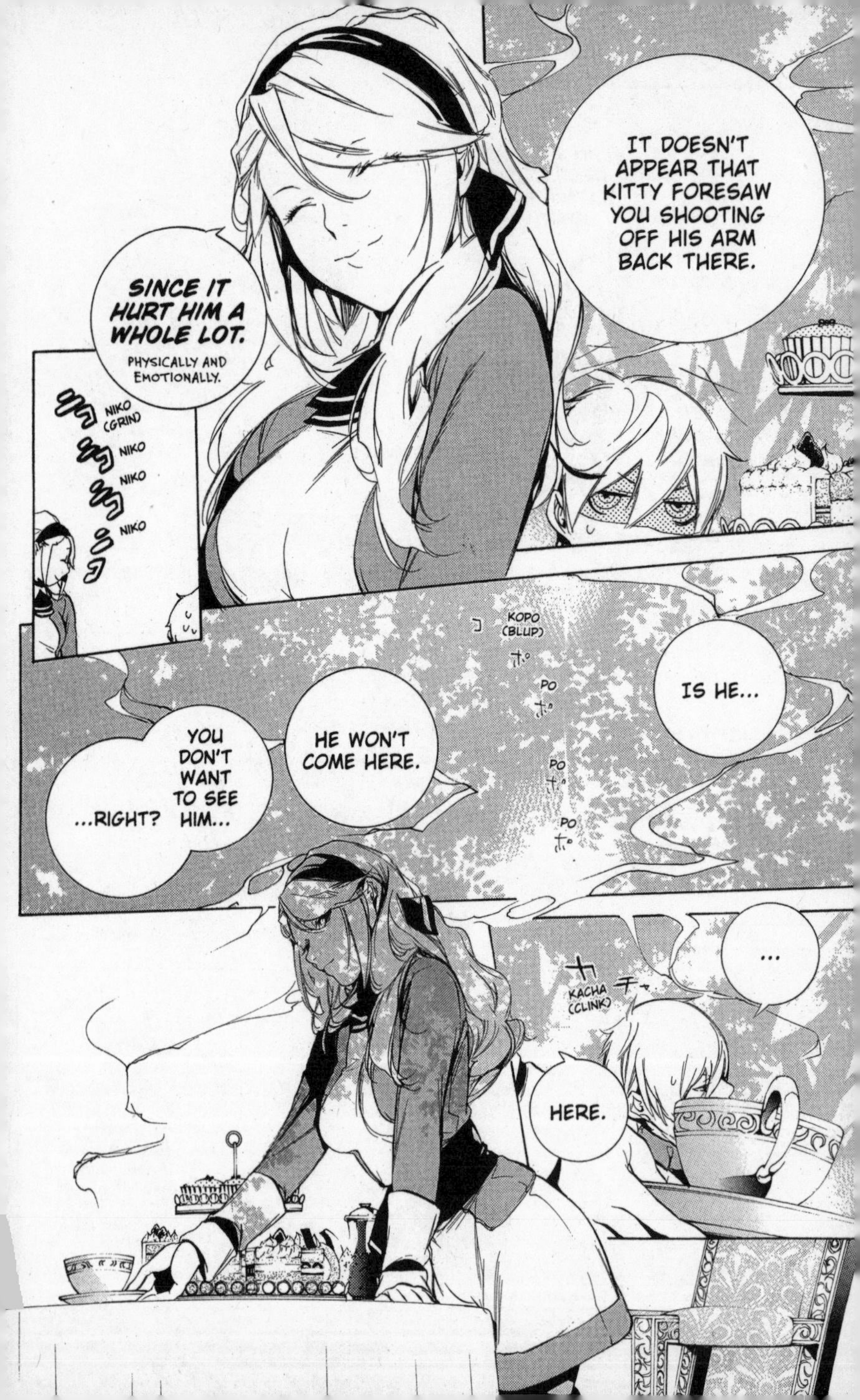
IT DOESN'T APPEAR THAT KITTY FORESAW YOU SHOOTING OFF HIS ARM BACK THERE.
SINCE IT HURT HIM A WHOLE LOT.
PHYSICALLY AND EMOTIONALLY.
NIKO (GRIN)
NIKO
NIKO
NIKO
KOPO (BLUP)
PO
PO
PO
IS HE...
HE WON'T COME HERE.
YOU DON'T WANT TO SEE HIM... ...RIGHT?
...
KACHA (CLINK)
HERE.

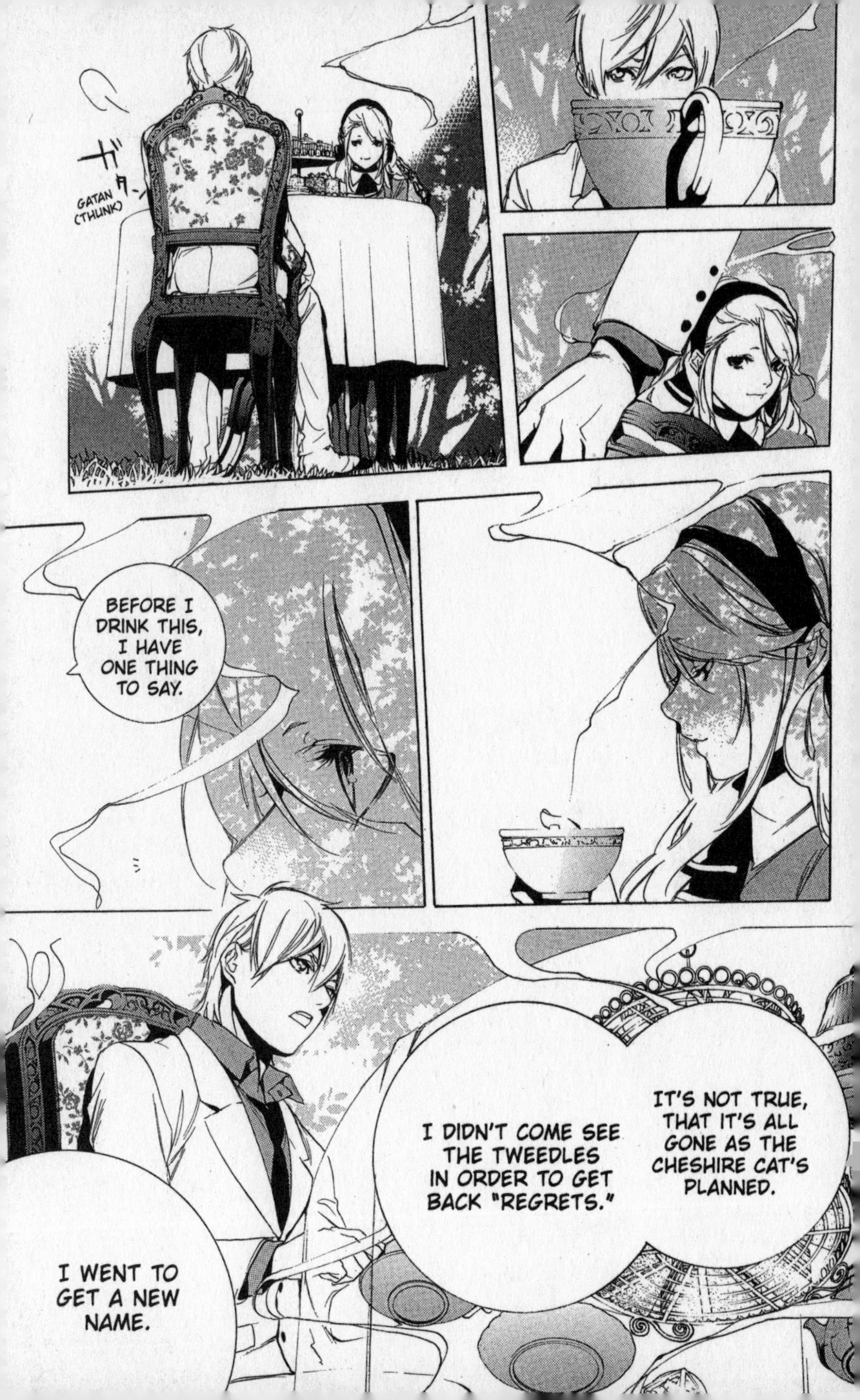
ガタ
GATAN (THUNK)
BEFORE I DRINK THIS, I HAVE ONE THING TO SAY.
IT'S NOT TRUE, THAT IT'S ALL GONE AS THE CHESHIRE CAT'S PLANNED.
I DIDN'T COME SEE THE TWEEDLES IN ORDER TO GET BACK "REGRETS."
I WENT TO GET A NEW NAME.

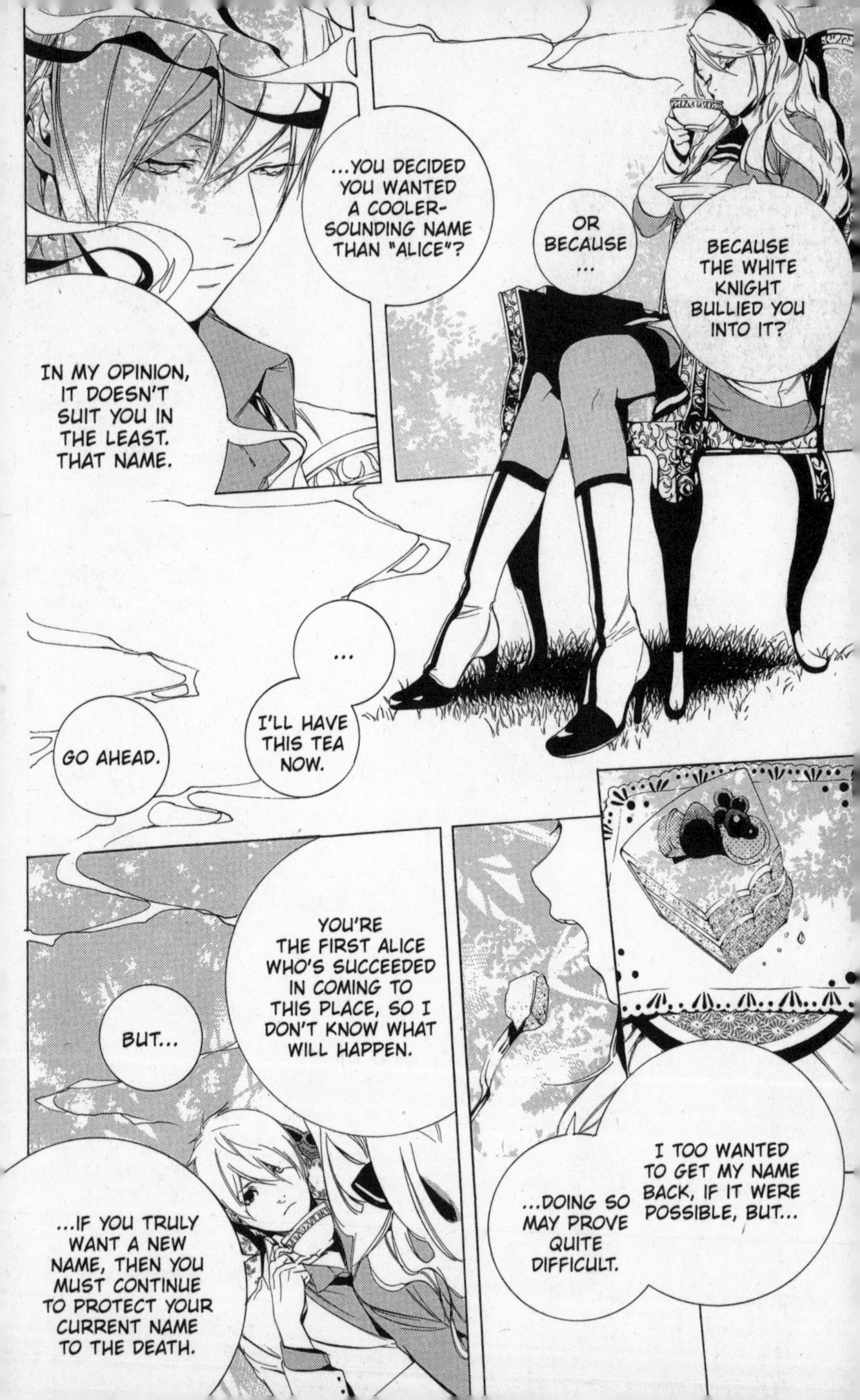
BECAUSE THE WHITE KNIGHT BULLIED YOU INTO IT?
OR BECAUSE ...
...YOU DECIDED YOU WANTED A COOLER-SOUNDING NAME THAN "ALICE"?
IN MY OPINION, IT DOESN'T SUIT YOU IN THE LEAST. THAT NAME.
...
I'LL HAVE THIS TEA NOW.
GO AHEAD.
I TOO WANTED TO GET MY NAME BACK, IF IT WERE POSSIBLE, BUT...
...DOING SO MAY PROVE QUITE DIFFICULT.
YOU'RE THE FIRST ALICE WHO'S SUCCEEDED IN COMING TO THIS PLACE, SO I DON'T KNOW WHAT WILL HAPPEN.
BUT...
...IF YOU TRULY WANT A NEW NAME, THEN YOU MUST CONTINUE TO PROTECT YOUR CURRENT NAME TO THE DEATH.

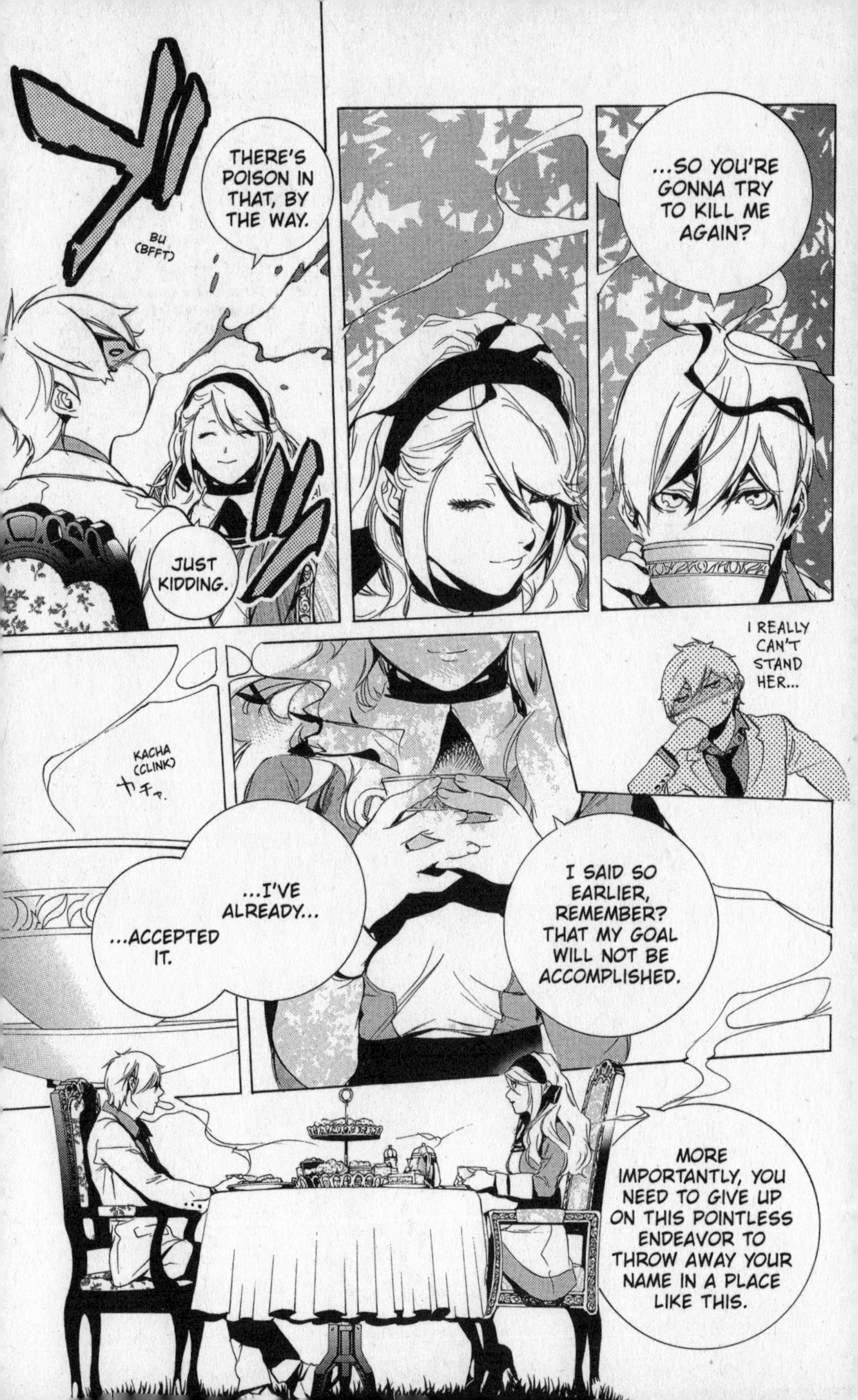
...SO YOU'RE GONNA TRY TO KILL ME AGAIN?
THERE'S POISON IN THAT, BY THE WAY.
BU (BFFT)
JUST KIDDING.
I REALLY CAN'T STAND HER...
KACHA (CLINK)
I SAID SO EARLIER, REMEMBER? THAT MY GOAL WILL NOT BE ACCOMPLISHED.
...I'VE ALREADY...
...ACCEPTED IT.
MORE IMPORTANTLY, YOU NEED TO GIVE UP ON THIS POINTLESS ENDEAVOR TO THROW AWAY YOUR NAME IN A PLACE LIKE THIS.

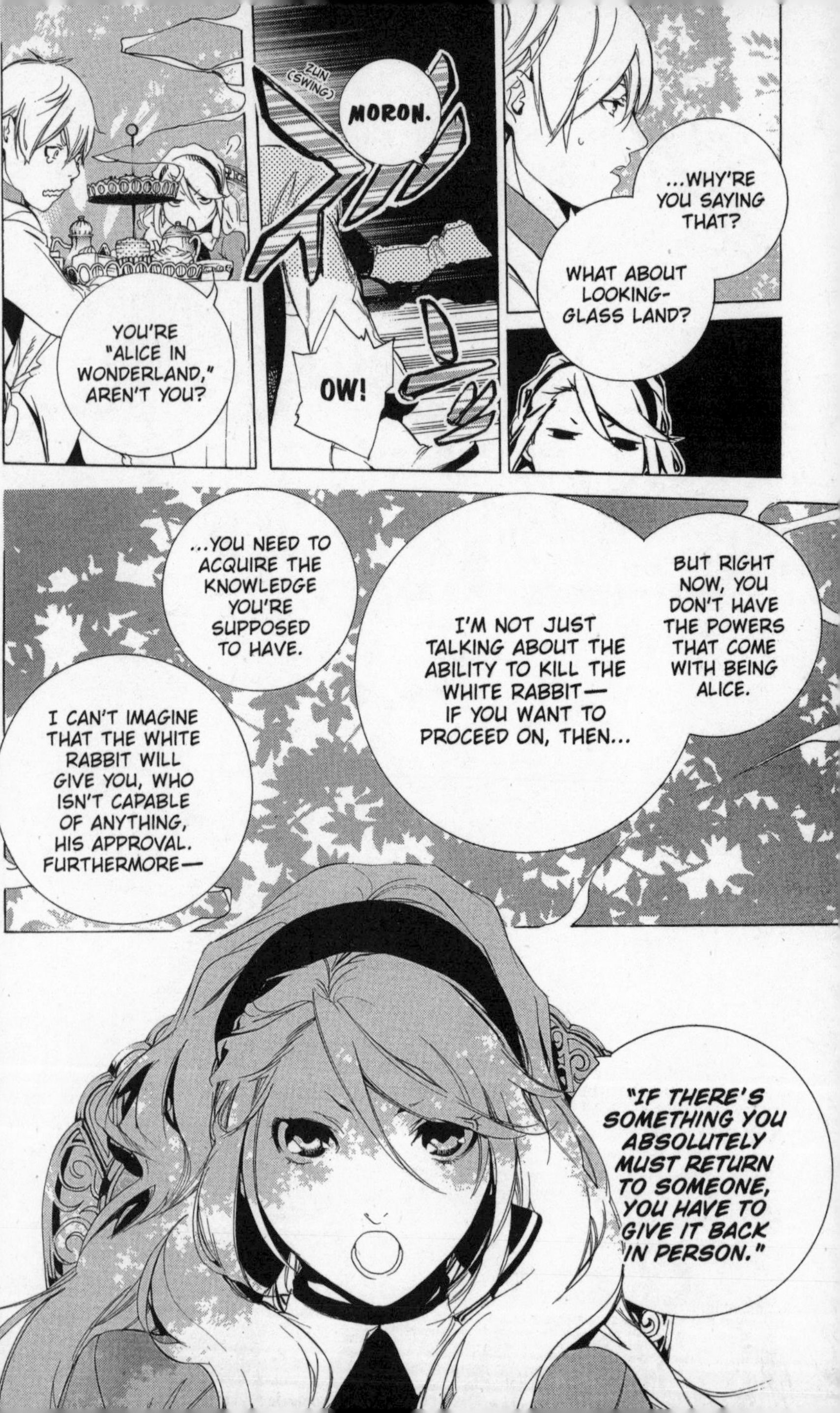
...WHY'RE YOU SAYING THAT?
WHAT ABOUT LOOKING-GLASS LAND?
ZUN (SWING)
MORON.
OW!
YOU'RE "ALICE IN WONDERLAND," AREN'T YOU?
BUT RIGHT NOW, YOU DON'T HAVE THE POWERS THAT COME WITH BEING ALICE.
I'M NOT JUST TALKING ABOUT THE ABILITY TO KILL THE WHITE RABBIT— IF YOU WANT TO PROCEED ON, THEN...
...YOU NEED TO ACQUIRE THE KNOWLEDGE YOU'RE SUPPOSED TO HAVE.
I CAN'T IMAGINE THAT THE WHITE RABBIT WILL GIVE YOU, WHO ISN'T CAPABLE OF ANYTHING, HIS APPROVAL. FURTHERMORE—
"IF THERE'S SOMETHING YOU ABSOLUTELY MUST RETURN TO SOMEONE, YOU HAVE TO GIVE IT BACK IN PERSON."

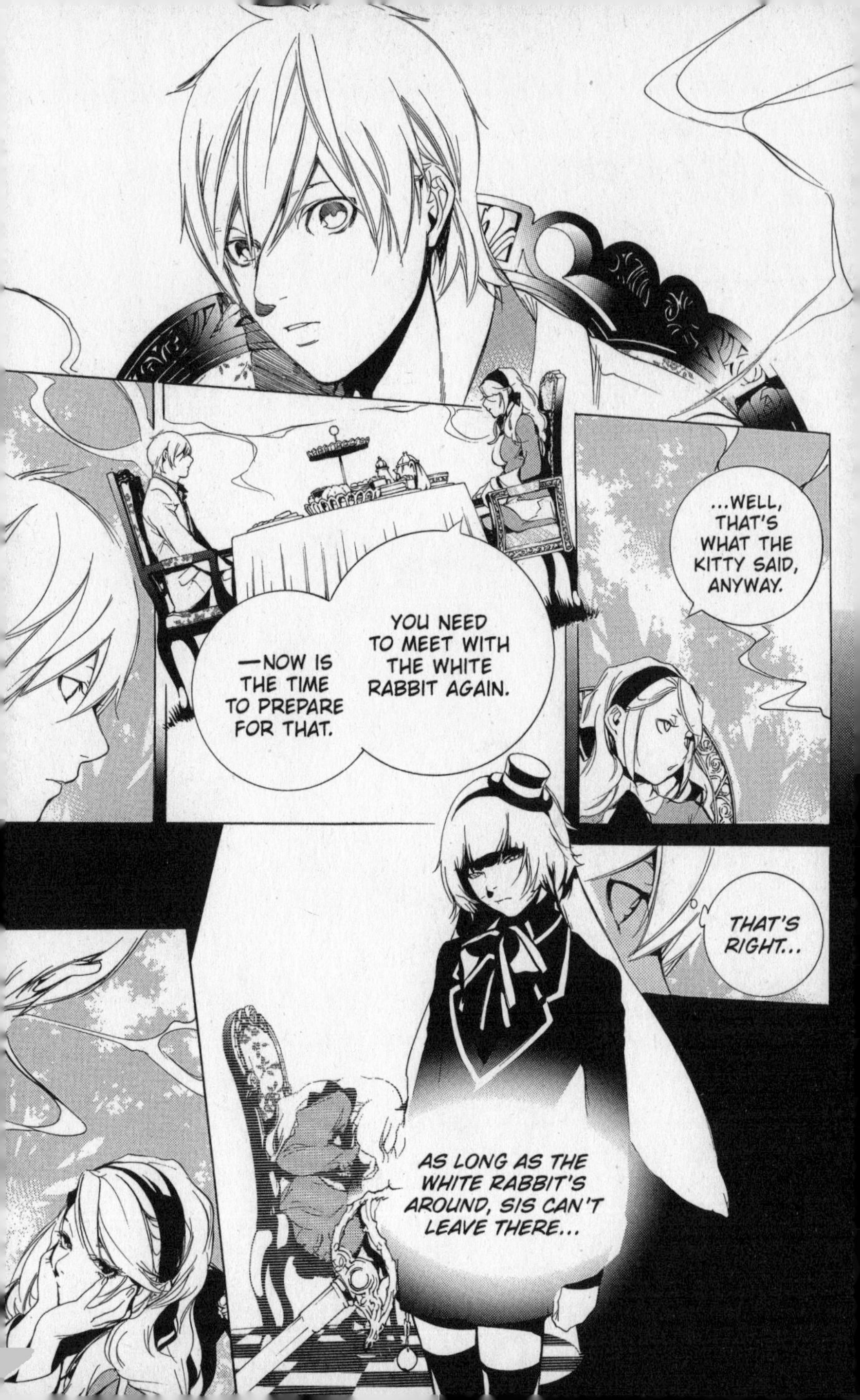
...WELL, THAT'S WHAT THE KITTY SAID, ANYWAY.
YOU NEED TO MEET WITH THE WHITE RABBIT AGAIN.
—NOW IS THE TIME TO PREPARE FOR THAT.
THAT'S RIGHT...
AS LONG AS THE WHITE RABBIT'S AROUND, SIS CAN'T LEAVE THERE...

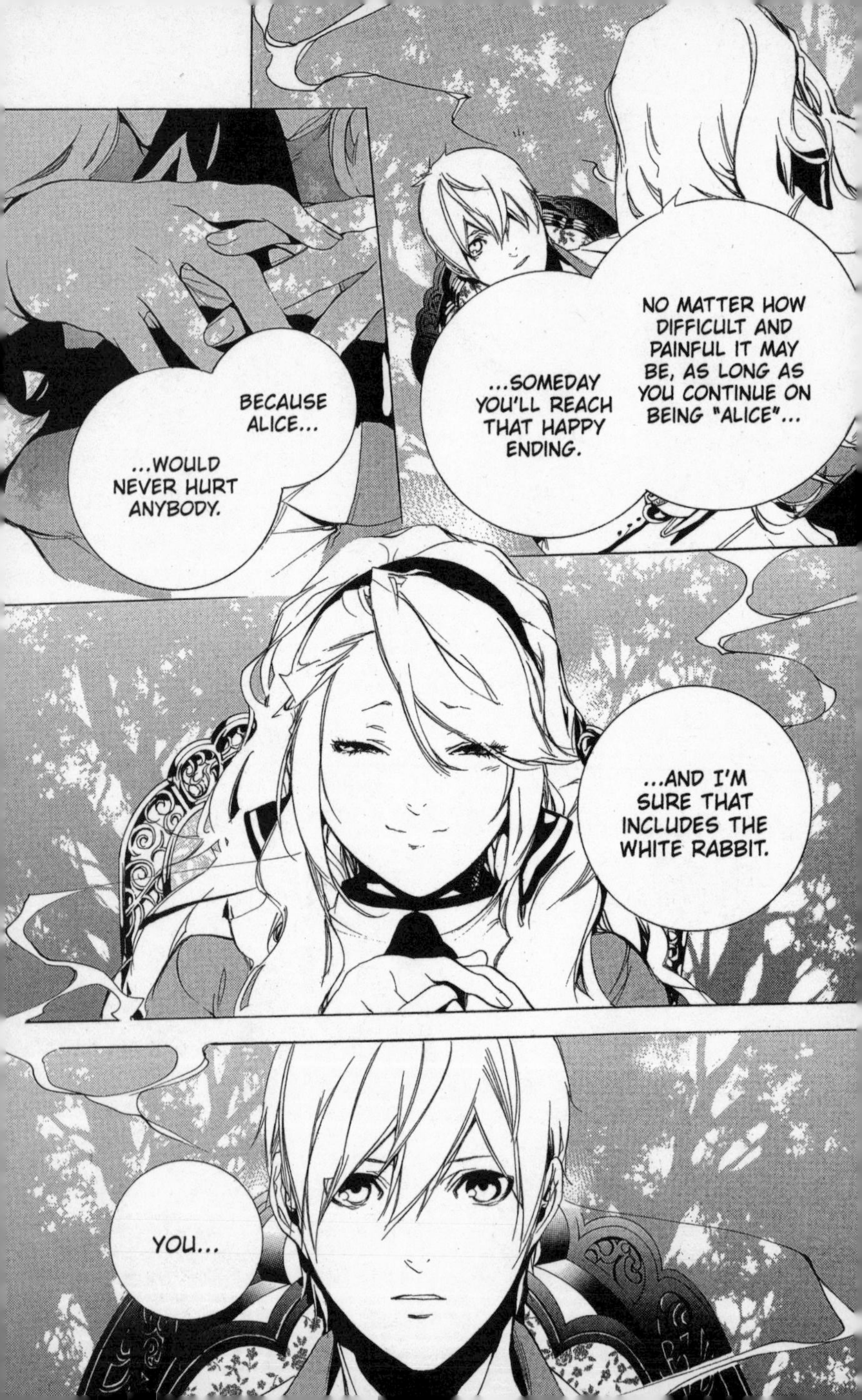
NO MATTER HOW DIFFICULT AND PAINFUL IT MAY BE, AS LONG AS YOU CONTINUE ON BEING "ALICE"...
...SOMEDAY YOU'LL REACH THAT HAPPY ENDING.
BECAUSE ALICE...
...WOULD NEVER HURT ANYBODY.
...AND I'M SURE THAT INCLUDES THE WHITE RABBIT.
YOU...

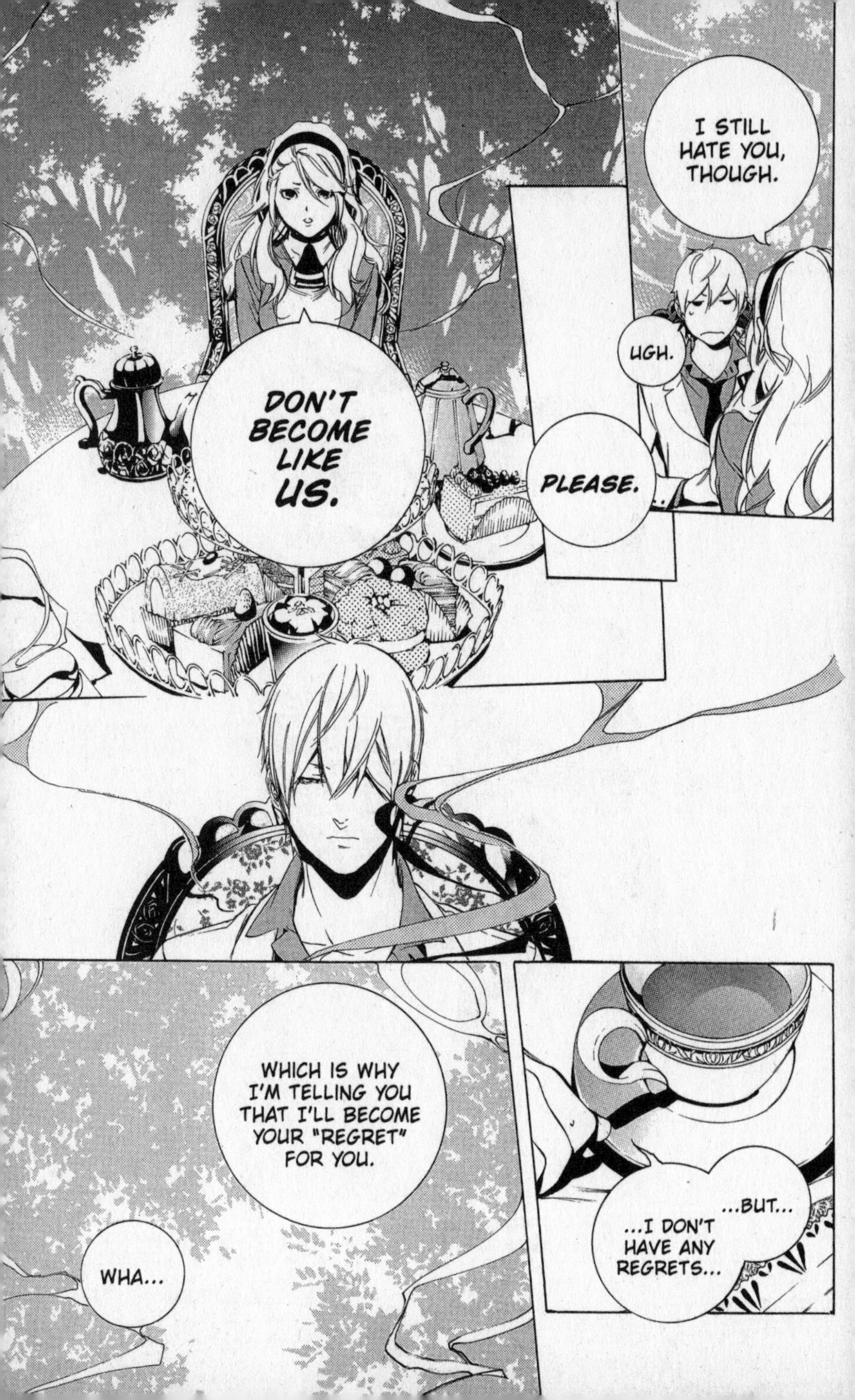
I STILL HATE YOU, THOUGH.
UGH.
PLEASE.
DON'T BECOME LIKE US.
...BUT...
...I DON'T HAVE ANY REGRETS...
WHICH IS WHY I'M TELLING YOU THAT I'LL BECOME YOUR "REGRET" FOR YOU.
WHA...

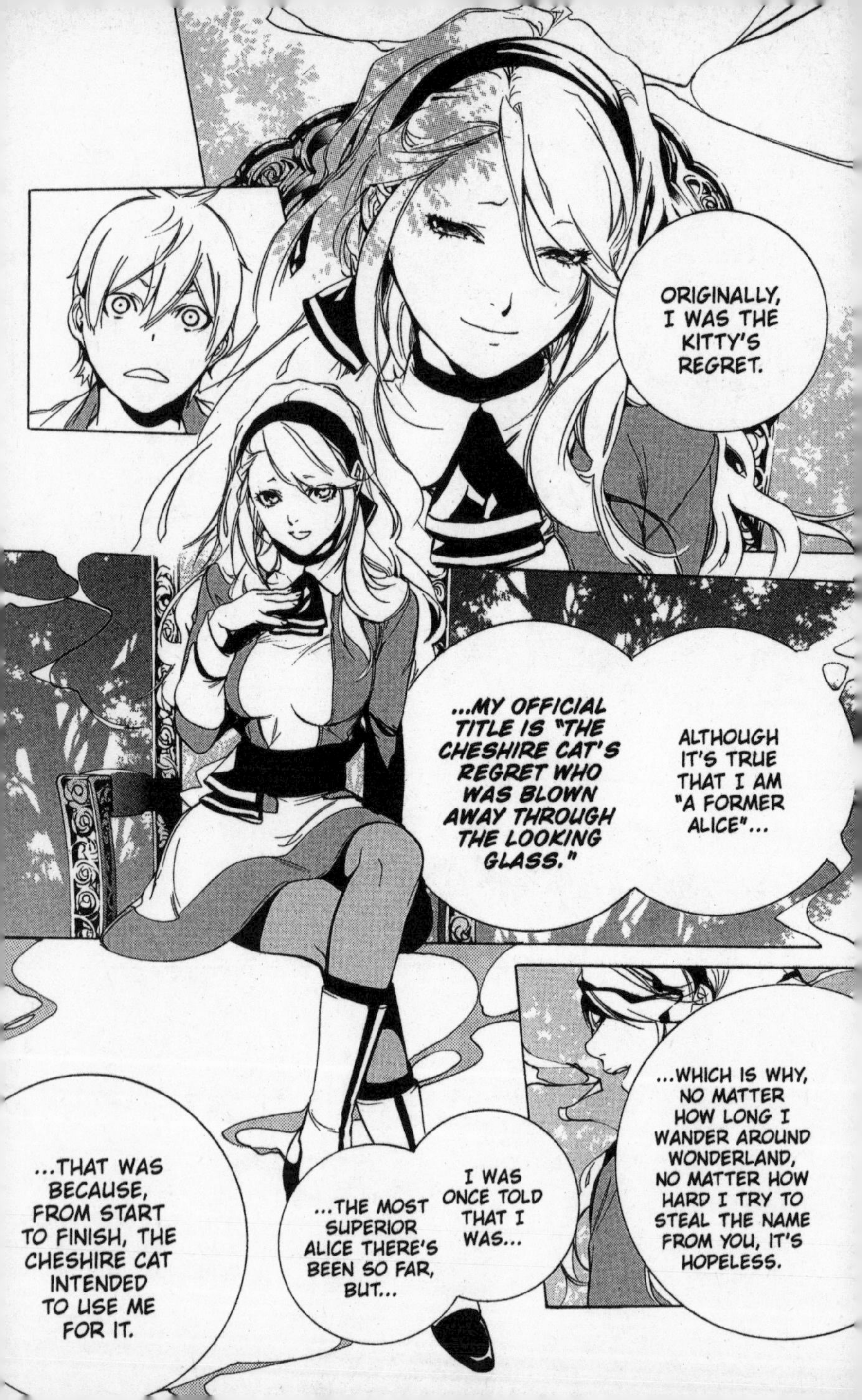
ORIGINALLY, I WAS THE KITTY'S REGRET.
ALTHOUGH IT'S TRUE THAT I AM "A FORMER ALICE"...
...MY OFFICIAL TITLE IS "THE CHESHIRE CAT'S REGRET WHO WAS BLOWN AWAY THROUGH THE LOOKING GLASS."
...WHICH IS WHY, NO MATTER HOW LONG I WANDER AROUND WONDERLAND, NO MATTER HOW HARD I TRY TO STEAL THE NAME FROM YOU, IT'S HOPELESS.
I WAS ONCE TOLD THAT I WAS...
...THE MOST SUPERIOR ALICE THERE'S BEEN SO FAR, BUT...
...THAT WAS BECAUSE, FROM START TO FINISH, THE CHESHIRE CAT INTENDED TO USE ME FOR IT.

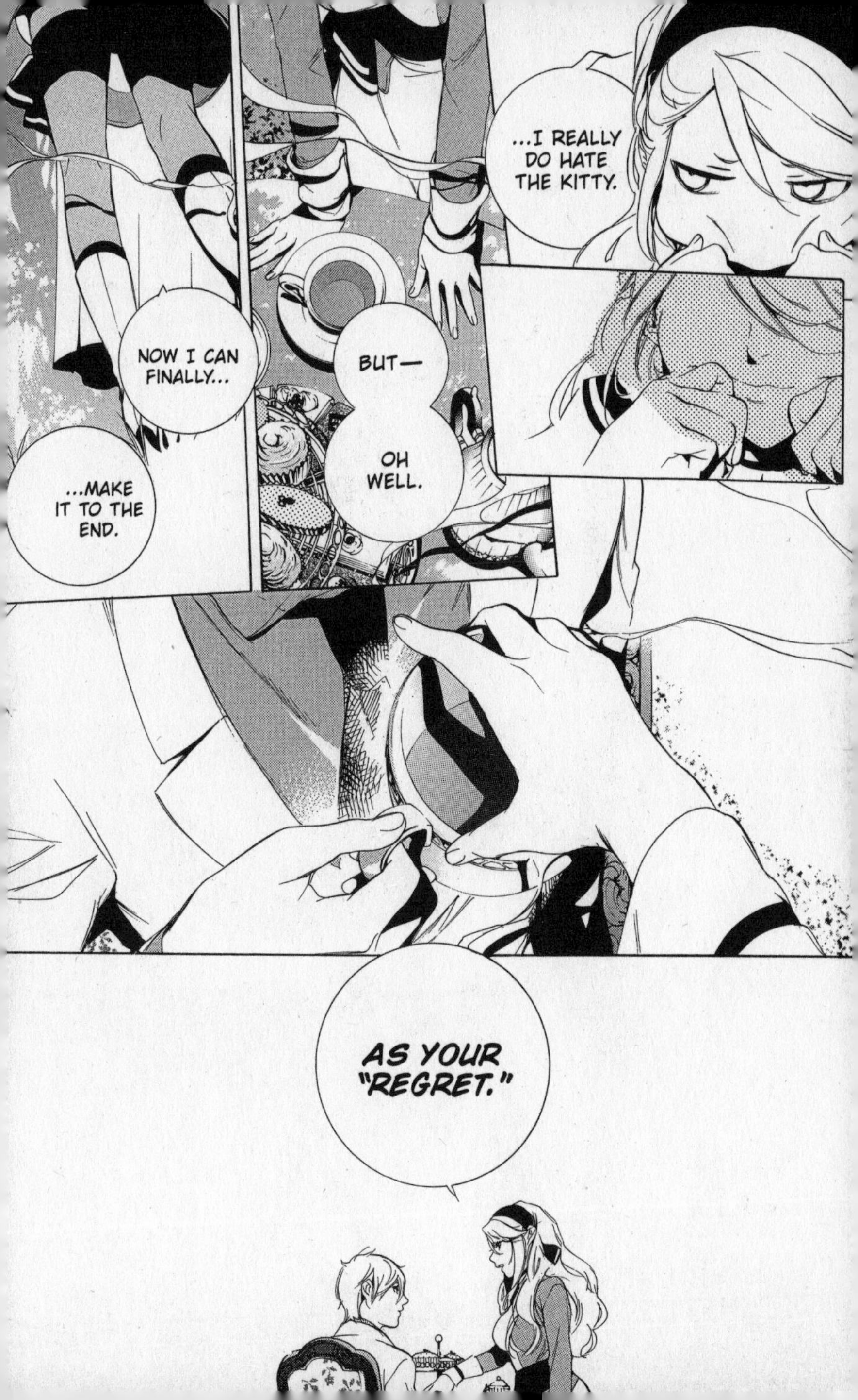
...I REALLY DO HATE THE KITTY.
BUT—
OH WELL.
NOW I CAN FINALLY...
...MAKE IT TO THE END.
AS YOUR "REGRET."

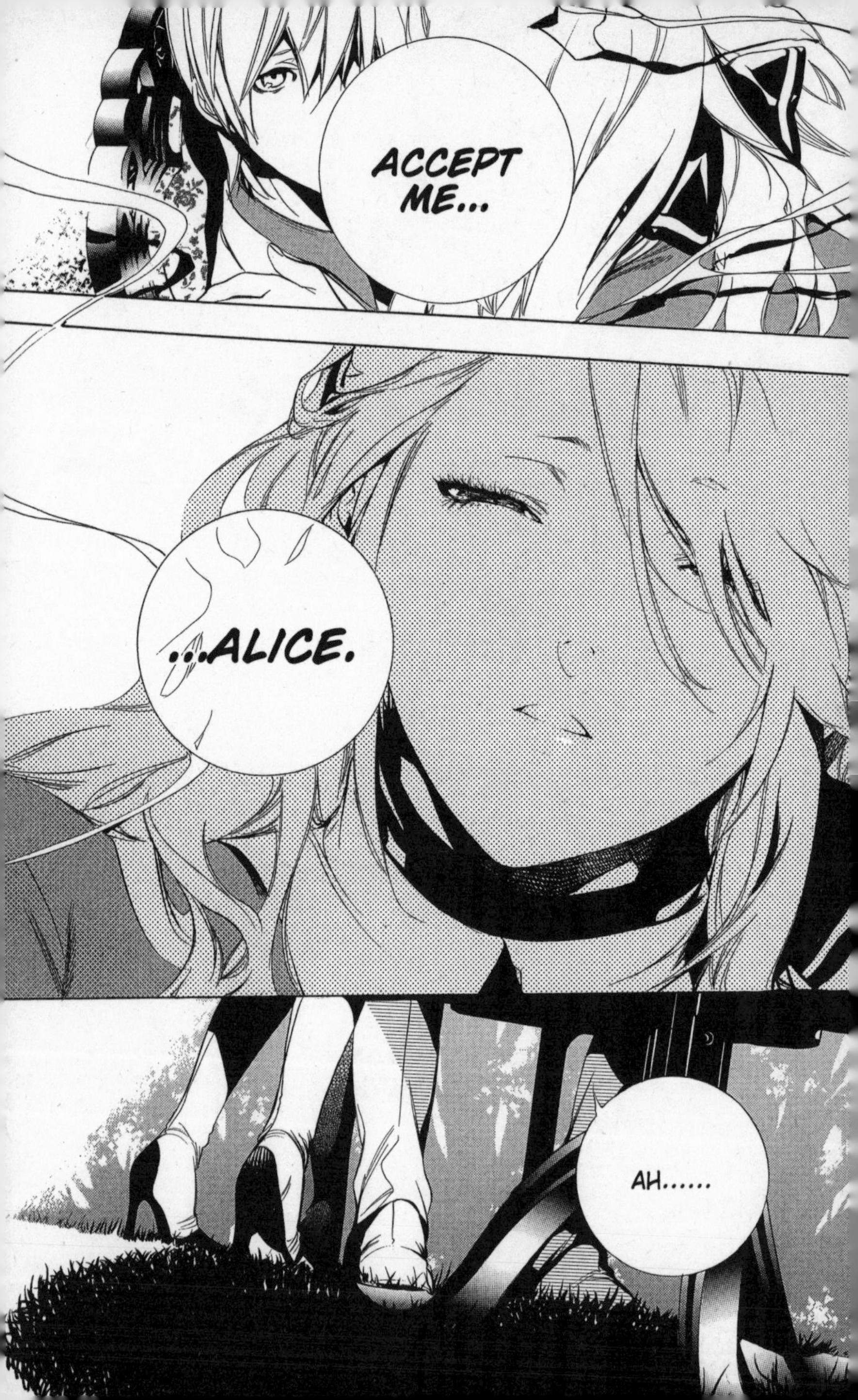
ACCEPT ME...
...ALICE.
AH......

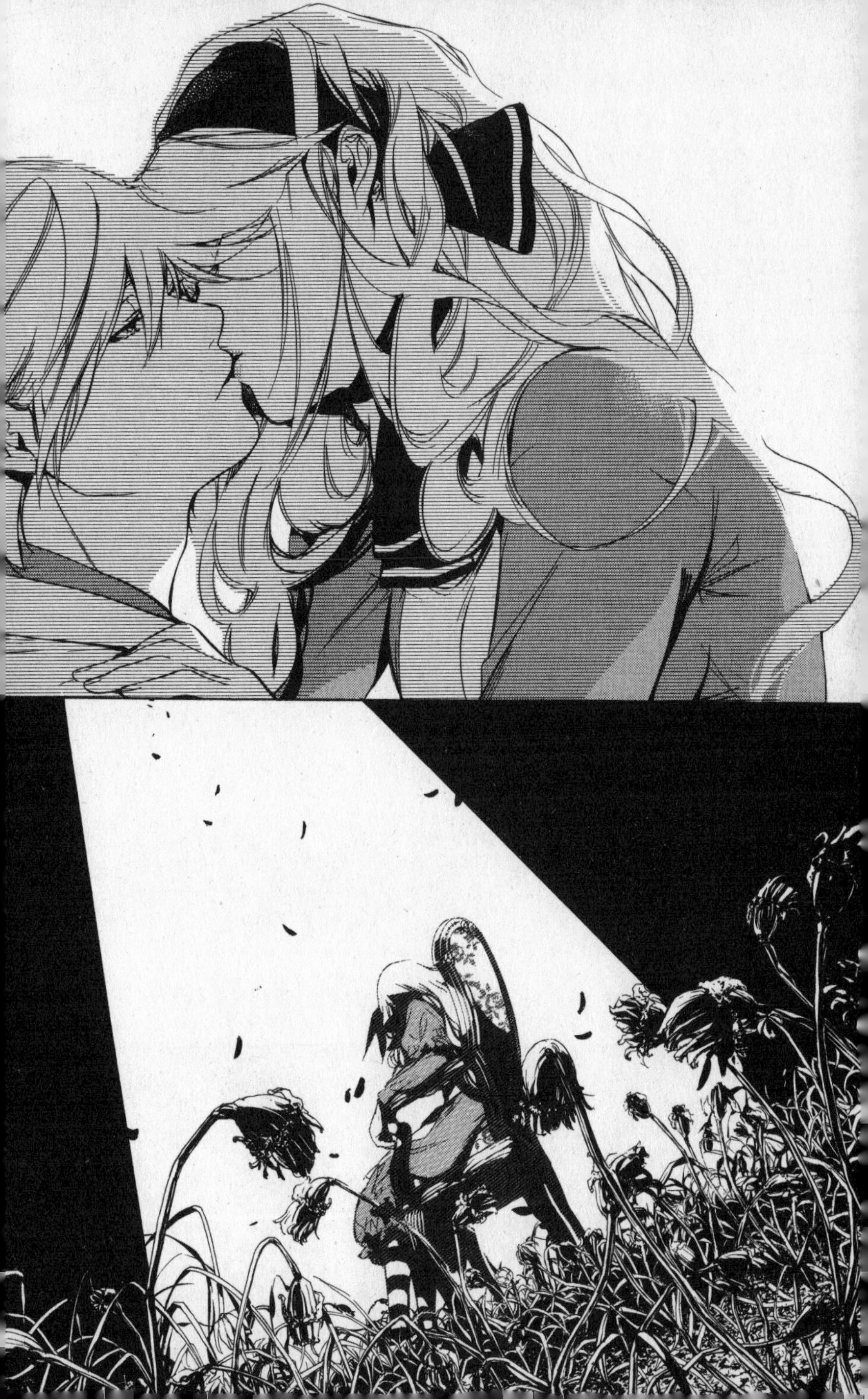

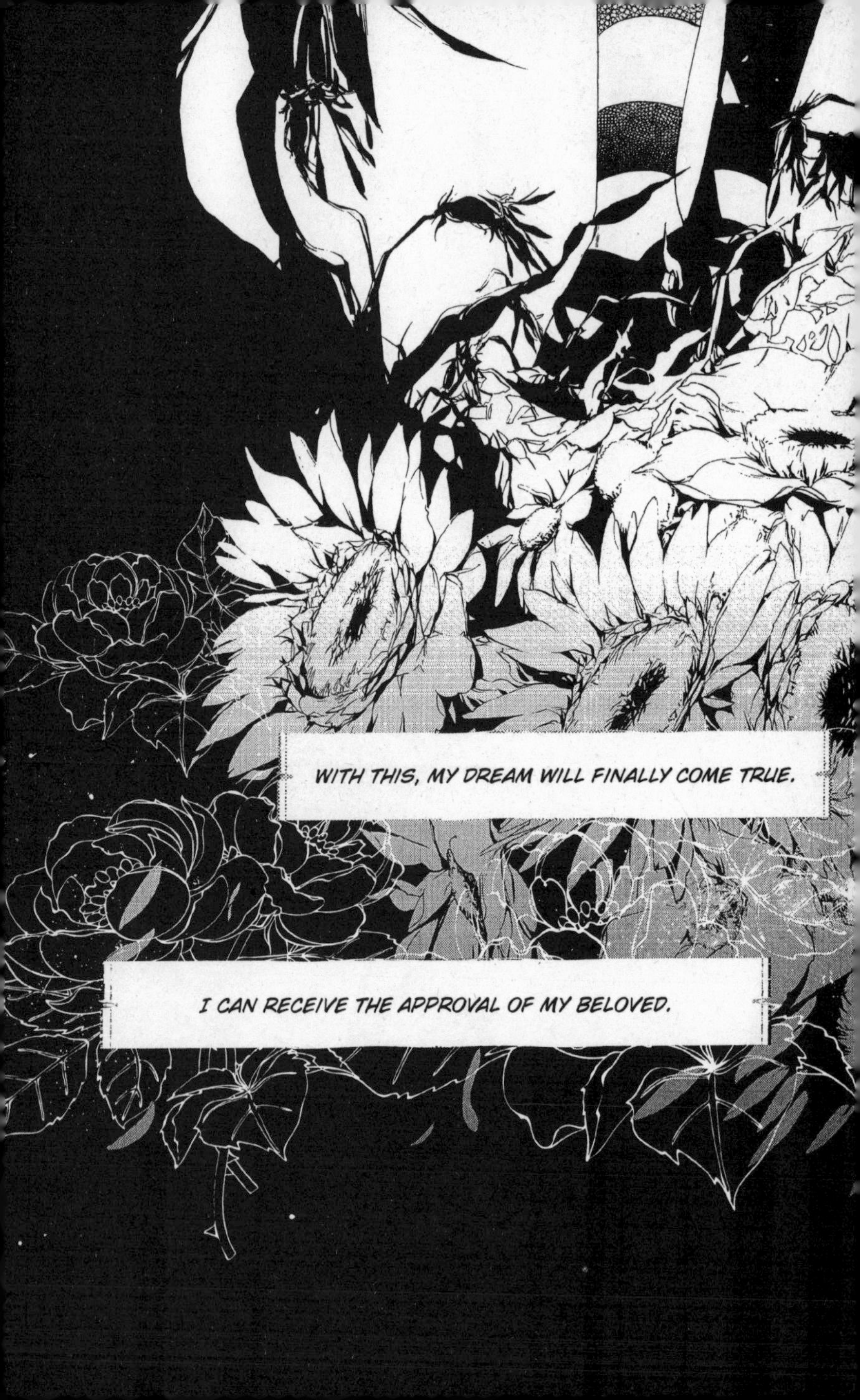
WITH THIS, MY DREAM WILL FINALLY COME TRUE.
I CAN RECEIVE THE APPROVAL OF MY BELOVED.

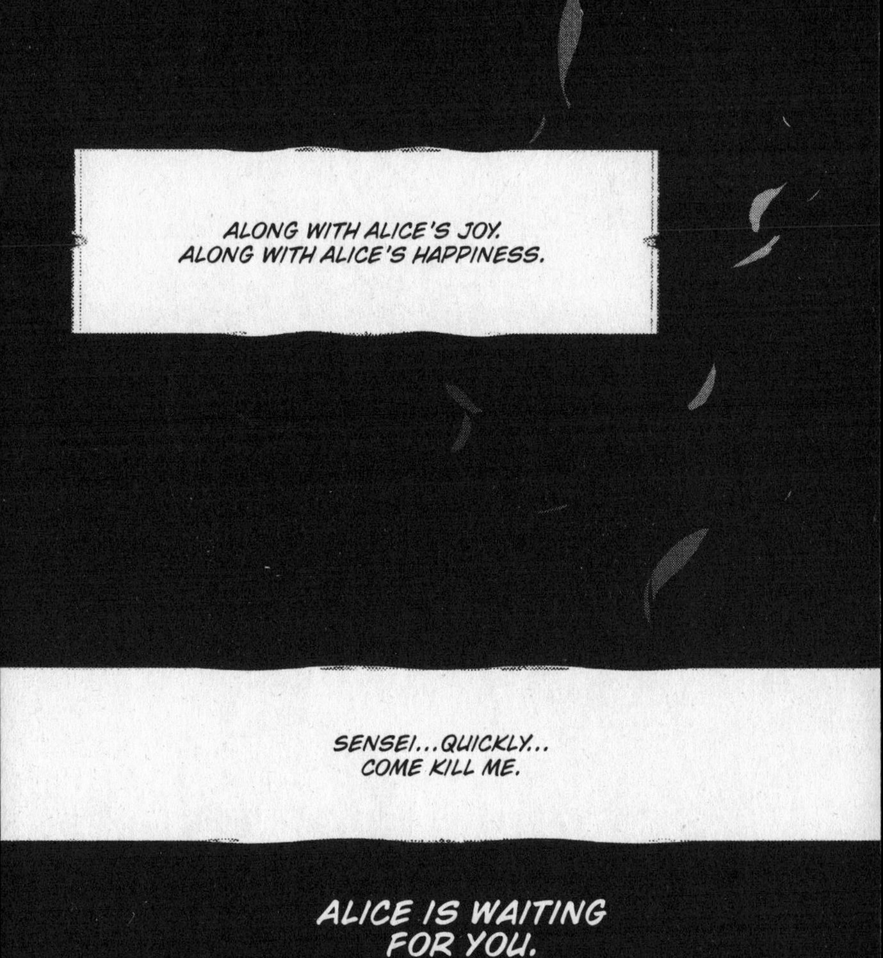
ALONG WITH ALICE'S JOY. ALONG WITH ALICE'S HAPPINESS.
SENSEI...QUICKLY... COME KILL ME.
ALICE IS WAITING FOR YOU.

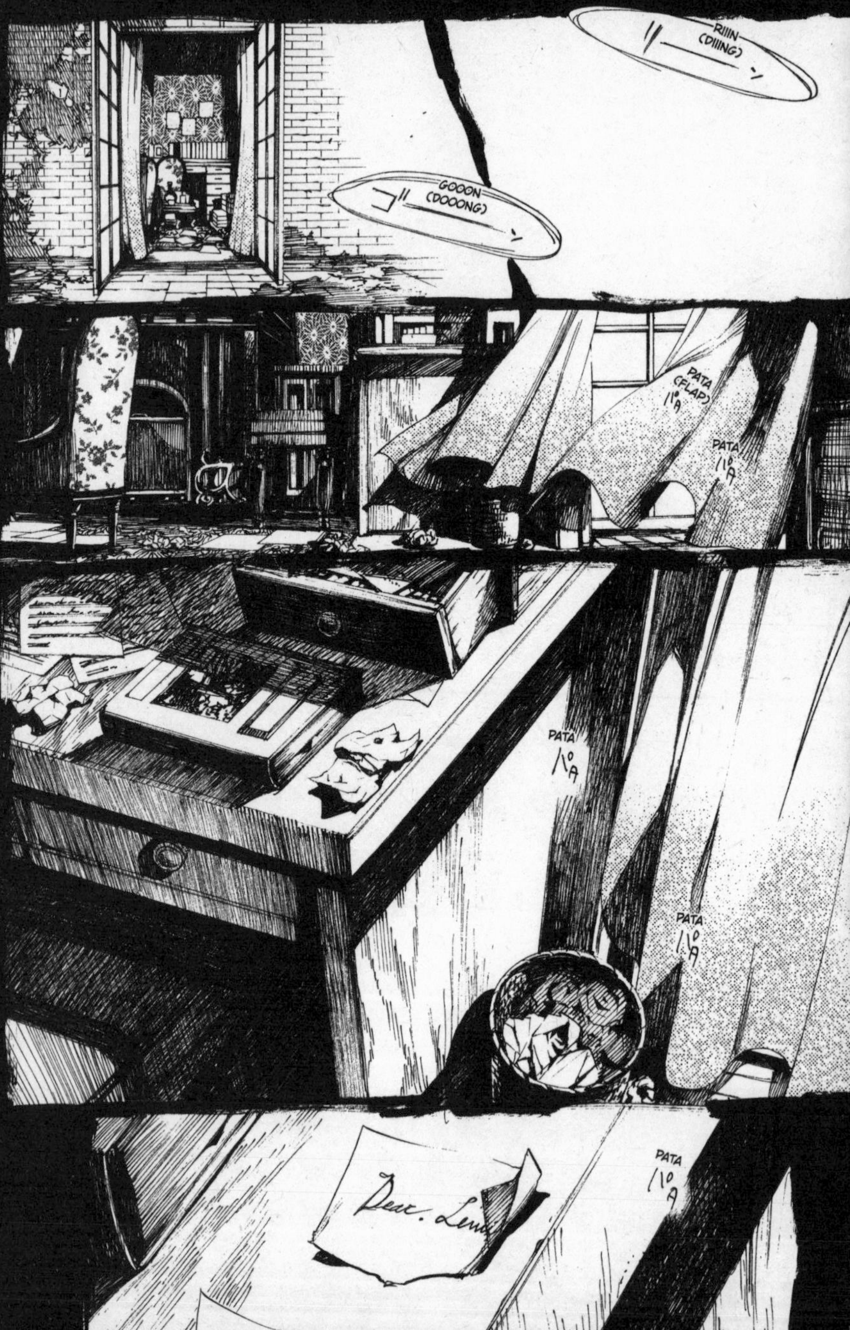
RIIN (DIIING)
GOOON (DOOONG)
PATA (FLAP)
PATA
PATA
PATA
PATA
Dear. Len

Chapter 48

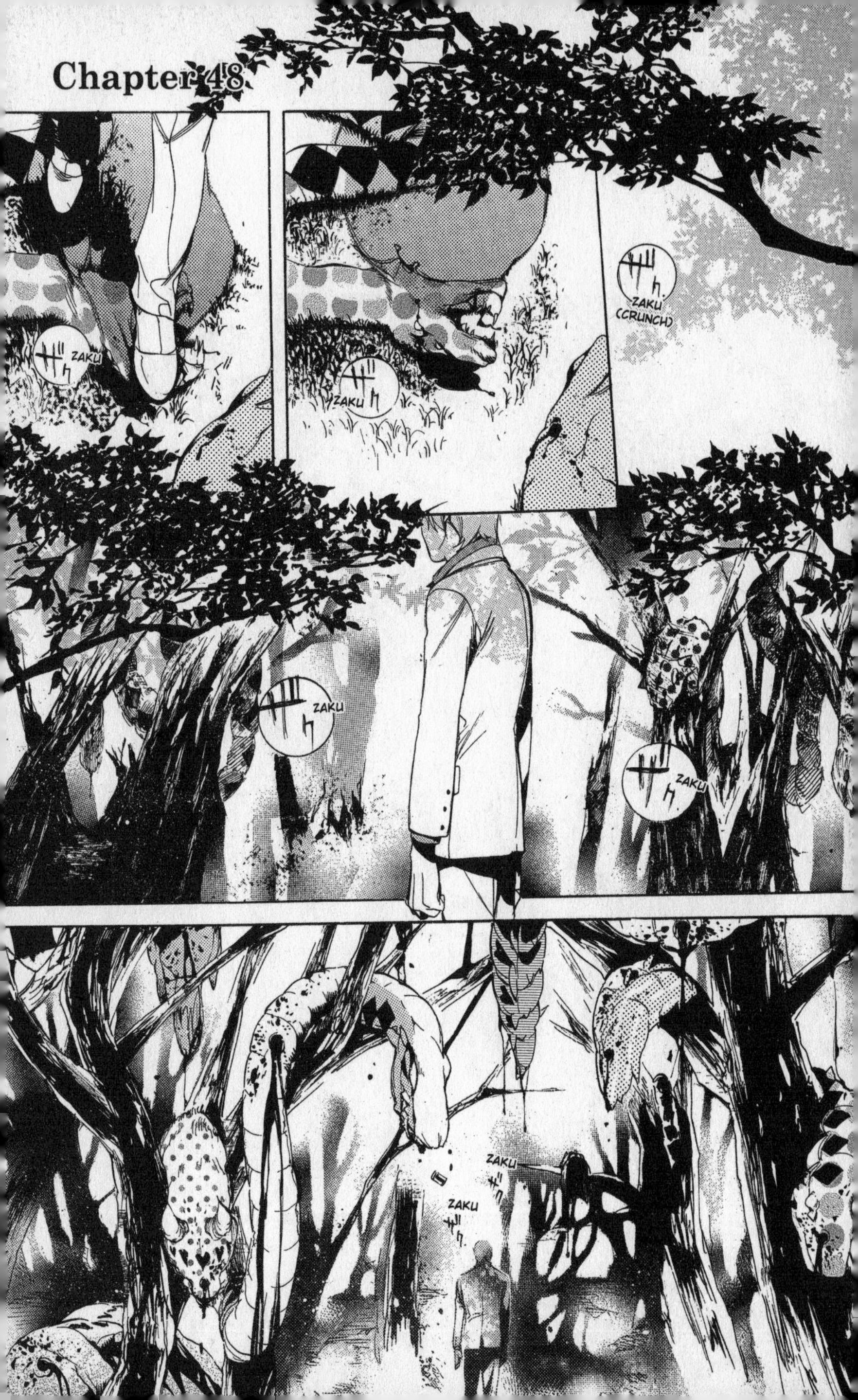
ZAKU (CRUNCH)
ZAKU
ZAKU
ZAKU
ZAKU
ZAKU
ZAKU

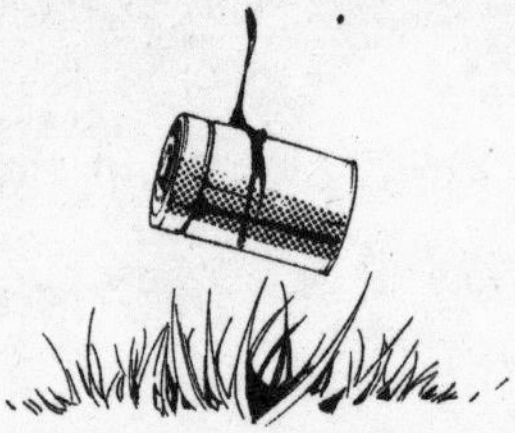

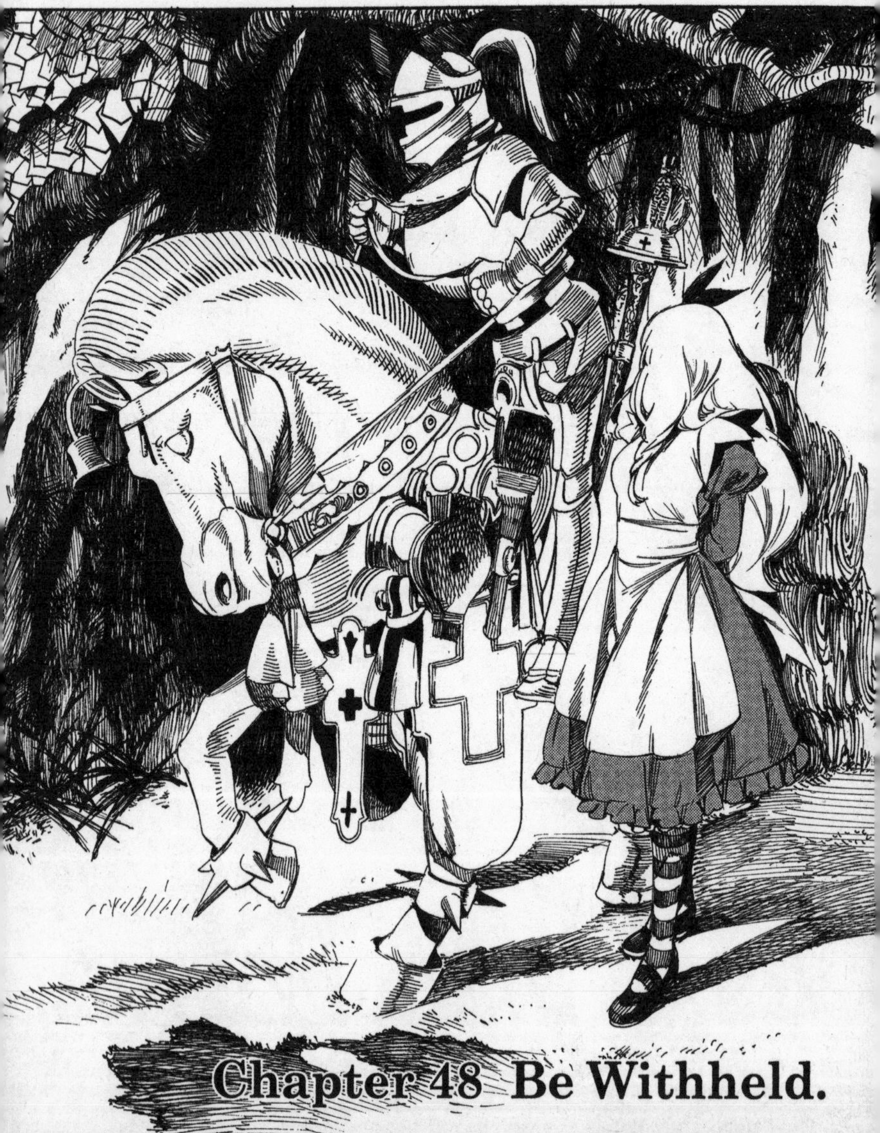

Chapter 48 Be Withheld.

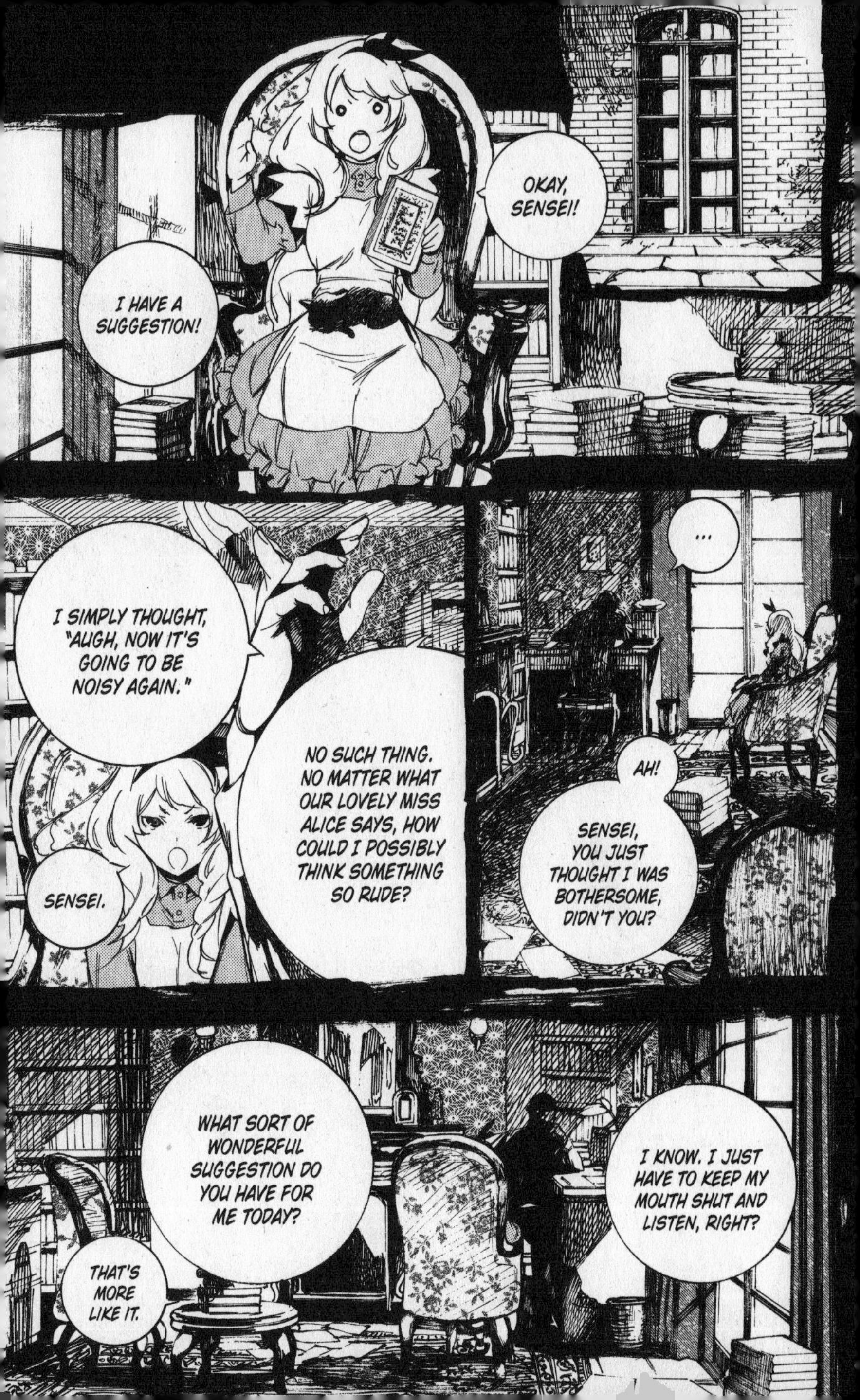
OKAY, SENSEI!
I HAVE A SUGGESTION!
...
AH!
SENSEI, YOU JUST THOUGHT I WAS BOTHERSOME, DIDN'T YOU?
NO SUCH THING. NO MATTER WHAT OUR LOVELY MISS ALICE SAYS, HOW COULD I POSSIBLY THINK SOMETHING SO RUDE?
SENSEI.
I SIMPLY THOUGHT, "AUGH, NOW IT'S GOING TO BE NOISY AGAIN."
I KNOW. I JUST HAVE TO KEEP MY MOUTH SHUT AND LISTEN, RIGHT?
THAT'S MORE LIKE IT.
WHAT SORT OF WONDERFUL SUGGESTION DO YOU HAVE FOR ME TODAY?

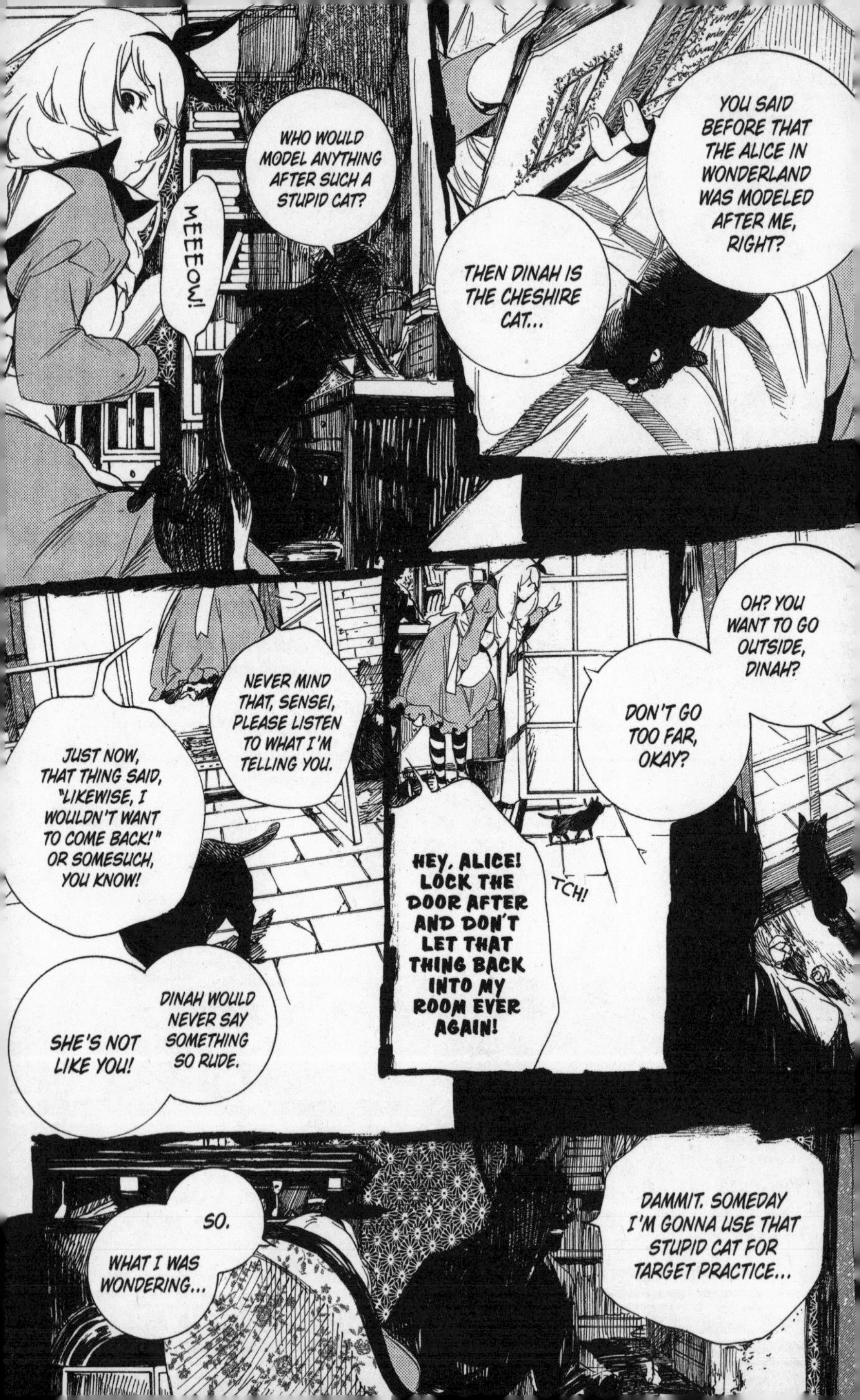
YOU SAID BEFORE THAT THE ALICE IN WONDERLAND WAS MODELED AFTER ME, RIGHT?
THEN DINAH IS THE CHESHIRE CAT...
WHO WOULD MODEL ANYTHING AFTER SUCH A STUPID CAT?
MEEEOW!
OH? YOU WANT TO GO OUTSIDE, DINAH?
DON'T GO TOO FAR, OKAY?
TCH!
HEY, ALICE! LOCK THE DOOR AFTER AND DON'T LET THAT THING BACK INTO MY ROOM EVER AGAIN!
NEVER MIND THAT, SENSEI, PLEASE LISTEN TO WHAT I'M TELLING YOU.
JUST NOW, THAT THING SAID, "LIKEWISE, I WOULDN'T WANT TO COME BACK!" OR SOMESUCH, YOU KNOW!
DINAH WOULD NEVER SAY SOMETHING SO RUDE.
SHE'S NOT LIKE YOU!
DAMMIT. SOMEDAY I'M GONNA USE THAT STUPID CAT FOR TARGET PRACTICE...
SO.
WHAT I WAS WONDERING...

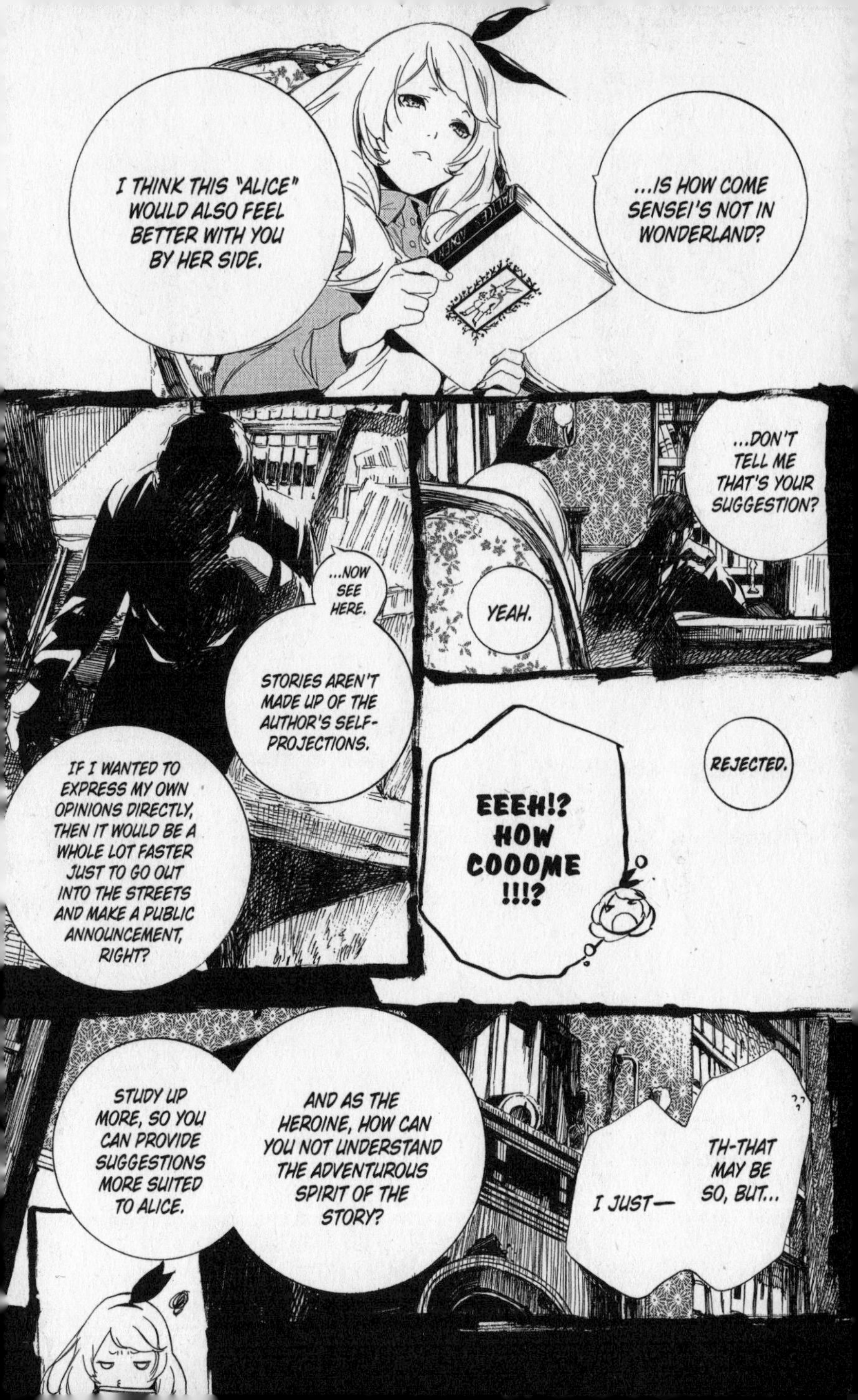
...IS HOW COME SENSEI'S NOT IN WONDERLAND?
I THINK THIS "ALICE" WOULD ALSO FEEL BETTER WITH YOU BY HER SIDE.
...DON'T TELL ME THAT'S YOUR SUGGESTION?
YEAH.
REJECTED.
EEEH!? HOW COOOME!!!?
...NOW SEE HERE.
STORIES AREN'T MADE UP OF THE AUTHOR'S SELF-PROJECTIONS.
IF I WANTED TO EXPRESS MY OWN OPINIONS DIRECTLY, THEN IT WOULD BE A WHOLE LOT FASTER JUST TO GO OUT INTO THE STREETS AND MAKE A PUBLIC ANNOUNCEMENT, RIGHT?
TH-THAT MAY BE SO, BUT...
I JUST—
AND AS THE HEROINE, HOW CAN YOU NOT UNDERSTAND THE ADVENTUROUS SPIRIT OF THE STORY?
STUDY UP MORE, SO YOU CAN PROVIDE SUGGESTIONS MORE SUITED TO ALICE.

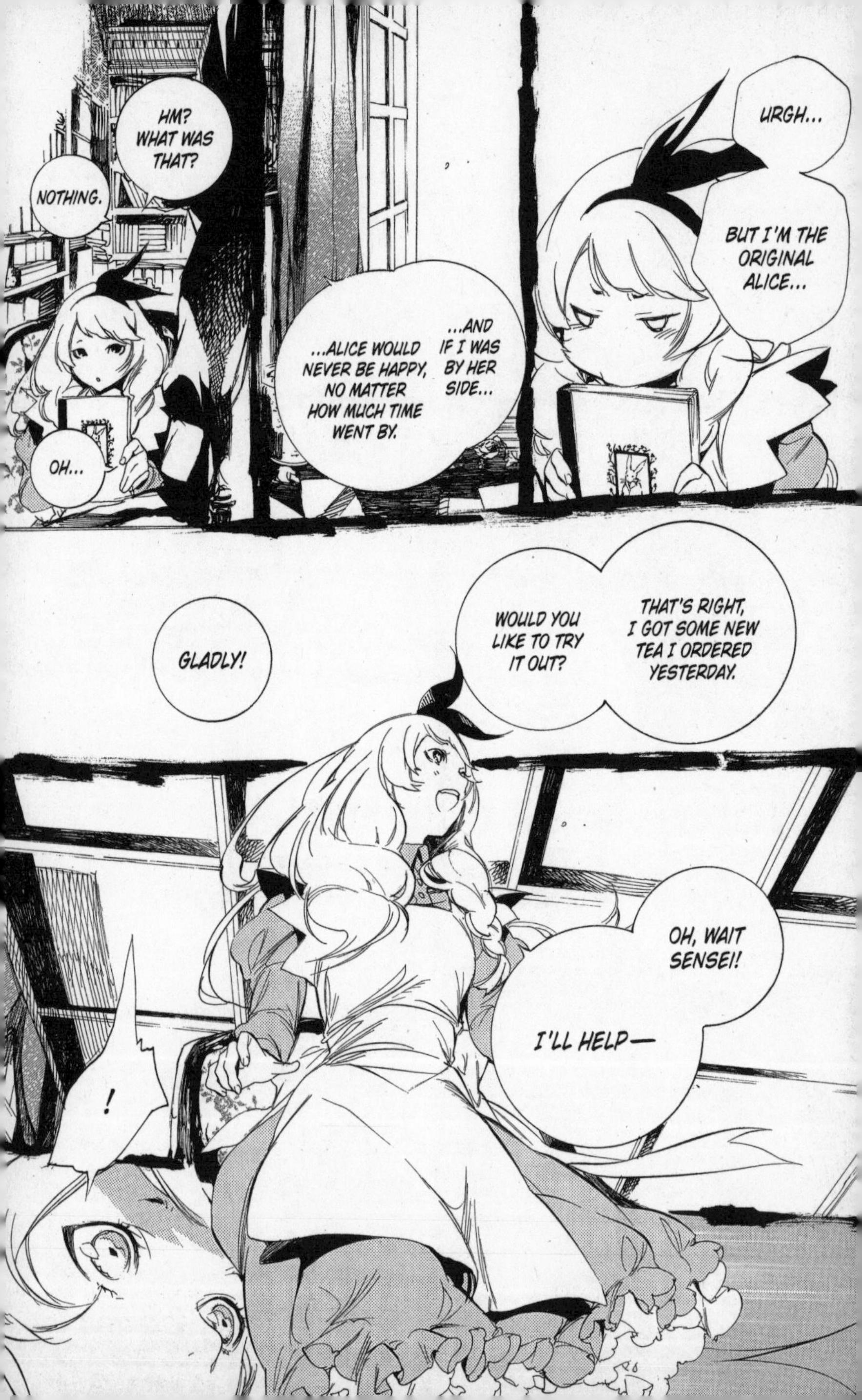
URGH...
BUT I'M THE ORIGINAL ALICE...
...AND IF I WAS BY HER SIDE...
...ALICE WOULD NEVER BE HAPPY, NO MATTER HOW MUCH TIME WENT BY.
HM? WHAT WAS THAT?
NOTHING.
OH...
THAT'S RIGHT, I GOT SOME NEW TEA I ORDERED YESTERDAY.
WOULD YOU LIKE TO TRY IT OUT?
GLADLY!
OH, WAIT SENSEI!
I'LL HELP—
!

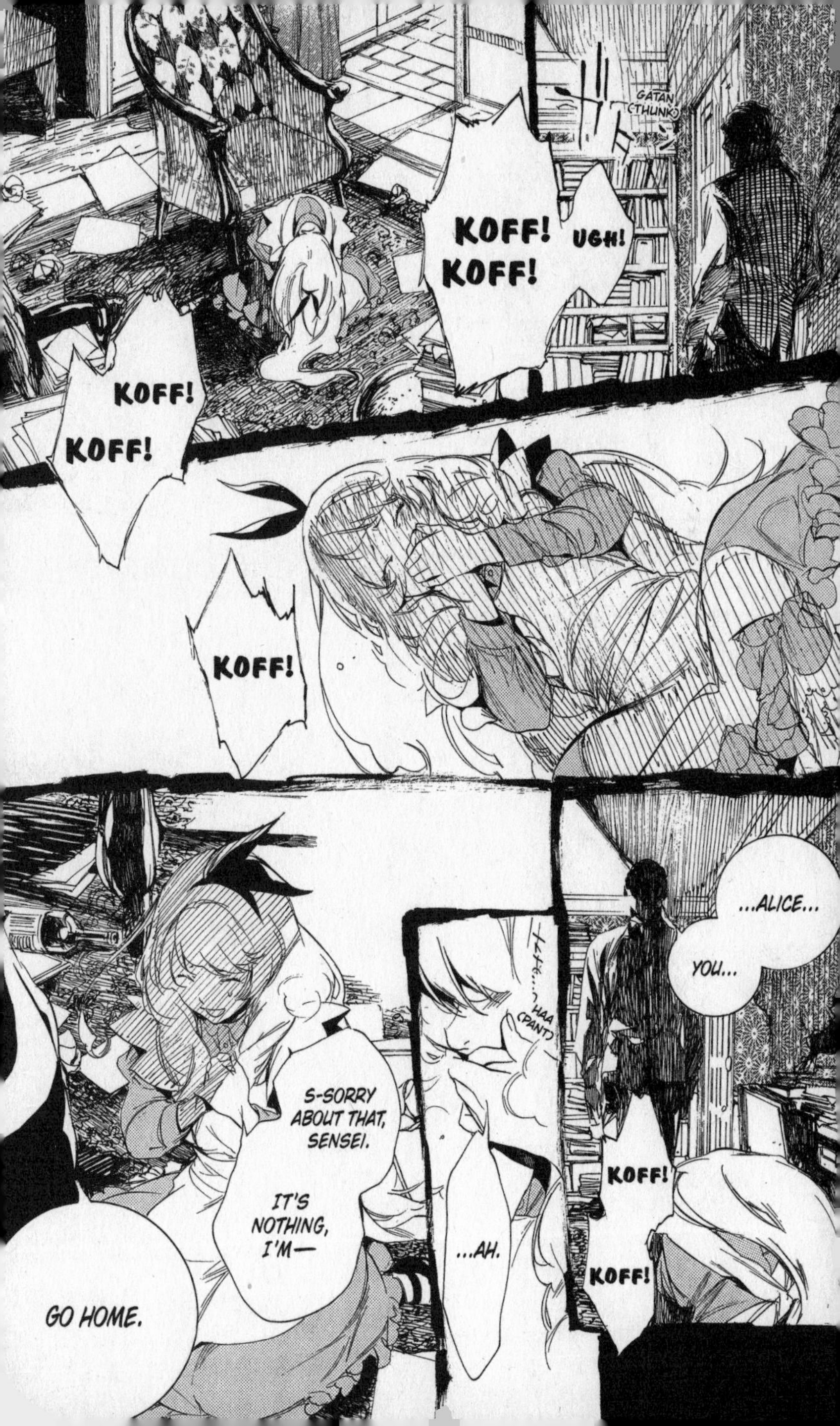
GATAN (THUNK)
UGH!
KOFF! KOFF!
KOFF! KOFF!
KOFF!
...ALICE...
YOU...
KOFF!
KOFF!
HAA (PANT)
...AH.
S-SORRY ABOUT THAT, SENSEI.
IT'S NOTHING, I'M—
GO HOME.

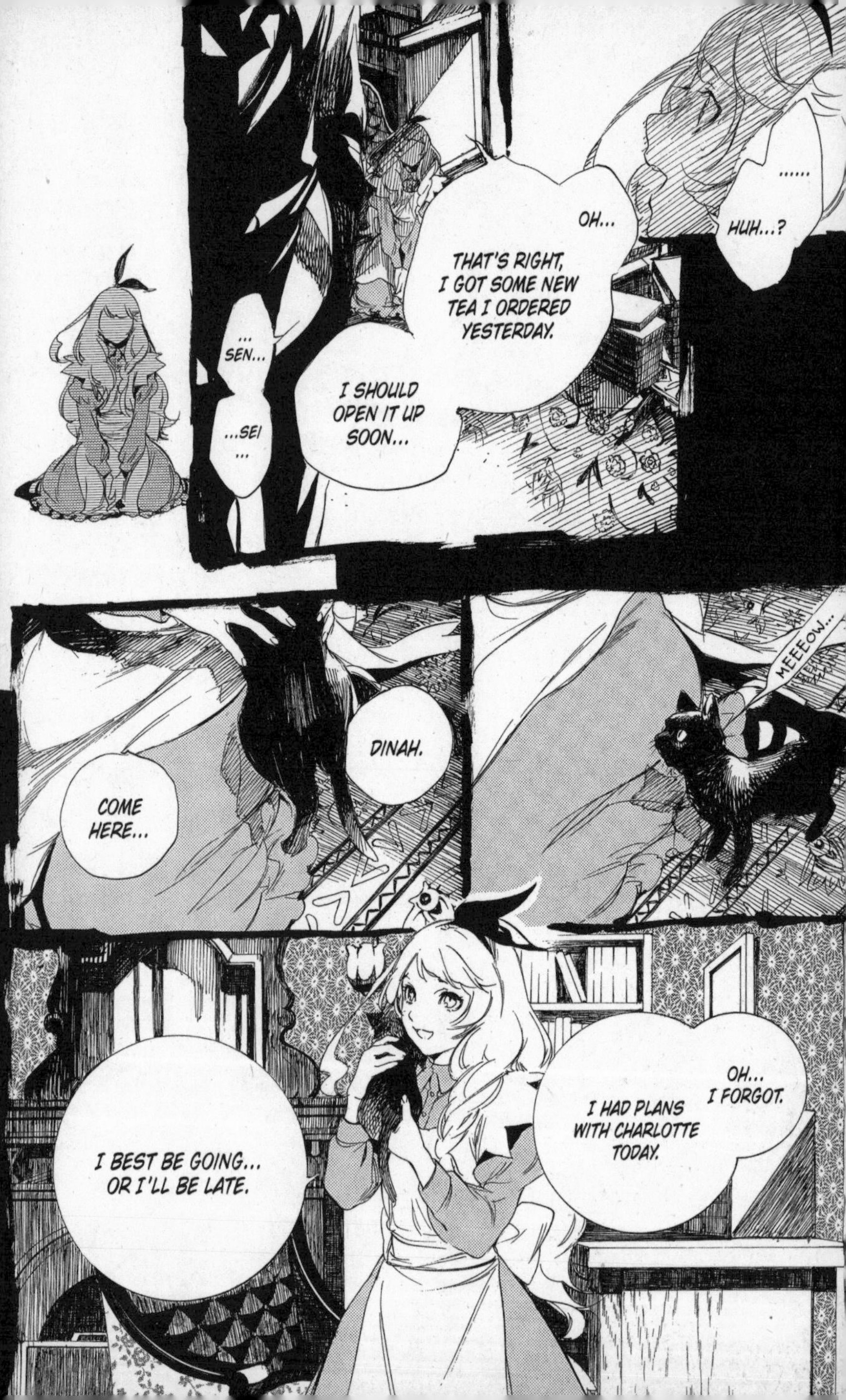
......
HUH...?
OH...
THAT'S RIGHT, I GOT SOME NEW TEA I ORDERED YESTERDAY.
I SHOULD OPEN IT UP SOON...
... SEN...
...SEI ...
MEEEOW...
DINAH.
COME HERE...
OH... I FORGOT.
I HAD PLANS WITH CHARLOTTE TODAY.
I BEST BE GOING... OR I'LL BE LATE.

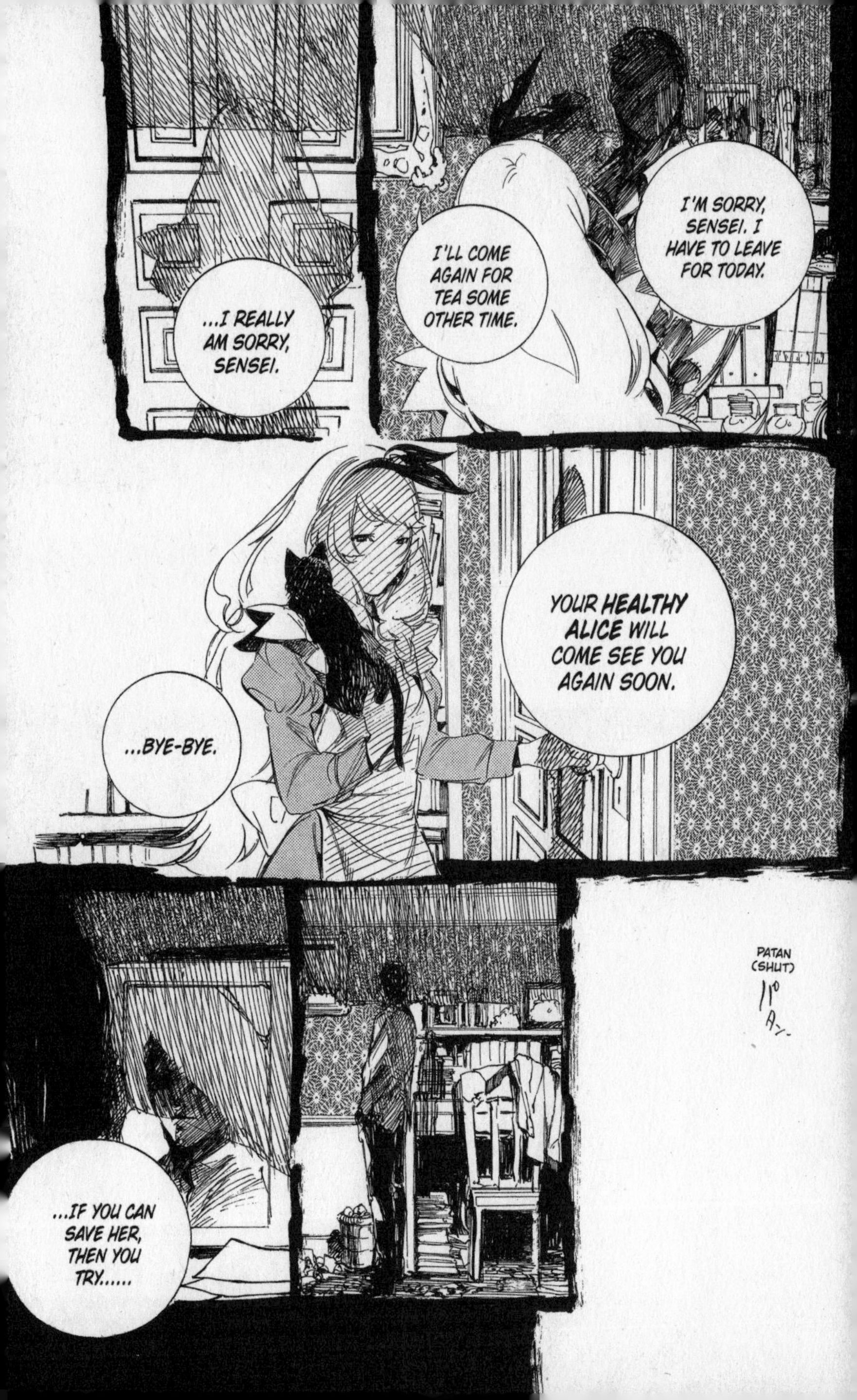
I'M SORRY, SENSEI. I HAVE TO LEAVE FOR TODAY.
I'LL COME AGAIN FOR TEA SOME OTHER TIME.
...I REALLY AM SORRY, SENSEI.
YOUR HEALTHY ALICE WILL COME SEE YOU AGAIN SOON.
...BYE-BYE.
PATAN (SHUT)
...IF YOU CAN SAVE HER, THEN YOU TRY......

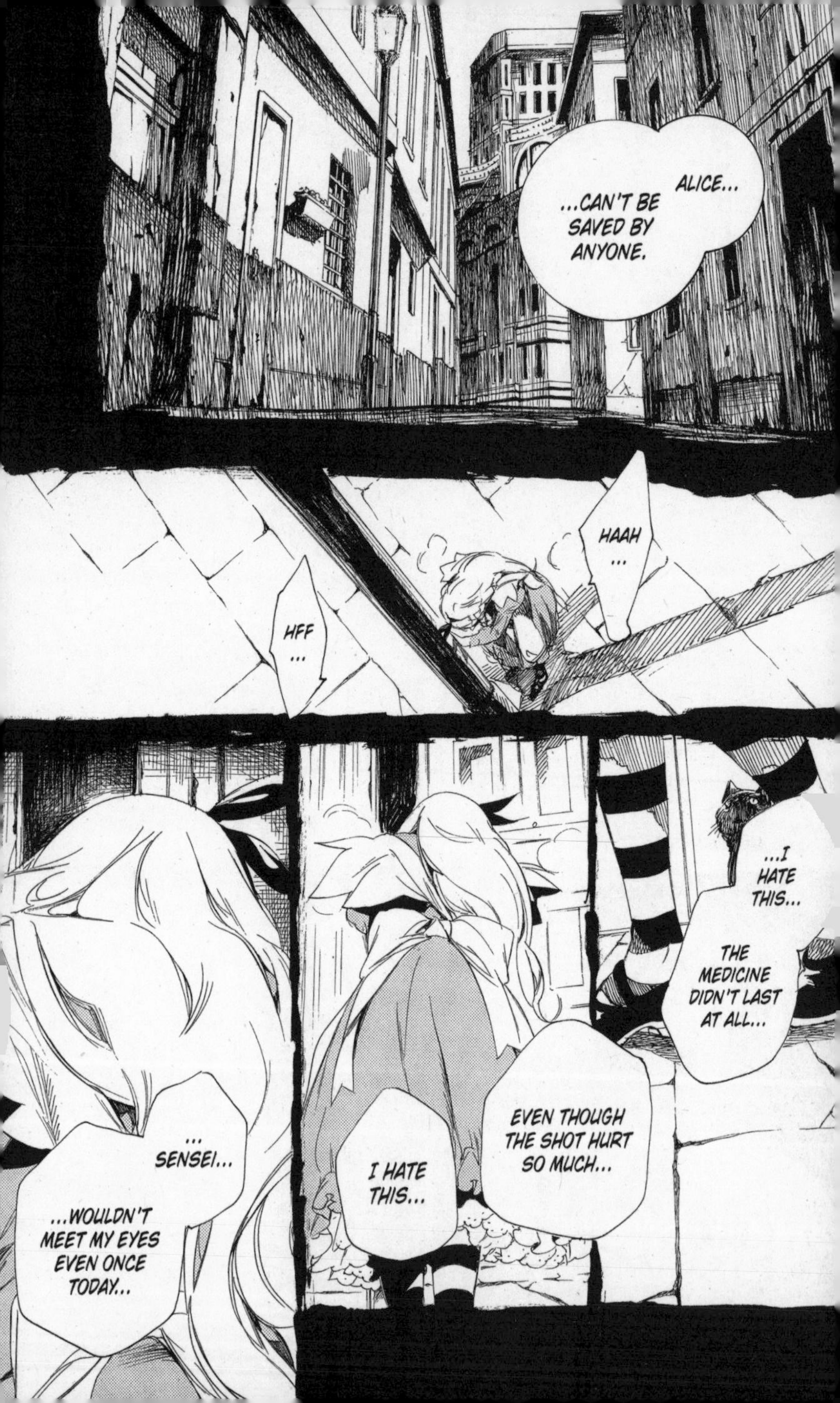
ALICE...
...CAN'T BE SAVED BY ANYONE.
HAAH ...
HFF ...
...I HATE THIS...
THE MEDICINE DIDN'T LAST AT ALL...
EVEN THOUGH THE SHOT HURT SO MUCH...
I HATE THIS...
... SENSEI...
...WOULDN'T MEET MY EYES EVEN ONCE TODAY...

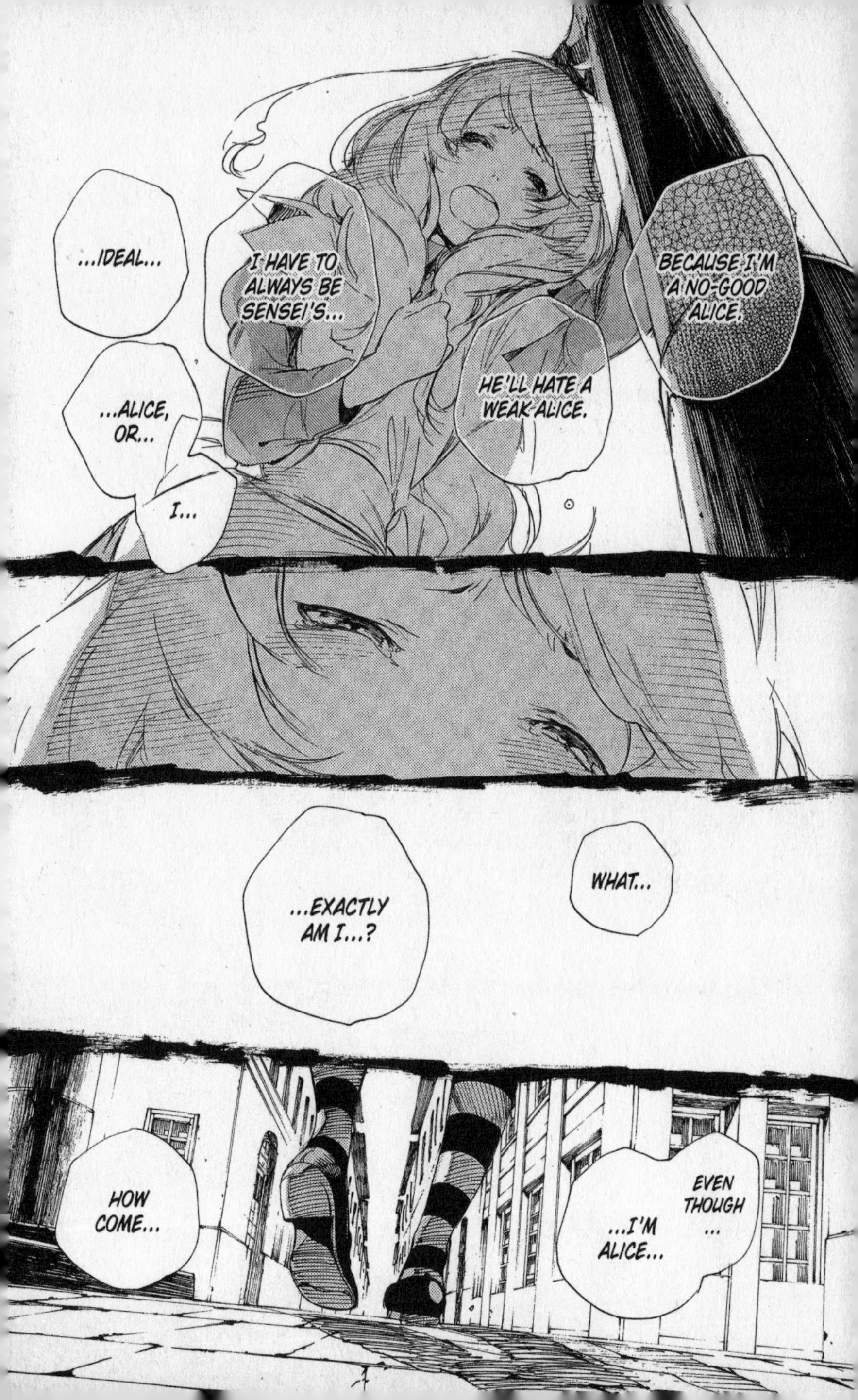
BECAUSE I'M A NO-GOOD ALICE.
HE'LL HATE A WEAK ALICE.
I HAVE TO ALWAYS BE SENSEI'S...
...IDEAL...
...ALICE, OR...
I...
WHAT...
...EXACTLY AM I...?
EVEN THOUGH ...
...I'M ALICE...
HOW COME...

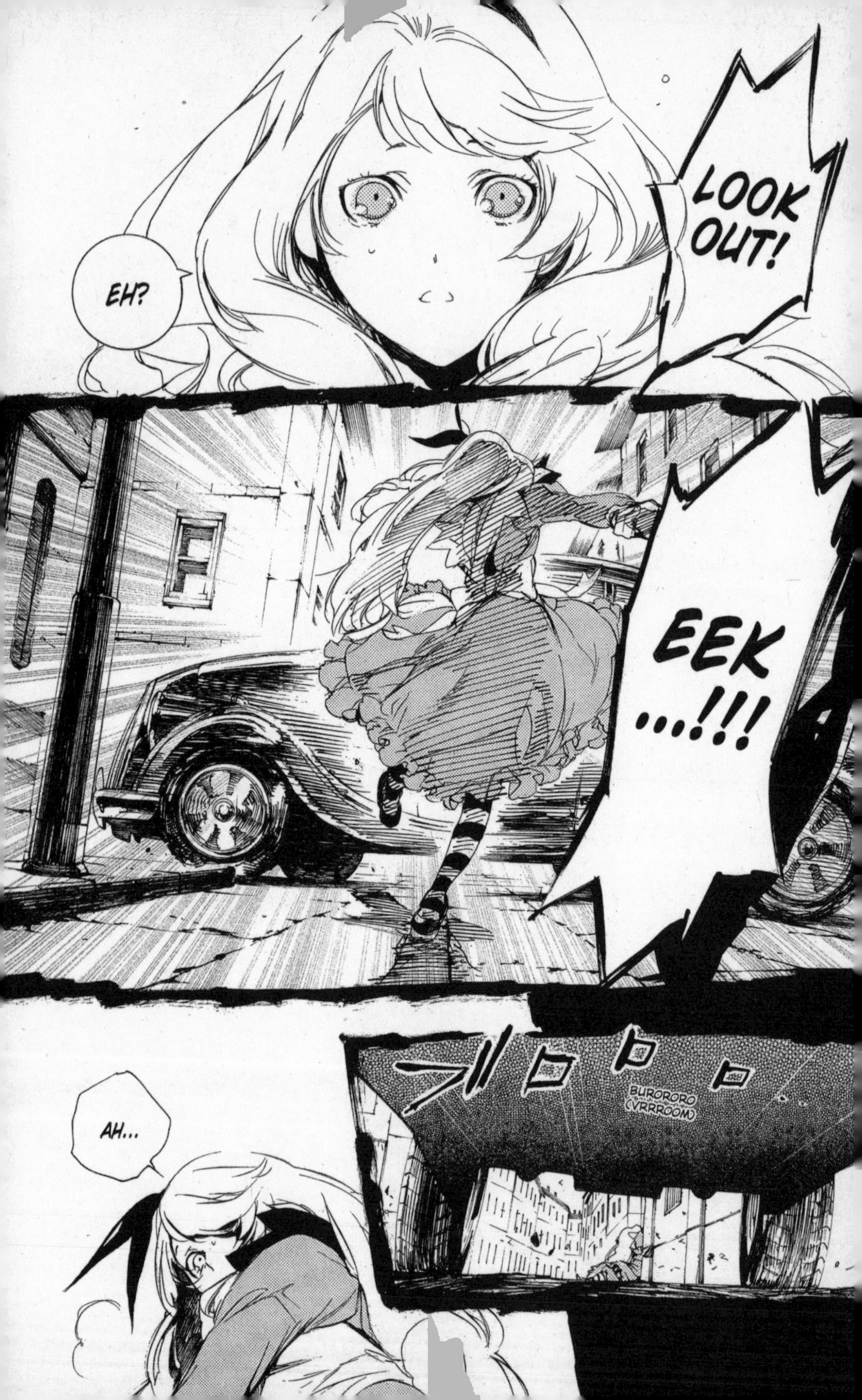
LOOK OUT!
EH?
EEK ...!!!
BURORORO (VRRROOM)
AH...

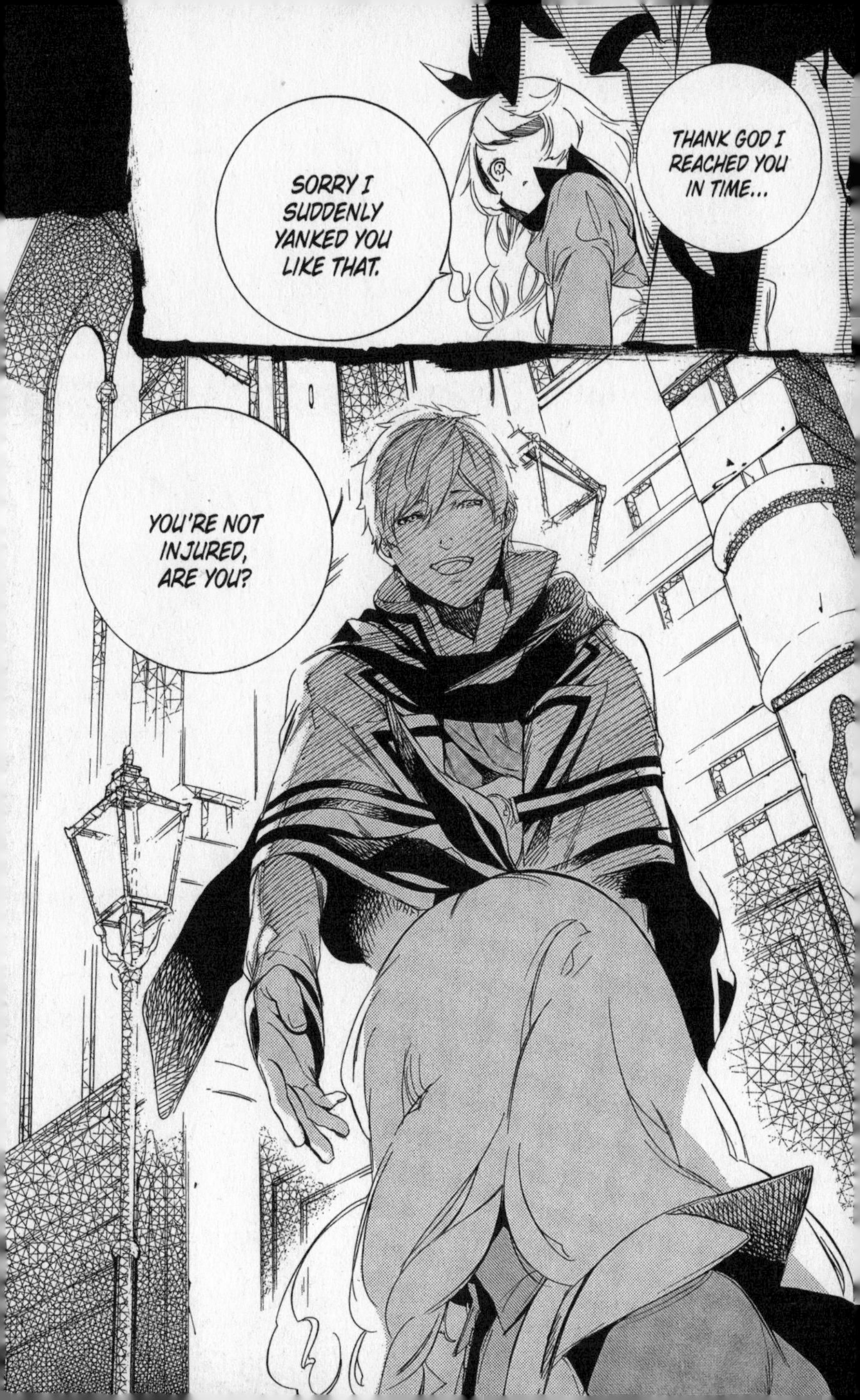
THANK GOD I REACHED YOU IN TIME...
SORRY I SUDDENLY YANKED YOU LIKE THAT.
YOU'RE NOT INJURED, ARE YOU?

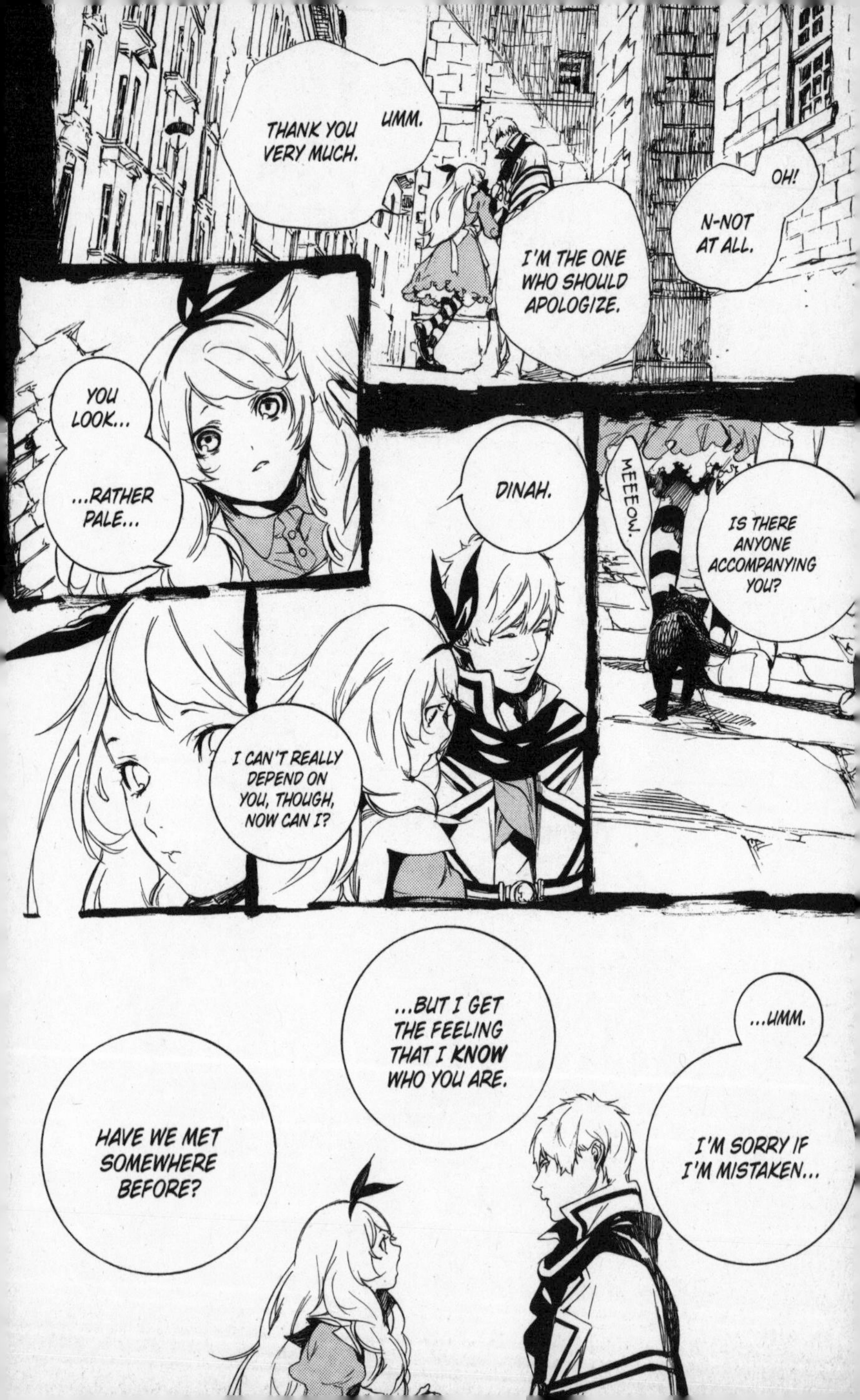
UMM.
THANK YOU VERY MUCH.
OH!
N-NOT AT ALL.
I'M THE ONE WHO SHOULD APOLOGIZE.
IS THERE ANYONE ACCOMPANYING YOU?
MEEEOW.
DINAH.
I CAN'T REALLY DEPEND ON YOU, THOUGH, NOW CAN I?
YOU LOOK...
...RATHER PALE...
...UMM.
I'M SORRY IF I'M MISTAKEN...
...BUT I GET THE FEELING THAT I KNOW WHO YOU ARE.
HAVE WE MET SOMEWHERE BEFORE?

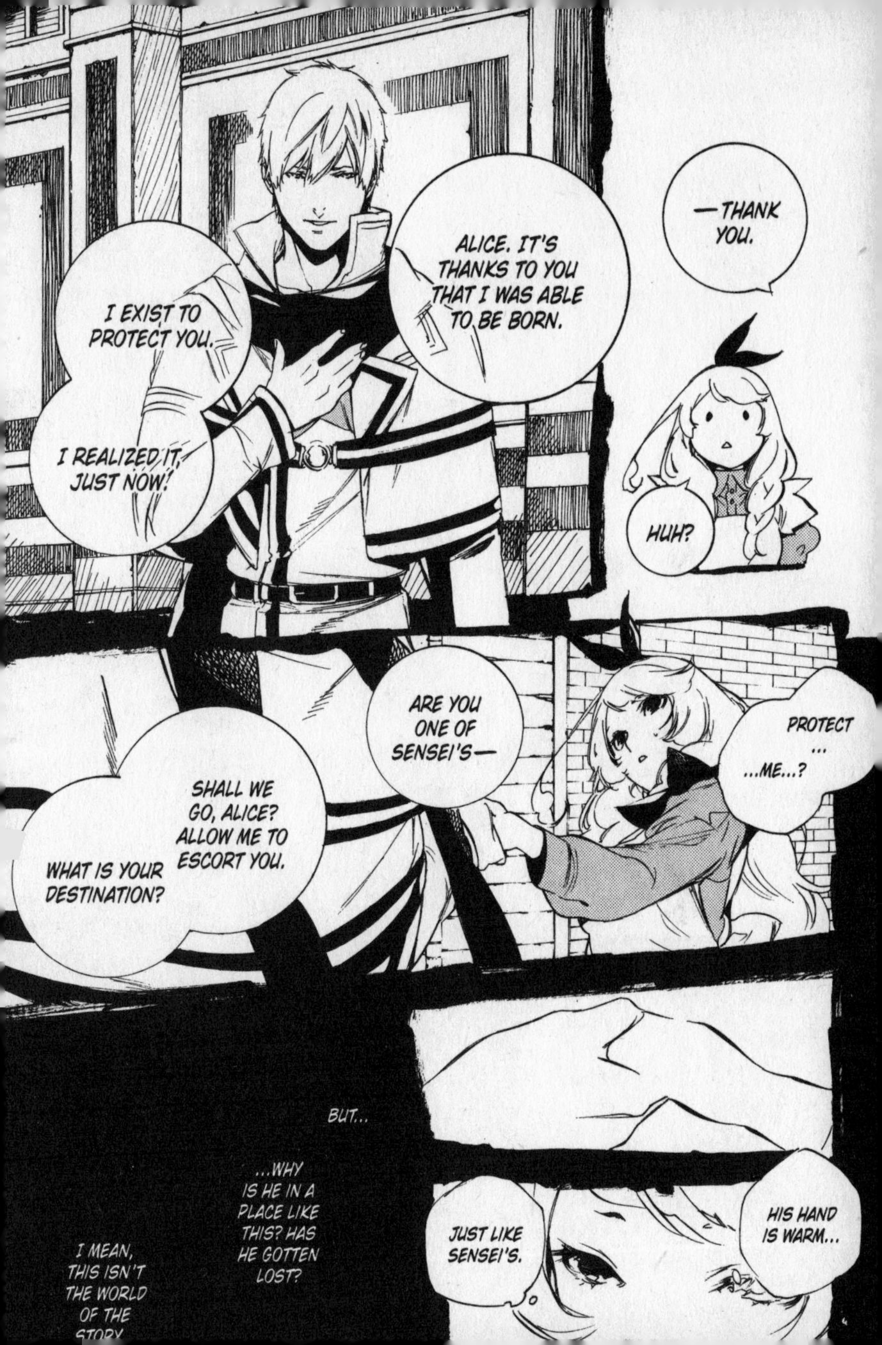
—THANK YOU.
ALICE. IT'S THANKS TO YOU THAT I WAS ABLE TO BE BORN.
I EXIST TO PROTECT YOU.
I REALIZED IT JUST NOW!
HUH?
PROTECT... ...ME...?
ARE YOU ONE OF SENSEI'S—
SHALL WE GO, ALICE? ALLOW ME TO ESCORT YOU.
WHAT IS YOUR DESTINATION?
HIS HAND IS WARM...
JUST LIKE SENSEI'S.
BUT...
...WHY IS HE IN A PLACE LIKE THIS? HAS HE GOTTEN LOST?
I MEAN, THIS ISN'T THE WORLD OF THE

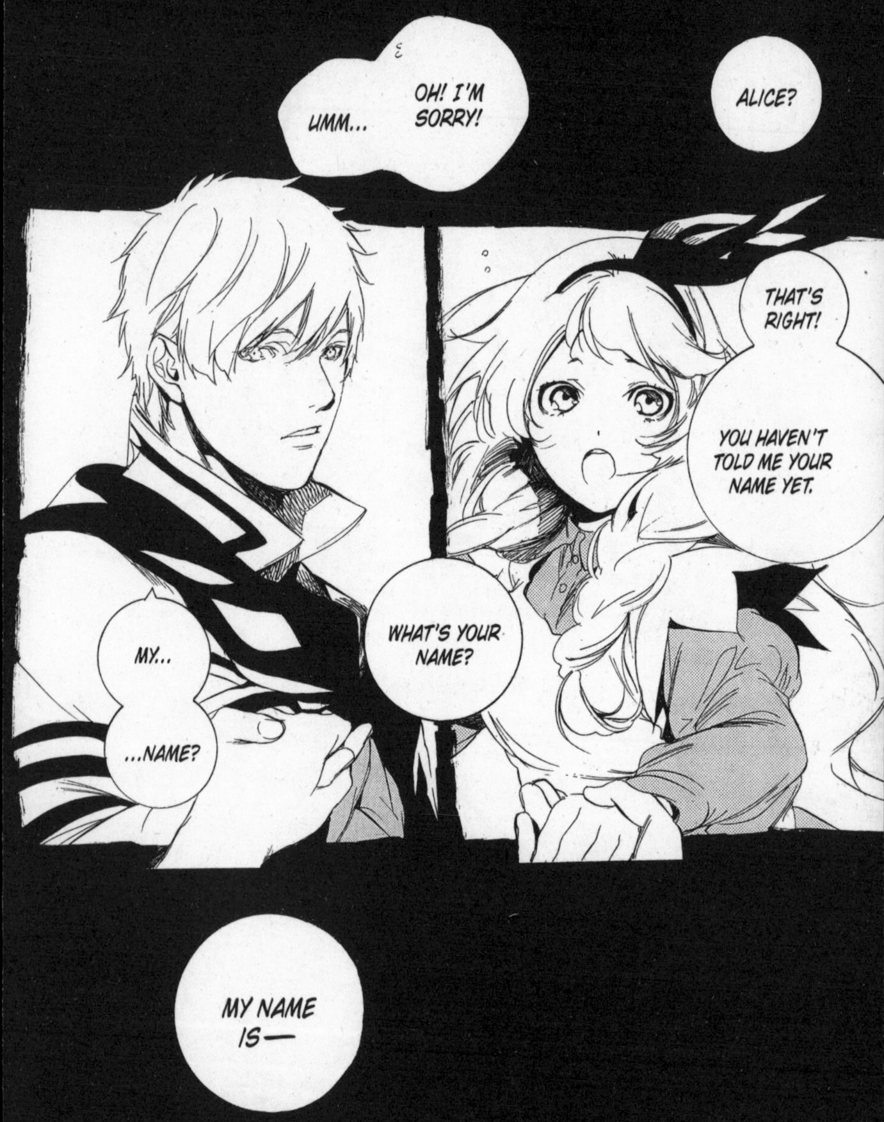
ALICE?
OH! I'M SORRY!
UMM...
THAT'S RIGHT!
YOU HAVEN'T TOLD ME YOUR NAME YET.
WHAT'S YOUR NAME?
MY...
...NAME?
MY NAME IS—

Chapter 49

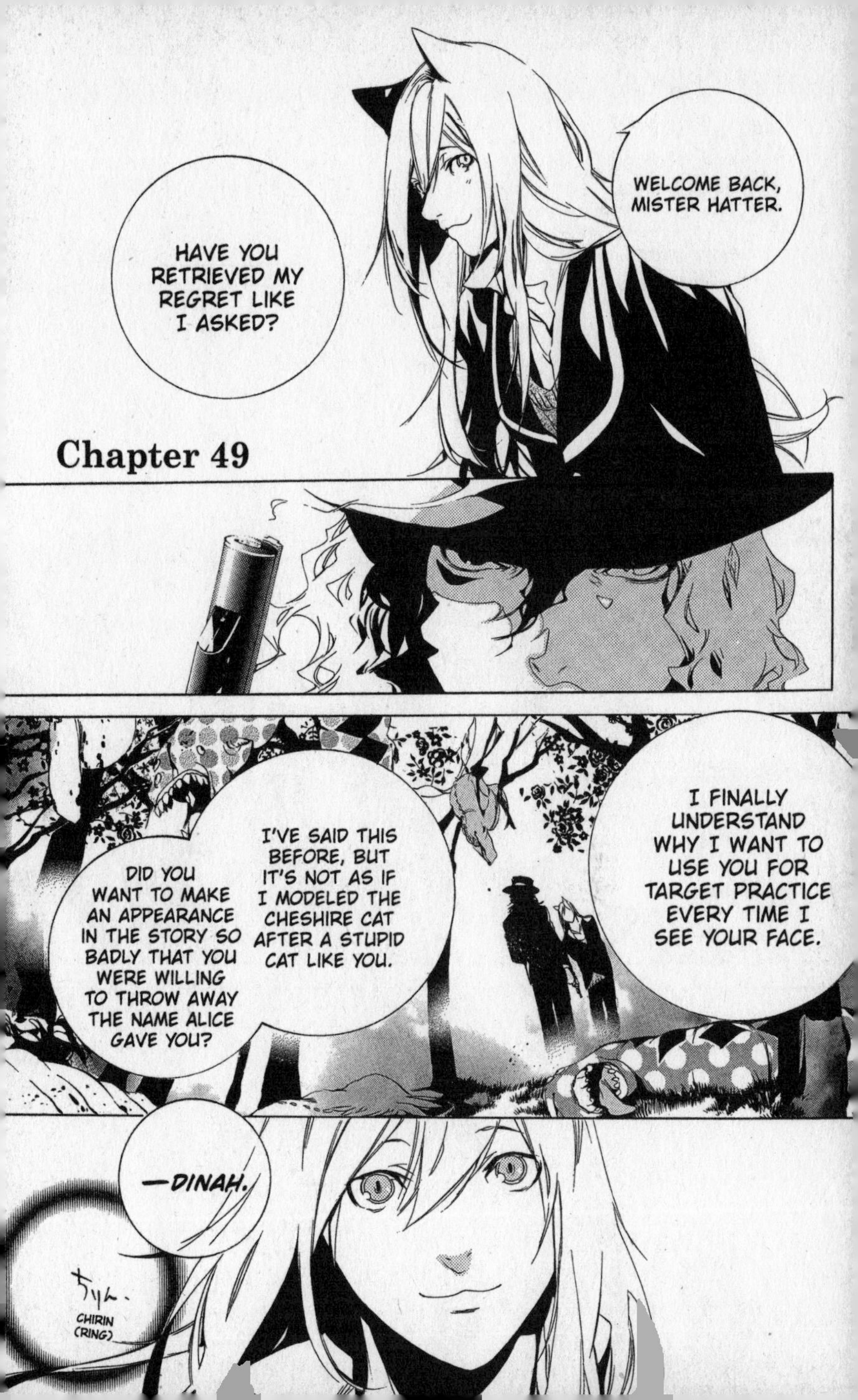
WELCOME BACK, MISTER HATTER.
HAVE YOU RETRIEVED MY REGRET LIKE I ASKED?
I FINALLY UNDERSTAND WHY I WANT TO USE YOU FOR TARGET PRACTICE EVERY TIME I SEE YOUR FACE.
I'VE SAID THIS BEFORE, BUT IT'S NOT AS IF I MODELED THE CHESHIRE CAT AFTER A STUPID CAT LIKE YOU.
DID YOU WANT TO MAKE AN APPEARANCE IN THE STORY SO BADLY THAT YOU WERE WILLING TO THROW AWAY THE NAME ALICE GAVE YOU?
—DINAH.
ちりん
CHIRIN (RING)

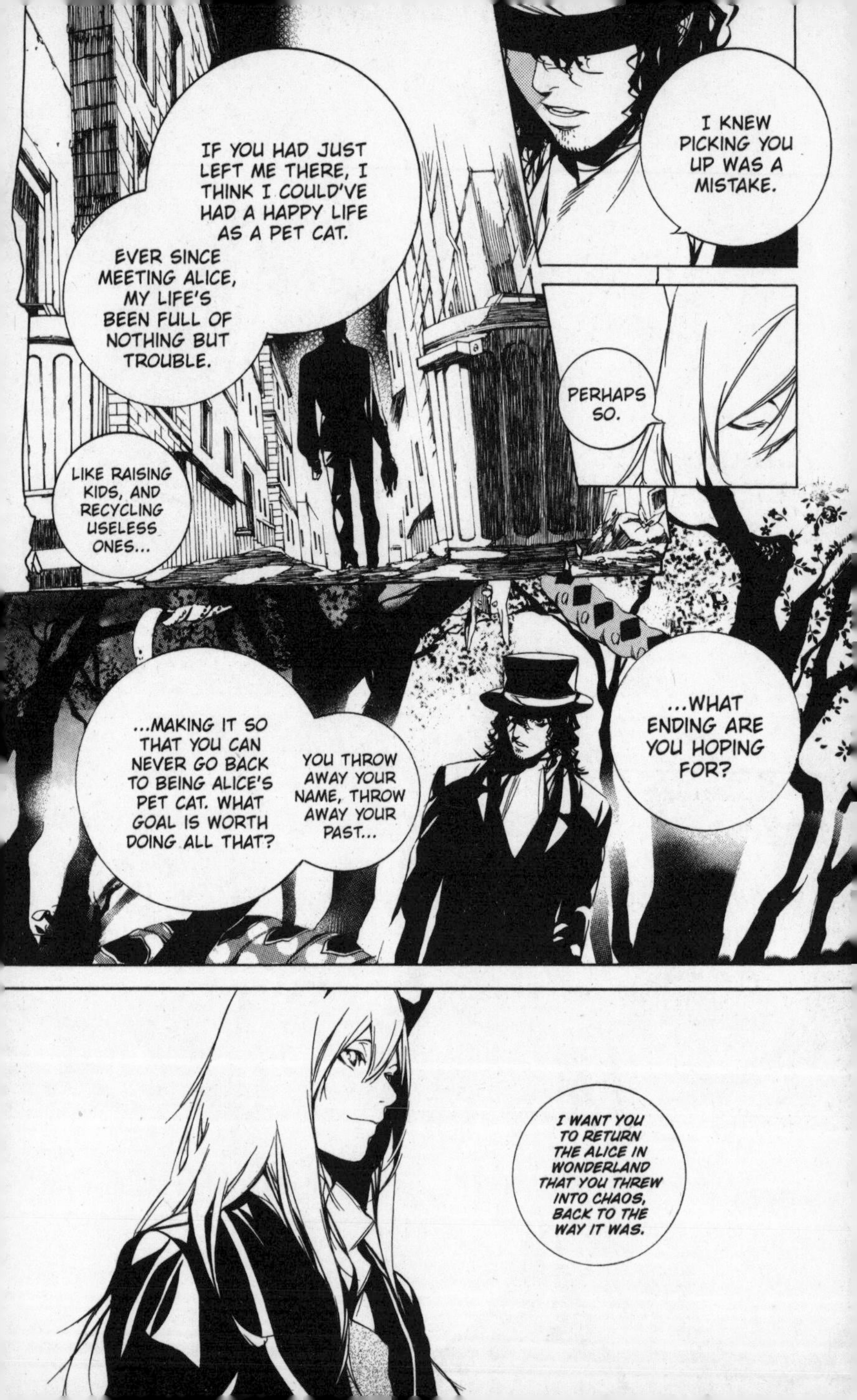
I KNEW PICKING YOU UP WAS A MISTAKE.
PERHAPS SO.
IF YOU HAD JUST LEFT ME THERE, I THINK I COULD'VE HAD A HAPPY LIFE AS A PET CAT.
EVER SINCE MEETING ALICE, MY LIFE'S BEEN FULL OF NOTHING BUT TROUBLE.
LIKE RAISING KIDS, AND RECYCLING USELESS ONES...
...WHAT ENDING ARE YOU HOPING FOR?
YOU THROW AWAY YOUR NAME, THROW AWAY YOUR PAST...
...MAKING IT SO THAT YOU CAN NEVER GO BACK TO BEING ALICE'S PET CAT. WHAT GOAL IS WORTH DOING ALL THAT?
I WANT YOU TO RETURN THE ALICE IN WONDERLAND THAT YOU THREW INTO CHAOS, BACK TO THE WAY IT WAS.

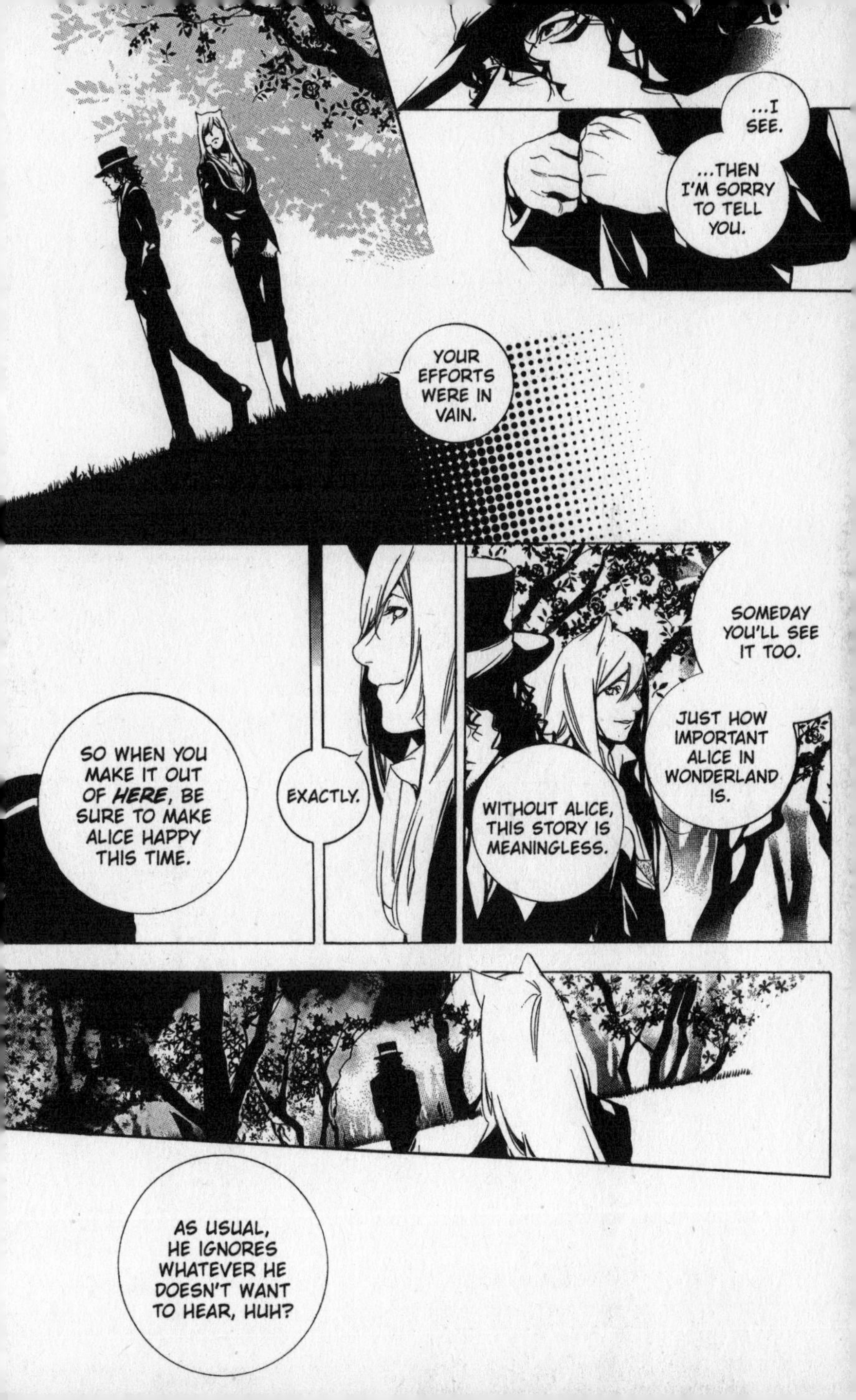
...I SEE.
...THEN I'M SORRY TO TELL YOU.
YOUR EFFORTS WERE IN VAIN.
SOMEDAY YOU'LL SEE IT TOO.
JUST HOW IMPORTANT ALICE IN WONDERLAND IS.
WITHOUT ALICE, THIS STORY IS MEANINGLESS.
EXACTLY.
SO WHEN YOU MAKE IT OUT OF *HERE*, BE SURE TO MAKE ALICE HAPPY THIS TIME.
AS USUAL, HE IGNORES WHATEVER HE DOESN'T WANT TO HEAR, HUH?

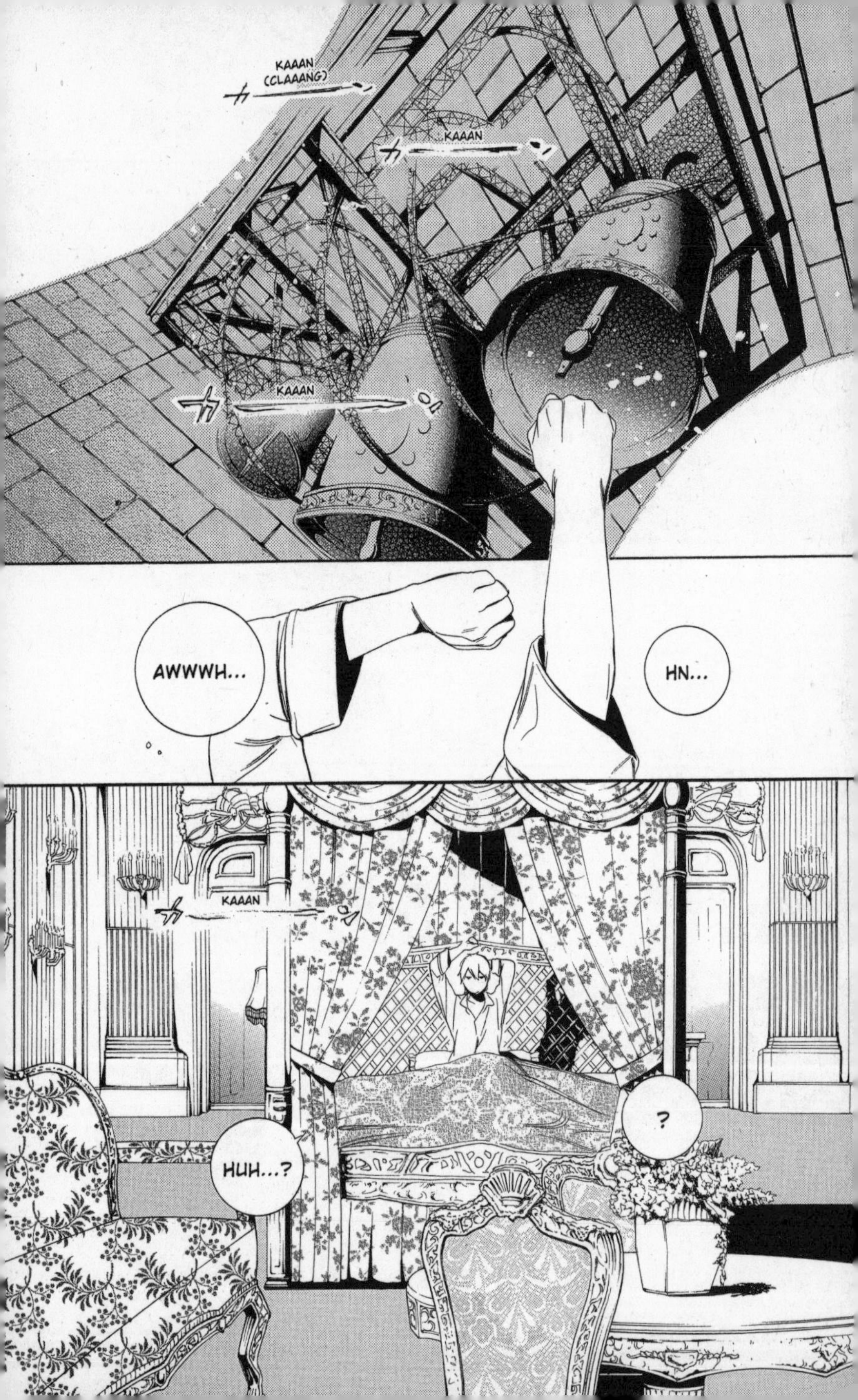
KAAAN (CLAAANG)
KAAAN
KAAAN
HN...
AWWWH...
KAAAN
?
HUH...?

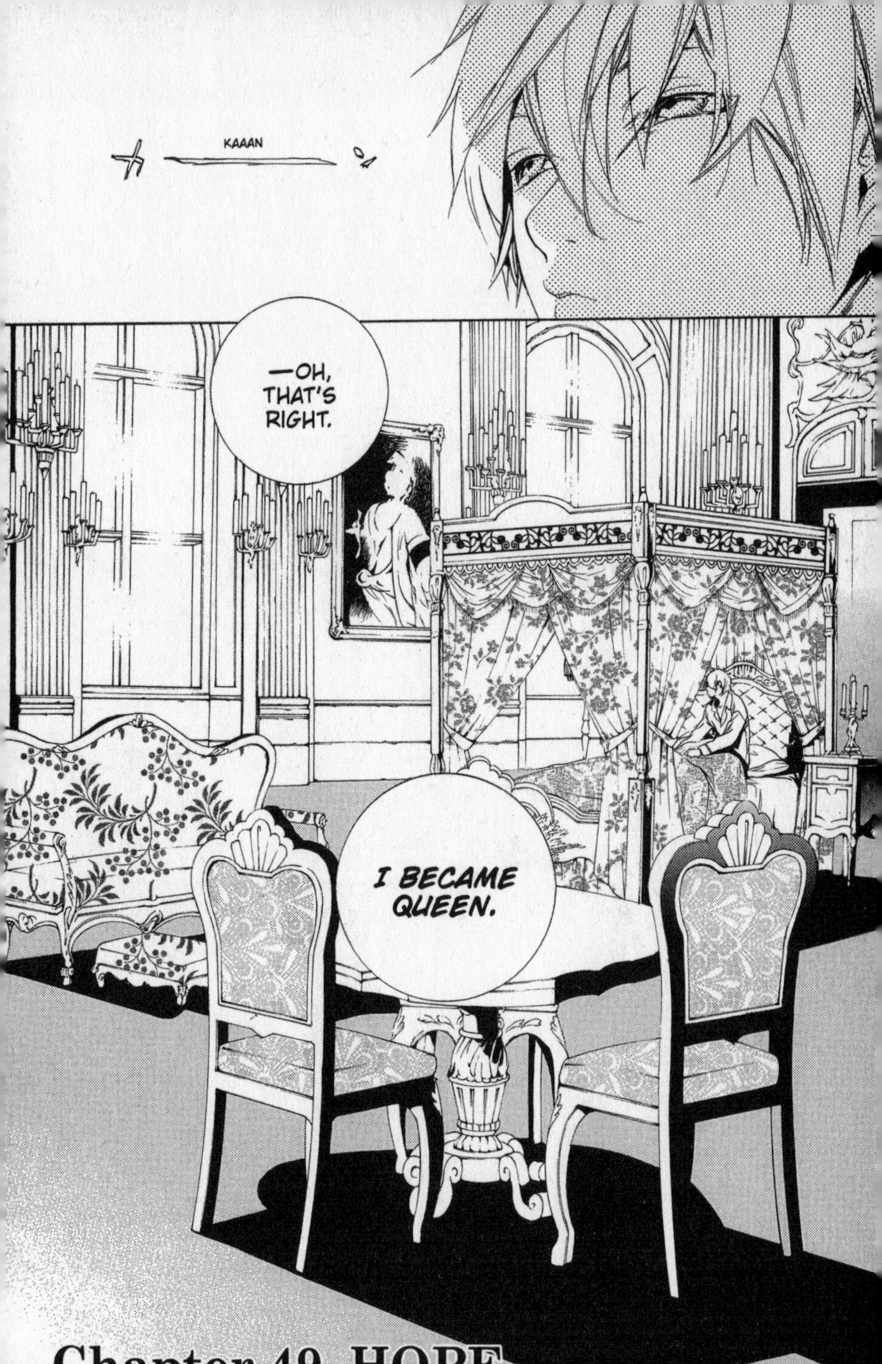
KAAAN
—OH, THAT'S RIGHT.
I BECAME QUEEN.

Chapter 49 HOPE.

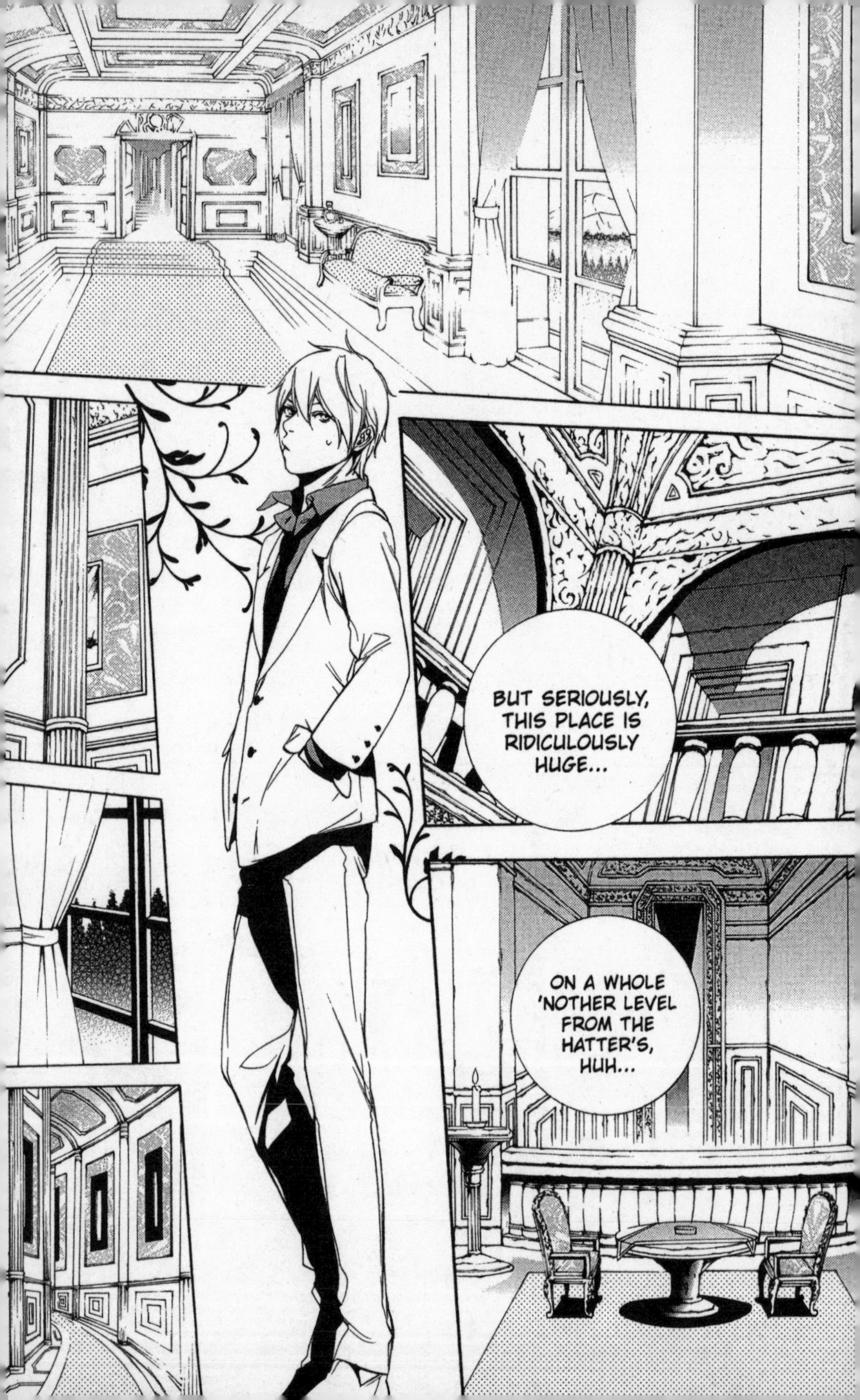
BUT SERIOUSLY, THIS PLACE IS RIDICULOUSLY HUGE...
ON A WHOLE 'NOTHER LEVEL FROM THE HATTER'S, HUH...

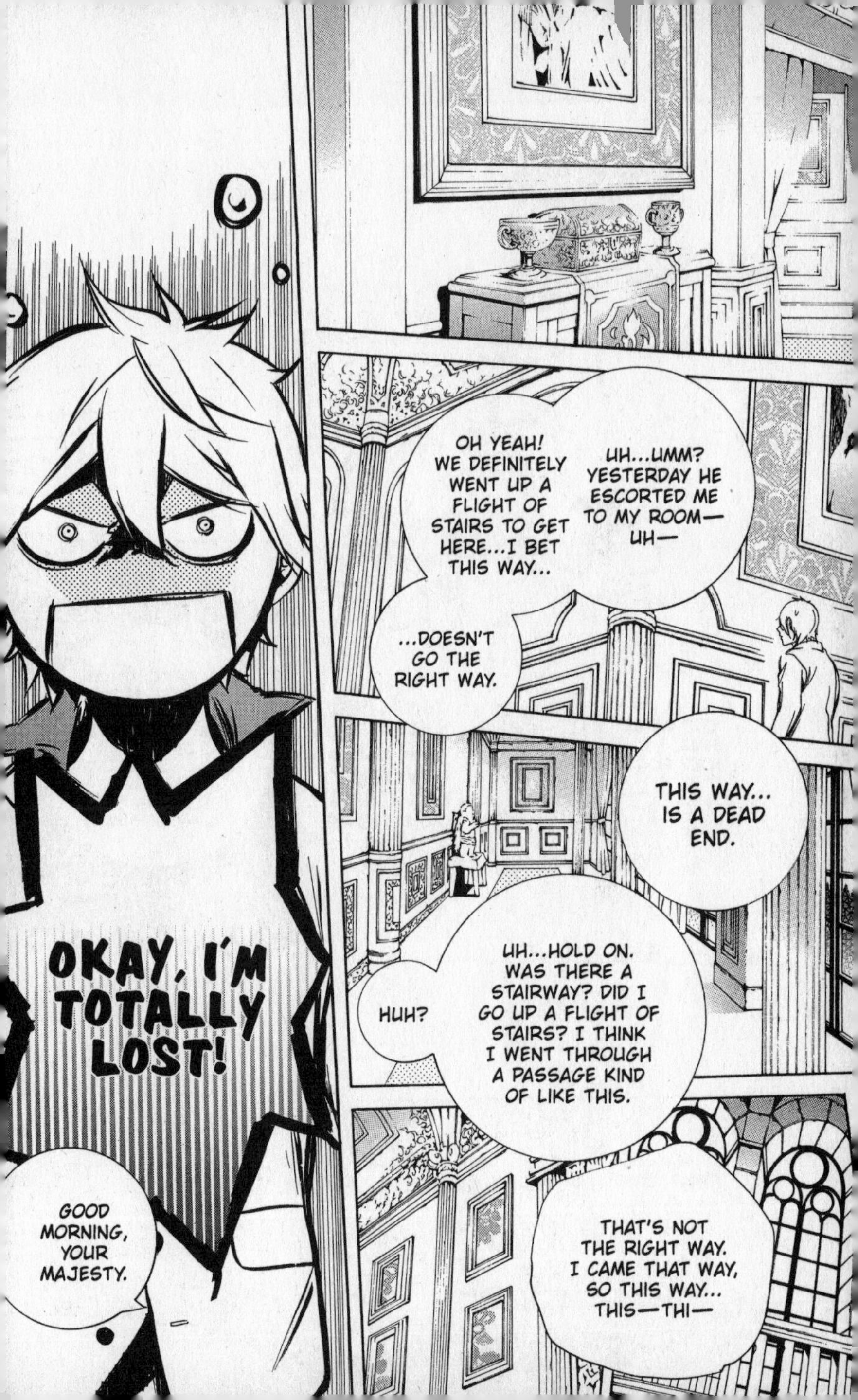
UH...UMM? YESTERDAY HE ESCORTED ME TO MY ROOM— UH—
OH YEAH! WE DEFINITELY WENT UP A FLIGHT OF STAIRS TO GET HERE...I BET THIS WAY...
...DOESN'T GO THE RIGHT WAY.
THIS WAY... IS A DEAD END.
UH...HOLD ON. WAS THERE A STAIRWAY? DID I GO UP A FLIGHT OF STAIRS? I THINK I WENT THROUGH A PASSAGE KIND OF LIKE THIS.
HUH?
THAT'S NOT THE RIGHT WAY. I CAME THAT WAY, SO THIS WAY... THIS—THI—
OKAY, I'M TOTALLY LOST!
GOOD MORNING, YOUR MAJESTY.

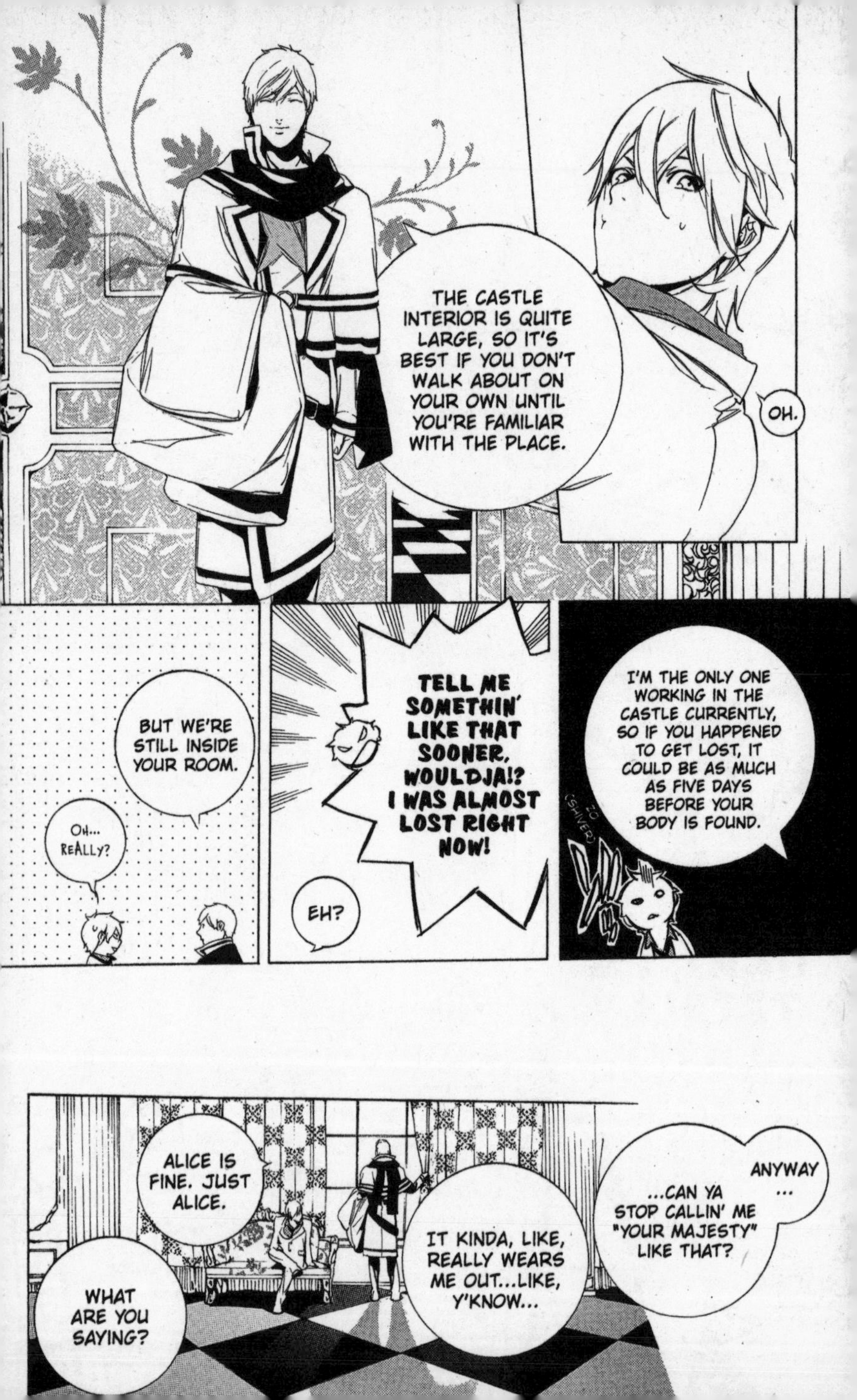
THE CASTLE INTERIOR IS QUITE LARGE, SO IT'S BEST IF YOU DON'T WALK ABOUT ON YOUR OWN UNTIL YOU'RE FAMILIAR WITH THE PLACE.
OH.
I'M THE ONLY ONE WORKING IN THE CASTLE CURRENTLY, SO IF YOU HAPPENED TO GET LOST, IT COULD BE AS MUCH AS FIVE DAYS BEFORE YOUR BODY IS FOUND.
ZO (SHIVER)
TELL ME SOMETHIN' LIKE THAT SOONER, WOULDJA!? I WAS ALMOST LOST RIGHT NOW!
EH?
BUT WE'RE STILL INSIDE YOUR ROOM.
OH... REALLY?
ANYWAY ...
...CAN YA STOP CALLIN' ME "YOUR MAJESTY" LIKE THAT?
IT KINDA, LIKE, REALLY WEARS ME OUT...LIKE, Y'KNOW...
ALICE IS FINE. JUST ALICE.
WHAT ARE YOU SAYING?

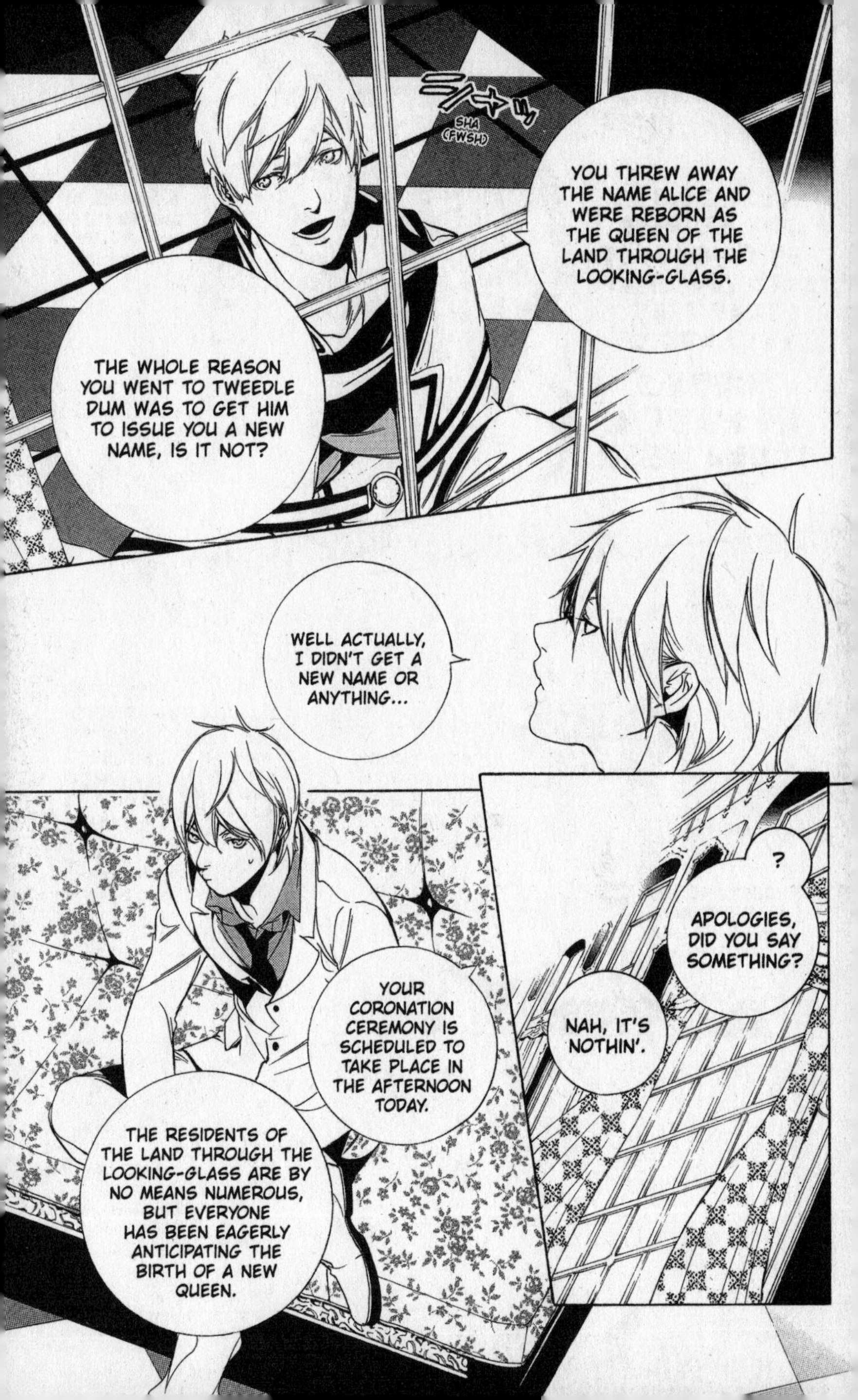
SHA (FWSH)
YOU THREW AWAY THE NAME ALICE AND WERE REBORN AS THE QUEEN OF THE LAND THROUGH THE LOOKING-GLASS.
THE WHOLE REASON YOU WENT TO TWEEDLE DUM WAS TO GET HIM TO ISSUE YOU A NEW NAME, IS IT NOT?
WELL ACTUALLY, I DIDN'T GET A NEW NAME OR ANYTHING...
?
APOLOGIES, DID YOU SAY SOMETHING?
NAH, IT'S NOTHIN'.
YOUR CORONATION CEREMONY IS SCHEDULED TO TAKE PLACE IN THE AFTERNOON TODAY.
THE RESIDENTS OF THE LAND THROUGH THE LOOKING-GLASS ARE BY NO MEANS NUMEROUS, BUT EVERYONE HAS BEEN EAGERLY ANTICIPATING THE BIRTH OF A NEW QUEEN.

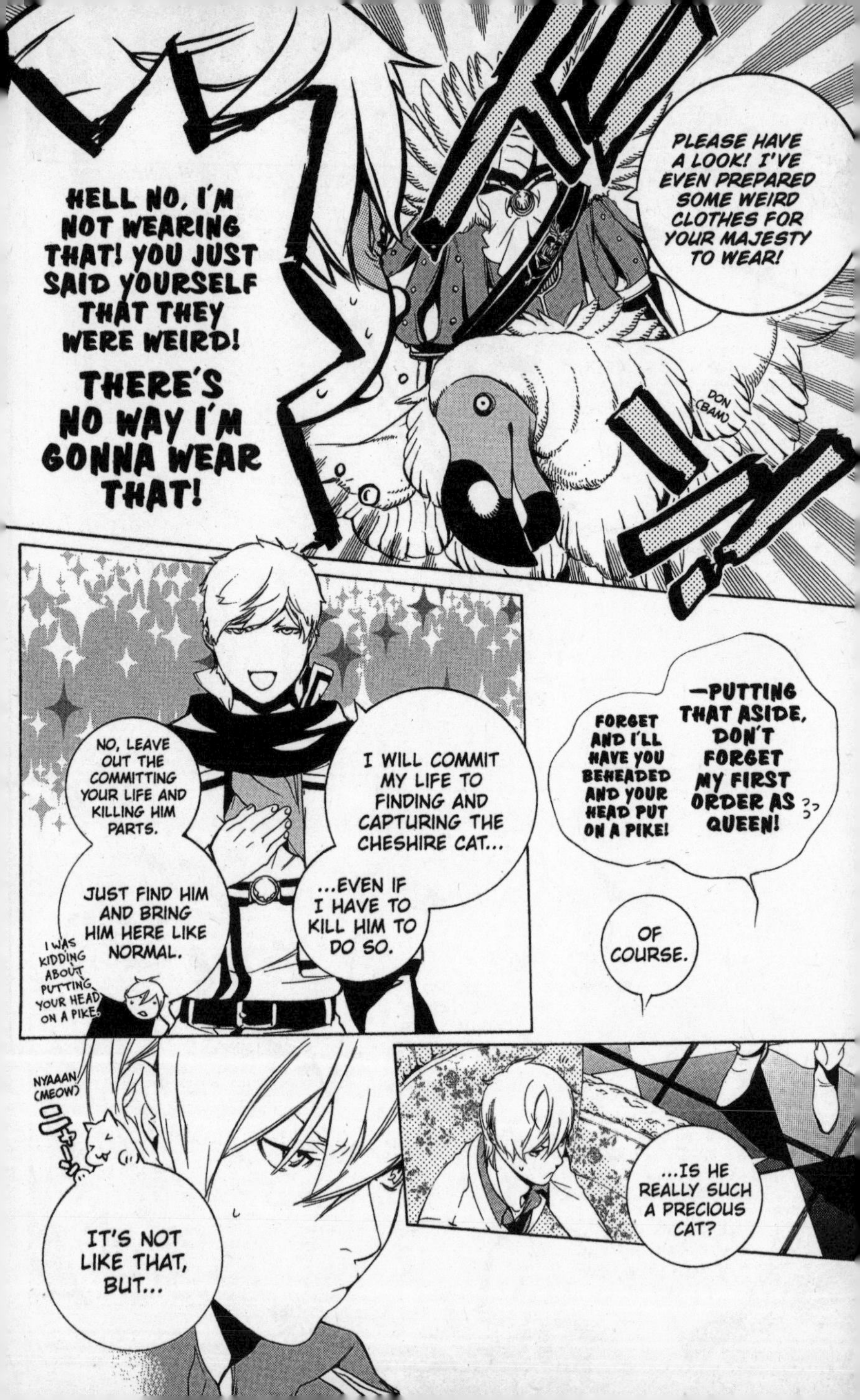
PLEASE HAVE A LOOK! I'VE EVEN PREPARED SOME WEIRD CLOTHES FOR YOUR MAJESTY TO WEAR!
DON (BAM)
HELL NO, I'M NOT WEARING THAT! YOU JUST SAID YOURSELF THAT THEY WERE WEIRD!
THERE'S NO WAY I'M GONNA WEAR THAT!
—PUTTING THAT ASIDE, DON'T FORGET MY FIRST ORDER AS QUEEN!
FORGET AND I'LL HAVE YOU BEHEADED AND YOUR HEAD PUT ON A PIKE!
OF COURSE.
I WILL COMMIT MY LIFE TO FINDING AND CAPTURING THE CHESHIRE CAT...
...EVEN IF I HAVE TO KILL HIM TO DO SO.
NO, LEAVE OUT THE COMMITTING YOUR LIFE AND KILLING HIM PARTS.
JUST FIND HIM AND BRING HIM HERE LIKE NORMAL.
I WAS KIDDING ABOUT PUTTING YOUR HEAD ON A PIKE.
...IS HE REALLY SUCH A PRECIOUS CAT?
NYAAAN (MEOW)
IT'S NOT LIKE THAT, BUT...

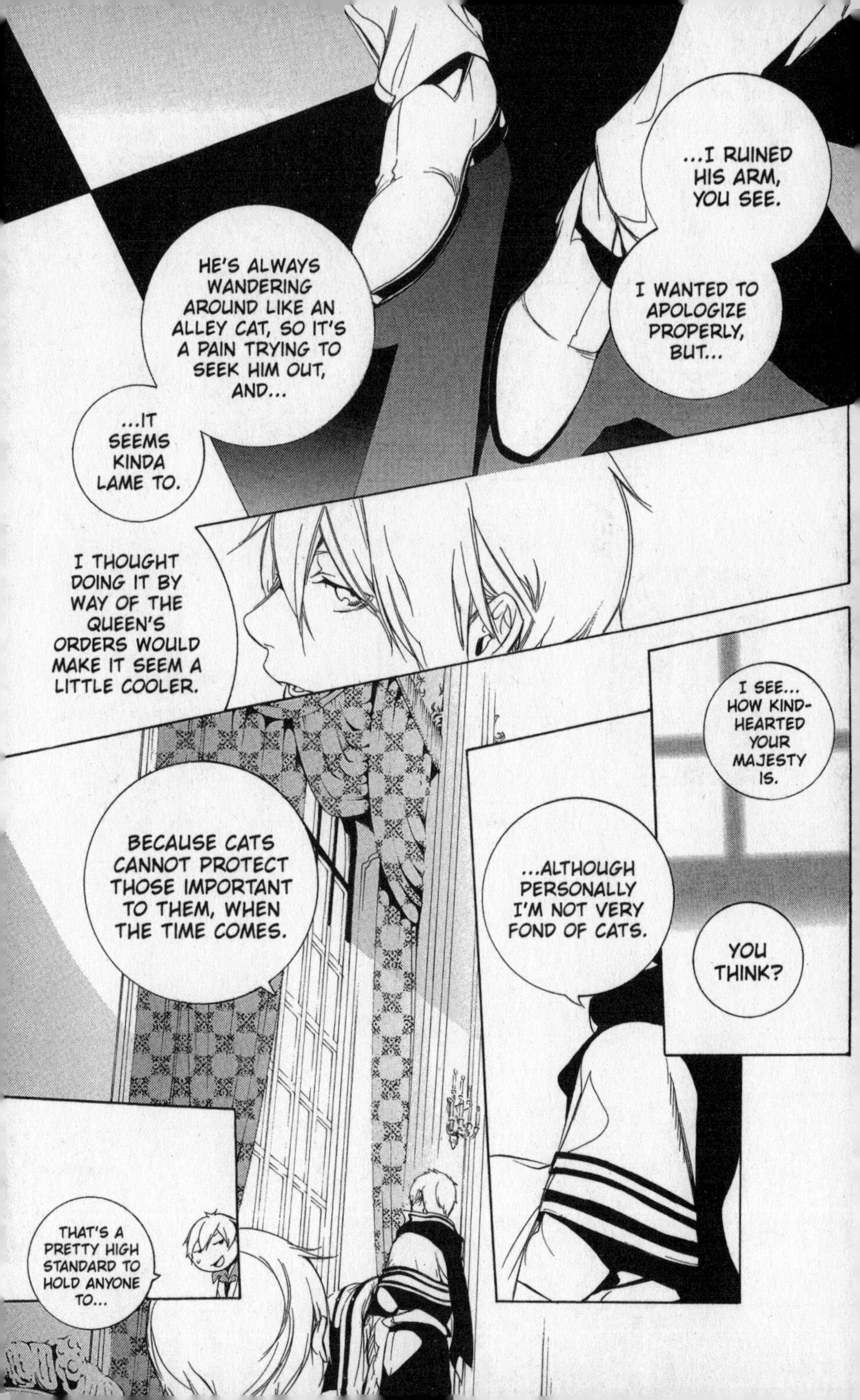
...I RUINED HIS ARM, YOU SEE.
I WANTED TO APOLOGIZE PROPERLY, BUT...
HE'S ALWAYS WANDERING AROUND LIKE AN ALLEY CAT, SO IT'S A PAIN TRYING TO SEEK HIM OUT, AND...
...IT SEEMS KINDA LAME TO.
I THOUGHT DOING IT BY WAY OF THE QUEEN'S ORDERS WOULD MAKE IT SEEM A LITTLE COOLER.
I SEE... HOW KIND-HEARTED YOUR MAJESTY IS.
YOU THINK?
...ALTHOUGH PERSONALLY I'M NOT VERY FOND OF CATS.
BECAUSE CATS CANNOT PROTECT THOSE IMPORTANT TO THEM, WHEN THE TIME COMES.
THAT'S A PRETTY HIGH STANDARD TO HOLD ANYONE TO...

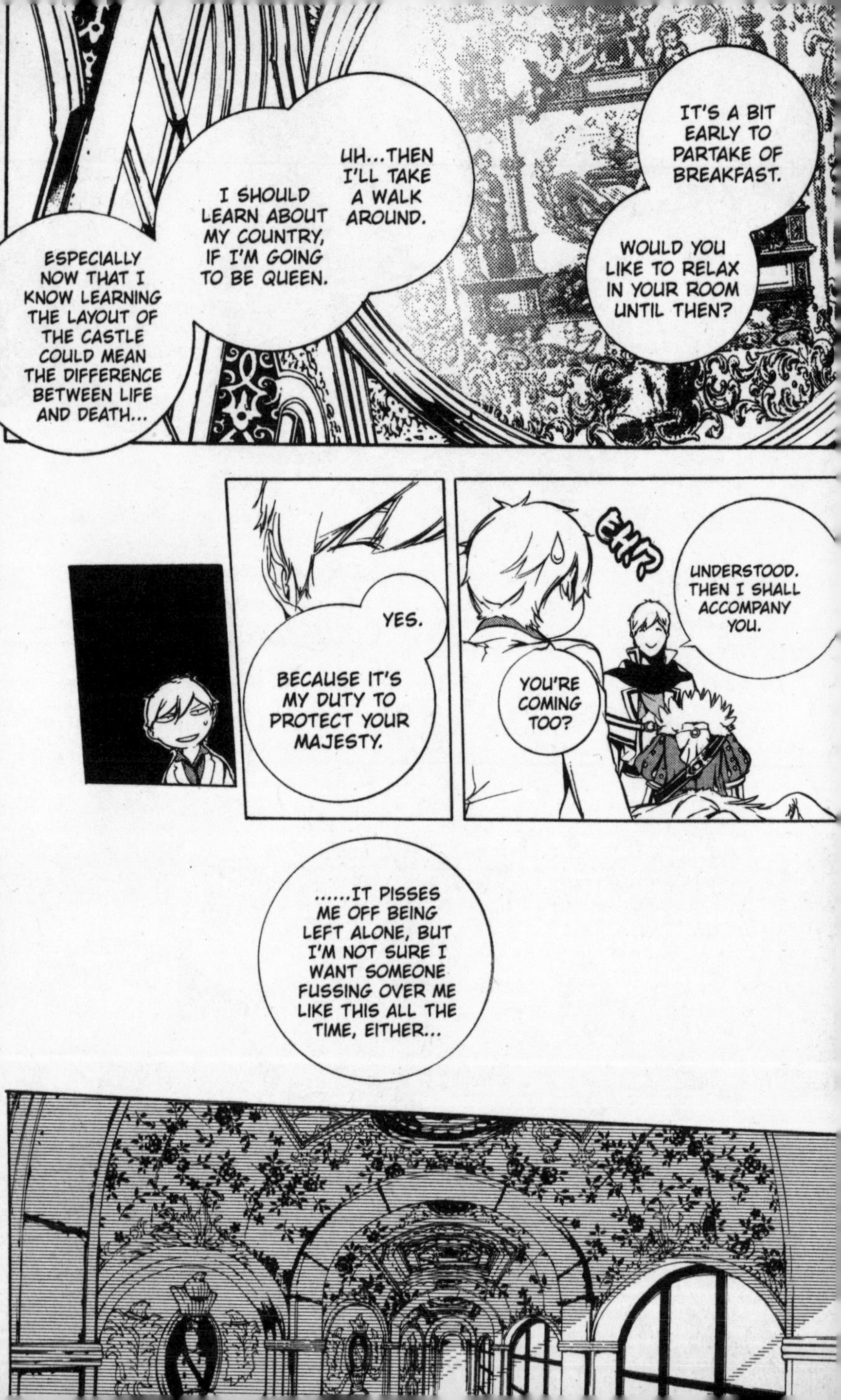
IT'S A BIT EARLY TO PARTAKE OF BREAKFAST.
WOULD YOU LIKE TO RELAX IN YOUR ROOM UNTIL THEN?
UH...THEN I'LL TAKE A WALK AROUND.
I SHOULD LEARN ABOUT MY COUNTRY, IF I'M GOING TO BE QUEEN.
ESPECIALLY NOW THAT I KNOW LEARNING THE LAYOUT OF THE CASTLE COULD MEAN THE DIFFERENCE BETWEEN LIFE AND DEATH...
UNDERSTOOD. THEN I SHALL ACCOMPANY YOU.
EH?
YOU'RE COMING TOO?
YES.
BECAUSE IT'S MY DUTY TO PROTECT YOUR MAJESTY.
......IT PISSES ME OFF BEING LEFT ALONE, BUT I'M NOT SURE I WANT SOMEONE FUSSING OVER ME LIKE THIS ALL THE TIME, EITHER...

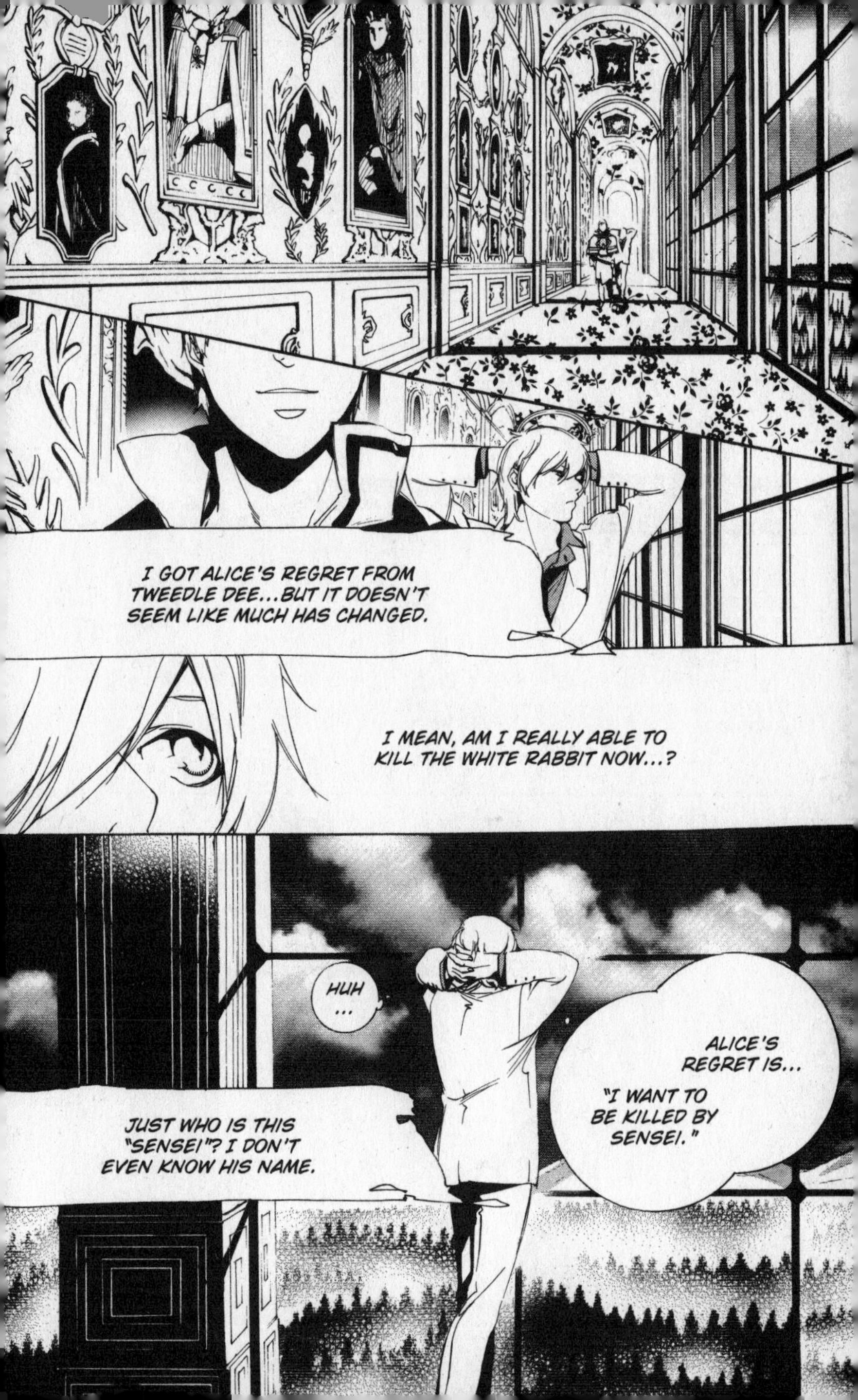
I GOT ALICE'S REGRET FROM TWEEDLE DEE...BUT IT DOESN'T SEEM LIKE MUCH HAS CHANGED.
I MEAN, AM I REALLY ABLE TO KILL THE WHITE RABBIT NOW...?
ALICE'S REGRET IS... "I WANT TO BE KILLED BY SENSEI."
HUH ...
JUST WHO IS THIS "SENSEI"? I DON'T EVEN KNOW HIS NAME.

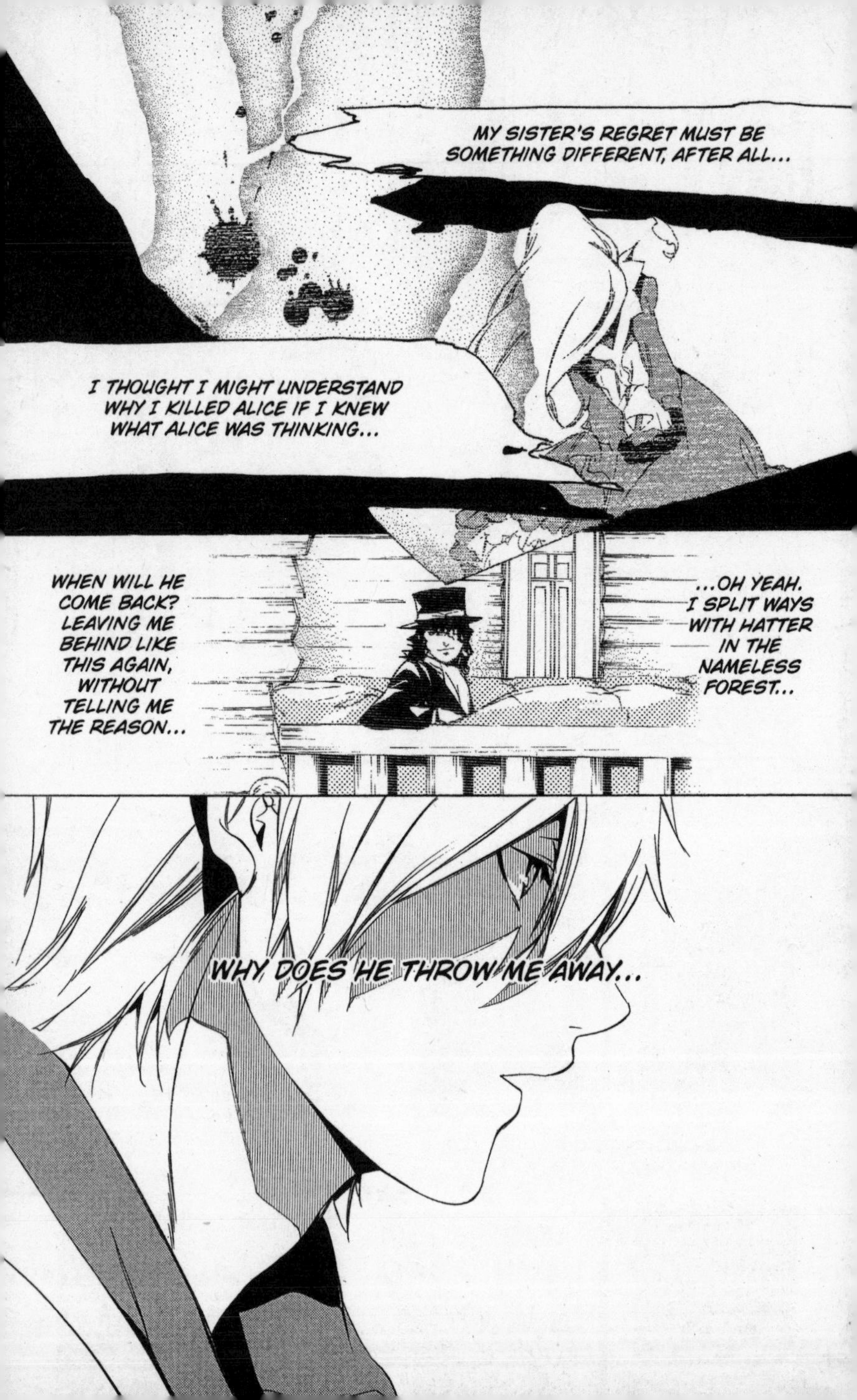
MY SISTER'S REGRET MUST BE SOMETHING DIFFERENT, AFTER ALL...
I THOUGHT I MIGHT UNDERSTAND WHY I KILLED ALICE IF I KNEW WHAT ALICE WAS THINKING...
...OH YEAH. I SPLIT WAYS WITH HATTER IN THE NAMELESS FOREST...
WHEN WILL HE COME BACK? LEAVING ME BEHIND LIKE THIS AGAIN, WITHOUT TELLING ME THE REASON...
WHY DOES HE THROW ME AWAY...

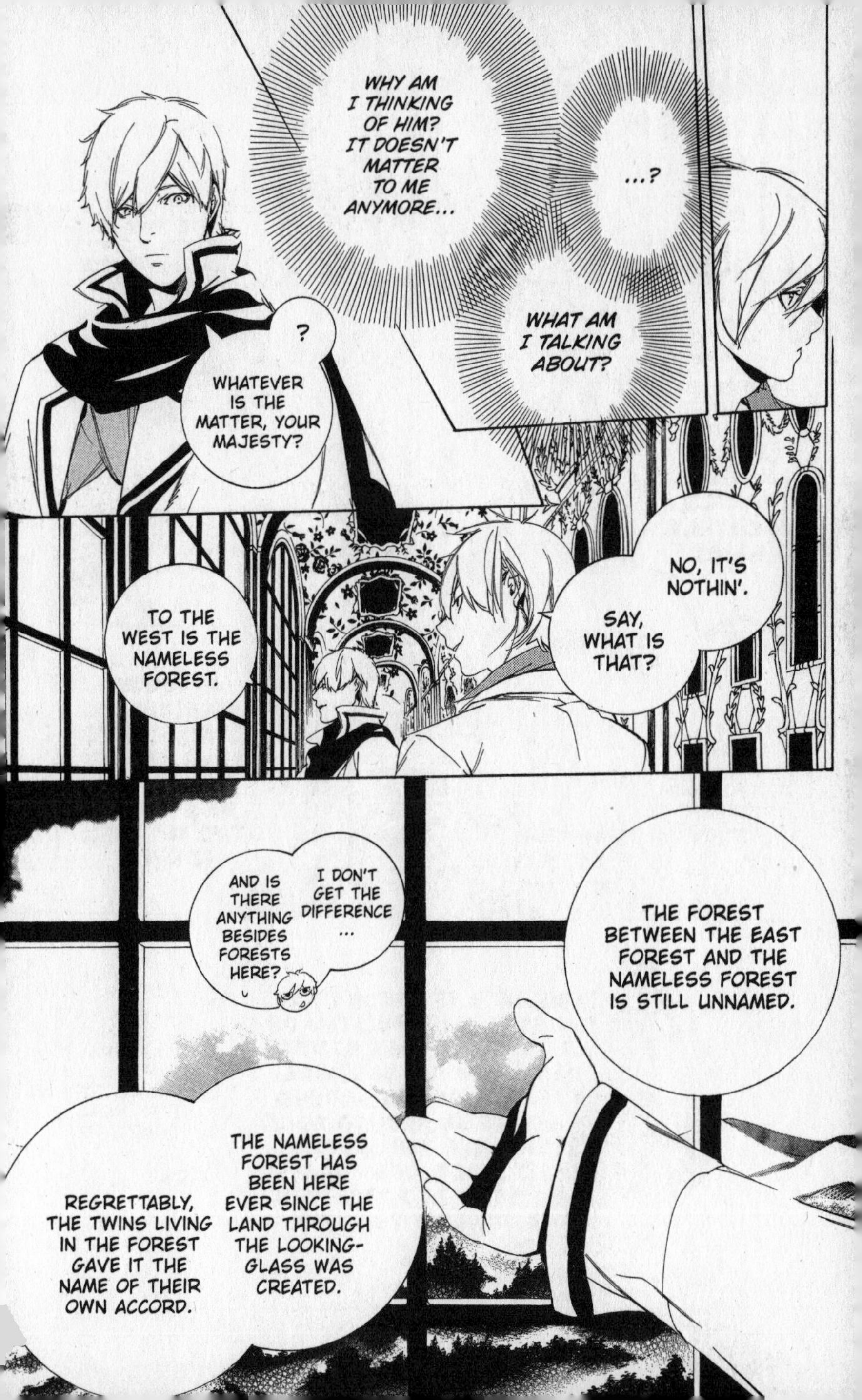
WHY AM I THINKING OF HIM? IT DOESN'T MATTER TO ME ANYMORE...
...?
WHAT AM I TALKING ABOUT?
?
WHATEVER IS THE MATTER, YOUR MAJESTY?
NO, IT'S NOTHIN'.
SAY, WHAT IS THAT?
TO THE WEST IS THE NAMELESS FOREST.
THE FOREST BETWEEN THE EAST FOREST AND THE NAMELESS FOREST IS STILL UNNAMED.
I DON'T GET THE DIFFERENCE...
AND IS THERE ANYTHING BESIDES FORESTS HERE?
THE NAMELESS FOREST HAS BEEN HERE EVER SINCE THE LAND THROUGH THE LOOKING-GLASS WAS CREATED.
REGRETTABLY, THE TWINS LIVING IN THE FOREST GAVE IT THE NAME OF THEIR OWN ACCORD.

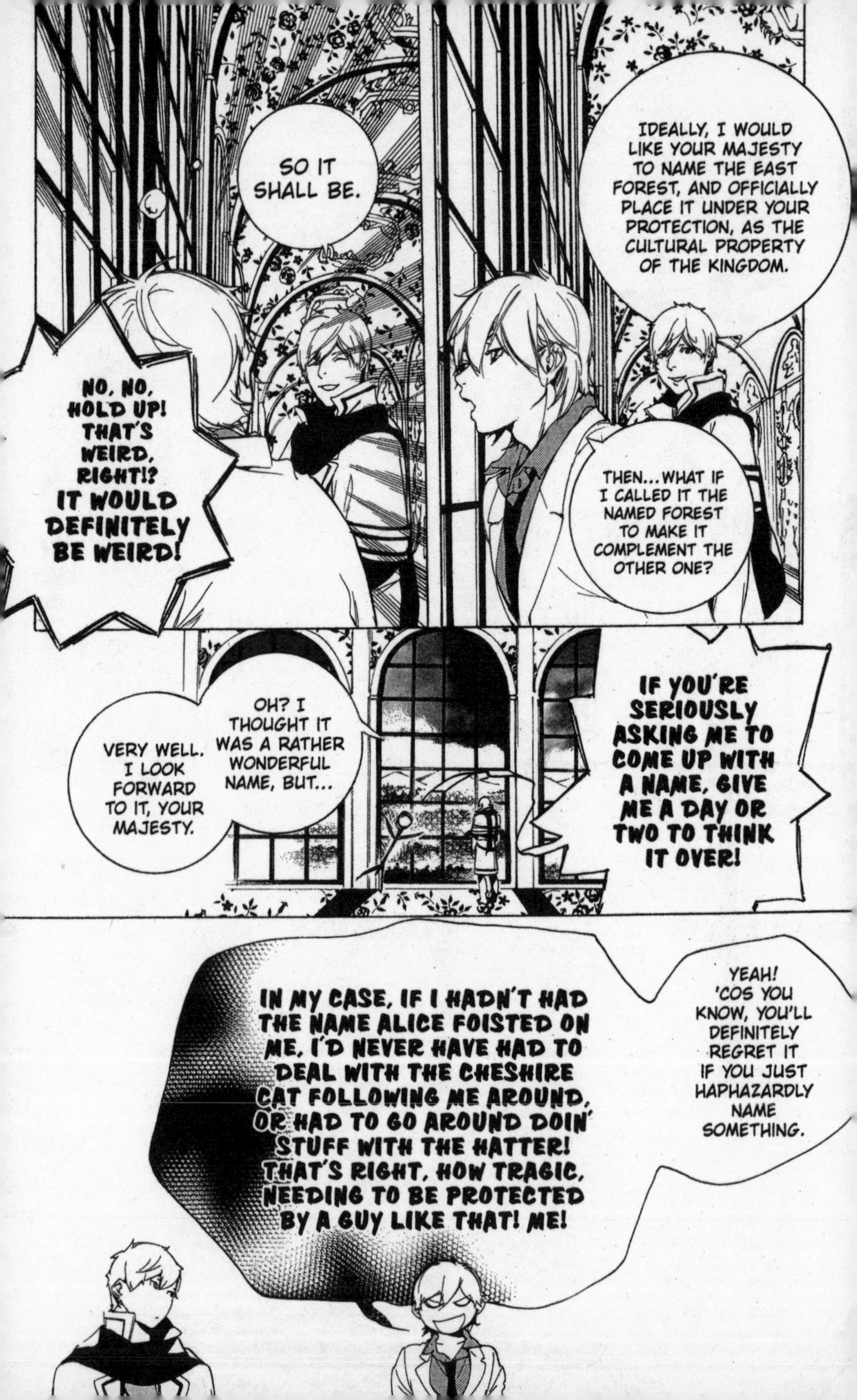
IDEALLY, I WOULD LIKE YOUR MAJESTY TO NAME THE EAST FOREST, AND OFFICIALLY PLACE IT UNDER YOUR PROTECTION, AS THE CULTURAL PROPERTY OF THE KINGDOM.
SO IT SHALL BE.
THEN...WHAT IF I CALLED IT THE NAMED FOREST TO MAKE IT COMPLEMENT THE OTHER ONE?
NO, NO, HOLD UP! THAT'S WEIRD, RIGHT!? IT WOULD DEFINITELY BE WEIRD!
IF YOU'RE SERIOUSLY ASKING ME TO COME UP WITH A NAME, GIVE ME A DAY OR TWO TO THINK IT OVER!
OH? I THOUGHT IT WAS A RATHER WONDERFUL NAME, BUT...
VERY WELL. I LOOK FORWARD TO IT, YOUR MAJESTY.
YEAH! 'COS YOU KNOW, YOU'LL DEFINITELY REGRET IT IF YOU JUST HAPHAZARDLY NAME SOMETHING.
IN MY CASE, IF I HADN'T HAD THE NAME ALICE FOISTED ON ME, I'D NEVER HAVE HAD TO DEAL WITH THE CHESHIRE CAT FOLLOWING ME AROUND, OR HAD TO GO AROUND DOIN' STUFF WITH THE HATTER! THAT'S RIGHT, HOW TRAGIC, NEEDING TO BE PROTECTED BY A GUY LIKE THAT! ME!

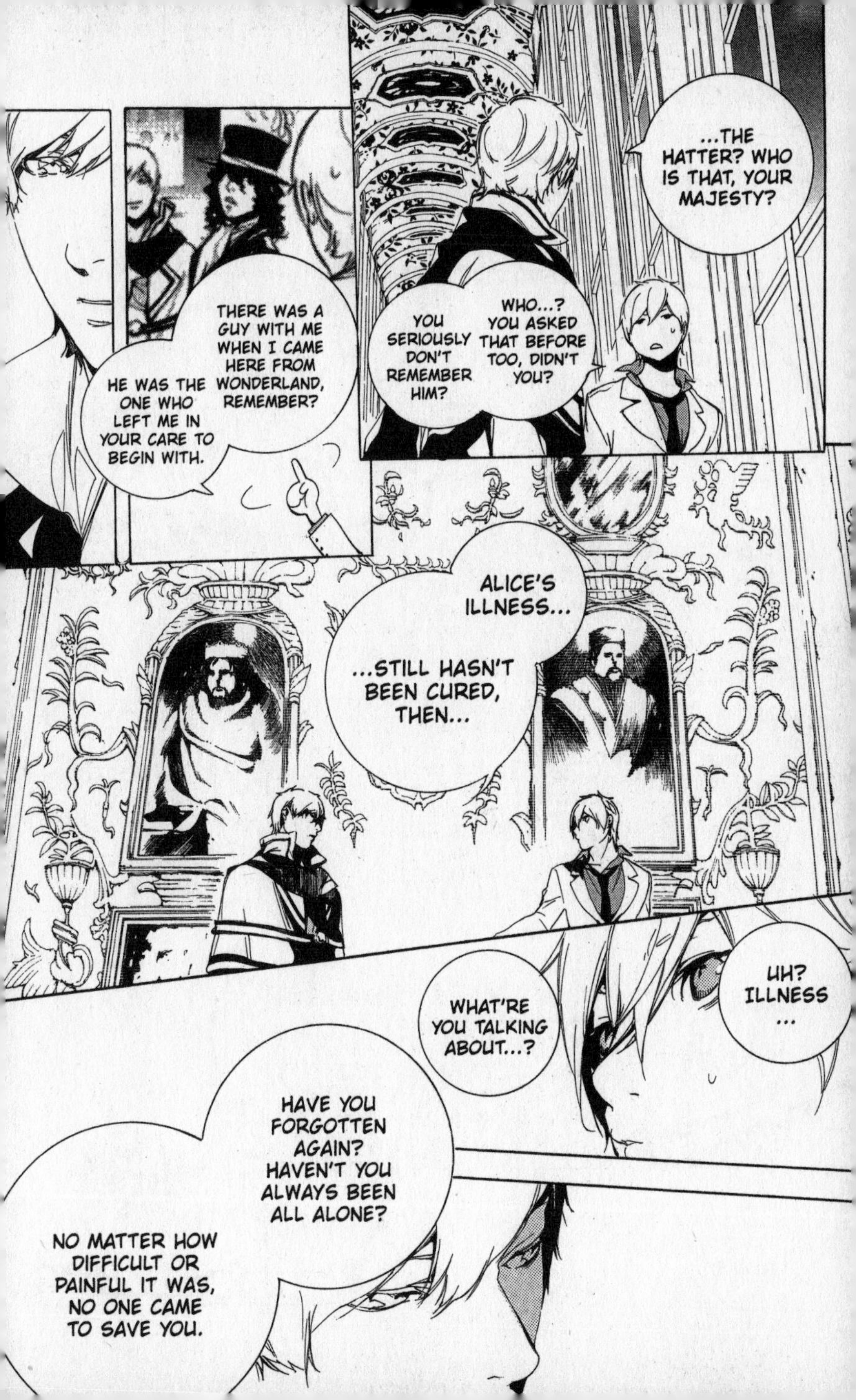
...THE HATTER? WHO IS THAT, YOUR MAJESTY?
WHO...? YOU ASKED THAT BEFORE TOO, DIDN'T YOU?
YOU SERIOUSLY DON'T REMEMBER HIM?
THERE WAS A GUY WITH ME WHEN I CAME HERE FROM WONDERLAND, REMEMBER?
HE WAS THE ONE WHO LEFT ME IN YOUR CARE TO BEGIN WITH.
ALICE'S ILLNESS...
...STILL HASN'T BEEN CURED, THEN...
UH? ILLNESS ...
WHAT'RE YOU TALKING ABOUT...?
HAVE YOU FORGOTTEN AGAIN? HAVEN'T YOU ALWAYS BEEN ALL ALONE?
NO MATTER HOW DIFFICULT OR PAINFUL IT WAS, NO ONE CAME TO SAVE YOU.

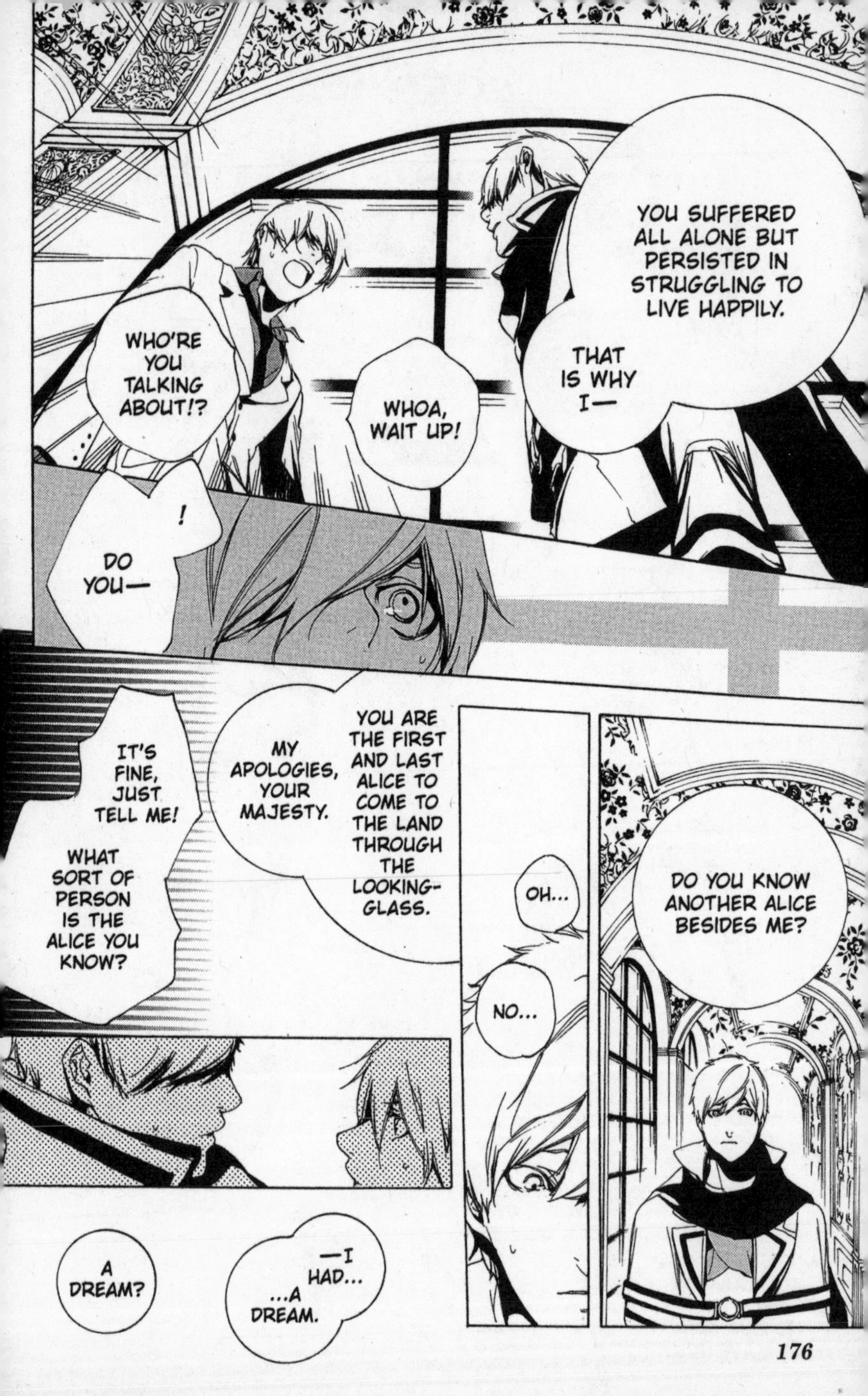
YOU SUFFERED ALL ALONE BUT PERSISTED IN STRUGGLING TO LIVE HAPPILY.
THAT IS WHY I—
WHOA, WAIT UP!
WHO'RE YOU TALKING ABOUT!?
!
DO YOU—
DO YOU KNOW ANOTHER ALICE BESIDES ME?
OH...
NO...
YOU ARE THE FIRST AND LAST ALICE TO COME TO THE LAND THROUGH THE LOOKING-GLASS.
MY APOLOGIES, YOUR MAJESTY.
IT'S FINE, JUST TELL ME!
WHAT SORT OF PERSON IS THE ALICE YOU KNOW?
—I HAD... ...A DREAM.
A DREAM?

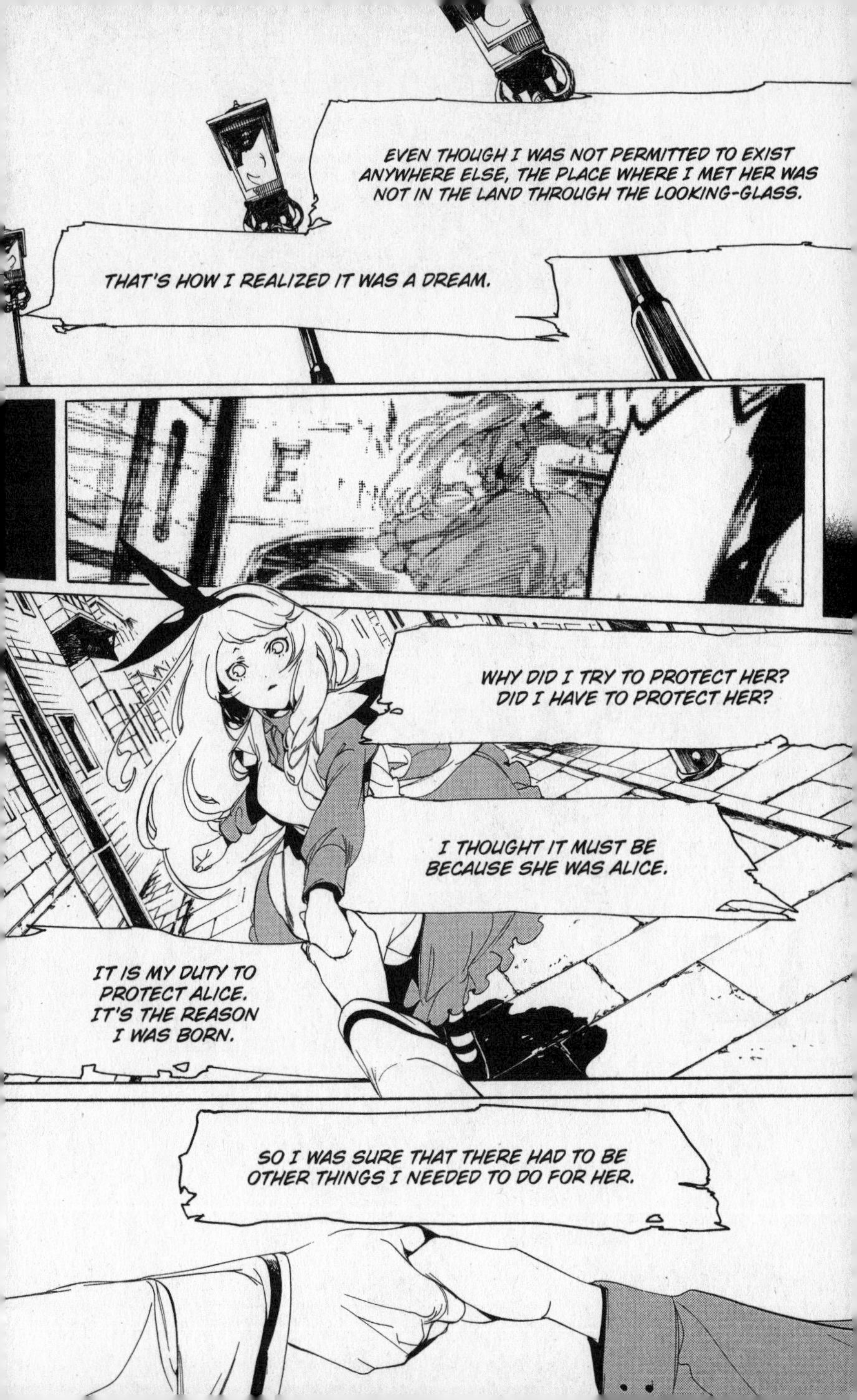
EVEN THOUGH I WAS NOT PERMITTED TO EXIST ANYWHERE ELSE, THE PLACE WHERE I MET HER WAS NOT IN THE LAND THROUGH THE LOOKING-GLASS.
THAT'S HOW I REALIZED IT WAS A DREAM.
WHY DID I TRY TO PROTECT HER? DID I HAVE TO PROTECT HER?
I THOUGHT IT MUST BE BECAUSE SHE WAS ALICE.
IT IS MY DUTY TO PROTECT ALICE. IT'S THE REASON I WAS BORN.
SO I WAS SURE THAT THERE HAD TO BE OTHER THINGS I NEEDED TO DO FOR HER.

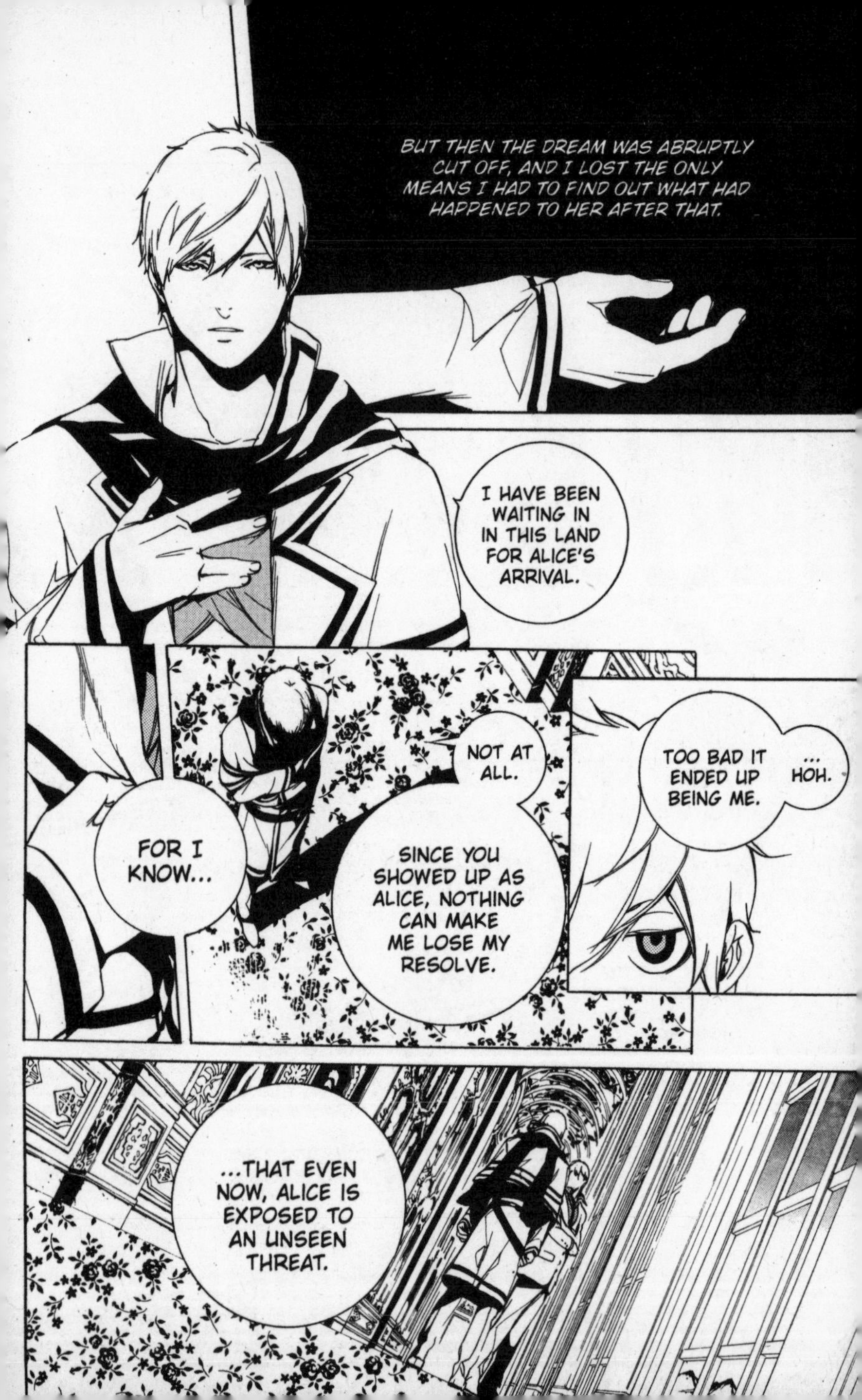
BUT THEN THE DREAM WAS ABRUPTLY CUT OFF, AND I LOST THE ONLY MEANS I HAD TO FIND OUT WHAT HAD HAPPENED TO HER AFTER THAT.
I HAVE BEEN WAITING IN IN THIS LAND FOR ALICE'S ARRIVAL.
...HOH.
TOO BAD IT ENDED UP BEING ME.
NOT AT ALL.
SINCE YOU SHOWED UP AS ALICE, NOTHING CAN MAKE ME LOSE MY RESOLVE.
FOR I KNOW...
...THAT EVEN NOW, ALICE IS EXPOSED TO AN UNSEEN THREAT.

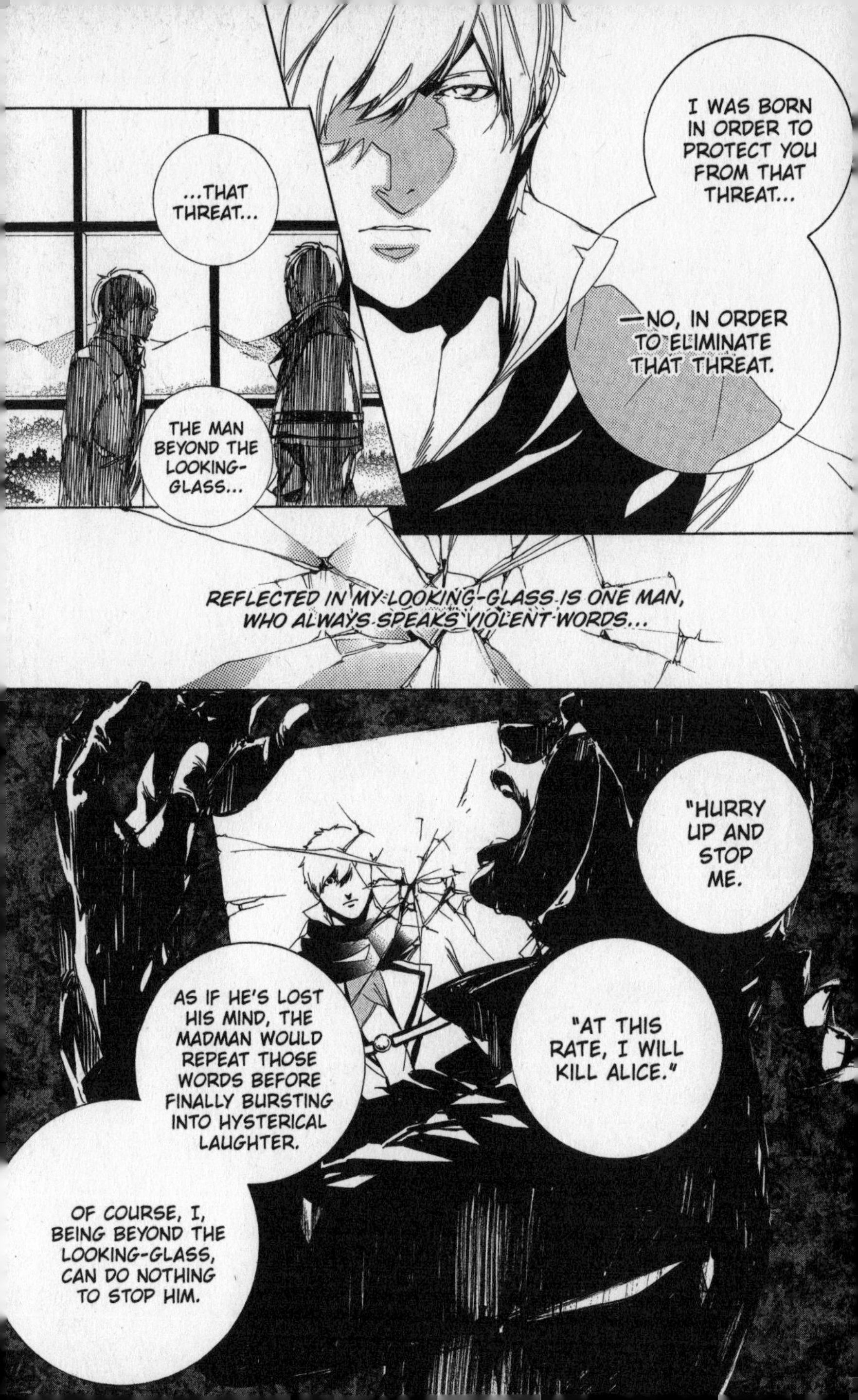
I WAS BORN IN ORDER TO PROTECT YOU FROM THAT THREAT...
—NO, IN ORDER TO ELIMINATE THAT THREAT.
...THAT THREAT...
THE MAN BEYOND THE LOOKING-GLASS...
REFLECTED IN MY LOOKING-GLASS IS ONE MAN, WHO ALWAYS SPEAKS VIOLENT WORDS...
"HURRY UP AND STOP ME.
"AT THIS RATE, I WILL KILL ALICE."
AS IF HE'S LOST HIS MIND, THE MADMAN WOULD REPEAT THOSE WORDS BEFORE FINALLY BURSTING INTO HYSTERICAL LAUGHTER.
OF COURSE, I, BEING BEYOND THE LOOKING-GLASS, CAN DO NOTHING TO STOP HIM.

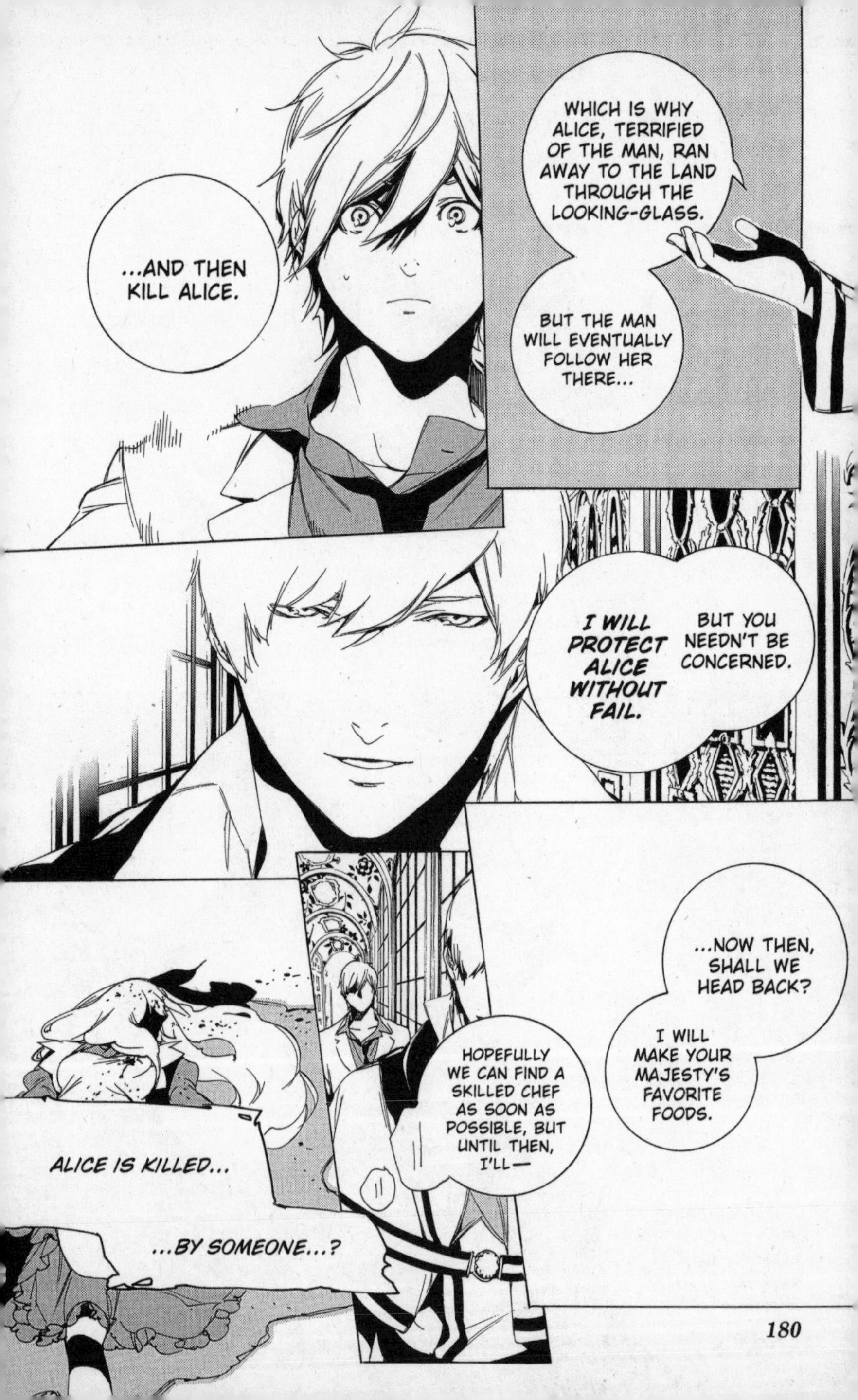
WHICH IS WHY ALICE, TERRIFIED OF THE MAN, RAN AWAY TO THE LAND THROUGH THE LOOKING-GLASS.
BUT THE MAN WILL EVENTUALLY FOLLOW HER THERE...
...AND THEN KILL ALICE.
BUT YOU NEEDN'T BE CONCERNED.
I WILL PROTECT ALICE WITHOUT FAIL.
...NOW THEN, SHALL WE HEAD BACK?
I WILL MAKE YOUR MAJESTY'S FAVORITE FOODS.
HOPEFULLY WE CAN FIND A SKILLED CHEF AS SOON AS POSSIBLE, BUT UNTIL THEN, I'LL—
ALICE IS KILLED...
...BY SOMEONE...?

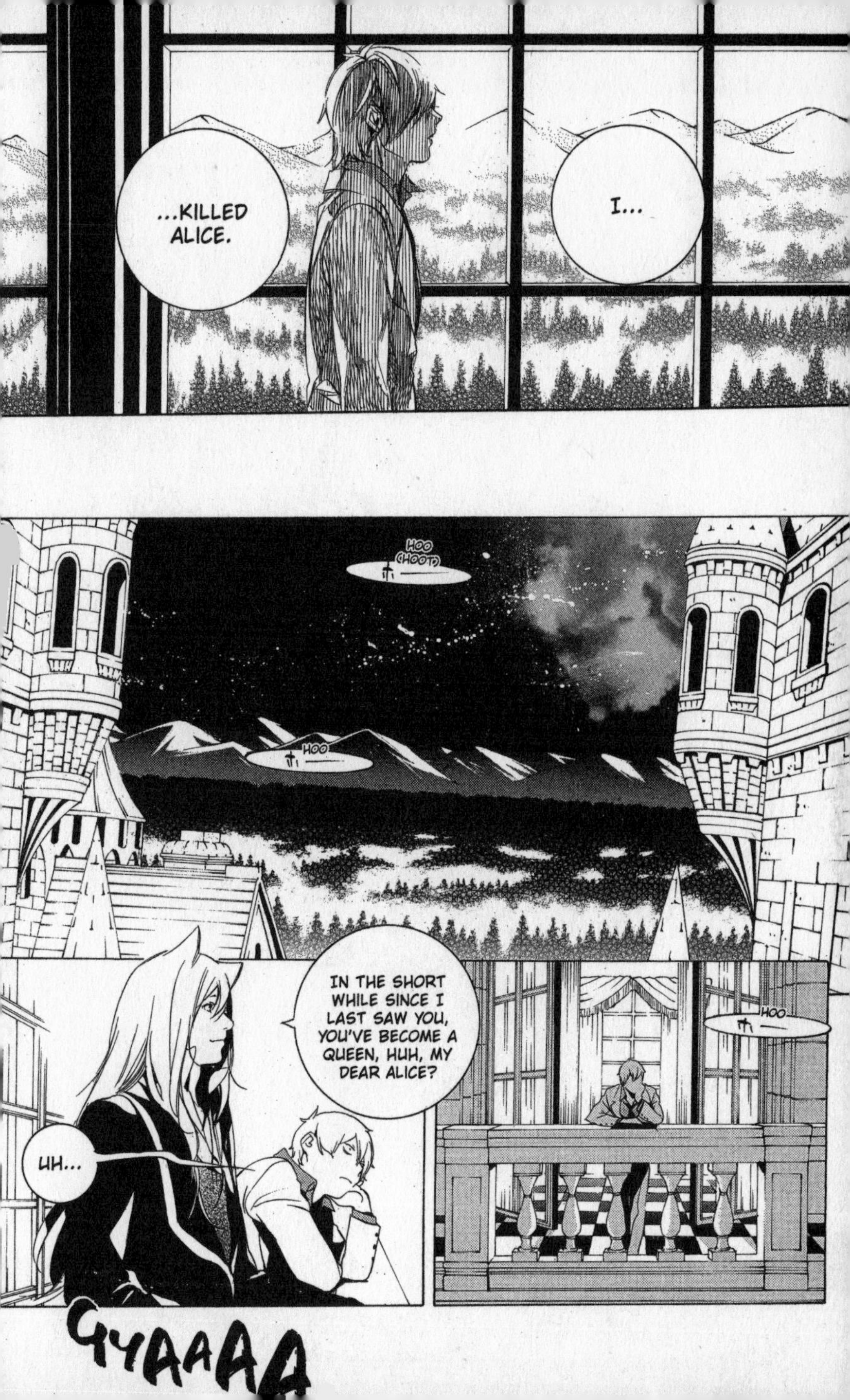
I...
...KILLED ALICE.
HOO (HOOT)
HOO
HOO
IN THE SHORT WHILE SINCE I LAST SAW YOU, YOU'VE BECOME A QUEEN, HUH, MY DEAR ALICE?
UH...
GYAAAA

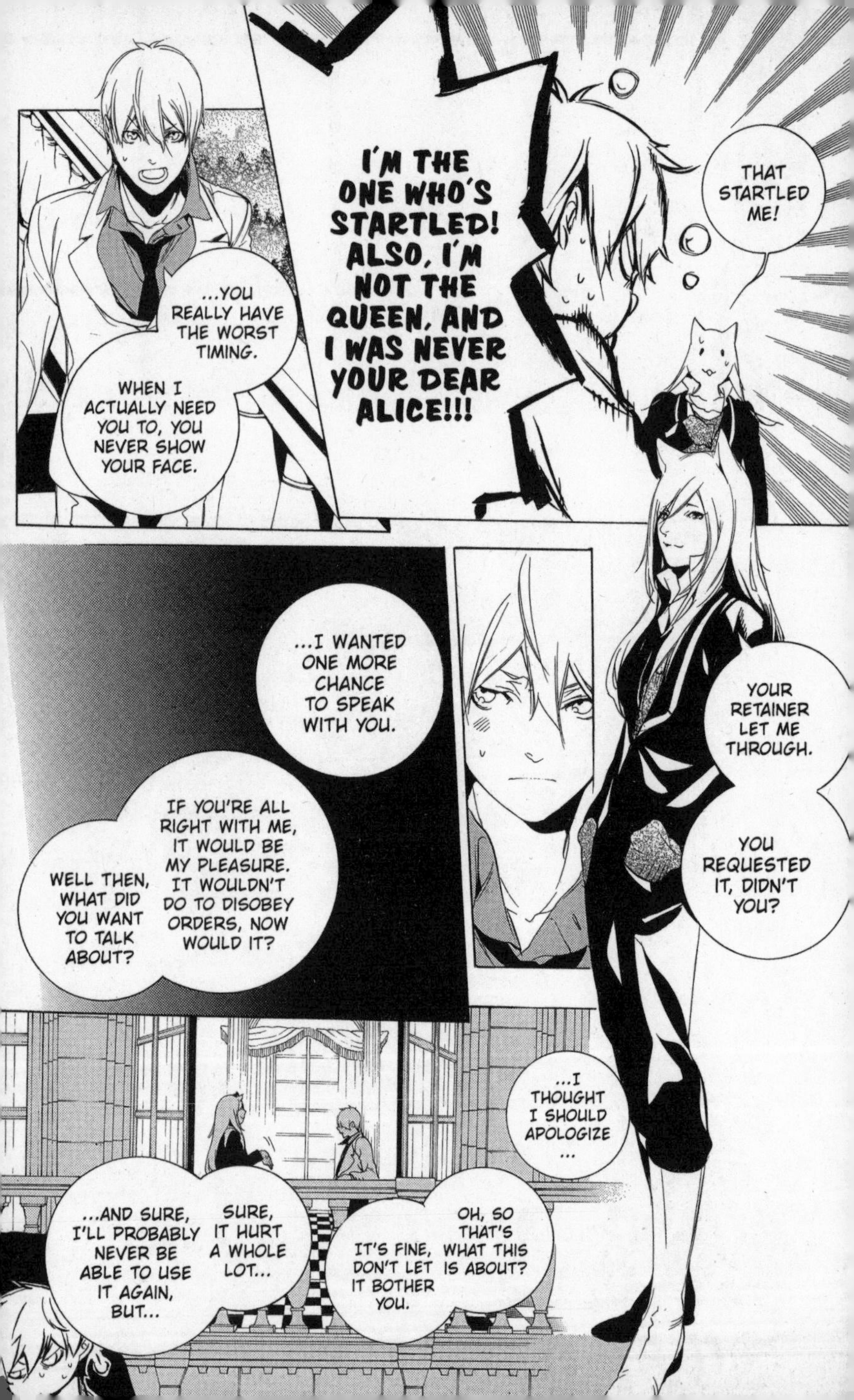
THAT STARTLED ME!
I'M THE ONE WHO'S STARTLED! ALSO, I'M NOT THE QUEEN, AND I WAS NEVER YOUR DEAR ALICE!!!
...YOU REALLY HAVE THE WORST TIMING.
WHEN I ACTUALLY NEED YOU TO, YOU NEVER SHOW YOUR FACE.
YOUR RETAINER LET ME THROUGH.
YOU REQUESTED IT, DIDN'T YOU?
...I WANTED ONE MORE CHANCE TO SPEAK WITH YOU.
IF YOU'RE ALL RIGHT WITH ME, IT WOULD BE MY PLEASURE. IT WOULDN'T DO TO DISOBEY ORDERS, NOW WOULD IT?
WELL THEN, WHAT DID YOU WANT TO TALK ABOUT?
...I THOUGHT I SHOULD APOLOGIZE...
OH, SO THAT'S WHAT THIS IS ABOUT?
IT'S FINE, DON'T LET IT BOTHER YOU.
SURE, IT HURT A WHOLE LOT...
...AND SURE, I'LL PROBABLY NEVER BE ABLE TO USE IT AGAIN, BUT...

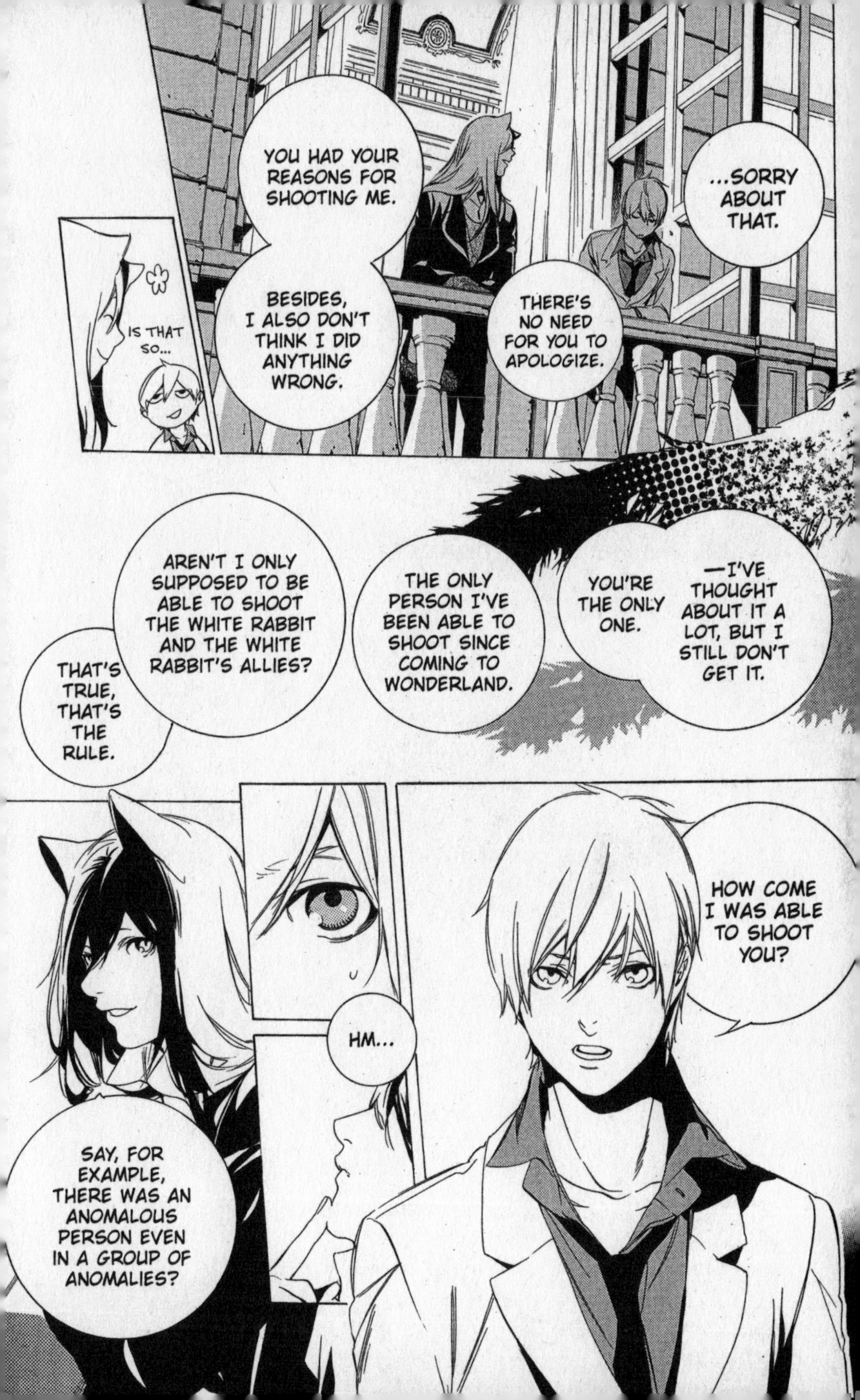
...SORRY ABOUT THAT.
THERE'S NO NEED FOR YOU TO APOLOGIZE.
YOU HAD YOUR REASONS FOR SHOOTING ME.
BESIDES, I ALSO DON'T THINK I DID ANYTHING WRONG.
IS THAT SO...
—I'VE THOUGHT ABOUT IT A LOT, BUT I STILL DON'T GET IT.
YOU'RE THE ONLY ONE.
THE ONLY PERSON I'VE BEEN ABLE TO SHOOT SINCE COMING TO WONDERLAND.
AREN'T I ONLY SUPPOSED TO BE ABLE TO SHOOT THE WHITE RABBIT AND THE WHITE RABBIT'S ALLIES?
THAT'S TRUE, THAT'S THE RULE.
HOW COME I WAS ABLE TO SHOOT YOU?
HM...
SAY, FOR EXAMPLE, THERE WAS AN ANOMALOUS PERSON EVEN IN A GROUP OF ANOMALIES?

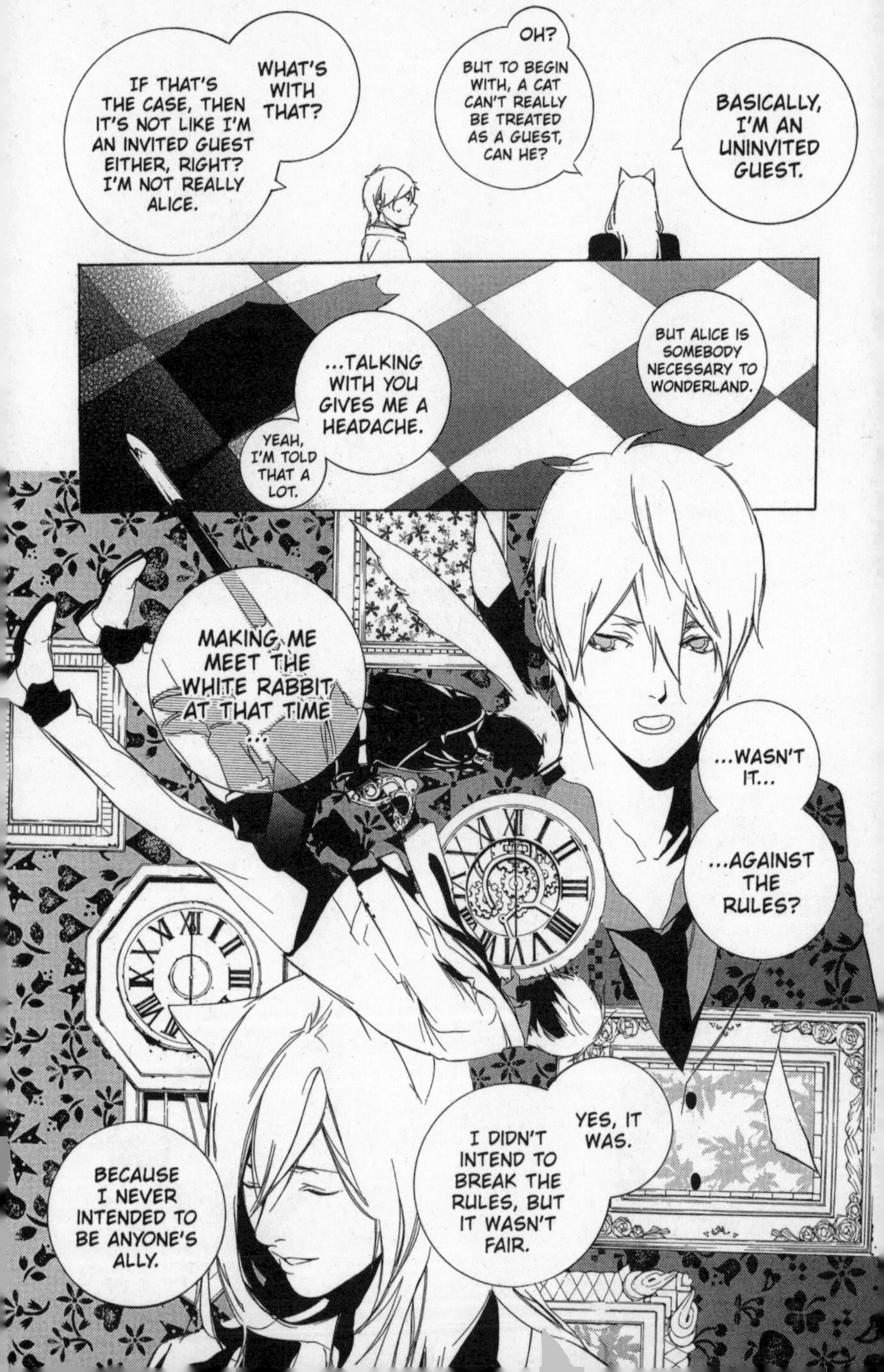
BASICALLY, I'M AN UNINVITED GUEST.
OH?
BUT TO BEGIN WITH, A CAT CAN'T REALLY BE TREATED AS A GUEST, CAN HE?
WHAT'S WITH THAT?
IF THAT'S THE CASE, THEN IT'S NOT LIKE I'M AN INVITED GUEST EITHER, RIGHT? I'M NOT REALLY ALICE.
BUT ALICE IS SOMEBODY NECESSARY TO WONDERLAND.
...TALKING WITH YOU GIVES ME A HEADACHE.
YEAH, I'M TOLD THAT A LOT.
MAKING ME MEET THE WHITE RABBIT AT THAT TIME ...
...WASN'T IT...
...AGAINST THE RULES?
YES, IT WAS.
I DIDN'T INTEND TO BREAK THE RULES, BUT IT WASN'T FAIR.
BECAUSE I NEVER INTENDED TO BE ANYONE'S ALLY.

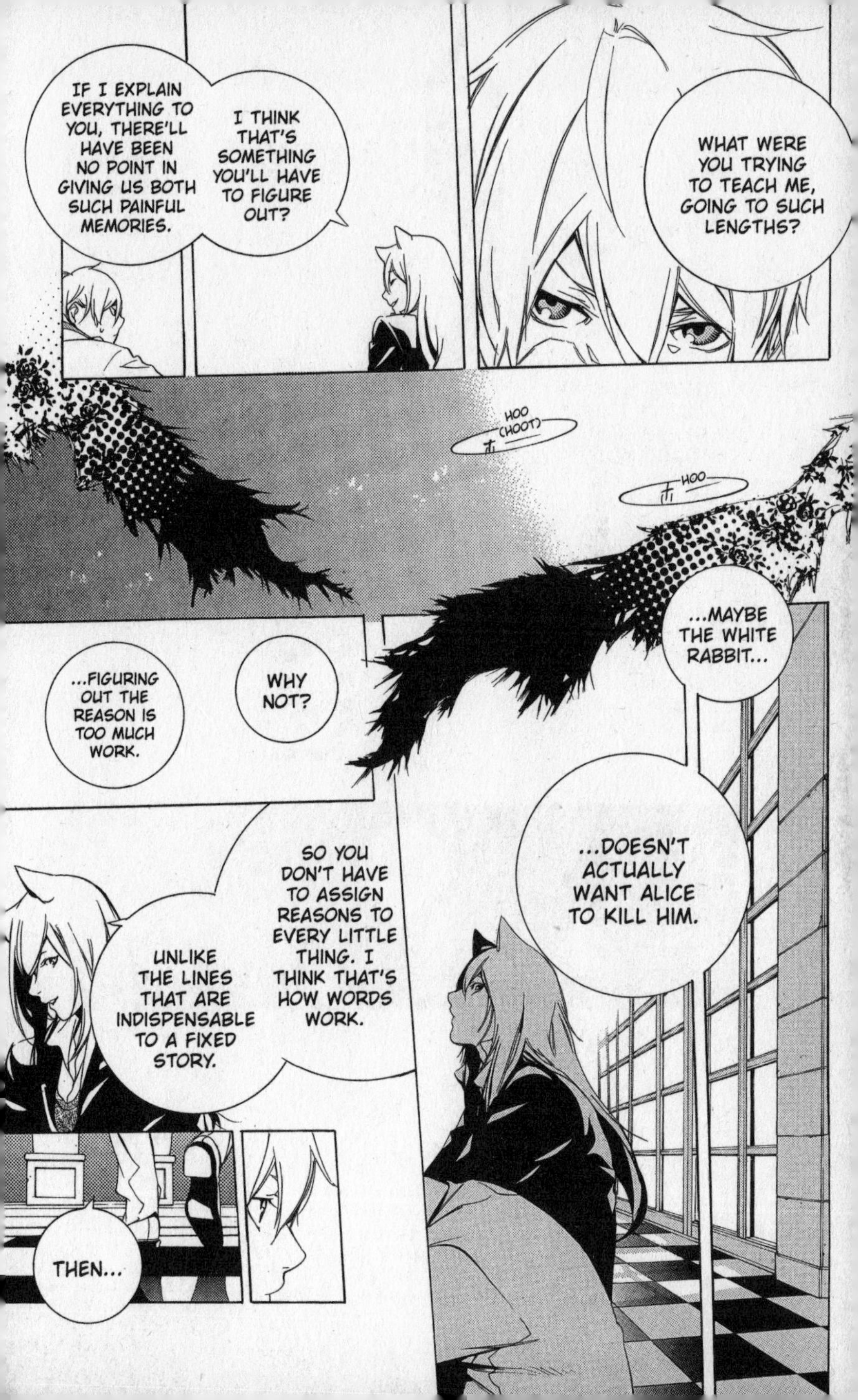
WHAT WERE YOU TRYING TO TEACH ME, GOING TO SUCH LENGTHS?
I THINK THAT'S SOMETHING YOU'LL HAVE TO FIGURE OUT?
IF I EXPLAIN EVERYTHING TO YOU, THERE'LL HAVE BEEN NO POINT IN GIVING US BOTH SUCH PAINFUL MEMORIES.
HOO
HOO (HOOT)
...MAYBE THE WHITE RABBIT...
...DOESN'T ACTUALLY WANT ALICE TO KILL HIM.
WHY NOT?
...FIGURING OUT THE REASON IS TOO MUCH WORK.
SO YOU DON'T HAVE TO ASSIGN REASONS TO EVERY LITTLE THING. I THINK THAT'S HOW WORDS WORK.
UNLIKE THE LINES THAT ARE INDISPENSABLE TO A FIXED STORY.
THEN...

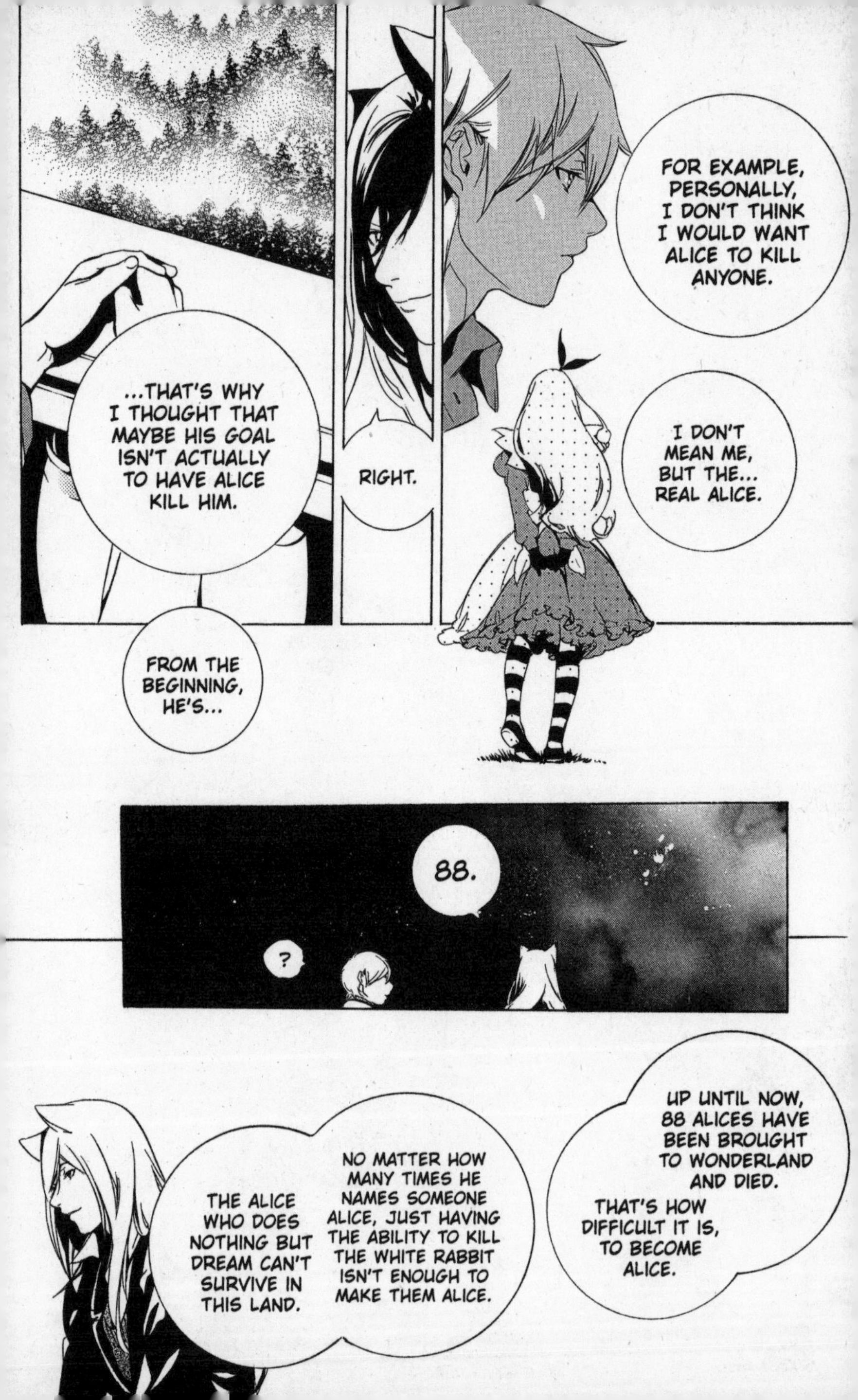
FOR EXAMPLE, PERSONALLY, I DON'T THINK I WOULD WANT ALICE TO KILL ANYONE.
I DON'T MEAN ME, BUT THE... REAL ALICE.
RIGHT.
...THAT'S WHY I THOUGHT THAT MAYBE HIS GOAL ISN'T ACTUALLY TO HAVE ALICE KILL HIM.
FROM THE BEGINNING, HE'S...
88.
?
UP UNTIL NOW, 88 ALICES HAVE BEEN BROUGHT TO WONDERLAND AND DIED.
THAT'S HOW DIFFICULT IT IS, TO BECOME ALICE.
NO MATTER HOW MANY TIMES HE NAMES SOMEONE ALICE, JUST HAVING THE ABILITY TO KILL THE WHITE RABBIT ISN'T ENOUGH TO MAKE THEM ALICE.
THE ALICE WHO DOES NOTHING BUT DREAM CAN'T SURVIVE IN THIS LAND.

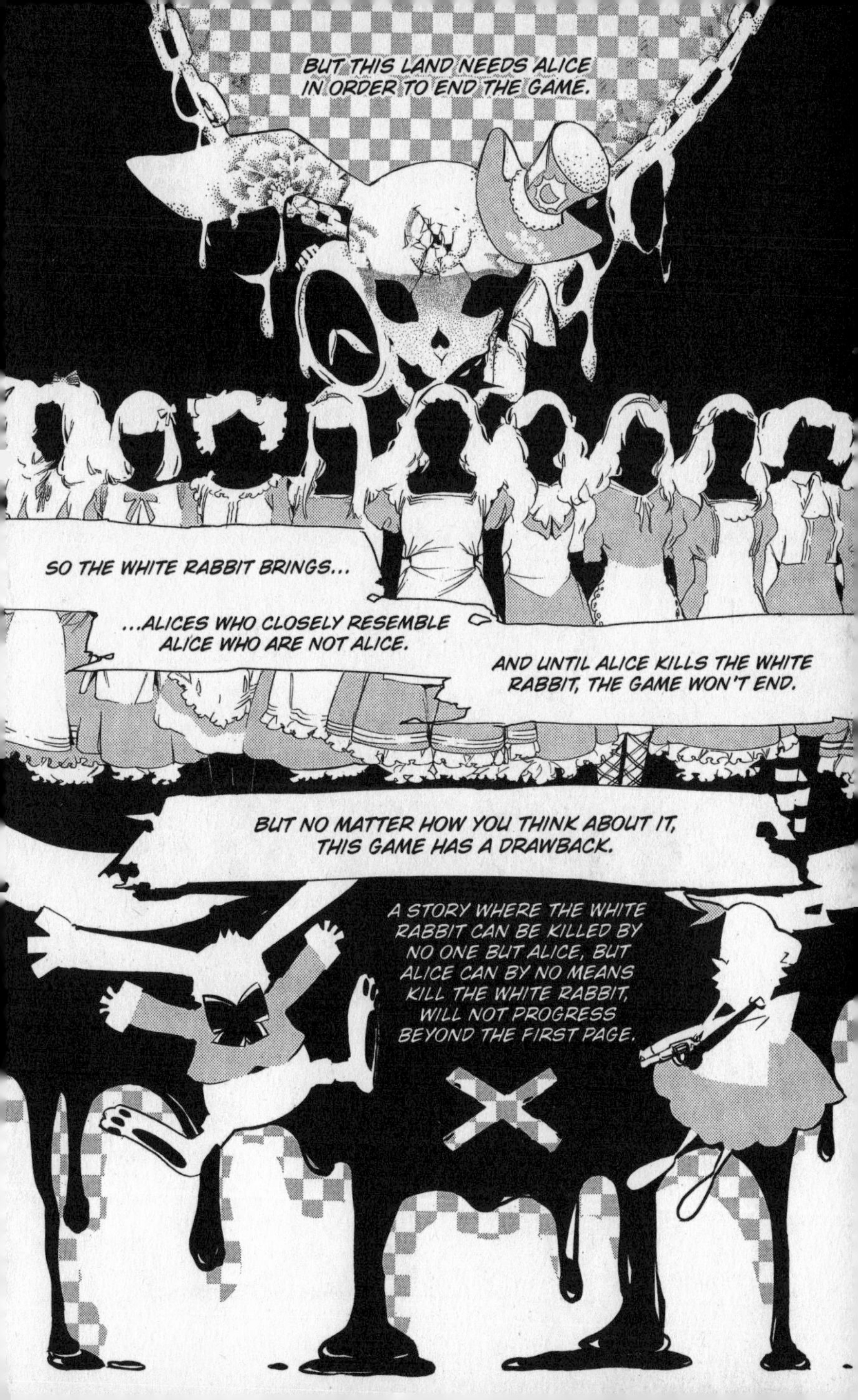
BUT THIS LAND NEEDS ALICE IN ORDER TO END THE GAME.
SO THE WHITE RABBIT BRINGS...
...ALICES WHO CLOSELY RESEMBLE ALICE WHO ARE NOT ALICE.
AND UNTIL ALICE KILLS THE WHITE RABBIT, THE GAME WON'T END.
BUT NO MATTER HOW YOU THINK ABOUT IT, THIS GAME HAS A DRAWBACK.
A STORY WHERE THE WHITE RABBIT CAN BE KILLED BY NO ONE BUT ALICE, BUT ALICE CAN BY NO MEANS KILL THE WHITE RABBIT, WILL NOT PROGRESS BEYOND THE FIRST PAGE.

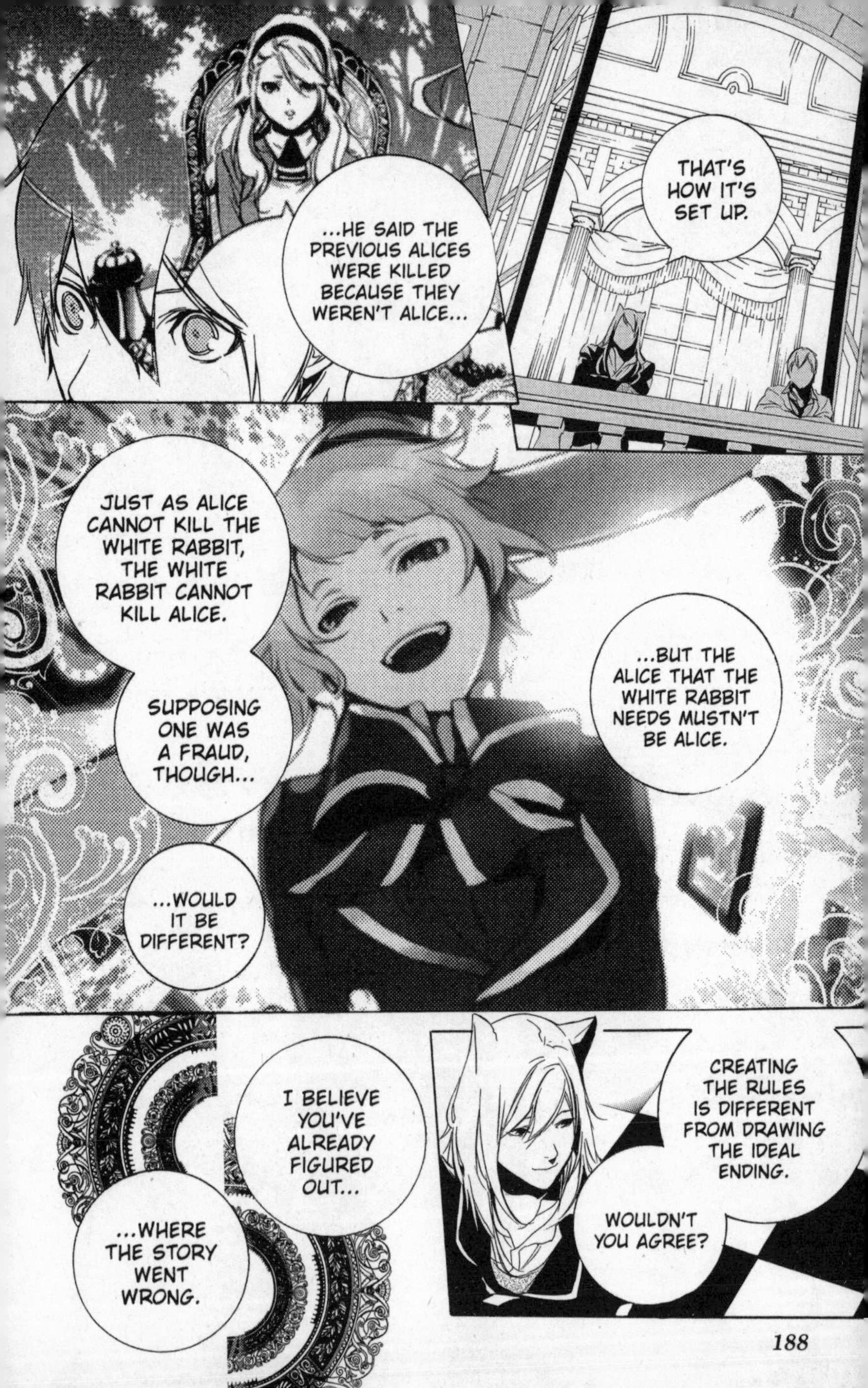
THAT'S HOW IT'S SET UP.
...HE SAID THE PREVIOUS ALICES WERE KILLED BECAUSE THEY WEREN'T ALICE...
...BUT THE ALICE THAT THE WHITE RABBIT NEEDS MUSTN'T BE ALICE.
JUST AS ALICE CANNOT KILL THE WHITE RABBIT, THE WHITE RABBIT CANNOT KILL ALICE.
SUPPOSING ONE WAS A FRAUD, THOUGH...
...WOULD IT BE DIFFERENT?
CREATING THE RULES IS DIFFERENT FROM DRAWING THE IDEAL ENDING.
WOULDN'T YOU AGREE?
I BELIEVE YOU'VE ALREADY FIGURED OUT...
...WHERE THE STORY WENT WRONG.

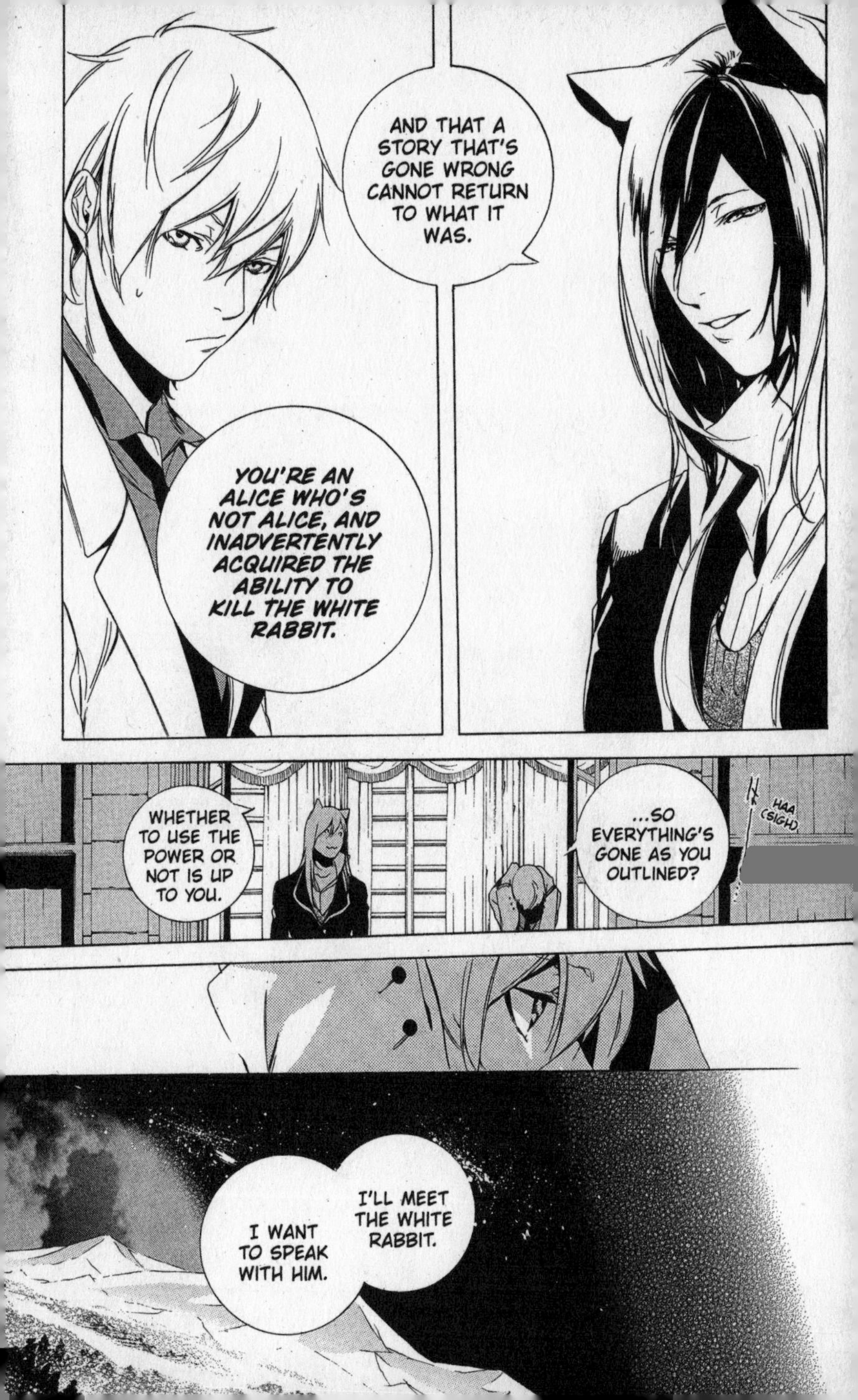
AND THAT A STORY THAT'S GONE WRONG CANNOT RETURN TO WHAT IT WAS.
YOU'RE AN ALICE WHO'S NOT ALICE, AND INADVERTENTLY ACQUIRED THE ABILITY TO KILL THE WHITE RABBIT.
HAA (SIGH)
...SO EVERYTHING'S GONE AS YOU OUTLINED?
WHETHER TO USE THE POWER OR NOT IS UP TO YOU.
I'LL MEET THE WHITE RABBIT.
I WANT TO SPEAK WITH HIM.

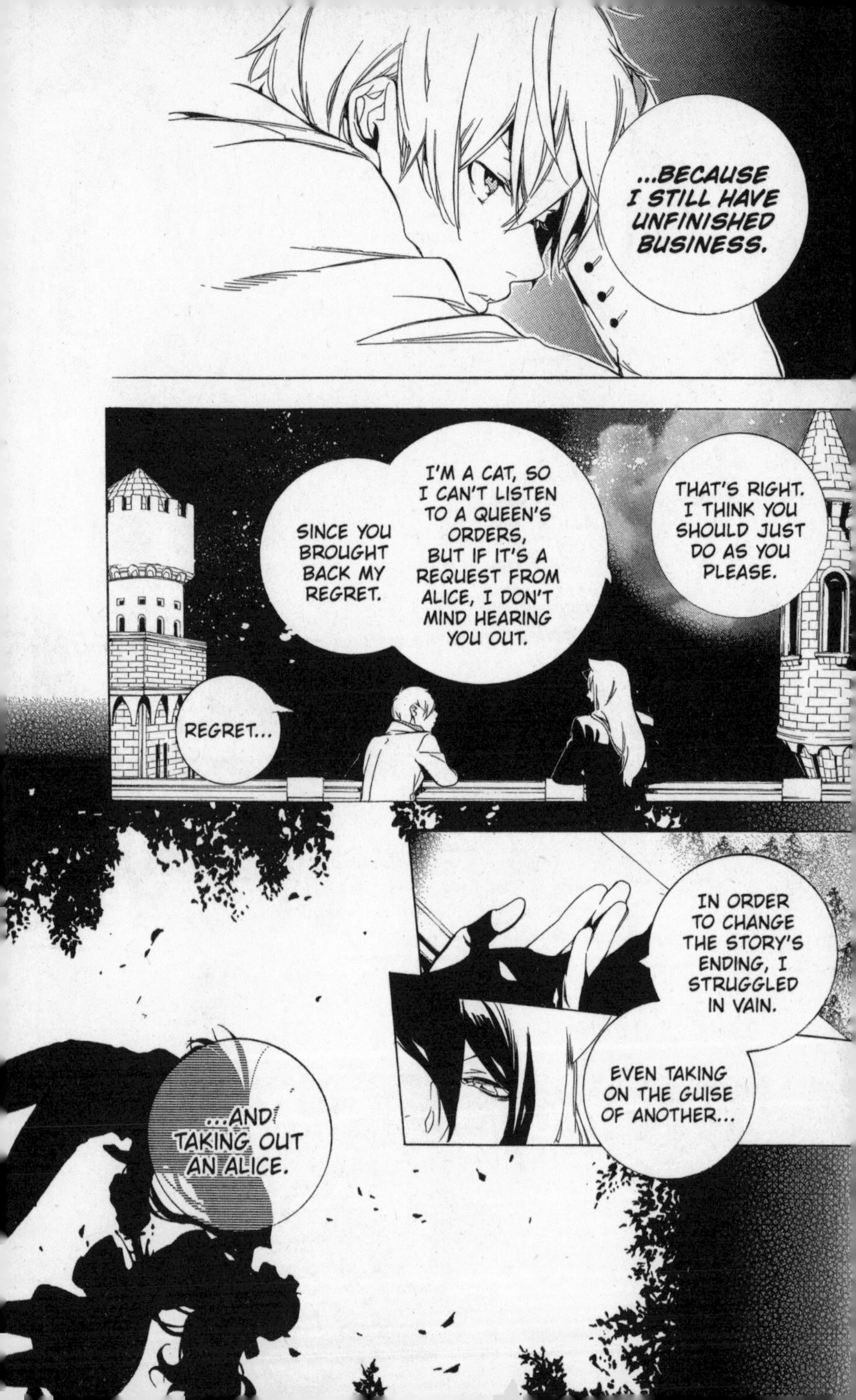
...BECAUSE I STILL HAVE UNFINISHED BUSINESS.
THAT'S RIGHT. I THINK YOU SHOULD JUST DO AS YOU PLEASE.
I'M A CAT, SO I CAN'T LISTEN TO A QUEEN'S ORDERS, BUT IF IT'S A REQUEST FROM ALICE, I DON'T MIND HEARING YOU OUT.
SINCE YOU BROUGHT BACK MY REGRET.
REGRET...
IN ORDER TO CHANGE THE STORY'S ENDING, I STRUGGLED IN VAIN.
EVEN TAKING ON THE GUISE OF ANOTHER...
...AND TAKING OUT AN ALICE.

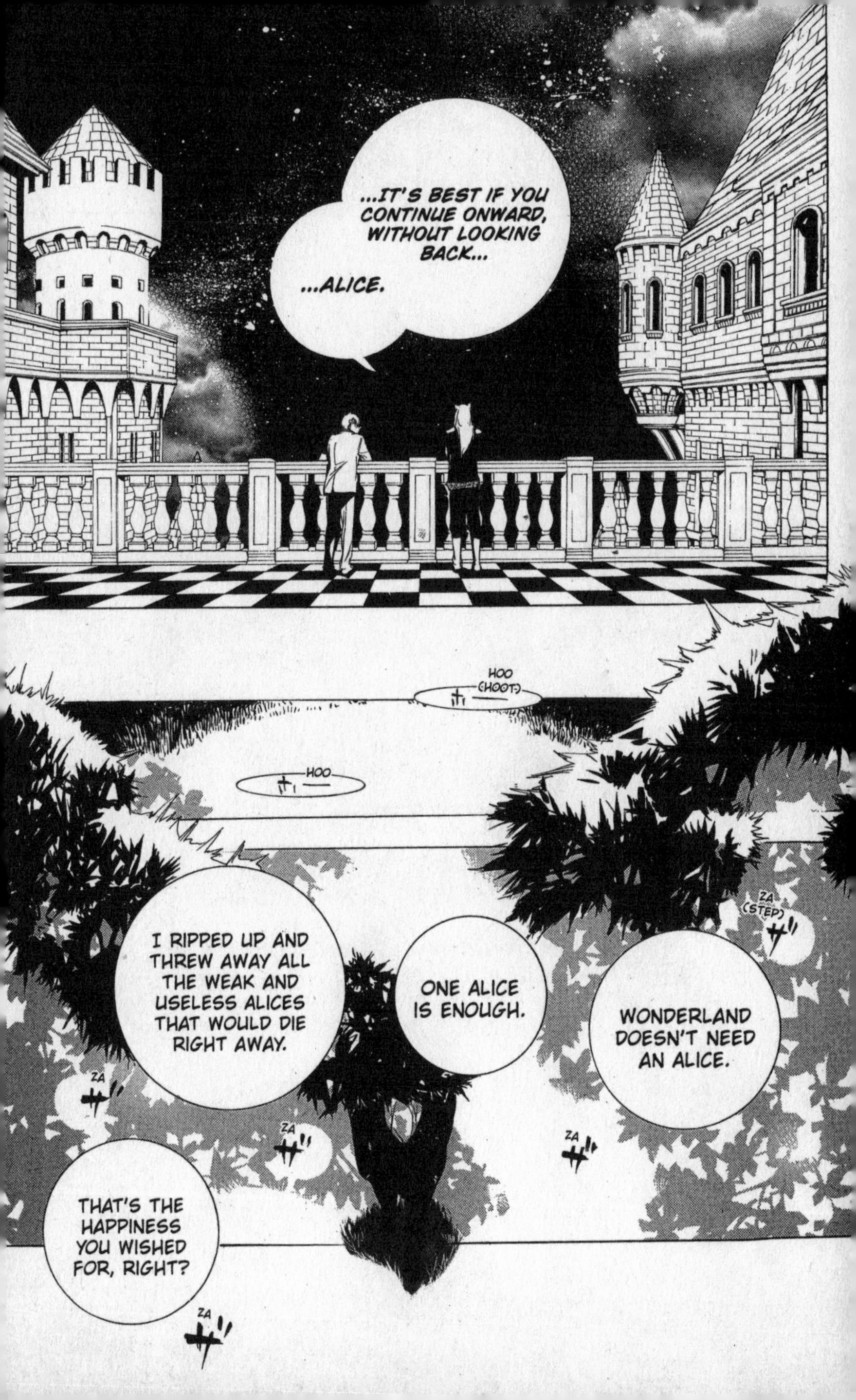
...IT'S BEST IF YOU CONTINUE ONWARD, WITHOUT LOOKING BACK...
...ALICE.
HOO (HOOT)
HOO
ZA (STEP)
WONDERLAND DOESN'T NEED AN ALICE.
ONE ALICE IS ENOUGH.
I RIPPED UP AND THREW AWAY ALL THE WEAK AND USELESS ALICES THAT WOULD DIE RIGHT AWAY.
ZA
ZA
ZA
THAT'S THE HAPPINESS YOU WISHED FOR, RIGHT?
ZA

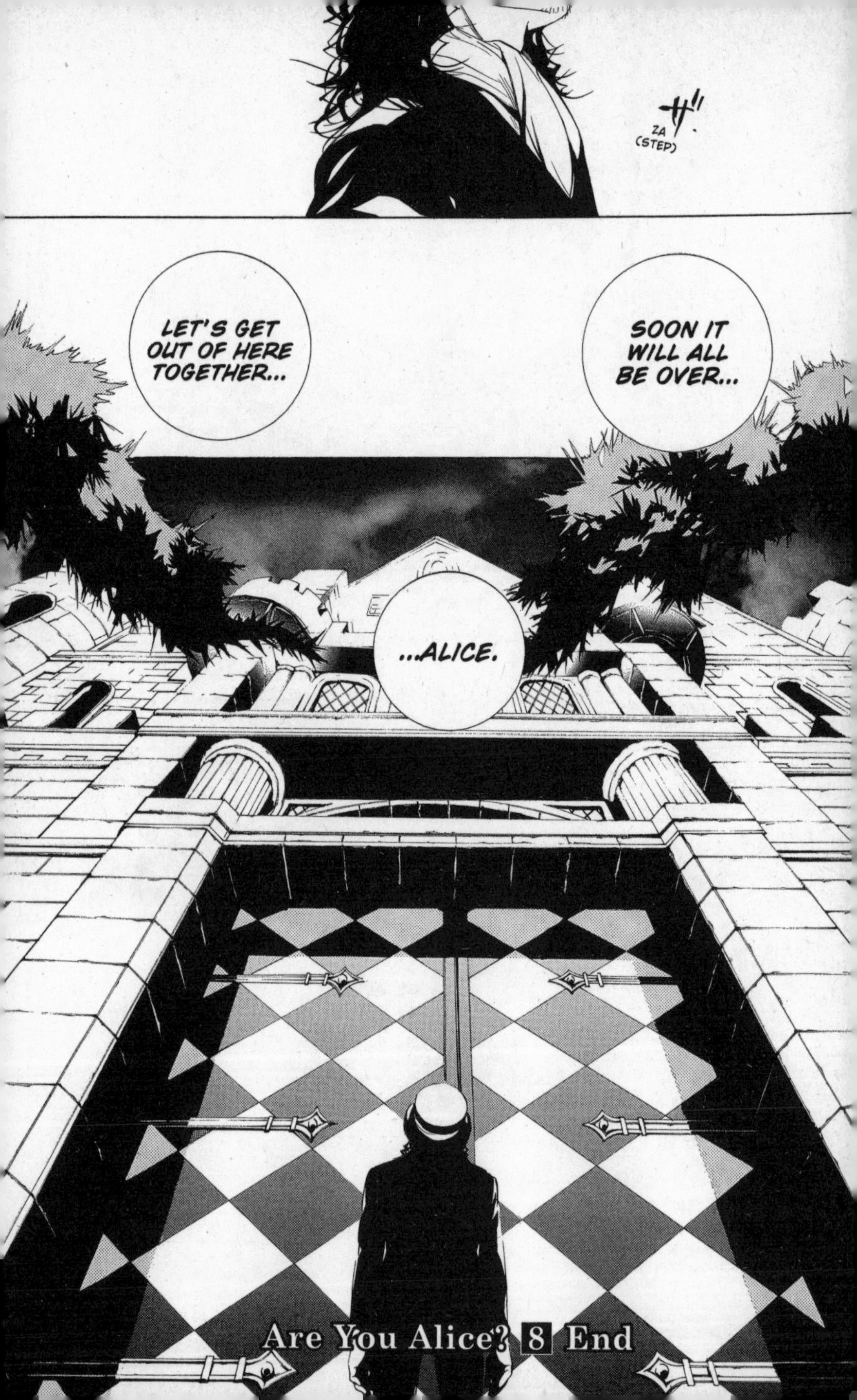
ZA (STEP)
SOON IT WILL ALL BE OVER...
LET'S GET OUT OF HERE TOGETHER...
...ALICE.
Are You Alice? 8 End

The Looking-Glass arc doesn't have many characters, and in the original drama CD, shadows slowly creep in. It has an all-encompassing sense of unease, but when I gave it a second read, I found it unexpectedly lively... The culprit is none other than...Alice!

And with that, I hope to see you again in Volume 9!

Ai Ninomiya

Translation Notes

Page 3
"Waste not, want not" ghosts
This is a reference to a PSA from the 1980s, entitled *Mottainai Obake*, where ghosts came out at night to terrify picky eaters who had wasted food.

Page 19
Name tag
Hatter asks if the regret has a *maigofuda*, which is actually an identification tag that parents will pin to a preschooler's clothes in case they get lost.

ARE YOU ALICE? 8

**IKUMI KATAGIRI
AI NINOMIYA**

Translation and Lettering: Alexis Eckerman

Are you Alice? © 2013 by Ai Ninomiya / Ikumi Katagiri. © IM/Re;no, Inc. All rights reserved. First published in Japan in 2013 by ICHIJINSHA. English translation rights arranged with ICHIJINSHA through Tuttle-Mori Agency, Inc., Tokyo.

Translation © 2015 by Hachette Book Group, Inc.

Yen Press
Hachette Book Group
1290 Avenue of the Americas
New York, NY 10104

www.HachetteBookGroup.com
www.YenPress.com

Yen Press is an imprint of Hachette Book Group, Inc. The Yen Press name and logo are trademarks of Hachette Book Group, Inc.

The publisher is not responsible for websites (or their content) that are not owned by the publisher.

First Yen Press Edition: March 2015

ISBN: 978-0-316-33989-6

10 9 8 7 6 5 4 3 2 1

BVG

Printed in the United States of America